STANDARD LOAN

UNLESS RECALLED BY ANOTHER READER
THIS ITEM MAY BE BORROWED FOR

FOUR WEEKS

To renew, telephone:
01243 816089 (Bishop Otter)
01243 812099 (Bognor Regis)

Inclusive and Heterogeneous Schooling

Assessment, Curriculum, and Instruction

edited by

Mary A. Falvey, Ph.D.
California State University, Los Angeles

·P·A·U·L·H·
BROOKES
PUBLISHING Co.

Baltimore • London • Toronto • Sydney

Paul H. Brookes Publishing Co.
Post Office Box 10624
Baltimore, Maryland 21285-0624

Typeset by Brushwood Graphics, Inc., Baltimore, Maryland.
Manufactured in the United States of America by
The Maple Press Co., York, Pennsylvania.

Portions of some chapters in this book appeared originally in M.A. Falvey, *Community-Based Curriculum: Instructional Strategies for Students with Severe Handicaps* (2nd ed.), Paul H. Brookes Publishing Co., 1989. This material appears by permission of the author and the publisher.

Library of Congress Cataloging-in-Publication Data

Inclusive and heterogeneous schooling : assessment, curriculum, and
   instruction / edited by Mary A. Falvey.
        p.   cm.
   Includes bibliographical references and index.
   ISBN 1-55766-202-9
   1. Handicapped children—Education—United States.   2. School
management and organization—United States.   3. Educational change—
United States.   4. Mainstreaming in education—United States.
I. Falvey, Mary A., 1950–
LC4031.I52   1995   94-36201
371.91'0973—dc20   CIP

British Library Cataloguing-in-Publication data are available from the
British Library.

CONTENTS

CONTRIBUTORS

EDITOR

Mary A. Falvey, Ph.D., is a professor in the Division of Special Education at California State University, Los Angeles. She was a teacher and administrator in the public schools responsible for teaching and administering programs for students with severe disabilities. She received her doctor of philosophy degree in 1980 from the University of Wisconsin–Madison. She has authored numerous chapters, several articles, and the first and second editions of *Community-Based Curriculum: Instructional Strategies for Students with Severe Handicaps*. She served on the TASH board of directors and is on the California TASH board. She provides workshops and technical assistance on inclusive education throughout the world.

CHAPTER AUTHORS

Peggy Ann Abernathy, B.A., is an inclusion facilitator in the Fullerton School District, a medium size district in Southern California. She is responsible for the development, coordination, and support of educational programs for elementary and junior high school students with severe disabilities in inclusive classrooms. As a former general educator, she is very interested in the merger of general and special education to best meet the needs of all children.

Sandra L. Amate, B.A., is a community specialist for C.H.O.I.C.E.S.S., an adult services agency in the Los Angeles area that provides support for adults with severe disabilities to live, work, and play as full participants in their communities. She has also been a teacher for students 18–22 years old in a community-based transition program, preparing young adults for life beyond the school system.

Kathryn D. Bishop, Ph.D., is an associate professor in the Special Education program at the University of San Diego. She is currently the director for the Special Education Credential and Master's Degree programs at the University of San Diego. She has worked with teachers and families to provide appropriate services to students with severe disabilities, particularly in the areas of inclusion and positive behavior support.

Jennifer J. Coots, Ph.D., coordinates a longitudinal research project investigating the adaptations made by families of children with disabilities. Her primary research interests are the involvement of families in their children's schooling and the impact of ecology and culture on family adaptations. Dr. Coots was a teacher of students with severe disabilities for 8 years in settings ranging from a state hospital to an integrated classroom on a regular campus. She served as a mentor teacher in her district and a demonstration teacher for her state department of education regarding functional curriculum and integrated educational opportunities. She presently consults and advocates for inclusive educational opportunities for all students.

Lori Eshilian, M.A., is a support teacher at Whittier High School, which has been restructured into "houses" and does not "track" students or place them in separate education settings. She was a co-director of a community-based program serving adults with severe disabilities. She formerly taught for Los Angeles County schools where she was instrumental in establishing integrated and community-based educational programs for junior and senior students with severe disabilities. She received her master of arts degree from California State University, Los Angeles.

Susann Terry Gage, M.A., is employed as a vocational specialist assisting secondary and postsecondary students and their families as they prepare for the transition from school to community work settings. She has previously been employed by the California State Department of Education as an independent consultant for numerous school districts in Los Angeles County developing both appropriate integrated and inclusive programs for students ranging from preschool age to young adults. She was a classroom teacher with Los Angeles County Office of Education for 6 years, where her primary focus was community-based instruction and vocational placements in integrated work settings. She is working on her doctor of philosophy degree at California State University, Los Angeles, and the University of California, Los Angeles. Her research focuses on social competence and peer interactions of young elementary-age children with disabilities.

Christine C. Givner, Ph.D., is an associate professor and co-coordinator of the Learning Handicapped and Resource Specialist Teacher Credential and Master's programs in the Division of Special Education at California State University, Los Angeles. Dr. Givner's research interests include collaboration between special and general educators in the development of effective inclusive learning environments, the use of the teacher as researcher in school restructuring, the challenges faced by minority teachers and teachers with disabilities, the use of authentic assessment with K–12 students with disabilities, the effective education of students with emotional/behavioral difficulties, and the use of technology in the education of students with learning difficulties.

Marquita Grenot-Scheyer, Ph.D., is an associate professor at California State University, Long Beach. She is primarily responsible for the coordination of the credential in severe disabilities. She is also co-director of The Consortium for Collaborative Research on Social Relationships: Inclusive Schools and Communities for Children and Youth with Diverse Abilities, a federally funded longitudinal study of children and youth with severe disabilities and their relationships and interactions with their peers without disabilities. Her research and publications are focused on the social relationships among children with and without severe disabilities in inclusive settings. Her community action activities have centered on assisting families to secure quality inclusive educational placements for their sons and daughters with the label of severe disabilities.

Diane Haager, Ph.D., co-coordinates the Learning Handicapped and Resource Specialist Teacher Credential and Master's programs at California State University, Los Angeles. Dr. Haager's research interests currently focus on the interface between general and special education. Her previous work has focused on general education teachers' adaptations and accommodations for students with special needs, as well as on the social and behavioral characteristics of students with learning disabilities.

Kimberlee A. Jubala, M.A., teaches in the San Diego Unified School District. As a special educator, she collaborated with colleagues to provide inclusive opportunities for her students. She is now a general educator of students with a wide range of abilities and backgrounds. She received her master of arts degree from the University of San Diego.

Christina H. Kimm, Ph.D., received her doctorate from the University of Minnesota, Department of Educational Psychology. She has an extensive background of research and research methodology in special education and rehabilitation. Dr. Kimm worked as a member of the interdisciplinary team to provide rehabilitation services for young adolescents with developmental disabilities and their families. Her primary area of research is the development of community-based services and rehabilitation programs for young minority adolescents with multiple disabilities to assist them in making a smooth transition into adulthood in the integrated environment. Dr. Kimm is also teaching and conducting research in rehabilitation and integration in the multicultural/multilingual perspectives.

Richard L. Rosenberg, Ph.D., is vocational coordinator and coordinator of training at Whittier Union High School District and the Career Assessment and Placement Centers Adult Services component, Whittier, California. He has established educational support plans and created supported living options for individuals by using the future planning process of MAPs, PATH, and Circles of Support. He received his doctorate in 1980 from the University of Wisconsin–Madison. He has provided technical assistance to a number of schools, adult services agencies, and individual families in Los Angeles and across the United States. For several years he has served as a board member of California's chapter of The Association for Persons with Severe Handicaps and as president of CHOICESS, a nonprofit adult support organization in Los Angeles.

Jacqueline S. Thousand, Ph.D., is a research associate professor in the Department of Education and the University Affiliated Program of Vermont, University of Vermont. Since 1986, she has coordinated a graduate training program that prepares integration facilitators, advanced educational leadership personnel who work with administrators, teachers, and families to redesign the delivery of special education services. This enables learners with extensive educational and psychological challenges to experience quality educational and social opportunities within their local general education and community environments. Dr. Thousand's most recent research is in the area of collaborative consultation and teaming, school-based systems change strategies, cooperative group learning and partner learning, transition planning, attitudinal change strategies, and international educational exchange.

Richard A. Villa, Ph.D., is President of the Bayridge Educational Consortium and an adjunct professor at the University of Vermont, Trinity College, and St. Michael's College; he teaches courses and supervises practica in the development of effective administrative and instructional skills for accommodating all students within general education classrooms in Colchester, Vermont. His primary field of expertise is the development of administrative support systems for educating all students within general education settings. Dr. Villa has taught a number of subjects at both the middle and secondary school levels, including biology, chemistry, physics, government, and special education; his administrative experiences include serving as a special education administrator, pupil personnel services director, and director of instructional services.

Pamela J. Villalobos, M.A., has worked for a number of years as a director of adult services and a transition instructor for the Whittier Union High School District. She is a high school teacher with the Grossmont Union High School District working to include students with severe disabilities in general education classes on the high school campus. She received her master of arts degree from California State University, Los Angeles.

Lisbeth J. Vincent, Ph.D., presently resides in Helena, Montana, and serves as a consultant to numerous local and state departments of health and education. She is active in helping design programs of ongoing staff development that foster the adoption of a family-centered model to service delivery. Previously, Dr. Vincent directed the SHARE Center for Excellence in Early Intervention at California State University–Los Angeles from 1988 to 1994. Dr. Vincent served on the Executive Board of the Division for Early Childhood of the Council for Exceptional Children from 1983 to 1991. She was the president in 1985–1986 and was involved in the development and passage of PL 99-457. Dr. Vincent was a founding member of The Association for Persons with Severe Handicaps and served on the executive board from 1978 to 1981. Her major area of emphasis has been program and personnel development for young children with disabilities and their families. She has contributed numerous articles, chapters, and monographs to the literature on community integration and active decision making by families.

Debbie Williamson is an inclusion facilitator in the Fullerton School District, a medium-size district in Southern California. She is responsible for the development, coordination, and support of educational programs for elementary students with severe disabilities in inclusive classrooms. As a former special day class teacher of 13 years, she has seen the benefits of inclusion for children with and without severe disabilities and is "not going back."

FOREWORD

As parents of a child who has multiple and significant challenges, our main concern has always been our son Caleb's quality of life. We wanted him to be known and cared about the way all children are known, cared about, and included, allowed to make choices, to fail, to succeed, and to learn. We knew that, because of our son's disabilities, achieving these goals would be very problematic. This was not necessarily because of *his* disability, but rather because of our culture's inability to be comfortable with his differences. For many years, persons with disabilities have been segregated into separate schools and classes, sheltered workshops for employment, and institutional living arrangements. With so little experience and exposure, how could a community feel comfortable around someone with such significant challenges?

Significant changes would have to take place in order for our son to be an accepted member of our society. Philosophies, therapies, and educational practices based on convenience would have to be recognized as such and changed. The underlying values they are based on would have to be challenged. Eventually, new practices based on valuing individuals above all else would have to stand paramount to all other issues. We had no idea how this was to happen.

We first met Mary Falvey in 1988. She was chairing the Integration Consortium of Los Angeles County—a grass roots organization seeking inclusive educational and community options for all persons. It was part of a broad social movement for equal access and respect regardless of ability. In the Los Angeles area, it was pivotal in the struggle for inclusive educational opportunities. Mary has been and continues to be an inspiration to families and educators who strive for an inclusive and just society.

Professor Falvey had written and compiled *Community-Based Curriculum: Instructional Strategies for Students with Severe Handicaps*. As more inclusive educational options were sought and became available, the reality of what happened in the classroom fell short of what was hoped for. Recognizing this deficiency, she saw the need for a book to cover instructional strategies in the full inclusion setting. *Inclusive and Heterogeneous Schooling: Assessment, Curriculum, and Instruction* brings forth ways to educate all children together without sacrificing the needs of any.

When we were first presented with the idea that our son might be fully included *in a regular classroom in his neighborhood school*, we as a couple had split opinions. Ben embraced it because of the value and benefit it had for all children. Renee questioned how it could be applied and wanted strategies. What was important was that neither of us could imagine our son growing as we hoped while he was in a segregated environment. Now, after more than 5 years of full inclusion, we have both seen the ability of all children to achieve what we, as adults, could not even imagine: acceptance. As for Caleb, his language and behaviors improved in the general education classroom and continue to do so. We have seen that as new problems surface, new strategies are developed to solve them. Everyone learns and grows. People like growing.

Full inclusion is a value, and there is something that moves us deeply when we speak about our values. Values should represent the principles and standards that we live by, not just ideals to talk about. Therefore, the means for accomplishing these values are as important as the outcome. Children are very good observers of the way educators model and demonstrate the value and importance of each student. They notice when a method is more important than the child. Methods providing immediate results are highly attractive, but may not account for individual differences and the many variables that occur in the classroom—learning styles and cultural, emotional, cognitive, and physical issues. Quick fixes and immediate results don't help people relate to and learn about each other. For long-term solutions, individuals must be willing to go through a process that develops their understanding, empathy, and positive regard for each other. It takes time to know and understand another person. Taking time to learn about another person suggests that the person has value and is worth the time invested to know him or her. Fundamental to that process must be the basic value that we all have something to learn from each other. When teachers treat all their students as worthy and with respect, they are teaching and *demonstrating* that everyone has a value and is deserving of respect.

Inclusive and Heterogeneous Schooling: Assessment, Curriculum, and Instruction places techniques and strategies in the regular education classroom. For full inclusion to work, students, parents, teachers, and educators must be willing to work as a team, problem solving together. This model requires collaborative participation on all levels. Different perceptions of the problem stimulate fresh insights and lead to previously unthought-of solutions. Numerous inputs continue to shape this model. The most functional communities work this way. The bottom line is that everyone's exposure and involvement with students having disabilities takes away the mystery surrounding these children. Being there and dealing with the everyday issues takes away the fear imposed by separation. Interaction breaks down barriers of all kinds.

Classroom management, instructional strategies, and positive behavior changes are presented in this book in a way that provides practical, applicable methods to use with students of all ages and abilities. The strategies are clearly and simply provided. The value is this: All students can learn. They may not all learn at the same pace or in the same way, but they can learn and change together.

As parents we want to see a world where all children, including those with differences as significant as our son's, can be appreciated. Our hope is that the sentiments and actions of all adults will someday reflect the empathy and friendship the children willingly extend to each other in the fully inclusive setting. We must look past the inconvenience of learning new ways to educate and the discomfort brought by change. We must accept failures as precursors to success, and we must let the children show us what they can and are willing to do.

Renee and Ben Adams
Los Angeles, California

PREFACE

This book is intended to assist in moving forward to change systems, people's attitudes, and community accessibility for people with disabilities. My two previous books, the first and second editions of *Community-Based Curriculum: Instructional Strategies for Students with Severe Handicaps*, focused on strategies for moving students with severe disabilities off segregated school campuses and into community settings. The pressure from parents, students, educators, and advocates has been strong enough to change this priority and has brought the discontinuation of the segregated school service delivery model in many communities. As a result of closing segregated schools, many segregated classrooms were created on general education campuses outside of students' neighborhoods, where the curriculum and instructional offerings do not provide students access to the core general education curriculum and where the assumption prevails that special educators are the only skilled educators who can effectively teach students with disabilities. Fortunately, educators, parents, students, and advocates have not been willing to accept this reality and have pushed systems to create neighborhood general education school curriculum and instructional access with the necessary supports of general and special educators, peers, parents, and community members to make inclusive education successful. This book is designed to assist educators, administrators, and parents to take the necessary next steps to create inclusive educational communities that support all students. Some of the original work contained in the two editions of *Community-Based Curriculum: Instructional Strategies for Students with Severe Handicaps* is retained in this new text; however, the principles and strategies addressed in this text are presented within the context of inclusive schooling.

This book uses the terms severe and significant disabilities interchangeably when referring to those students with these labels. However, disability labels are generally not useful when developing relationships or when designing educational interventions.

ACKNOWLEDGMENTS

This book would not have been possible if it were not for the many people who support me in my daily professional and personal life. The chapter contributors have lent their incredible expertise to create a much more comprehensive and credible text than I could have completed alone. The collaborative efforts and the contributions of general and special educators, administrators, parents, and students to this text are impressive, and they are what make it so sensitive and real. A special thanks to Katie, Jenni, and Marquita for their tremendous assistance, as painful and laborious as it seemed at times; they assisted in providing the conceptual framework for the book. I want to specifically thank Marquita for her input and insight in the Friendship Chapter and Jenni for the same in the Friendship and Communication Chapters.

I would also like to thank my students, both those at California State University, Los Angeles, and those at the numerous colleges, universities, and other educational communities where I have had the opportunity to teach. Much of the material in this text came from you, our discussions, and questions that always push me to think harder and more clearly. A special acknowledgment to Susann; I know these writing experiences will hold you in good stead once you complete your doctoral studies and move on.

To my new colleagues at California State University, Los Angeles, who contributed to this text, Chris, Christina, and Diane: I look forward to our ongoing collaborative relationship, which will more directly and effectively train educators to contribute to the success of inclusive educational settings. Lori, you are such a terrific teacher and friend; thanks for all you give me. To Lisbeth, for making sure the needs of young children were addressed in this book, thanks. To my great pals (and my children's great pals) "Richy Rich" and Jacque, who trusted me and I them, that what we do individually and collectively will support and not distract from our agenda! To the students, those with and without labels, and their families, many of whom are my trusted friends, you have given me so much; and if we can just learn to "listen" to you more often we will hear, see, feel, and understand the solutions. I especially thank Sue Rubin, who has taught me so much about hope and courage.

Ben and Renee, the words in the Foreword are thoughtful and insightful as always. You have been such a strength for our family in our struggles to create supports for children that enhance their abilities, gifts, and talents. Thanks for all you do for Caleb, our children, other children, and their families and for the way you live your lives, which reflects the principles of justice, equality, and freedom.

To the Paul H. Brookes Publishing Company staff, including Paul, thanks for all your support and trust in me. Especially thanks to Melissa, who as usual demonstrated her phenomenal knowledge and skills in editing the manuscript not only for writing style, but also for content. You continue to impress and amaze me. To Lyn, welcome to Brookes and thanks for all your fresh insight; it always helped.

Most authors and editors at this point thank their family for putting up with them during the writing process, and I must follow suit. I cannot imagine a more helpful and supportive partner than Richard; he has been my best and most committed colleague and friend for the past 20 years. There were times, many times, when he cared more about this project than I did! Thanks for keeping me on track. Nathan and Anthony, you two have had to be the most patient without really understanding why—thanks for that, and you have your mom back!

This text is dedicated to all the children, but particularly to my children and my nieces and nephews, Nathan, Anthony, Tara, Sean, Shannon, Mikel, Diedre, Darcy, Colin, Jeanette, Laurel and Marissa with faith that you all will be respected as learners with strengths, talents, and gifts and that you will all experience, teach, and be models of justice, equality, and freedom for all throughout your lives.

INTRODUCTION

JACQUELINE S. THOUSAND, RICHARD A. VILLA, AND MARY A. FALVEY

As a people, we strive to make progress through the ages toward justice, equality, and freedom for all. To experience lifestyles that truly reflect these principles, however, requires constant vigilance. Change comes slowly and not always in the desired direction. This has been true in how society responds to people with disabilities.

Everything has changed, but nothing has changed.

> *Children and adults with disabilities have greater possibilities to be welcomed into their communities than past generations.*

> *Yet thousands of children and adults with disabilities are still forced into segregated services within schools, work, and housing arrangements.*

Everything has changed, but nothing has changed.

> *We have technology (computers, fax machines, cellular phones, electronic communication aids, calculators, spell checkers, and so on) to assist us in daily lives that become increasingly complex.*

> *Yet technological resources are also allocated in ways that bring modern conveniences only to those who can afford them, applied in ways that gratify self-interests (e.g., economic status), and misapplied in life and death situations (e.g., terminating an infant's support in a neonatal care unit), rather than used to support and assist people who most need the new resources.*

Everything has changed, but nothing has changed.

> *The United States of America has had a civil rights law, the American with Disabilities Act, since 1990 that guarantees the rights of people with disabilities.*

Yet the accessibility rights of children and adults with disabilities continue to be denied in school, work, housing, transportation, and community life.

Everything has changed, but nothing has changed.
We have begun to recycle and become more aware of Earth's precious natural beauty and our responsibility to protect it.

Yet filth, pollution, and poison still spoil our rivers, streams, and oceans, and litter our city streets and parks.

Everything has changed, but nothing has changed.
People with disabilities are moving out of institutions and into the community.

Yet nursing homes, groups homes, and other congregate housing arrangements, in which care providers control and manage people with disabilities, continue to flourish as the common housing arrangement available to persons with severe disabilities.

Everything has changed, but nothing has changed.

What does all this mean? What can each of us contribute? This book is designed to illuminate some of the ways we can work within the education arena for justice, equality, and freedom in *all* students' lives.

Throughout history, education has been for the elite. In the United States, for example, the first attempt to provide education to a larger proportion of the population was Thomas Jefferson's 1779 plan for 3 years of public education for poor white boys and girls of Virginia with continued education for poor "gifted" white boys. Although Jefferson's plan was clearly undemocratic, it was the most liberal of the time. Unfortunately, Jefferson's plan was rejected, the well-to-do refusing to finance the education of the poor.

More than 100 years later, education became state supported, but inequities continued. Native and African Americans who received education, received it separately. Ability tracking became popular, with children from low socio-economic groups and racial and ethnic minorities routinely put in low tracks. The 1954 landmark Supreme Court *Brown v. Board of Education* ruling, "separate is not equal," helped to address these inequities. It opened integrated education for African Americans and other minorities, and it focused attention on the exclusion of students with disabilities.

Education for Americans with disabilities had begun in 1817 with Gallaudet's Asylum for the Education and Instruction of the Deaf and Dumb. From asylums and residential institutions to special schools and classes, access to education for students with disabilities made halting progress. More than 20 years after the *Brown* decision, the U.S. Congress finally passed PL 94-142 in 1975, the Education for All Handicapped Children Act. Promised a "free, appropriate public education" in the "least restrictive environment," students with disabilities finally began to move toward partial and full inclusion in community and school life. Experiments in educating students with varying challenges in regular classrooms yielded documented benefits for students with and without disabilities, their teachers, and their families. And so arrived the notion and practice of "inclusive education"—*all* children having equal access to shared experiences in their local school and community. To paraphrase Lilly (1988), the move from segregated to inclusive education for all children is more than a passing fad. It is the culmination of nearly 180 years of development of services for students with learning and behavior problems that increasingly were based in a democratic value system of public education for all.

Inclusive education, then, might be considered a predictable moment in educational history that simultaneously reflects and pushes forward human rights and personalized educational philosophy and practice for everyone. To achieve inclusive education requires those who believe in it to employ strategies likely to foster the desired change in beliefs, dispositions, and actions of people who work for and in school systems.

Traditional Native American educational philosophy has been described as a powerful tool to guide educational and child development theory and practice (Brendtro, Brokenleg, & Van Bockern, 1990). It offers yet another representation of progress in schooling. Native Americans' approaches to education emerged from a culture where the main purpose of existence is to educate and empower children. It is a holistic approach with a central goal of fostering self-esteem. Coopersmith (1967) identified four components of self-esteem: *significance*, derived from the acceptance and affection of others; *competence*, developed through mastery of the environment and a satisfaction and sense of efficacy derived from success; *power*, experienced through demonstrations of self-control and the gaining of others' respect; and *virtue*, or worthiness as judged by the culture's values. Traditional Native American education attempts to address all four bases of self-esteem through four practices or goals of Native education known as the Circle of Courage (Brendtro et al., 1990, p. 34):

1. *Belonging*—the nurturing of significance in a culture that recognizes a universal need for belonging
2. *Mastery*—ensurance of competence through guaranteed opportunities to develop and demonstrate mastery
3. *Independence*—the fostering of a sense of power through encouragement to express personal independence
4. *Generosity*—the experiencing of worthiness by practicing the highly valued virtue of generosity toward others

This philosophy continues to guide school communities in the delivery of educational services for all students and in the process of changing systems from segregated to inclusive environments that acknowledge and emphasize the whole person.

This text has been written to enlighten and empower educators, related services staff, parents, students, and administrators to design and implement effective educational programs that meet the needs of all students. Chapters 1 and 2 provide historical accounts of the events leading up to contemporary education in both the general and the special education systems. This provides a backdrop for the inclusive educational strategies delineated in subsequent chapters.

Chapter 3 discusses the importance of collaboration—why and how educators, parents, administrators, students, and other community members must work together when designing educational plans for students. All key stakeholders need to be involved in the planning and monitoring of educational programs if they are to be effective. This chapter details strategies for such planning and monitoring.

Through the gathering of meaningful, ongoing assessment information, educators, students, administrators, and parents are provided with the information critical to designing effective educational practices based on individual students' needs. Chapter 4 provides the reader with this foundation. Specific strategies that can be used to efficiently and comprehensively obtain such assessment information are also reviewed.

Chapters 5, 6, and 7 discuss strategies for increasing the probability of students' active participation in the learning process. Chapter 5 delineates strategies teachers can use to organize their classrooms effectively and enlist students' participation in establishing rules and norms for the class. Chapter 6 includes a detailed discussion of the various instructional strategies that have been used successfully to facilitate students' acquisition of new skills and maintenance of previously learned skills. A discussion of the importance of using positive rather than previously punishing procedures to facilitate students' learning is detailed in Chapter 7. This chapter also includes specific strategies for implementing such positive procedures, especially with students who have experienced significant behavior challenges in their lives.

Teaching students personal care, motor, and communication skills is the focus of Chapters 8 and 9. Specific strategies for incorporating personal care, motor, and communication objectives into the general education curriculum are provided in these two chapters. Strategies for facilitating students' development of friendships are delineated in Chapter 10.

Chapters 11, 12, 13, and 14 address the assessment, curriculum, and instructional needs of students across ages. Chapter 11 focuses on preschoolers, Chapter 12 turns to the needs of elementary students, and Chapter 13 examines the needs of secondary-age students. Students who are post high school are the subject of Chapter 14.

The book concludes with a chapter on strategies for changing systems to better respond to innovations in education, particularly those associated with the provision of inclusive education. This chapter includes an example of one school district's plan and a description of the implementation strategies used during the change process.

Edmonds (1979) stated that "(a) We can, whenever we choose, successfully teach all children whose schooling is of interest to us; (b) We already know more than we need to know to do that; and (c) Whether or not we do it must finally depend on how we feel about the fact that we haven't so far" (p. 22). In other words, the will or motivation to change systems to be more responsive and equitable to all children and adults is really up to each of us. The knowledge of how to change exists, and much of it is included in this text. The critical and current question becomes, will we respond to the needs of all students, and if so, when?

REFERENCES

Brendtro, L., Brokenleg, M., & Van Bockern, S. (1990). *Reclaiming youth at risk: Our hope for the future*. Bloomington, IN: National Education Service.

Coopersmith, S. (1967). *The antecedents of self esteem*. San Francisco: W.H. Freeman.

Edmonds, R. (1979). Effective schools for the urban poor. *Educational Leadership, 37*(1), 15–24.

Lilly, S. (1988). The regular education initiative: A force for change in general and special education. *Education and Training in Mental Retardation, 23*, 253–260.

Practices in General Education: Past and Present

Jennifer J. Coots, Kathryn D. Bishop,
Marquita Grenot-Scheyer, and Mary A. Falvey

Reform and restructuring of our educational system have long been topics of discussion within the field of education. The responses have been both emotional and provocative. A long "troubled crusade against ignorance," for example, were Ravitch's (1983) words for our efforts at educational reform; Tharp and Gallimore (1988) described reform-minded dialogues in the 1980s as "only the most recent of the irregular series of national spasms that, from time to time, grip the nation" (p. 1). Frady (1985) said that

> our system of public schools, that fundamental national institution is itself poised on the threshold of a decade of peril—a precarious moment of truth which could decide the survival or final decay of our whole concept of public schooling. (p. 4)

Bastian, Frutcher, Gittell, Greer, and Haskins (1986) said that the "current ferment in public education arises within a national climate of resurgent conservatism" (p. 13). Kozol (1991) wrote of the "savage inequalities" in our public school system. The height of emotion is not surprising considering that, ultimately, these discussions revolve around mapping out the future for our society's children and future generations. Clearly, there is concern about our public education, whatever the emotion shared and the terminology used. The fundamental question appears to be: How do we best educate all students and help each to achieve his or her full potential? This question must be asked, addressed, and answered for all students, including those with significant disabilities.

There have been many and varied responses to the question of how to best educate all students, with little agreement among respondents. The varied responses reflect an ongoing struggle between effectively meeting the needs of each individual as well as efficiently meeting the needs of groups of students in our attempt to provide education for an entire citizenry. One initial answer to striking a balance between meeting the needs of individuals and groups was the development of dual systems of education: general education and special education. However, at present, some reforms in both special and general education are moving toward a unified, inclusive system of education where the education of all students will become the concern of the entire school system. This chapter provides a historical perspective on reforms in general education; a chapter on historical perspectives on special education follows. We do this so that the reader will develop an understanding of the parallel reform efforts in general and special education that have compelled us to envision a unified system where the needs of all students are effectively addressed. The end goal is a system of education that more accurately reflects and prepares all students to learn to function in our diverse, pluralistic society.

HISTORICAL PERSPECTIVE

The present organization of our schools can be likened to a factory system. Such a factory model, where children move down an educational assembly line and progress to a new grade each year, was seen as an efficient way to provide effective educational services to the masses and was based upon similar models developed during the industrial revolution (Finkelstein, 1992). To keep the assembly line running efficiently, students who could not "keep up" or who required additional assistance to achieve were placed in separate programs. The development of these dual programs was thought to be a key element in the efficient operation of the factory-model system.

A formal, organized system of public education evolved slowly. Historically, education occurred within the family setting. Needed skills were passed from an experienced family member to children, including the skills necessary to hunt, farm, raise livestock, read, write, and so forth. Over time towns hired teachers to teach many of these skills, and finally communities organized public systems of education. The social and economic benefits of a well educated citizenry led to increasing standardization of educational programs (Ravitch, 1983). School systems therefore grew into centralized, professionalized bureaucracies in an attempt to provide systematic, standardized educational services for all children.

Limitations of Traditional School Models

Unfortunately, traditional school models and systems have been found by many to be ineffective in meeting the educational needs of the diverse student body in most classrooms and schools in the 1990s (e.g., Capper, 1993; Kozol, 1991; United States Department of Education, 1991). The increasing cultural, ethnic, and economic diversity in our society results in great variation in the experiences students have outside school settings (Ogbu, 1974; Orfield & Paul, 1987–1988). The experiences and expectations for children at home, including behavioral, social, and educational experiences, are often inconsistent with the experiences and expectations for them at school (Delgado-Gaitan, 1992; Greenfield, 1984). Many children are therefore not prepared to face the different and often rigid rules, demands, and expectations of the school system. Our traditional models of schooling present other limitations for certain groups of students as well. For example, lowered expectations and class differences in instruction have resulted in a less challenging or "watered down" curriculum for some economically disadvantaged students (Goldenberg, 1991; Levin, 1988; Moll, 1992).

Traditional models have also been criticized for their inability to prepare many students to participate fully as adults in their communities. Students who went into special education programs were often not prepared to reenter the community mainstream once they left the school system (Brown et al., 1986; Wehman, Hill, Wood, & Parent, 1987). Yet many children identified as having a disability or as unable to complete school tasks function effectively outside the school setting (Berryman, 1993; Mercer, 1973). Clearly, the expectations for students within the system and preparation provided by the school setting have not met the needs and expectations of the community outside the school setting. Many students graduate schools today ill prepared to meet even the most mundane demands of the work world, such as functional use of literacy and numeracy skills (Berryman, 1993; De La Garza, 1992). Some students drop out of school before graduating because they find it difficult to envision how the training provided will help them to function in the world outside of school or fulfill adult roles and responsibilities (Calathes, 1991; Pallas, 1993).

Another limitation of traditional models of education is the increasing isolation of teachers. In the prevailing school model, individual teachers direct and guide the education for groups of students within individual classrooms. Teachers of special education (specialists) and teachers of regular education (generalists) operate within separate systems, classrooms, and often separate schools. The actions of all of these teachers are directed by rules and regulations set by school boards in addition to state and federal agencies. Such a model places limits on decision making by individual teachers at the classroom level. It also provides few opportunities for collaboration and sharing of expertise, though the benefits of collaboration among classroom teachers and other school staff are many (Harris, 1990; Tharp & Gallimore, 1988).

Efforts to Restructure

After release of the federal report *A Nation at Risk* (National Commission on Excellence in Education, 1983), educational reformists intensified their calls for increased time on task as well as more accountability, evaluation, and regulation from state governments. It was thought that our educational systems could work more effectively and efficiently through increasing regulations and accountability from the top down (e.g., Smith & O'Day, 1991). Since the publication of *A Nation at Risk*, reformists have suggested a more broad-based reworking of the structure of our educational system (e.g., Cohen, 1988; Darling-Hammond, 1993; Goodlad, 1984). Such broad-based reform requires thoughtful restructuring of beliefs and practices at district, school, and classroom levels involving students, teachers, parents, administrators, and community members. The suggested reorganization includes modifying and changing the roles and responsibilities of all members of the educational community, along with restructuring and modifying curriculum and instruction.

Changing Roles and Responsibilities

As noted earlier, traditional school models do not reflect a system of collaboration where the performance of each individual in the system is assisted by competent others in an ongoing, collaborative fashion. Rather, teachers, schools, and districts have often operated in isolation, with decision-making responsibility in some areas but with many activities regulated by others in the system hierarchy. In addition, the dual nature of the present general education program and specific categorical programs, such as special education, has tended to limit the amount of collaboration between generalists and specialists.

Sailor (1991a) has suggested that the restructuring should shift the power over the daily routines of schools and classrooms away from the district level to each individual school-site community. According to Sailor, this level of restructuring must reflect the following four components: 1) organizational support and relational autonomy at the school-site and classroom level, 2) full infusion and coordination of all available resources (e.g., special and general education) to all students and classrooms, 3) site-based management and shared decision making among students, teachers, parents, and community members, and 4) community participation in the life of the school.

Where districts have been able to shift power to individual schools via Sailor's (1991a) four components, increasingly collaborative roles have emerged for school administrators (Capper, 1993; Villa, Thousand, Stainback, & Stainback, 1992). New models of administration such as site-based management and shared decision making call for administrators to become more facilitative than directive. These new models also call for administrators to promote visions and values, and to support and encourage positive action on the part of students, teachers, parents, and community members. Other new administrative roles include identifying and articulating the needs of inclusive schools and providing an important link between the schools and the larger community.

New roles for teachers (as included in Sailor's [1991b] four components) have also emerged, reflecting increased collaboration and consultation for both general and special education teachers (Bishop, Foster, & Jubala, 1993). These changing roles have several positive outcomes. First, infusing needed resources into a single system of diverse classrooms rather than operating dual systems allows for lower teacher–student ratios, as well as provides teachers with access to a wider variety of materials and technological support in the classroom. Second, collaborative efforts among teachers with varying areas of specialization has resulted in increased available expertise for all teachers in meeting the academic, physical, and socioemotional needs of all students. Third, participation in shared decision making empowers teachers and leads teachers and students to be more active participants in daily decisions about teaching and learning.

Business leaders and other persons in the community have also taken on new roles by becoming increasingly involved in raising money for schools, supplying equipment and technical assistance, and facilitating volunteer teaching by their employees to public school students. As employment needs have changed, business leaders have had a more vested interest in the curriculum and activities of the schools (Harris, 1990; Sailor, 1991a). Developing relationships between local schools and businesses can result in broader community ownership and support of schooling as well as better preparation of students for employment in the community.

Curricular and Instructional Reform

Suggested reforms for organizational systems have been accompanied by efforts to introduce reform in curriculum and instruction. Central to these efforts has been a change in focus from short- to long-term outcomes of schooling. This practice is sometimes referred to as "outcomes-based education" (OBE). As this shift in focus to long-term outcomes occurs, educators, parents, students and other community members are working collaboratively to determine what students should know, do, and be like when they have completed school. Outcomes-based education has received attention, both positive and negative, from educators, administrators, school boards, and local communities. Though still controversial, such attention to long-term outcomes has been credited with leading to more functional and more applied curriculum as well as to instruction that is more diverse and more reflective of the learning opportunities outside of school. Other reforms that have arisen from focusing on long-term outcomes include increased attention to teaching values and social skills in school curricula. Each of these suggested reforms is described below.

Learning to apply basic academic skills and higher order thinking skills in a functional manner is of value to all students, although such a balance has not been typical in school programs (Berryman, 1993; Gehrke, Knapp, & Sirotnik, 1992; Graham, 1992; Stipp, 1992). For example, traditional math curricula typically focus on short-term outcomes of basic skill acquisition in isolation from real-life applications. Yet students can benefit greatly from being taught how to approach and eventually solve complex, real-life problems by applying math skills integrated with skills learned from other areas of the curriculum (e.g., language arts, science, social studies). Curricula addressing such a long-term outcome for the application and integration of math skills might involve teaching students how to balance a checkbook, track stock market investments, or develop a budget for grocery shopping.

Besides a focus on curriculum, reform efforts have also targeted the style of instruction. Adapting school instruction to be more like the style of instruction found in everyday learning experiences outside of school is of value to students for developing thinking skills and for learning to apply information taught at school to everyday life (Berryman, 1993; Goldenberg, 1991; Goodlad & Anderson, 1987; Tharp & Gallimore, 1988). Traditionally, classroom styles of instruction have been teacher directed and have relied on large-group instruction that offers little opportunity to recognize the individual learning needs of students. This approach can result in disconnected conversations and interactions, referred to as *disconnected discourse* and places students in a passive role. Through effective use, instead, of extensive discussion and connected discourse, teachers can successfully facilitate students' skill acquisition by designing instructional procedures that are compatible with students' learning styles and needs. In connected discourse, the teacher and students discover shared understanding through genuine interaction, discussion, and dialogue.

In a related approach that is sensitive to individual learning styles, teachers can employ individualized learning contracts that allow students to learn at their own pace, using types of materials and instructional techniques that best meet their learning styles. An example of such a contract might be one that requires each student to develop a *portfolio*, that is, a product that represents the students' learning on a particular topic. For instance, following a visit to a local mission and time for other study on California missions, students might draw pictures of several missions, participate in the development of a dramatic play regarding the missions, and complete a computer-generated journal that summarizes both the visit and other research conducted (e.g., information gathered from encyclopedias, other written sources, and interviews with knowledgeable people). The use of such ongoing portfolios as assessment tools has dramatically increased in recent years. Portfolios are often more authentic and comprehensive assessment tools than traditional tests because portfolios can provide a rich picture of a student's strengths and needs and can tap multiple ways of knowing.

Increased attention to teaching values within the curriculum presented to all students is another area of reform (Noddings, 1992; Strike, 1991). Although it is sometimes difficult to identify shared values within an increasingly diverse society, many school districts now work to include the explicit teaching of values within their curriculum. For example, some school districts focus on values of cooperation and serving the greater community by adding community service experience as a graduation requirement (Nazario, 1992). Other districts promote discussion and study of values reflecting a variety of national, cultural, ethnic, religious, and personal perspectives (Strike, 1991).

The focus on individual achievement and competition characteristic of most American schools has been criticized (Bastian et al., 1986). This criticism has led to calls for fostering peer relationships and social skills development within school settings. Such instructional arrangements as cooperative learning groups, town meetings, Tribes, and Circles of Friends are effective means to build both academic skills and social skills and are described in Chapters 5, 10, and 12.

As roles and responsibilities are redefined and curriculum and instruction change, our educational system is being restructured. The fundamental purpose of schooling and the practices that best achieve those purposes must constantly be reexamined for continued growth and improvement in providing educational services for students with and without disabilities in common settings. One way to design and deliver appropriate educational services is to determine the general components that are necessary for "good" schools, those that include and effectively educate *all* students. The following sections discuss what makes a school good and outline a number of components essential to those good schools.

WHAT MAKES A GOOD SCHOOL?

A good school is one in which teachers and principals want to work and that parents want their children to attend. In addition, the school is an integral part of the community (Barth, 1990; Levin, 1992). A good school is a place where everyone is learning and teaching and where everyone receives the supports necessary to develop.

A good school also respects differences in gender, race, ethnic backgrounds, languages spoken, religion, sexual orientation, abilities, and so on. Those differences are highlighted, attended to, and celebrated as valuable opportunities for learning (National Coalition of Advocates for Students, 1991). Students develop an understanding of different values and lifestyles through daily interactions with a variety of people. Through such opportunities, students benefit from a strong foundation of skills necessary to live successfully in a diverse, global community (National Coalition of Advocates for Students, 1991).

As adapted from Barth (1990) and *The Good Common School* (National Coalition of Advocates for Students, 1991), a good school includes the following characteristics:

- All students are provided *free access* to schools that are safe, attractive, and without prejudice.
- Educational settings are *integrated, heterogeneous, and responsive* to different learning styles and abilities.
- *Equal educational opportunity* is supported by the provision of necessary resources for all students.
- *A broad range of support services* are provided to address the individual needs of all students.
- Teachers, other personnel, and parents *collaborate* to deliver educational services.
- Teachers hold *high expectations* for all students and are *prepared* to meet the challenges presented by diverse classrooms.

- *Comprehensive, sensible, culturally supportive, and developmentally appropriate teaching strategies and curricula* are presented.
- All students have access to a *common body of knowledge* and the opportunity to acquire *higher-order skills.*
- *Assessment of progress is broad based*, and evaluation structures enhance individual strengths and potential.
- *Peer interactions and relationships* are valued and facilitated.

Each of these characteristics is more fully described below.

All Students Are Provided *Free Access* to Schools that Are Safe, Attractive, and without Prejudice

Good schools adhere to the value of freedom of access for all students; that is, all students have the right to attend school. The right to attend school, while necessary, is not sufficient. The schools all children attend should be safe, attractive, and free from prejudice. No one should be summarily excluded or separated based upon race, social class, ethnicity, culture, gender, disability, primary language, religious beliefs, or sexual orientation. Although the Supreme Court decided in *Brown v. Board of Education* (1954) that separate was not equal, schools continue to separate students by such characteristics as class, race, IQ, disability, and primary language (Calathes, 1991). In addition, all students do not attend schools that are safe, attractive, and free from prejudice (Kozol, 1991). Such practices do not reflect free access for *all* students.

The decision to develop inclusive educational models with free access for all to safe and attractive schools that are without prejudice is ultimately a question of values and beliefs (Goodlad & Levitt, 1993). For the future of the society, schools must teach, model, and promote the understanding and appreciation of diversity and engage in practices that result in the successful inclusion of *all* students, without exception (see Chapter 5).

Educational Settings Are *Integrated, Heterogeneous, and Responsive* to Different Learning Styles and Abilities

Children must have access to integrated, heterogeneous educational settings that are responsive to individual differences in learning styles and needs. Historically, children have been grouped homogeneously for their learning: Spanish-speaking children placed in separate bilingual education programs; children identified as gifted placed in separate or advanced placement programs; and children with disabilities placed in separate special education classes and schools. Particularly in junior and senior high school general education programs, students are often "tracked"; that is, they are assigned to classes based upon their past performance (Kozol, 1991; Oakes, 1985). Although this practice was intended to facilitate instruction responsive to varying learning styles and abilities, there is limited evidence that it has led to positive achievement and attitudinal outcomes for students (Gursky, 1990). This practice has also contributed to the perpetuation of a society that segregates and separates its members according to differences.

In order to create a community that truly values and respects all of its members, students must be explicitly taught to value and respect one another. Where school systems continue to segregate students by various characteristics, students may be inadvertently learning that segregation is acceptable and necessary. The impact of this experience will likely remain with students for the rest of their lives. If, however, schools model the appreciation of diversity and acceptance of all students and respond to varying needs of students, students can learn to understand, respect, and value all members of their community and learn the skills necessary to create inclusive and caring communities (see Chapters 4 and 6).

Equal Educational Opportunity Supported by the Provision of Necessary Resources for All Students

Equal educational opportunity means that each student is given the support he or she requires to achieve his or her full potential. Equal educational opportunity does not refer to the even distribution of resources over an uneven foundation (National Coalition of Advocates for Students, 1991). Providing an equal educational opportunity requires a careful allocation of funds and resources. It is necessary but not enough to offer greater general access by building ramps, widening doorways, offering instruction in different languages, adding signs in Braille throughout the school, and so forth. Adequate and needed supports must be provided for each student based on his or her individual needs. With dwindling resources available for education, decisions about how to best allocate those resources are made all the more challenging. Such decisions are made even more complex by an increase in the number and types of supports needed for individual students to reach their full potential, due to the increasing diversity in today's schools and classrooms. Although such decisions about resource allocation can be challenging due to the tough budgetary constraints faced by most schools today, all students must be provided with equally favorable learning conditions, as well as equal opportunities to benefit from these conditions, for our schools to be effective (Calathes, 1991; Ogbu, 1974) (see Chapter 15).

A Broad Range of Support Services Are Provided to Address the Individuals Needs of All Students

The increasing diversity of students in classrooms today means an increase in the number and types of supports needed for individual students to reach their full potential. For students with disabilities, supports may include adapted educational materials (e.g., pictorial vs. written directions), peer supports, technological devices (e.g., computers), and consultants to assist with the designing of individualized instructional programs. For students who are economically disadvantaged, supports may include supplemental nutrition, counseling, and health-care assistance. For students whose primary language is other than

English, supports may include instruction that builds on skills in their native language and respects their ethnic and cultural skills, as well as teaching them to speak, understand, read, and write in English.

Past practices have too often confused intensity of services with location of service delivery (Taylor, 1988). That is, students who required additional support services to achieve and learn were served in programs separated from general education programs. Recently, researchers and educators have advocated that such support services can be brought to children within general education programs (e.g., Lipsky & Gartner, 1989; Stainback & Stainback, 1990, 1992). Therefore, good schools bring services to all children who need them within general education settings, rather than requiring that the students go to the services (see Chapters 8 and 9).

Teachers, Other Personnel, and Parents *Collaborate* to Deliver Educational Services

The supports needed for all students to reach their full potential can best be provided in a collaborative system where general educators, specialists, and parents each bring their specific areas of expertise to the process of defining needs and arranging supports to meet those needs (Rainforth, York, & Macdonald, 1992). Areas that can benefit from a collaborative sharing of expertise from different disciplines include mental health counseling, health services, behavior management, instructional adaptations to facilitate full participation by all students in classroom activities, personnel supports for secondary or post–secondary age students, and so forth. School personnel must make a concerted effort to facilitate collaboration, as implementing such a change requires more than a single in-service. Such changes require ongoing support and fundamental changes in the daily lives of teachers (Goldenberg & Gallimore, 1991). Skills for effective collaboration must be taught and practiced on a daily basis. School personnel must make special effort to facilitate meaningful parent involvement by acknowledging parents' expertise regarding the needs and abilities of their children, allowing for variety in the types and amount of involvement expected, and being sensitive to the multiple demands families must balance as they organize their daily routines (Bernheimer, Gallimore, & Weisner, 1990; Vincent & Salisbury, 1988) (see Chapters 3 and 15).

Teachers Hold *High Expectations* for All Students and Are *Prepared* to Meet the Challenges Presented by Diverse Classrooms

The diversity of contemporary classrooms and schools is well documented in both the professional literature and public media. "The challenges faced daily by classroom teachers have heightened exponentially during the past decade as intensified student needs are compounded by increasingly diverse student cultures and languages" (National Coalition of Advocates for Students, 1991, p. 248). With this increasing diversity, the challenge is to develop strategies that can be used to effectively teach all students. Unfortunately, the strategy often used for students who have not been successful in the classroom, students who are at risk for failing, female students, students with disabilities, or students whose cultural practices and language are different from the school majority has been to lower expectations by "watering-down" the curriculum or teaching concepts and skills at a slower rate than other students (Brandt, 1992; Levin, 1988).

Alternative strategies that teachers should be prepared to use to effectively meet the challenges presented by a diverse student population are described throughout this text. These include a knowledge of second language acquisition, whole-language approaches to integrate the curriculum, and knowledge of augmentative modes of communication to facilitate language and communication skills in all students. In addition, teachers should have a basic understanding of the important role culture and language play in shaping learning and the attitudes students hold toward one another. Teachers should then utilize materials and resources that reflect the experiences of all students, including those who are culturally and linguistically diverse. Classroom learning experiences should be used as opportunities to build respect, trust, and responsibility among students. As high expectations are intertwined with good teaching, schools will have high expectations for all their students, including those identified as having a disability, being a minority, or being economically disadvantaged (Brophy, 1983; Levin, 1992; also see Chapters 11–14).

Comprehensive, Sensible, Culturally Supportive, and Developmentally Appropriate Teaching Strategies and Curricula Are Presented

Contemporary classrooms and schools also require the use of varied approaches by teachers to meet the diverse learning styles and strengths present among students. These approaches include curriculum and instruction where learning is hands-on rather than passive. Learning is experiential so that students gather knowledge by doing, communicating, thinking, and experimenting while drawing upon real objects, experiences, and environments. With such varied approaches, instructional experiences extend beyond classroom walls.

Good schools invite exploration and allow for many possible outcomes instead of directing children to single, predetermined outcomes. Good schools also provide meaningful, functional, and age-appropriate learning experiences keyed into children's cultural backgrounds and personal interests. Curiosity and energy are honored and facilitated and serve as key sources of motivation (see Chapters 11–13).

All Students Have Access to a Common Body of Knowledge and the Opportunity to Acquire Higher-Order Skills

Students, regardless of their current ability levels, are entitled to an academic curriculum that is rich and stimulating. As mentioned earlier, too often students with disabilities, those who are not fluent in English, and others are restricted to curriculum and instructional strategies that are oversimplified, redundant, and rigid. All children should be afforded the joy of learning that stems from creative and dynamic instructional strategies, a rich and multifaceted curriculum, interactive settings, and involvement of families and other community members. In a good school, children share a common curriculum and work interactively to solve challenges and create their own knowledge base. They experience a learning process that promotes basic as well as higher-order thinking skills and establishes a foundation for cooperation and collaboration (see Chapters 12 and 13).

Broad Based Evaluation Structures
Enhance Students' Strengths and Potential

Student progress must be evaluated using procedures that are fair, yield meaningful results, and provide information about student strengths and needs. Traditional assessments, particularly standardized tests, do not typically provide such meaningful, broad-based information, and too often they focus on what students cannot do. Information about what students *can* do is essential for designing meaningful and comprehensive educational programs. The types of testing procedures that provide relevant and meaningful assessment information include conferences and home visits with parents, authentic assessment procedures such as portfolio evaluations, and structured and informal classroom observations (see Chapter 4).

Peer Interactions and Relationships Are Valued and Facilitated

In order for students to learn to function effectively in a social world, good schools must explicitly facilitate positive peer interactions and relationships and move away from a focus on individual achievement and competition. Instructional arrangements such as cooperative learning groups have been found to be effective means to build both academic and social skills. Working in groups and encouraging child-to-child interactions can promote a sense of belonging and valued interdependence. With such strategies, educators can make full use of peer resources and "power" to allow for student-to-student learning. Additional strategies that can facilitate positive peer interactions and relationships, including Circles of Friends, student collaboration, and peer tutoring, are described in coming chapters. Students can be creative problem solvers and can assist teachers in designing ways for all students to become accepted and meaningfully involved in class activities (Giangreco & Putnam, 1991). Such strategies should be based upon the notion of developing and using natural peer supports to learn to function effectively across multiple environments and activities (see Chapter 10). These natural supports for school-age children have been described as

> those components of an educational program—philosophy, policies, people, materials and technology, and curricula that are used to enable all students to be fully participating members of regular classroom, school, and community life. Natural

supports bring children closer together as friends and learning partners rather than isolating them. (Jorgensen, 1992, p. 183)

CONCLUSION

Our vision of good schools includes the encouragement and facilitation of flexible teaching styles. Teachers use varied approaches to allow for and encourage genuine interaction between students and teachers. This greater interaction allows teachers to monitor progress, provide feedback, and be more responsive to individual needs. Collaboration among staff and students is encouraged, so that specific areas of expertise are shared to meet the needs of all students. Peer resources and "power" are used to allow for student-to-student learning. Basic skills as well as higher-order skills are infused and systematically taught throughout the curriculum for all students. Parents are provided with opportunities to be full and valued participants in all educational decision making.

The reality of today's schools is disconcerting and requires that we question how to best reform or restructure our educational systems. A plethora of analyses, reports, and postulates have led to the conclusion that there are grave problems with the American educational system. Politicians, parents, academics, educators, and members of grass-roots organizations continue to create visions of a different nature. Their vision for all children and members of the community is a future of fulfilled human and community potential, security, belonging, and valued interdependence leading to meaningful contributions. Small steps are being accomplished that can create highly powerful changes in the quality of life of some individuals. Larger steps that will support universal change for all individuals are sure to follow. The remainder of this volume describes the reforms and specific strategies necessary to achieve those universal changes in the quality of schooling and life for all members of our society, particularly those with severe disabilities.

REFERENCES

Barth, R.S. (1990, March). A personal vision of a good school. *Phi Delta Kappan,* pp. 512–516.

Bastian, A., Frutcher, N., Gittell, M., Greer, C., & Haskins, K. (1986). *Choosing equality: The case for democratic schooling.* Philadelphia: Temple University Press.

Bernheimer, L.P., Gallimore, R., & Weisner, T.S. (1990). Ecocultural theory as a context for the Individual Family Service Plan. *Journal of Early Intervention, 14*(3), 219–233.

Berryman, S.E. (1993). Learning for the workplace. In L. Darling-Hammond (Ed.), *Review of research in education* (pp. 343–404). Washington, DC: American Educational Research Association.

Bishop, K.D., Foster, W.A., & Jubala, K.A. (1993). The social construction of disability in education: Organizational considerations. In C. Capper (Ed.), *Educational administration in a pluralistic society* (pp. 173–202). Albany, NY: SUNY Press.

Brandt, R. (1992). On building learning communities: A conversation with Hank Levin. *Educational Leadership, 50*(1), 19–23.

Brophy, J. (1983). Research on the self-fulfilling prophecy and teacher expectations. *Journal of Educational Psychology, 75*, 631–661.

Brown, L., Rogan, P., Shiraga, B., Albright, K.Z., Kessler, K., Bryson, F., Vandeventer, P., & Loomis, R. (1986). A vocational follow-up evaluation of the 1984–86 Madison Metropolitan School District graduates with severe intellectual disabilities. *Monographs of The Association for Persons with Severe Handicaps, 2*(2).

Brown v. Board of Education, 347 U.S. 483 (1954).

Calathes, W. (1991). Perpetuating social inequalities. *Thought and action: The NEA Higher Education Journal, 7*(2), 137–153.

Capper, C. (Ed.). (1993). *Educational administration in a pluralistic society.* Albany, NY: SUNY Press.

Cohen, M. (1988). *Restructuring the education system: Agenda for the 1990's.* Washington, DC: National Governors Association.

Darling-Hammond, L. (1993). Introduction. In L. Darling-Hammond (Ed.), *Review of research in education* (pp. xi–xxii). Washington DC: American Educational Research Association.

De La Garza, V. (1992). Improving the lives of children: Business must take a proactive approach now to create an effective workforce for tomorrow. *Investing in Education, A Supplement to the Los Angeles Business Journal,* p. A5.

Delgado-Gaitan, C. (1992). School matters in the Mexican-American home: Socializing children to education. *American Educational Research Journal, 29*(3), 459–513.

Finkelstein, B. (1992). Education historians as mythmakers. In G. Grant (Ed.), *Review of research in education* (pp. 255–297). Washington, DC: American Educational Research Association.

Frady, M. (1985). *To save our schools, to save our children: The approaching crisis in America's public schools.* Far Hills, NJ: New Horizon Press.

Gehrke, N.J., Knapp, M.S., & Sirotnik, K.A. (1992). In search of the school curriculum. In G. Grant (Ed.), *Review of research in education* (pp. 51–110). Washington, DC: American Educational Research Association.

Giangreco, M.F., & Putnam, J.W. (1991). Supporting the education of students with severe disabilities in regular education environments. In L.H. Meyer, C.A. Peck, & L. Brown (Eds.), *Critical issues in the lives of people with severe disabilities* (pp. 245–270). Baltimore: Paul H. Brookes Publishing Co.

Goldenberg, C. (1991). *Instructional conversations and their classroom application.* Washington, DC: National Center for Research on Cultural Diversity and Second Language Learning.

Goldenberg, C., & Gallimore, R. (1991). Changing teaching takes more than a one-shot workshop. *Educational Leadership, 49*(13), 69–72.

Goodlad, J. (1984). *A place called school: Prospects for the future.* New York: McGraw-Hill.

Goodlad, J.I., & Anderson, R.H. (1987). *The nongraded elementary school* (rev. ed.). New York: Teachers College Press.

Goodlad, J.I., & Levitt, T.C. (Eds.). (1993). *Integrating general and special education.* New York: Merrill.

Graham, E. (1992, September 11). Digging for knowledge: "Active learning" classes follow a difficult rule: student as worker, teacher as coach. *Wall Street Journal,* p. B1.

Greenberg, P. (1989). Parents as partners in young children's development and education: A new American fad? Why does it matter? *Young Children, 44*(4), 61–75.

Gursky, D. (1990). On the wrong track? *Teacher Magazine, 1*(8), 43–51.

Harris, K. (1990). Meeting diverse needs through collaborative consultation. In W. Stainback & S. Stainback (Eds.), *Support networks for inclusive schooling: Interdependent integrated education* (pp. 139–150). Baltimore: Paul H. Brookes Publishing Co.

Jorgensen, C.M. (1992). Natural supports in inclusive schools: Curricular and teaching strategies. In J. Nisbet (Ed.), *Natural supports in school, at work, and in the community for people with severe disabilities* (pp. 179–216). Baltimore: Paul H. Brookes Publishing Co.

Kozol, J. (1991). *Savage inequalities: Children in America's schools.* New York: Harper Perennial.

Lave, J. (1988). *Cognition in practice.* New York: Cambridge University Press.

Levin, H. (1988). *Accelerated schools for at-risk students.* [Brochure]. New Brunswick, NJ: Center for Policy Research in Education, Rutgers University.

Levin, H. (1992). Accelerating the education of all students. *Restructuring brief.* Santa Rosa, CA: Redwood Region Consortium for Professional Development.

Lipsky, D.K., & Gartner, A. (1989). School administration and financial arrangements. In S. Stainback, W. Stainback, & M. Forest (Eds.), *Educating all students in the main stream of regular education* (pp. 105–120). Baltimore: Paul H. Brookes Publishing Co.

Mercer, J.R. (1973). *Labeling the mentally retarded.* Berkeley, CA: University of California Press.

Moll, L.C. (1992). Bilingual classroom studies and community analysis: Some recent trends. *Educational Researcher, 21*(2), 20–24.

National Coalition of Advocates for Students. (1991). *The good common school: Making the vision work for all children.* Boston: Author.

National Commission on Excellence in Education. (1983). *A nation at risk.* Washington, DC: United States Department of Education.

Nazario, S.L. (1992, September 11). Right and wrong: Teaching values makes a comeback, as schools see a need to fill a moral vacuum. *Wall Street Journal,* p. B6.

Noddings, N. (1992). *The challenge to care in schools: An alternative approach to education.* New York: Teachers College Press.

Oakes, J. (1985). *Keeping track: How schools structure inequity.* New Haven, CT: Yale University Press.

Ogbu, J.U. (1974). The next generation: *An ethnography of education in an urban neighborhood.* New York: Academic Press.

Orfield, G., & Paul, F. (1987–1988, Fall/Winter). Declines in minority access. *Educational Record,* pp. 60–72.

Pallas, A.M. (1993). Schooling in the course of human lives: The social context of education and the transition to adulthood in industrial society. *Review of Educational Research, 63*(4), 409–447.

Rainforth, B., York, J., & Macdonald, C. (1992). *Collaborative teams for students with severe disabilities: Integrating therapy and educational services.* Baltimore: Paul H. Brookes Publishing Co.

Ravitch, D. (1983). *The troubled crusade.* New York: Basic Books.

Sailor, W. (1991a). Community school. In L.H. Meyer, C.A. Peck, & L. Brown (Eds.), *Critical issues in the lives of people with severe disabilities* (pp. 379–385). Baltimore: Paul H. Brookes Publishing Co.

Sailor, W. (1991b). Special education in the restructured school. *Remedial and Special Education, 12*(6), 8–22.

Smith, M., & O'Day, J. (1991). Systemic school reform. In S. Fuhrman (Ed.), *The politics of curriculum and testing* (pp. 47–68). Philadelphia: Falmer Press.

Stainback, S., & Stainback, W. (Eds.). (1992). *Curriculum considerations in inclusive classrooms: Facilitating learning for all students.* Baltimore: Paul H. Brookes Publishing Co.

Stainback, W., & Stainback, S. (Eds.). (1990). *Support networks for inclusive schooling: Interdependent integrated education.* Baltimore: Paul H. Brookes Publishing Co.

Stipp, S. (1992, September 11). Reinventing math: Active learning promises radical changes, as teachers say the rote approach doesn't add up. *Wall Street Journal,* p. B4.

Strike, K.A. (1991). The moral role of schooling in a liberal democratic society. In G. Grant (Ed.), *Review of research in education* (pp. 413–483). Washington, DC: American Educational Research Association.

Taylor, S.J. (1988). Caught in the continuum: A critical analysis of the principle of least restrictive environment. *Journal of The Association for Persons with Severe Handicaps, 13*(1), 41–53.

Tharp, R.G., & Gallimore, R. (1988). *Rousing minds to life.* New York: Cambridge University Press.

United States Department of Education. (1991). *America 2000: An education strategy sourcebook* (ED/0591–13). Washington, DC: Author.

Villa, R.A., Thousand, J.S., Stainback, W., & Stainback, S. (Eds.). (1992). *Restructuring for caring and effective education: An administrative guide to creating heterogeneous schools.* Baltimore: Paul H. Brookes Publishing Co.

Vincent, L.J., & Salisbury, C.L. (1988). Changing economic and social influences on family involvement. *Topics in Early Childhood Special Education, 8*(1), 48–59.

Wehman, P., Hill, M., Wood, W., & Parent, W. (1987). A report on competitive employment histories of persons labeled severely mentally retarded. *Journal of The Association for Persons with Severe Handicaps, 12*(1), 11–18.

SERVICES FOR STUDENTS WITH DISABILITIES: PAST AND PRESENT

MARY A. FALVEY, MARQUITA GRENOT-SCHEYER,
JENNIFER J. COOTS, AND KATHRYN D. BISHOP

People with disabilities, especially those with significant disabilities, have had to endure a history of rejection and forced segregation within society, including within the public school system. Despite litigation and legislation intended to eliminate such rejection and discrimination, large numbers of school-age students with disabilities have continued to be excluded from participating in schools and classrooms attended by their brothers, sisters, and neighbors without disabilities (*Fourteenth Annual Report to Congress on the Implementation of the Individuals with Disabilities Education Act* 141, 1992). Increasing advocacy efforts and research regarding effective education challenge these exclusionary practices (Cole & Meyer, 1991; York, Vandercook, Macdonald, Heiss-Neff, & Caughey, 1992). Therefore, the current educational trend is toward developing models of service delivery that include *all* students in common settings. The remainder of this book focuses on presenting the rationale for this practice and delineates the strategies that will assist in the development and implementation of successful inclusive models of education.

This chapter provides teachers, parents, administrators, related services staff, students, and others with a historical perspective on service delivery models for persons with severe disabilities. The following areas are discussed: implications of using disability labels; litigation and legislation; family and consumer-driven advocacy; past educational models; and current trends in service delivery, specifically inclusive classrooms and schools.

IMPLICATIONS OF USING DISABILITY LABELS

At present, labels such as "trainable," "severe and profound mental retardation," "autism," and "multiple handicaps" are used in many school districts to describe

23

persons with severe disabilities. These labels are used, for example, in discussions of individual differences, to define research samples, and to determine eligibility for services. However, the definitions for each of these labels are also the topic of frequent debate. As our scientific understanding of disabilities and our social constructions of disabilities change, our generally accepted definitions also change (Biklen & Duchan, 1994). An example is the definition of mental retardation that was approved by the Board of Directors for the American Association on Mental Retardation (AAMR) in 1992 (AAMR, 1992). This change represents a significant departure—a "paradigm shift"—from past conceptualizations of mental retardation. AAMR has published this definition in *Mental Retardation: Definition, Classification, and Systems of Supports,* 9th ed. (1992):

> Mental retardation refers to substantial limitations in present functioning. It is characterized by significantly subaverage intellectual functioning, existing concurrently with related limitations in two or more of the following applicable adaptive skill areas: communication, self-care, home living, social skills, community use, self-direction, health and safety, functional academics, leisure, and work. Mental retardation manifests before age 18. (p. 1)

This definition is in accord with the conceptualization of mental retardation presented by Marc Gold (1980), a leading early contributor in the design of services for persons with disabilities. He defined mental retardation as the "level of power needed in the training process required for the individual to learn, and not by limitations in what he or she can learn" (p. 5). Gold further stated: "The height of a retarded person's level of functioning is determined by the availability of training technology and the amount of resources society is willing to allocate and not by significant limitations in biological potential" (1980, p. 5). Within the new AAMR classification, mental retardation is no longer viewed as an absolute trait of an individual and distinctions are no longer made regarding "level of disability." Within this new definition, distinctions focus on the level and intensity of *support* needed by the individual. The designations for pattern and intensity of supports included in this definition are intermittent, limited, extensive, and pervasive. In other words, supports can be provided on a full-time or intermittent basis, and supports can range from minimal (or limited) to extensive or pervasive.

However, even with a more enlightened definition of mental retardation, using definitions to label people raises many concerns. One of the main concerns is that there are swift and often irreparable effects of the continued use of labels for individuals with disabilities (Armstrong, 1987; Biklen, 1992; Miller, 1993; Taylor, 1991). For example, a student having difficulties in school may be labeled a "mentally retarded" student, a "learning disabled" student, or an "emotionally disturbed" student. Those who interact with the student then may have trouble seeing a person first; instead, they see the disability and "all the stereotypes associated with the status" (Biklen, 1989, p. 13). The disability label and associated stereotypes can result in a single-minded approach to the education of the student, without regard to the whole individual. The label emphasizes a single attribute of a person and detracts from other attributes. Labels and simplistic stereotypes can create a negative and devalued identity for the person by members of his or her community. Labels can also become part of the common culture and can be used in a pejorative manner.

Even the most global terms used to describe a person, such as "handicapped" or "disabled," have been criticized due to their semantic origins. For example, the term "handicapped" originates from the phrase "cap in hand," a reference to people who beg for money by holding out a cap in their hand with the intention of receiving a charitable donation. The expression "cap in hand" conjures up an image of pity and disdain. The term "disabled" is used more frequently today than the term "handicapped," but this term also has the negative connotation of being "not able."

Numerous authors have suggested that labels provide an excuse for school systems who fail diverse student populations by placing the blame for "failure" on the students (Jones, 1972; Keogh, 1975; Sapon-Shevin, 1989). In addition, disability labels can imply a permanent deficit within an individual (Harry, 1992). If educators focus on these deficits and assume their permanence, expectations for a student may be lowered. Kindergarten teacher Anne Martin (1988) described how labels can "obscure children's potential":

> Early in the school year, I was asked to meet with school personnel who had administered a screening test to my new kindergarten children during the first weeks of school. To my surprise, test results indicated that fully half of my young students were considered to be "at risk" in one or more crucial developmental areas. One of my brightest students was said to be possible "learning disabled," and my most skilled artist deficient in fine motor ability. My most cooperative learner was "oppositional" and displayed "negative attitudes." (p. 489)

Martin was not willing to accept the test results about her students because her personal observations provided competing evidence of her students' potential. Another teacher might have assumed that the test results were a reflection of permanent deficits and subsequently expected less of her students.

There are major conceptual problems inherent in the development and use of labels. Current classification systems for disability labels are plagued with problems, as indicated by disagreement among professionals and demographic variation in identification practices (Biklen, 1989; Ysseldyke, Algozzine, & Epps, 1983). These problems include difficulties with the reliability and validity of fitting individuals into disability categories (e.g., Blashfield, 1973). In addition, the existence of disability labels and the assignment of those labels to individuals are as much sociocultural phenomena as medical, biologically based, or organic phenomena (Levine & Langness, 1986). The process of giving an individual a disability label is affected by social values, cultural belief systems, and political forces as much as any objective reality about that individual. Examples of the social, cultural, and political factors that affect the labeling process include available funding, school system structures, increasing scientific understanding of disabling conditions and their causes, changes in social constructions of disabilities, advocacy efforts, language used by an assessor as well as the primary language of the person being assessed, and the environment in which the individual is functioning. That these factors affect who is given a label at any point in time supports the premise that there are basic conceptual difficulties with labels and the labeling process.

Another concern regarding labels involves their limited usefulness to educators and parents, as they do not provide information that leads to informed programmatic, curricular, and instructional decisions (Sapon-Shevin, 1992). As noted in federal legislation mandating education for all students with disabilities, effective educational interventions must be based on an individual's needs rather than on a given disability label. Evans (1991) suggests that in addition to limited usefulness for schooling decisions, the designation of "mental retardation" or other related disability labels has little implication for housing, community life, or type of work. Sapon-Shevin (1989) argues that there are no individuals with disabilities in any absolute sense. As a result of our predisposition to label, we create disabilities by how we view and relate to students and through the ways we think about people and their differences. Too often, differences are equated with deviance. Such assumed "deviance" has often led to separation and segregation.

LEGISLATION AND LITIGATION

Separation and segregation in educational programs were initially criticized in the United States of America in relation to segregated schools for students of diverse racial and ethnic backgrounds. The first U.S. court case to revolutionize the principle of "equal citizenship" was *Brown v. Board of Education* (1954), frequently referred to as the *"Brown* decision." This decision effectively overturned the 1896 *Plessy v. Ferguson* decision in which the court agreed that segregation of nonwhites was constitutional as long as the services offered were equal. In declaring their legal opinion in the *Brown* decision, the United States Supreme Court overturned *Plessy v. Ferguson* and stated that separate educational facilities are inherently unequal. This segregation:

> generate[s] a feeling of inferiority as to [children's] status in the community that may affect their hearts and minds in a way unlikely ever to be undone. This sense of inferiority . . . affects the motivation of a child to learn . . . [and] has a tendency to retard . . . educational and moral development. (Warren, 1954, p. 493)

Similar equal citizenship rights were initially legislated for persons with disabilities in 1973 when Congress passed the Rehabilitation Act (PL 93-112), in particular Section 504 of the act. This law bars any agency receiving federal funds from discriminating against persons with disabilities. Specifically, the act states:

> A recipient [any agency receiving federal funds] shall provide educational services to each qualified handicapped person who resides in the recipient's jurisdiction, re-

gardless of the nature or severity of the person's handicap, in the most normal setting feasible and may not remove a handicapped person from, or place such a person in a setting other than, the regular educational environment except when the nature or severity of the person's handicap is such that education in regular classes with the use of supplementary aids and services is demonstrated by the recipient not to be in the best interest of such person. (*Federal Register*, Vol. No. 96, 1976)

In 1990, broader civil rights protections were legislated for persons with disabilities as the Americans with Disabilities Act (ADA), PL 101-336, was passed and signed into law. This law provides civil rights protections to all individuals with disabilities. While Section 504 of the Rehabilitation Act targeted agencies receiving federal funds, ADA requires that all businesses, public and private, comply with its mandates of "nondiscriminatory" practices. This is the true "Civil Rights Bill" for people with disabilities. The ADA guarantees equal opportunity for individuals with disabilities in employment, public accommodations, transportation, state and local government services, and telecommunications. Specifically, this law requires that employers; transportation systems; public utility companies; and private entities, such as hotels, restaurants, and retail stores, not discriminate against individuals with disabilities. These entities must provide "reasonable accommodations" to ensure an individual's access to and participation in community life. This law has been hailed as the final legislated protection against discrimination and prejudicial policies, procedures, and actions against persons with disabilities.

Although Section 504 and the ADA have had a broad impact upon civil rights and services for persons with disabilities, other landmark legislation has focused specifically upon educational services. In 1975, PL 94-142, the Education for All Handicapped Children Act, was signed into law. Subsequent amendments, including the 1990 amendment that changed its title to the Individuals with Disabilities Education Act (IDEA) (PL 101-476), require school districts to develop and offer a free, appropriate public education for all children and youth with disabilities in the least restrictive environment. Since PL 94-142 was first passed, *least restrictive environment* has been defined as:

> to the maximum extent appropriate, handicapped children, including those children in public and private institutions or other care facilities, are educated with children who are not handicapped, and that special classes, separate schooling, or other removal of handicapped children from the regular educational environment occurs only when the nature or severity of the handicap is such that education in regular classes with the use of supplementary aids and services cannot be achieved satisfactorily. (Section 1412[5][B])

Following the passage of this legislation, several federal court cases have attempted to clarify the full intent of the law, specifically the principles of special education law (Turnbull, 1990).

One of the principles recently clarified in a court case was the "zero-reject" principle (Turnbull, 1990). In this case, the School District of Rochester, New Hampshire, contended that Timothy W. was not entitled to the benefits of IDEA as he was "too disabled" and not "educable." They argued that he should be excluded from their educational programs as he would not benefit from an education. In 1988, the United States Court of Appeals in New Hampshire reversed a lower court finding in the question of the "educability" of this child. The United States Court of Appeals required that the school district assume the responsibility to educate all children residing in the school district, including Timothy W. This case specified that the term "all" in the amendments to IDEA meant "all" children with disabilities, without exception.

The least restrictive environment (LRE) principle of IDEA and its amendments is perhaps one of the most controversial and has therefore led to much litigation. One of the first major cases to clarify the meaning of LRE was the *New York State Association for Retarded Children v. Carey* (612F.2d 644, 2d Cir. 1979). The Second Circuit Court of Appeals upheld a district court order that refused to allow New York City Schools to segregate 48 students who were carriers of hepatitis B as a result of having once lived at Willowbrook State Institution (Gilhool, 1989). The following excerpt reflects the United States Court of Appeals decision regarding this case:

> The formation of special classes for this small group of children will naturally lead to a decrease in the curricular options that are available for each child . . . . Separation of the carrier children will also limit the extent to which they can participate in school-wide activities such as meals, recess, and assemblies, and will reinforce the stigma to which these children have already been subjected. (612F.2d. at 650-51).

In *Roncker v. Walter* (1983), a family in Cincinnati, Ohio, requested that the school district educate their 9-year-old son, categorized as severely retarded, with his peers without disabilities. They felt he would benefit from contact with his peers. The school district disagreed and recommended that the Roncker child attend a segregated school. The case was resolved in favor of the integrated placement because the court felt it was feasible to provide the required specialized educational services in the integrated setting. This has been referred to as the "principle of portability": "if a desirable service currently provided in a segregated setting can feasibly be delivered in an integrated setting, it would be inappropriate under PL 94-142 to provide the service in a segregated environment" (700 F. 2d at 1063).

Litigation has also occurred to clarify "education in regular classes with the use of supplementary aids and services." On May 28, 1993, the United States Court of Appeals for the Third Circuit upheld the right of students with disabilities to be included in "regular" education classes with peers without disabilities using supplementary aids and services. In this case, *Rafael Oberti v. Board of Education of Clementon, New Jersey* (1993), the Appeals court affirmed a federal district court ruling that Rafael Oberti, an 8-year-old child with Down syndrome, be provided with an education in a regular school in his neighborhood while receiving adequate and necessary support services in order to participate success-fully. United States Circuit Court Judge Edward R. Becker wrote:

> We construe the Individuals with Disabilities Education Act (IDEA), PL 101-476, mainstreaming requirement to prohibit a school from placing a child with disabilities outside of a regular classroom if educating the child in the regular classroom, with supplementary aids and support services, can be achieved satisfactorily. In addition, if placement outside of a regular classroom is necessary for the child to receive edu-cational benefit, the school may still be violating IDEA if it has not made sufficient efforts to include the child in school programs with nondisabled children whenever possible.

The Court of Appeals clarified that the law made a presumption in favor of inclu-sion and that the burden of proving compliance with IDEA's mainstreaming re-quirement is on the school district, not the parents. As Judge Becker wrote:

> The Act's strong presumption in favor of mainstreaming . . . would be turned on its head if parents had to prove that their child was worthy of being included, rather than the school district having to justify a decision to exclude the child from the reg-ular classroom.

The court ruled that children with disabilities must be included in school pro-grams with children without disabilities whenever possible. The ruling also states that districts must take meaningful steps to include children with disabilities in regular classes.

In a dispute over the right to an inclusive education for Rachel Holland, a 9-year-old girl with developmental disabilities (*Sacramento Unified School District v. Rachel Holland, 1994*), a United States district judge, the Honorable David Levi, upheld the administrative law judge's decision that the Sacramento Unified School District must create an education for Rachel in general education, with the provision of the necessary supplementary aids and services. Judge Levi indicated that when school districts determine the placement of students with dis-abilities, the starting point and presumption is mainstreaming. Although the school district appealed the district court's decision and the subsequent federal appellate court's equally favorable decision, the United States Supreme Court de-nied review of the Holland decision, thereby establishing standards that promote inclusive education.

FAMILY AND CONSUMER ADVOCACY

Service delivery models and changes in those models have been, over the years, influenced not only by legislation and litigation, as described above, but also by family advocacy efforts. The pre-1950s can be characterized by a lack of services and programs for individuals with disabilities, particularly those described as having significant and/or extremely challenging disabilities. However, in 1950, parents organized the Association for Retarded Children (currently known as The

Arc: A National Organization on Mental Retardation). This national organization, consisting of hundreds of local chapters, served as a support and information network for parents. Efforts of this organization and others led to the development and delivery of school services and other related programs for children and adults with disabilities in the late 1950s. These early programs were designed to give parents respite from the care of their child as well as to provide education and training, because the public schools had denied them access. The settings were typically segregated; often children and/or adults with disabilities attended "school" together in church basements or vacant schools. In the 1960s and 1970s, school districts and adult services providers began assuming responsibility for these programs, which had been developed by parent groups and Arc chapters.

In 1974, an advocacy organization, the American Association for the Education of the Severely and Profoundly Handicapped, now called The Association for Persons with Severe Handicaps (TASH) was formed. TASH is an international organization that had fewer than three dozen members in 1974 and now has more than 9,000. Since its founding, TASH has helped shape changes in service delivery for persons with severe disabilities. TASH has been instrumental in promoting inclusion of persons with severe disabilities into community life through its journal, newsletter, annual conference, service briefs, and lobbying efforts at the federal, state, and local levels, as well as through active involvement in litigation, local chapters, and individual member advocacy. TASH's mission statement reflects its purpose and commitment. In addition, TASH has passed a number of critical resolutions that have guided its efforts and activities over the years.

A great deal of the advocacy efforts in this country and throughout much of the world have been based upon the principle of normalization. In 1969, N.E. Bank-Mikkelsen, then director of the Danish Mental Retardation Services, defined normalization as providing opportunities for people identified as mentally retarded to obtain and maintain an existence in proximity to, and in a manner as similar as possible to, the "normal" population (Bank-Mikkelsen, 1969; Wolfensberger, 1970). Bengt Nirje (1969) elaborated on this principle and facilitated the development of Swedish laws governing normalized provision of services for persons with mental retardation. In the United States and Canada, Wolf Wolfensberger was responsible for the application of the principle of normalization to individuals labeled mentally retarded. He elaborated upon this principle by introducing the "culturally normative" concept. Viewing human services delivery through culturally normative lenses means that, to the greatest degree possible, services should be provided so that they reflect the culture of people without disabilities. When designing services and supports for persons with disabilities, Wolfensberger (1970) suggested that service providers use those "means which are as culturally normative as possible, in order to establish and/or maintain personal behaviors and characteristics which are as culturally normative as possible" (p. 28). Furthermore, persons with disabilities should be "enabled to emit behaviors and an appearance appropriate (normative) within that culture for persons of similar characteristics, such as age and sex" (Wolfensberger, 1979, p. 28). Wolfensberger later renamed this concept "social role valorization" (Wolfensberger, 1985). The focus of this principle is not, however, on forcing persons with disabilities to fit narrow standards of "normalcy." Rather, the focus is on the provision of culturally valued opportunities.

PAST EDUCATIONAL PRACTICES

While families and advocates were organizing programs for persons with disabilities, curricula were being developed for those programs. Prior to the 1980s, curricula for students with severe disabilities were based upon sequences of skills found in typical development. Students were taught the activities and skills typically exhibited by persons of the same "developmental age," without regard for their chronological age. For example, a 10-year-old assessed as "functioning" at a 2-year-old level would be taught the skills of a 3-year-old. (For examples, see Greer, Anderson, & Odle, 1982; Smith, 1968; Stephens, 1971.) The reliance upon a student's developmental age in decisions about what to teach contributed to the selection of chronological age–inappropriate activities. The use of such age-inappropriate activities limited the effectiveness of educational programs in that students left such programs with few skills of use in their daily lives, valuable time was wasted teaching skills that were not useful, interactions between students with and without disabilities of the same chronological age were limited, and the number and types of environments accessible to students were also limited. Therefore, in the late 1970s and 1980s, an emphasis on teaching functional and age-appropriate skills emerged in the literature (e.g., Brown et al., 1979; Goetz, Guess, & Stremel-Campbell, 1987; Horner, Meyer, & Fredericks, 1986).

Age-Appropriate Curricula

Chronological age–appropriate curricula provide students with opportunities to participate in activities that are performed by same-age peers without disabilities regardless of the students' mental or developmental ages. The concept of age appropriateness extends beyond school curricula; it also applies to the expectations and interaction styles that teachers display. That is, preschoolers with disabilities should be allowed to "act" like other 3- and 4-year-old children and not be held to more rigorous behavioral standards sometimes seen in specialized educational settings. Adults with disabilities should have access to and use those environments, materials, and activities that adults without disabilities use (e.g., attending and working at a community college, living in an apartment with friends). Age appropriateness also involves treating adults with disabilities as adults, giving them the full range of choices and options available to adults without disabilities in regard to where they live and work, the relationships they hold, and the people who provide them with support.

Functional Curricula

The term functional curricula refers to teaching skills that have direct and immediate utility in students' lives within their communities. In order to determine if a curricular activity is immediately functional, teachers can ask themselves: If the student does not learn to perform a particular activity, will someone else have to do it for him or her (Brown et al., 1979)? If the answer is yes, the activity is more likely to be functional than if the answer is no. For example, Canisha, a 17-year-old student with significant disabilities, was directed by her teacher to sort different shaped blocks. When she did not do so, it was not necessary for someone else to do it for her. However, when Canisha was not systematically taught to sort items for the purpose of recycling as part of her high-school health class, someone else had to do it for her. Sorting for the purpose of recycling would therefore be a functional skill for Canisha, while sorting blocks would not.

During the 1970s and 1980s, research was also being conducted on the general learning characteristics of persons with severe disabilities (Stokes & Baer, 1977). Stokes and Baer and other researchers found that persons with severe disabilities, particularly with mental retardation and autism, did not generalize well. In other words, when a person learned a skill in one setting, that same person had difficulty and sometimes could not demonstrate that same skill in another setting. Research on the difficulties of generalized learning (Donnellan & Mirenda, 1983; Stokes & Baer, 1977) influenced the development of "community-based" school and adult services delivery models that did not infer transfer of information. These community-based or community-referenced models provided instruction to students with severe disabilities in "real" community environments such as grocery stores, laundromats, public buses, and post offices (Falvey, 1989).

Shortcomings of Segregated Services

Although the characteristics associated with chronological age–appropriate, functional, and community-based instruction provided community access, educational programs reflecting these practices offered students varying degrees of integration with their peers without disabilities. They generally did not provide full participation and membership in the same settings as their peers without disabilities; rather, students were placed in segregated special schools or self-contained special classes. These practices were criticized for several reasons. First, segregated service delivery models limited opportunities for individuals with disabilities to develop the social skills necessary for increased independence as adults in work and community settings (Greenspan & Shoultz, 1981). Second, parents and teachers of students with disabilities expressed concern about the limited number and types of relationships available to students who were forced to attend segregated schools and classrooms. Friendships and other relationships provide critical opportunities to develop social and cognitive skills (Guralnick, 1980; Hartup,

1983; Rubin, 1982), provide nurturance and support (Berndt & Perry, 1986; Weiss, 1974), and form the basis of a social network that will allow students to participate in school and live in the community (Falvey, Forest, Pearpoint, & Rosenberg, 1994). A prerequisite for students developing and maintaining friendships with their peers is that they have *close proximity* and *frequent opportunity* to interact with peers (Hartup, 1975; Howes, 1983). Therefore, students with disabilities attending the same schools and classes as their same-age neighbors are more likely to develop friendships with a range of peers, both with and without disabilities (Falvey, Coots, Bishop, & Grenot-Scheyer, 1989).

INCLUSIVE EDUCATIONAL PRACTICES

Current trends in service delivery for all persons with disabilities focus primarily on inclusive models of education. In these models, students with and without disabilities go to school together and share the same classes, while each student receives the support needed to learn and develop. The rationale for creating inclusive schooling can be traced to developments described earlier in this chapter on legislation and litigation, the implications of using disability labels, and limitations of past service delivery models.

Current models of inclusive education have been influenced by the regular education initiative (REI) (Lloyd, Singh, & Repp, 1991; Will, 1986). The REI concept was conceived by Madeleine Will, the former Assistant Secretary in the U.S. Office of Special Education and Rehabilitative Services. Will (1986) stated that new strategies were called for in education due to the large numbers of students not making adequate progress. She reported that many students were excluded from programs offering needed individual help because they did not fit the eligibility criteria for compartmentalized special education programs. She therefore argued for the provision of preventive, early intervention through a restructured educational system for students having difficulty in school. In this restructured system, general and special educators would collaborate and share responsibility for all students.

Through the 1980s and early 1990s, inclusive models of education expanded. Most recently the term "inclusive education" has been used to describe educational services for students with disabilities, including those with severe disabilities, that are located in the student's neighborhood and within general education classes. The research on recommended practices has documented a growing number and wider variety of supplementary aids and services successfully used to facilitate the education of students with disabilities, including those with significant disabilities, in "general" education settings (Biklen, Ferguson, & Ford, 1989; Giangreco, Cloninger, & Iverson, 1993; Goodlad & Lovitt, 1993; Hunt, Farron-Davis, Beckstead, Curtis, & Goetz, 1994; Lipsky & Gartner, 1989; Meyer, Peck, & Brown, 1991; Rainforth, York, & Macdonald, 1992; Stainback &

Stainback, 1990; Stainback, Stainback, & Forest, 1989; Villa, Thousand, Stainback, & Stainback, 1993). Based upon this growing literature base, inclusive models of education are considered the current recommended practice in service delivery for students with severe disabilities.

In this text, inclusion refers to the placement of students with disabilities in chronological age–appropriate, general education home/neighborhood schools and classes, while providing the necessary supports to students to allow successful participation in events and activities offered to and expected of classmates without disabilities. Inclusion does not necessarily require additional funds to implement; rather, it requires a different way of organizing special education supports, services, and fiscal resources (Salisbury & Chambers, 1994). Instead of viewing special education as a "place" where students and staff are congregated, full inclusion assumes special education is a "service" that should be brought to the student in his or her general education neighborhood school (Taylor, 1988).

Inclusion has sometimes been confused with the "mainstreaming" model. The mainstreaming model often resulted in students being "dumped" in general education classes without any supports or transition services. Inclusion, in contrast, requires that support services be provided to students with disabilities within general education settings. The staff at the Parent Education and Assistant for Kids (PEAK) Parent Training Center have described what inclusion is *not*:

- Dumping students with disability labels into general education classes without the supports and services they need to be successful
- Trading off the quality of a student's education for inclusion or the intensive support services they may need
- Doing away with or cutting back on special services
- Ignoring each student's unique learning needs
- Requiring all students to learn the same thing, at the same time, and in the same way
- Expecting general education teachers to teach students with disability labels without the support they need to effectively teach all their students
- Sacrificing the education of students without disabilities so that the students with disabilities can be included (Schaffner, Buswell, Summerfield, & Kovar, 1988, p. 9).

At present, parents, teachers, schools, and districts are struggling with how to best provide inclusive educational opportunities for all students. The research and practice literature concerning how to provide those inclusive educational opportunities continues to grow. We expect to learn more about how to implement inclusive models, but at present we can identify some key components of inclusion. These components include the following:

Placement of *all* students in age-appropriate general education classrooms in neighborhood schools

Comprehensive assessment of students' individual learning styles, strengths, and needs, and the development of individualized education programs based upon those assessment results

Collaboration among families, general education teachers, special education teachers, administrators, paraprofessionals, and related service personnel to apply each of their areas of expertise in effectively meeting the needs of *all* students

Classroom management strategies to motivate students and create supportive and caring educational environments

Systematic arrangement of general education instructional settings and specialized support, along with adaptations of general education curriculum to meet these individual needs

Positive behavior management strategies to motivate students and create supportive educational environments

Infused teaching of basic motor, personal care, communication, social interaction, and academic skills within general education activities and routines

Use of age-appropriate settings, activities, and materials provided to students in preschools, elementary and secondary schools, and throughout their postsecondary years

Collaborative and innovative strategies to assist schools to make the systemic "paradigm shift" that is necessary to create schools that effectively includes and teaches *all* of its students

CONCLUSION

Our belief is that successful inclusive models of education are really models of education that are good for *all* students. The reforms in general education described in the previous chapter coupled with the special education reforms described in this chapter should result in educational opportunities where all students are learning. Successful implementation rests upon a belief that inclusive schooling is a moral obligation, and without it, equity within the schools does not and cannot exist. The remainder of this book offers strategies that will assist in the development and implementation of successful inclusive models of education. These strategies are not intended as recipes or formulas that can be uniformly applied to every school community. All communities can and must create inclusive schooling for all students. The strategies for each community must be individualized to reflect the needs of each student, family, school, and community. The implementation strategies that will prove successful in each situation will ultimately depend upon the combined commitment, abilities, and expertise of the entire community.

REFERENCES

American Association on Mental Retardation. (1992). *Mental retardation: Definition, classification, and systems of supports.* (9th ed.). Washington, DC: Author.

Americans with Disabilities Act of 1990 (ADA), PL 101-336. (July 26, 1990). Title 42, U.S.C. 12101 et seq: *U.S. Statutes at Large, 104,* 327–378.

Armstrong, T. (1987). *In their own way.* Los Angeles: Jeremy P. Tarcher, Inc.

Bank-Mikkelsen, N.E. (1969). A metropolitan area in Denmark: Copenhagen. In R. Kugel & W. Wolfensberger (Eds.), *Changing patterns in residential services for the mentally retarded* (pp. 227–254). Washington, DC: U.S. Government Printing Office.

Berndt, T.J., & Perry, T.B. (1986). Children's perceptions of friendships as supportive relationships. *Developmental Psychology, 22*(5), 636–648.

Biklen, D. (1989). Redefining schools. In D. Biklen, D. Ferguson, & A. Ford (Eds.), *Schooling and disability: Eighty-eighth Yearbook of the National Society for the Study of Education,* (pp. 1–24). Chicago, IL: University of Chicago Press.

Biklen, D. (1992). *Schooling without labels.* Philadelphia: Temple University Press.

Biklen, D., & Duchan, J.F. (1994). "I am intelligent": The social construction of mental retardation. *Journal of The Association for Persons with Severe Handicaps, 19*(3), 173–184.

Biklen, D., Ferguson, D.L., & Ford, A. (1989). *Schooling and disability: Eighty-eighth yearbook of the National Society for the Study of Education.* Chicago: University of Chicago Press.

Blashfield, R. (1973). An evaluation of DSM-II classification of schizophrenia as a nomenclature. *Journal of Abnormal Psychology, 82*(3), 382–389.

Brown, L., Branston, M.B., Hamre-Nietupski, S., Pumpian, I., Certo, N., & Gruenewald, L. (1979). A strategy for developing chronological age appropriate and functional curricular content for severely handicapped adolescents and young adults. *Journal of Special Education, 13*(1), 81–90.

Brown v. Board of Education, 347 U.S. 483 (1954).

Cole, D., & Meyer, L.H. (1991). Social integration and severe disabilities: A longitudinal analysis of child outcomes. *Journal of Special Education, 25*(3), 340–351.

Donnellan, A., & Mirenda, P. (1983). A model for analyzing instructional components to facilitate generalization for severely handicapped students. *Journal of Special Education, 17,* 317–331.

Education for All Handicapped Children Act of 1975, PL 94-142. (August 23, 1977). Title 20, U.S.C. 1401 et seq: *U.S. Statutes at Large, 89,* 773–796.

Evans, I. (1991). Testing and diagnosis: A review and evaluation. In L.H. Meyer, C.A. Peck, & L. Brown (Eds.), *Critical issues in the lives of people with severe disabilities* (pp. 25–44). Baltimore: Paul H. Brookes Publishing Co.

Falvey, M.A. (1989). *Community-based curriculum: Instructional strategies for students with severe disabilities.* Baltimore: Paul H. Brookes Publishing Co.

Falvey, M.A., Coots, J., Bishop, K.D., & Grenot-Scheyer, M. (1989). Educational and curricular adaptations. In S. Stainback, W. Stainback, & M. Forest (Eds.), *Educating all students in the mainstream of regular education* (pp. 143–158). Baltimore: Paul H. Brookes Publishing Co.

Falvey, M.A., Forest, M., Pearpoint, J., & Rosenberg, R.L. (1994). Building connections. In J.S. Thousand, R.A. Villa, & A.I. Nevin (Eds.), *Creativity and collaborative learning: A practical guide to empowering students and teachers* (pp. 347–368). Baltimore: Paul H. Brookes Publishing Co.

Fourteenth Annual Report to Congress on the Implementation of the Individuals with Disabilities Education Act, 141 (1992).

Giangreco, M.F., Cloninger, C.J., & Iverson, V.S. (1993). *Choosing options and accommodations for children*. Baltimore: Paul H. Brookes Publishing Co.

Gilhool, T.K. (1989). The right to an effective education. In D.K. Lipsky & A. Gartner (Eds.), *Beyond separate education: Quality education for all* (pp. 243–253). Baltimore: Paul H. Brookes Publishing Co.

Goetz, L., Guess, D., & Stremel-Campbell, K. (Eds.). (1987). *Innovative program design for individuals with dual sensory impairments*. Baltimore: Paul H. Brookes Publishing Co.

Gold, M. (1980). *Try another way manual*. Champaign, IL: Research Press.

Goodlad, J.I., & Lovitt, T.C. (1993). *Integrating general and special education*. New York: Merrill.

Greenspan, S., & Shoultz, B. (1981). Why mentally retarded adults lose their jobs: Social competence as a factor in work adjustment. *Applied Research in Mental Retardation, 2*, 23–28.

Greer, J.G., Anderson, A.M., & Odle, S.J. (1982). *Strategies for helping severely and multiply handicapped citizens*. Baltimore: University Park Press.

Guralnick, M. (1980). Social interactions among preschool children. *Exceptional Children, 46*(4), 248–253.

Harry, B. (1992). *Cultural diversity, families, and the special education system*. New York: Teachers College Press.

Hartup, W.W. (1975). The origins of friendship. In M. Lewis & L.A. Rosenblum (Eds.), *Friendships and peer relations* (pp. 11–27). New York: John Wiley & Sons.

Hartup, W.W. (1983). Peer relations. In P.H. Mussen (Ed.), *Handbook of child psychology: socialization, personality, and social development* (4th ed.) (pp. 103–196). New York: John Wiley & Sons.

Horner, R.H., Meyer, L.H., & Fredericks, H.D.B. (Eds.). (1986). *Education of learners with severe handicaps: Exemplary service strategies*. Baltimore: Paul H. Brookes Publishing Co.

Howes, C. (1983). Patterns of friendship. *Child Development, 54*, 1041–1053.

Hunt, P., Farron-Davis, F., Beckstead, S., Curtis, D., & Goetz, L. (1994). Evaluating the effects of placement of students with severe disabilities in general education versus special classes. *Journal of The Association for Persons with Severe Handicaps, 19*(3), 200–214.

Individuals with Disabilities Education Act of 1990 (IDEA), PL 101-476. (October 30, 1990). Title 20, U.S.C. 1400 et seq: *U.S. Statutes at Large, 104*, 1103–1151.

Jones, R.L. (1972). Labels and stigma in special education. *Exceptional Children, 38*(7), 553–564.

Keogh, B. (1975). Social and ethical assumptions about special education. In K. Wedell (Ed.), *Orientations in special education* (pp. 1–15). New York: John Wiley & Sons.

Levine, H.G., & Langness, L.L. (1986). Conclusions: Themes in an anthropology of mild retardation. In L.L. Langness & H.G. Levine (Eds.), *Culture and retardation: Life histories of mildly retarded persons in American society*. Dordrecht: D. Reidel Publishing.

Lipsky, D.K., & Gartner, A. (Eds.). (1989). *Beyond separate education: Quality education for all*. Baltimore: Paul H. Brookes Publishing Co.

Lloyd, J.W., Singh, N.N., & Repp, A.C. (1991). *The regular education initiative: Alternative perspectives on concepts, issues, and models*. Sycamore, IL: Sycamore.

Martin, A. (1988). Teachers and teaching. Screening, early intervention, and remediation: Obscuring children's potential. *Harvard Educational Review, 58*, 488–501.

Meyer, L.H., Peck, C.A., & Brown, L. (Eds.). (1991). *Critical issues in the lives of people with severe disabilities*. Baltimore: Paul H. Brookes Publishing Co.

Miller, L. (1993). *What we call smart: A new narrative for intelligence and learning*. San Diego: Singular.

New York State Association for Retarded Children v. Carey, 612F. 2d 644, 2d Cir. (1979).

Nirje, B. (1969). The normalization principle and its management implications. In R. Kegel & W. Wolfensberger (Eds.), *Changing patterns in residential services for the mentally retarded* (pp. 51–57). Washington, DC: U.S. Government Printing Office.

Oberti v. Board of Education of the Borough of Clemington School District, 995 F.2d 1204 (3rd Cir. 1993).

Plessy v. Ferguson, 163 U.S. 537 (1896).

Rainforth, B., York, J., & Macdonald, C. (1992). *Collaborative teams for students with severe disabilities: Integrating therapy and educational services.* Baltimore: Paul H. Brookes Publishing Co.

Rehabilitation Act of 1973, PL 93-112. (September 26, 1973). Title 29, U.S.C. 701 et seq: *U.S. Statutes at Large, 87,* 355–394.

Roncker v. Walter, 700 F.2d 1058, cert. denied, 104 S.Ct. 196 (1983).

Rubin, Z. (1982). *Children's friendships.* Cambridge, MA: Harvard University Press.

Sacramento City Unified School District v. Rachel Holland, No. 92-15608 (9th Cir. 1994).

Salisbury, C., & Chambers, A. (1994). Instructional costs of inclusive education. *Journal of The Association for Persons with Severe Handicaps, 19*(3), 215–222.

Sapon-Shevin, M. (1989). Mild disabilities: In and out of special education. In D. Biklen, D.L. Ferguson, & A. Ford (Eds.), *Schooling and disability: Eighty-eighth yearbook of the National Society for the Study of Education* (pp. 77–107). Chicago: University of Chicago Press.

Sapon-Shevin, M. (1992). Celebrating diversity, creating community: Curriculum that honors and builds on differences. In S. Stainback & W. Stainback (Eds.), *Curriculum considerations in inclusive classrooms: Facilitating learning for all students* (pp. 19–36). Baltimore: Paul H. Brookes Publishing Co.

Schaffner, B., Buswell, B., Summerfield, A., & Kovar, G. (1988). *Discover the possibilities.* Colorado Springs, CO: PEAK Parent Center, Inc.

Schapps, E., & Solomon, D. (1990). Schools and classrooms as caring communities. *Educational Leadership, 48*(3), 38–42.

Smith, R.M. (1968). *Clinical teaching: Methods of instruction for the retarded.* New York: McGraw-Hill.

Stainback, S., Stainback, W., & Forest, M. (Eds.). (1989). *Educating all students in the mainstream of regular education.* Baltimore: Paul H. Brookes Publishing Co.

Stainback, W., & Stainback, S. (Eds.). (1990). *Support networks for inclusive schooling: Interdependent integrated education.* Baltimore: Paul H. Brookes Publishing Co.

Stephens, B. (Ed.). (1971). *Training the developmentally young.* New York: John Day Co.

Stokes, T.R., & Baer, D.M. (1977). An implicit technology of generalization. *Journal of Applied Behavior Analysis, 10,* 341–367.

Taylor, S.J. (1988). Caught in the continuum: A critical analysis of the principle of least restrictive environment. *Journal of The Association for Persons with Severe Handicaps, 13,* 41–53.

Taylor, D. (1991). *Learning denied.* Portsmouth, NH: Heinemann.

Timothy, W. v. Rochester, New Hampshire School District, 875 F.2nd 954 (1st Cir. 1989).

Turnbull, H.R. (Ed.). (1990). *Free appropriate education, the law and children with disabilities* (4th ed.). Denver, CO: Love.

Villa, R.A., Thousand, J.S., Stainback, W., & Stainback, S. (Eds.). (1993). *Restructuring for caring and effective education: An administrative guide to creating heterogeneous schools.* Baltimore: Paul H. Brookes Publishing Co.

Warren, E. (1954). *Brown v. Board of Education of Topeka.* 347 U.S. 483, 493.

Weiss, R.S. (1974). The provisions of social relationships. In Z. Rubin (Ed.), *Doing unto others* (pp. 17–20). Englewood Cliffs, NJ: Prentice Hall.

Will, M.C. (1986). Educating children with learning problems: A shared responsibility. *Exceptional Children, 52,* 411–416.

Wolfensberger, W. (1970). The principle of normalization and its implications to psychiatric services. *American Journal of Psychiatry, 127,* 291–296.

Wolfensberger, W. (1979). *The principle of normalization in human services.* Toronto: National Institute on Mental Retardation.

Wolfensberger, W. (1985). An overview of social role valorization and some reflections on elderly mentally retarded persons. In M.P. Janicki & H.M. Wisniewski (Eds.), *Aging and developmental disabilities: Issues and approaches* (pp. 61–76). Baltimore: Paul H. Brookes Publishing Co.

York, J., Vandercook, T., Macdonald, C., Heisse-Neff, C., & Caughey, E. (1992). Feedback about integrating middle-school education students with severe disabilities in general education classes. *Exceptional Children, 58*(3), 244–258.

Ysseldyke, J., Algozzine, B., & Epps, S. (1983). A logical and empirical analysis of current practice in classifying students as handicapped. *Exceptional Children, 50,* 160–166.

STRATEGIES FOR EFFECTIVE COLLABORATION

CHRISTINE C. GIVNER AND DIANE HAAGER

Recent concerns regarding the segregation of students with disabilities in special schools or classes have stemmed from moral, ethical, legal, educational, and personal perspectives and have been discussed in previous chapters. Whichever perspective has motivated the implementation of inclusion, the adoption of a collaborative framework is essential to meeting the needs of all students. Although the Education for All Handicapped Children Act of 1975, Public Law (PL) 94-142, mandates that a multidisciplinary team make the decisions in the program planning and implementation for individuals with disabilities, the members of these teams have historically contributed their separate expertise and carried out their responsibilities individually and independently. Hierarchical status structures have evolved in this decision-making process, and some important members, especially parents and students, have felt excluded, alienated, and lacking in importance (Skrtic, 1991; Turnbull & Turnbull, 1986; Vaughn, Bos, Harrell, & Lasky, 1988). There has been no mandate for collaboration or collegiality among general and special educators, community agents, parents, and students; yet it is apparent that all stand to benefit from a collaborative approach to planning inclusive education for students with disabilities.

This chapter defines collaboration and teams and addresses the basic questions of "why," "what," and "how" regarding collaborative teaming for fully including students with disabilities in school and community settings. The benefits for all involved, as well as the potential roles and contributions of team members, are delineated.

WHAT IS COLLABORATIVE TEAMING?

Collaborative teaming is at the heart of the inclusion process. In order to discuss strategies for effective collaboration, the concepts of collaboration and teams must first be defined. Simply stated, a *team* is a group of people working together to achieve a common purpose. Friend and Cook (1992) describe *collaboration* "as a style for direct interaction between at least two coequal parties voluntarily engaged in shared decision making as they work toward a common goal" (p. 5). A *collaborative team*, then, is a group of persons working together to achieve a common goal (e.g., inclusion) and using a specific style of interaction; that is, a collaborative style. Most view collaborative teaming as a group process involving shared ownership of responsibilities and goals.

Collaborative teaming is a vehicle used to develop realistic and meaningful strategies for including students with diverse needs in community and school settings. Even more important, this approach is fundamental to the process of developing and implementing viable inclusion strategies. Collaborative teaming is a synergistic whole that is strengthened by the contribution of each of its working parts. In other words, through the process of combining separate expertise and skills to achieve a common goal, a collaborative team is able to accomplish much more together than the individuals could accomplish working alone. As individuals work together in a team effort with a common vision or goal, drawing upon the resources and strengths of each individual involved, their ability to achieve their purpose is enhanced.

These characteristics (or prerequisites) are essential aspects of collaboration: 1) voluntary participation, 2) parity among participants, 3) mutual goals, 4) shared responsibility for participation and decision making, 5) shared resources, and 6) shared accountability (Friend & Cook, 1992). A shortcoming in any of these areas weakens the synergistic power of a collaborative team. Optimally, as various invested constituents, or stakeholders, meet to develop a set of associated strategies for maximizing the full participation of a student with disabilities in the school and/or community, these defining characteristics might well be discussed and agreed upon to lay the foundation for an effective working team. For example, in the process of arriving at an inclusion strategy such as establishing a peer coach to assist in content area reading or a buddy to assist in navigating the wheelchair down the hall between classes, the team may have to discuss and implement these essential elements of teaming.

Traditionally, invested participants (e.g., parents, students, teachers) have come to student-related meetings fearful of being told the bad news by the "experts" (i.e., what the "symptoms" are and what the particular student will not be able to do). These participants have felt powerless to influence the situation. When the collaborative prerequisites outlined above are in place, there is an opportunity for all involved to use their imaginations and resources to help the student participate as fully as possible in the school and community settings. This is the power that collaboration has for inclusion.

A SYSTEMS APPROACH

The lives of children and adults are not static, and neither are the systems (i.e., school and community) in which they live. The ongoing problem-solving process must be viewed from a dynamic systems perspective. Senge (1990) states that all human endeavors are systems. These systems

> are bound by invisible fabrics of interrelated actions, which often take years to fully play out their effects on each other. Since we are part of that lacework ourselves, it's doubly hard to see the whole pattern of change. Instead, we tend to focus on snapshots of isolated parts of the system, and wonder why our deepest problems never seem to get solved. (p. 7)

The collaborative team must continually identify the stressors, variables, and dynamics in the changing context that resist or limit inclusion, and the team must develop appropriate solutions that are not quick fixes but instead consider the complexity of the situation. Thus, it is of critical importance that the team consider itself a "learning team."

The collaborative team that meets to address the student's ongoing needs and goals must become a learning team. Team learning hinges on the ability of members to exchange dialogue with one another and to suspend assumptions and begin "thinking together." Successful teams do not just happen. Effective collaborative teams are created and developed over time.

WHY COLLABORATE?

Collaborative team efforts are essential to the success of inclusive education. The curriculum in segregated special education classes and schools has been fragmented and incompatible with that in most general education classrooms (Algozzine, Morsink, & Algozzine, 1988; McGill-Franzen & Allington, 1991; Pugach & Warger, 1993). General educators tend to have little knowledge of the content and methods used by special educators, and vice versa (Johnston, Allington, & Afflerbach, 1985). In order to facilitate inclusion of students with disabilities into general education settings, it is clear that all educators responsible for students with disabilities must increase their communication and knowledge of each other's expertise.

In addition, important parties (e.g., parents, related service personnel, significant others) have typically felt alienated from decision-making roles in traditional approaches to special education. Cultural differences can exacerbate such feelings of exclusion among team members. For instance, in an investigation involving Spanish-speaking Puerto Rican–American families, parents reported feeling misinformed by school personnel and became distrustful of the system despite the efforts of school personnel to ensure adequate communication (Harry, 1992). Family members often assume the role of being receivers or providers of information rather than decision makers (Bos & Van Reusen, 1986; Vaughn et al., 1988). Students too are often omitted from the decision-making process despite evidence that they have significant contributions to make regarding their education (Vaughn, Schumm, & Kouzekanani, 1993; Vaughn, Schumm, Niarhos, & Gordon, 1993; Thousand, Villa, & Nevin, 1994). When a team approach is adopted, with all parties equally sharing the responsibility for making decisions and with all parties contributing their own expertise to the process, a synergistic whole stronger than the sum of the individual parts is created.

COLLABORATIVE ROLES AND SYSTEMS

Potential Roles

The members of the collaborative team will vary depending upon the needs of the student. The most common configuration of a team is parents, student, friends or peers, general and special educators, and any other school and community support personnel deemed necessary. Students should be given primary responsibility for developing and communicating their current and future goals. Professionals need to listen attentively in order to understand what students want for themselves. Students' use of verbal and nonverbal communication must be considered. Parents provide unique and rich perspectives concerning the strengths and needs of their son or daughter, as do the students' peers and siblings. Parents have a longitudinal perspective that includes an intimate understanding of the student's past personal experiences, present personal and functional strengths, and future dreams. Parents are active advocates for crafting potential life goals and guiding their son or daughter to meet these goals.

General and special educators provide educational expertise. Educators' roles include assisting parents to understand their rights and identifying needed resources for parents. Connecting parents with pertinent support agencies and services is also an appropriate role for educators. Teachers have the unique perspective of seeing the student in formal school settings with peers. Teachers have knowledge of the student's ability to follow directions and his or her self-management skills, specific skills in academic and functional areas, and communication skills and abilities. Teachers should also be able to provide suggestions as to how tasks and activities can be adapted to maximize the student's involvement and learning.

School support personnel, including speech (or language or communication) specialists, physical therapists, occupational therapists, physical education teachers, music teachers, art teachers, and nurses, are also important members of the team. These support personnel contribute knowledge from their specific areas of expertise to develop appropriate activities within general education classrooms that address the unique talents and needs of students with disabilities. The speech specialist assesses the student's present and future expressive and receptive communication needs and develops recommendations to facilitate the student's improvement and success in communicating in school and community settings. Physical therapists, occupational therapists, and physical education teachers contribute important information concerning the gross and fine motor needs of students and assist parents and teachers to incorporate motor components into daily routines and activities. These personnel are also valuable resources when activities need to be physically adapted or accommodated to the specific individual needs of the student. Music and art teachers may have precise information concerning the student's interests in art or music as well as how these interests may be used to facilitate involvement in various learning activities. Nurses have critical knowledge about how medication or medical conditions might affect students' learning. The nurse also assesses students to determine visual or auditory needs.

Significant peers (i.e., friends, classmates, or siblings) should be ongoing members of the team. Peers provide valuable insight and unique knowledge from an age-appropriate perspective. An age-mate's solution to a difficulty concerning a student can be the most creative and appropriate solution. Often peers have interests, experiences, and world views similar to those of the student with a disability and are able to provide a sensitivity to the issues of inclusion that professionals and parents may miss.

Community members to be included in a collaborative team might be prospective employers interested in training and/or hiring students; rehabilitation, college, and university personnel who can assist in a student's transition to postsecondary education settings; recreational leaders or community organization leaders who are affiliated with organizations and services in which students may be interested in participating (e.g., Boy or Girl Scout leader, YMCA program director, minister); and others as considered appropriate.

Sharing Roles and Responsibilities

By definition, collaborative teaming requires sharing ideas and working together. Traditionally, various educational and community professionals have provided their isolated, independent, and specific expertise to the student with disabilities. This piecemeal approach to providing services to students has been found to be less than effective, although unfortunately it is tolerated in segregated service delivery systems. The inclusion of students with disabilities in schools and communities can be successful only if all team members work together. Parents, educators, peers, and community members need to share their expertise and contextual knowledge of the student to ensure consistency and effectiveness of intervention and support across settings. Segregated services are being replaced by collaborative teams working in concert to support the successful inclusion of students in general education. With increased collaboration, the separateness of various roles is being replaced by an overlapping and sharing of roles and responsibilities. All constituents involved in the education of students with disabilities must be prepared for the changes in their present roles.

Changes in Special Educators' Roles

Traditionally, special educators have been prepared to be the sole instructional leader and manager of students with disabilities in separate classrooms and resource rooms, with little focus placed on the collaborative role of special educators. Now special educators are being asked to assume a greater variety of roles in the education of students with disabilities. Separate classrooms and schools are diminishing. More and more, students with disabilities are being educated in general education with support services. Special educators are providing direct remedial and other adapted instruction within general education classrooms to groups of students who need specific intervention or instruction. Special educators are being asked to facilitate and coordinate inclusion teams that involve participants from the school and community.

Special educators are spending more time in general education classrooms consulting with classroom teachers about appropriate ways to structure lessons to accommodate the needs of students with disabilities. In addition, special educators are spending more time team teaching with general educators, implementing instruction that is meaningful and sensitive to the individual needs of students. In addition to these new and expanded roles, special educators continue to maintain primary responsibility for developing individualized education programs (IEPs) and documenting student progress on instructional objectives.

Changes in General Educators' Roles

Traditionally, general educators have been primarily responsible for implementing the appropriate grade level curriculum and being the instructional leader and manager in the classroom. When students have experienced serious learning difficulties, the classroom teacher has referred the student for psychoeducational evaluation and possible placement in separate special education classrooms or schools. Today general educators are adapting and accommodating instruction for students with disabilities. General educators are participating as full partners with special educators, parents, and others in efforts toward inclusion of students with disabilities. General educators are assuming shared responsibility for implementing students' IEPs.

No longer are general educators isolated in classrooms where the doors are shut. More and more general and special educators team teach, more parents participate daily in their classrooms as volunteers, and special education instructional assistants are increasingly assigned to general education classrooms. General educators have increased responsibility for coordinating the activities of the other adults in their classrooms. As inclusion of students with disabilities becomes more prominent, the roles of all education professionals will evolve into more collaborative arrangements.

COLLABORATION STRATEGIES

Collaborative Teams: Process, Not Method

There are no recipes for success in collaborative efforts, but proactive steps can be taken to facilitate the process and avoid common pitfalls. A group's success depends on multiple factors, including the team's purpose(s), the nature of the collaborative process, and contextual elements that are specific to the situation. By understanding the dynamic nature of these factors and making a commitment to a collaborative ethic, team members will make valuable contributions to inclusive education for students with disabilities. The collaborative ethic involves joint responsibility for problems, joint accountability for and recognition of problem resolution, a belief that pooling talents and resources is mutually advantageous, and a belief that teacher or student problem solving merits an investment of resources such as time and energy (Phillips & McCullough, 1990).

Purpose Setting

No matter what events or factors have precipitated the formation of a collaborative team, it is critical to the success of the group that all members acknowledge and accept a common purpose for the group. During the group initiation phase, a certain amount of effort must be dedicated to clearly defining the purpose in order to focus and direct the group. The purpose of the group, however, is not static and must be continually reviewed and refined throughout the process. The purpose and tasks of the collaborative team are then shaped into concrete goals and objectives; that is, the action plan is developed.

Prior to IEP implementation, the focus of the collaborative team is on assessing the student's instructional needs and developing an appropriate IEP. Once the IEP has been signed by all relevant team members, the purpose of the team becomes that of identifying specific strategies and activities to implement the IEP. The purpose of the collaborative team might initially be focused on creating accessibility for a student who is physically challenged. The team's purpose might evolve from these issues to issues related to curriculum task modifications that are beneficial for the student.

Group members should be equally responsible for establishing a purpose; however, a group facilitator may act to monitor and guide the group. It is important to establish and state the purpose of the collaboration periodically. This process not only helps to maintain the focus of the group, but it also serves to refine and redefine the purpose as it changes over time. New goals and objectives may need to be established as the team begins to implement the purpose, and the process continues.

Team Membership

Collaboration for the purpose of including students with disabilities in the classroom and/or community should involve a representative of each concerned party.

Group membership should be determined based on the individual's function in the group and should involve these considerations: 1) those who have the needed expertise, 2) those who are affected by the decisions, and 3) those who have an interest in participating (Thousand & Villa, 1992). All members of the team need to have a sense of ownership for the work of the group. Each member must be invested in helping to facilitate the success of the student.

Team Building

Regardless of the team membership or the overall purpose of the collaborative team, some elements of the process remain the same. How the group embarks upon the process is critical to its eventual success; yet a successful launching of a collaborative team is only the beginning. Through careful monitoring, reflection, and evaluation, the team can continue to be productive and focused.

As the working group begins, not only are procedures and guidelines set forth that will influence all later proceedings, but also a group "climate" is established. The unique climate of each team occurs as a result of factors such as the mix of personalities of group members, each team member's work style, and the degree of interpersonal and facilitation skills possessed by one or more members of the team. Teams that do not take the time to establish those elements are generally not very successful or productive. Team members need to establish as a shared value that disagreements among themselves should not be taken personally and that the diversity of the various perspectives of group members are more likely to lead to creative solutions. For the sake of productivity, different perspectives and healthy disagreement should be encouraged and valued rather than feared and avoided.

Shared Vision   One of the most important aspects of a well-functioning collaborative group is a shared vision, which is different from a purpose. A shared vision is the group's common image of how a situation should be in an ideal scenario. For example, a team's purpose might be to include Angela, a second-grade student with Down syndrome, in her neighborhood second-grade class. The shared vision of that collaborative team would evolve from the mental images that team members communicate to each other and share regarding what that best inclusive learning environment would look like for Angela. These images might include the following: 1) with the help and support of classmates, Angela will be able to read at an age-appropriate level; 2) Angela will be able to write a letter to her grandmother in Alaska; and 3) Angela will actively participate in a group project on kangaroos with her same-age peers.

Underlying Assumptions and Values   After establishing a shared vision, it is also helpful for the team to brainstorm and establish a set of underlying assumptions or values about their work together. This process might establish the value of the expertise of each member, the value of a problem-solving perspective, the importance of completing a task when one makes a commitment to do it, and the idea that differences of perspective can be very positive in a problem-solving task. This process helps to establish the collaborative spirit or climate immediately. The team leader or facilitator may play an integral role in focusing on achieving this climate. Trust begins to develop as team members begin to discover more about their colleagues through the verbal process of establishing a vision and an explication of values and assumptions about their work together.

Common Language   Because teams consist of people from different disciplines, diversity in the personal perspectives of team members is likely. Establishing a common language that allows participants to understand each other facilitates communication within the group. This process involves the elaboration of ideas and terminology at the outset. For example, when the team has its initial meetings to determine the supports necessary to include Angela in the second-grade classroom, the teacher states that she has never worked with a "mongoloid" child before. Angela's mother finds this term offensive, and she explains the implication of describing her daughter with the disability as the first and only descriptor used. She also mentions the inappropriate use of a racial descriptor to describe a disability. She respectfully asks the teacher to use "student-first" language and to use "Down syndrome" rather than "mongoloid." The teacher apologizes and agrees to make a conscious effort to correct her use of labels and terms. This initial investment of time is well spent because team members are then able to communicate more effectively as their work progresses. All group members will subsequently be comfortable in describing Angela's disability because they share a common language regarding Down syndome.

Trust Building   A good collaborative team has a sense of being "in it together." Establishing a shared vision, underlying values, and a common language are the foundation for a strong community sense. In order for team learning to become a reality, however, the group must establish a history of working and struggling together. Group history develops much like any other interpersonal relationship, but with more than one person at a time. Shared experiences provides the team members with a better sense of how the different personalities in the group will function together and assist with anticipating future challenges. A sense of trust builds over time in the dynamic process of collaborative work (Michelson, 1992).

Time   Initially, spending time together is necessary for team members to learn each others' perspectives, to establish a purpose and a set of working rules, and to establish the collaborative process. Regularly scheduled meeting times of adequate duration are needed to thoroughly process the information so that the group can be effective problem solvers. As previously stated, time is also required for the group process to evolve.

Self-Evaluation   A critical component of team learning is for the team to have regular opportunities for self-evaluation. It is important to monitor the group process itself, to consider how the team is operating, and, based on this information, to refine and redefine goals. Part of learning to think together is having an opportunity for critical reflection. The team needs time to gain perspective, to step back and take stock of the bigger picture. For example, a student support team has been meeting regularly every 2 weeks for the last 6 months, and there have been two instances during this time in which team members have had extreme differences of opinion. Although these differences have been amicably resolved, some residual tension remains. The last 30 minutes of this week's meeting has been set aside to review how members are feeling about the effectiveness of their work. Each member is asked to respond to the following questions and then share their responses with the group. 1) What has been our greatest accomplishment in the work we have done? 2) What is your greatest frustration in the work we have done? 3) What might we do differently to resolve this frustration? 4) What issue do you think we should address next? Again, the designated facilitator should play an integral role in the periodic recapping and surveying of the group perspective.

Effective Meetings

Meetings are established work sessions, a time for thinking together, making decisions regarding how to implement the next goal or objective, and problem solving together as challenges arise. In a collaborative team that is just beginning or is not functioning well, meetings can be frustrating or even uncomfortable. When collaborative teams are functioning well, the experience can be exhilarating and productive. The following sections describe variables that have been found to enhance the effectiveness of meetings.

Frequency   Teams need to establish regularly scheduled times to meet. Because team members have busy lives, personally and professionally, and their collaborative work is but one of the many priorities in their lives, establishing a routine time enhances the possibility that team members will attend meetings consistently. Additional whole group or smaller group meetings may have to be scheduled as the need arises. The frequency of meetings depends on factors such as how dynamic or changing the setting is and on the overall school schedule. Team meetings should be regularly scheduled so that ongoing communication and joint problem solving become routine. Adjustments of time and duration should be made as the team determines appropriate.

Physical Environment   Meetings should be held in an environment that is pleasant and conducive to thinking and learning together. The temperature (not too hot or too cold) and lighting (not too glaring or too dim) should be adjusted to maintain a comfortable working environment. The most important physical variable is to arrange the seating in a circle, preferably at a large round table. This arrangement encourages the sense of equal working partners. Adequate resources such as flipchart and markers (or similar visual devices) for the brainstorming and initial recording of group ideas are also critical.

Guidelines for Meetings   The team should establish a set of rules and procedures for meetings to facilitate the effective use of time. During an initial meeting, the team can brainstorm a list of these rules. This process also encourages ownership of the basic social contract regarding how members are to behave. Examples of meeting rules or guidelines include the following: 1) a rule about being on time for meetings, 2) procedures for reporting a necessary absence, 3) a format for giving input for future meeting agendas, 4) steps for recording action minutes that document all decisions made or actions taken at the meeting, 5) rules for individual participation in discussion (e.g., no interrupting someone who is talking), and 6) methods to use for reaching consensus during decision making.

Core Roles Another important meeting variable is the various roles team members assume during meetings. In team collaboration, shared or distributed leadership is often practiced and encouraged. Various participant roles have been identified. Each collaborative team should identify the roles that are necessary for their group functioning. The following examples describe some core roles:

1. *Facilitator*—the person responsible for guiding and directing the meeting discussions and decision-making process. This is usually the person who writes the brainstorming ideas on the flipchart and keeps the discussion on track.
2. *Secretary*—the person responsible for recording the action minutes, distributing minutes after the meeting, and collecting ideas for future agenda items.
3. *Encourager*—the person specifically responsible for giving appropriate positive reinforcement to the group as a whole and to individual members

The assignment of or volunteering for various roles can and should change over time, even as often as each meeting. In this way, the team functions more as equal participants who share responsibilities than as a structured group in which tiers of status or authority are established.

Agenda Building Another critical factor in effective meetings is developing procedures and a format for establishing an agenda (with time referents) for meetings, for recording action minutes, for establishing the next meeting place, and for documenting and updating the working action plan. Team members need a means for ensuring that their concerns and issues will be addressed. The last few minutes of every meeting should be set aside for the purpose of deciding what needs to be discussed at the next meeting. Often team members think of an issue for the next meeting after the last meeting has occurred. The designated secretary (i.e., the person who keeps the action minute notebook) might be contacted for adding issues to the next agenda. In the case of an agenda with too many items for one meeting, the facilitator might prioritize the items and identify a tentative time frame for all items. The secretary could send out the tentative agenda and request that team members come prepared for discussion of the items identified on the agenda. These suggested routines and techniques optimize the potential for effective use of meeting time. The important variable is that routines and procedures for agenda setting are established and agreed upon by the group. In this way, frustration is minimized and joint ownership for the agenda is maximized.

Action Minutes   Traditional meeting minutes provide a narrative summary of the issues that were discussed and the actions or votes that were taken. Action minutes (see Figure 1 for a sample) are usually more succinct, written in

---

ACTION MINUTES

Persons Present: ____   Persons Absent: ____
_____   _____
_____   _____
_____   _____
_____

Agenda

Item   Time Frame
1.

2.

3.

4.

Actions Taken

Action/Task/Item   Person(s) Responsible   Time to be Completed
1.

2.

3.

4.

Tentative Agenda for Next Meeting

Date: _____ Place: _____ Time: _____

Item
1.

2.

3.

Figure 1. Sample action minutes format. (Adapted from Thousand and Villa [1992].)

outline form, with a focus on documenting critical information from the last meeting. Typically, these minutes list team member attendance, agenda topics, action plan and person(s) responsible, time frame for the plan, and a tentative agenda for the next meeting. The team should develop and refine a format for action minutes that is suitable and efficient for their specific style and purpose.

Action Plan   An action plan is used to document the collaborative team's working plan of action, with goals, objectives, tasks, person(s) responsible, and tentative or actual time frames. As shown in Figure 2, an action plan format resembles an IEP. An IEP establishes the overarching academic, social-behavioral, and functional annual goals and short-term objectives that must be addressed.

Student:

ACTION PLAN

Task/activity	Person(s) responsible	Time to be completed

Figure 2. Sample action plan format. (Adapted from *Interactions: Collaboration skills for school professionals*, by Marilyn Friend and Lynne Cook. Copyright © 1992 by Longman Publishers, USA. Used with permission.)

The action plan establishes the concrete support activities, tasks, and human and materials resources needed by the team to implement the IEP objectives.

Developing and maintaining a format for documenting the work of the group serves several purposes. As a working document, the action plan makes public what the team has agreed upon in terms of goals and objectives, facilitating accountability as well as tracking when actions need to be accomplished. Traditional meetings, in which participants have not done their homework or no one recalls what was even decided at the last meeting, are all too common and ineffective. Action plans reduce the possibility that this will occur. In addition, action plans can be used to evaluate the effectiveness of actions or tasks accomplished to date as the group decides what needs to be done next or what additional goals and objectives need to be added or changed.

Decision Making   The decision-making processes used by collaborative teams can make or break the cohesiveness and productivity of the group. In coming together to plan, implement, evaluate, and redesign, the team must develop decision-making processes that facilitate collective creativity and expertise. These are important in generating meaningful strategies for accomplishing established team goals or redesigning goals as necessary. There are several specific strategies to facilitate decision making.

First, the collaborative team needs to develop a means of working through the day-to-day, week-to-week challenges that arise as the student with disabilities is included in the life of the classroom, school, and community. Using a step-by-step problem-solving process provides the team with a structure through which productive dialogue can occur. For example, Dettmer, Thurston, and Dyck (1993) describe such a format, which they refer to as *POCS*. POCS includes problem identification (P), generating options (O), determining consequences (C), and planning the solution (S). This procedure assists the team in its effort to learn together how to successfully support the student.

Suppose that one of Jon's IEP objectives states, "Given verbal directions and appropriate materials, Jon will distribute the morning snack to each of his classmates." The staff are having difficulty implementing this objective. Using POCS, the team defines the *p*roblem as: The team is having difficulty teaching Jon to complete this task. He becomes distracted by other events occurring in the classroom, fails to pass out the snacks to all of his classmates, and becomes angry when told that he has not completed the task correctly. The team then generates possible *o*ptions and probable *c*onsequences of each option. The teacher could provide Jon with direct physical and verbal assistance, but this strategy might increase Jon's dependence on teacher support when one of the goals for Jon is to increase his independence and active participation in various class activities. The team brainstorms several options and consequences and decides that Jon should choose a classmate each day to help him complete the snack administration. They plan the *s*olution in detail, determining when and how peers should provide cues to Jon to help him complete the task.

The second strategy for facilitating decision making is building consensus, which is an essential component of decision making. Consensus can be defined as the collective agreement on any course of action or decision, usually after the issue has been thoroughly discussed from various perspectives, negotiated, and agreed upon. These underlying values and guidelines facilitate consensus building: 1) openness to participation, 2) openness to diversity, 3) openness to conflict, 4) openness to reflection, and 5) openness to mistakes (Patterson, 1993). Guidelines that assist in building consensus also include ensuring that each member speaks uninterrupted, moving to a point of tension and then problem solving in a nonthreatening way, focusing on best-case outcomes, generating creative solutions to these outcomes, and using a variety of techniques to move the group toward consensus. Consensus guarantees full team support of decisions made and illustrates that we are smarter and more effective collectively than we are individually (Patterson, 1993).

Third, resolving conflict by majority rule when consensus cannot be attained is a critical aspect of decision making. Procedures should be established to guide majority group decision making when the group fails to reach consensus. The group needs to agree on what majority rule means. For example, the group may decide that a majority rule is reached with 80% agreement. When majority rule is used, it is helpful to team learning to review the dissenting opinion concerning the issue within a certain period of time after the initial decision is made. This review serves a number of purposes. The review process demonstrates a respect for the dissenting opinion (Patterson, 1993). Also, during the time after the initial majority rule, the strategies implemented may reveal additional information that will further shape future decisions. It is important that the dynamic nature of designing and implementing effective inclusive education be continually emphasized. Solutions change as the contexts change and the group learns.

Individual Accountability

Individual accountability is a critical variable in maintaining the integrity and vitality of the collaborative team. Members of the team must be committed to taking the action that has been decided upon during the meetings. Because many issues and decisions may be made during the same meeting, documentation through action minutes and the transfer of pertinent decisions to the working action plan are extremely important. One of the functions of the action plan is to document and make official all strategies generated, which one or more of the team members is responsible for the implementation of the strategy, and the time frame for completing the assigned task. If there is no agreed-upon commitment to implement the activity or strategy, the team will not be effective in facilitating inclusion.

Ongoing Evaluation and Redesign of Group

Collaboration is a cyclical process. The team proposes and agrees upon strategies, implements those strategies, assesses the effectiveness of those strategies, and then decides what needs to happen next. As members of a collaborative team, the group continually reinvents or redesigns strategies needed to include students with disabilities in all aspects of school and community life.

CONCLUSION

Collaboration for the purpose of including all students ensures that support services, adaptations, and/or accommodations that are required are implemented in a holistic manner that respects the individuality and worth of each student. Collaborative teams, as a functional framework, require greater orchestration and coordination of resources than was demanded in the traditional isolated and segregated educational model. With this additional effort, however, comes tremendous benefits for students. Students with disabilities have an opportunity to share in the actual life of the school as full participants. Self-esteem can blossom in a learning environment that is both challenging and sensitive to the needs of each student, with or without disabilities. As teams of educators focus more on students as individuals and not as labels in implementing an inclusive service delivery model, education will be humanized and become more effective for all students. Collaborative teams functioning to support students in inclusive settings will focus resources where they are most needed—in the classroom— so that every student's needs and talents can be addressed.

REFERENCES

Algozzine, B., Morsink, C.V., & Algozzine, K.M. (1988). What's happening in self-contained special education classrooms? *Exceptional Children, 55*(3), 259–265.

Bos, C.S., & Van Reusen, A.K. (1986). *Effects of teaching a strategy for facilitating student and parent participation in the IEP process* (Partner Project Final Report). Tucson: University of Arizona, Department of Special Education.

Dettmer, P., Thurston, L.P., & Dyck, N. (1993). *Consultation, collaboration, and teamwork for students with special needs.* Needham Heights, MA: Allyn & Bacon.

Education for All Handicapped Children Act of 1975, PL 94-142. (August 23, 1977). Title 20, U.S.C. 1401 et seq: *U.S. Statutes at Large, 89,* 773–796.

Friend, M., & Cook, L. (1992). *Interactions: Collaboration skills for school professionals.* White Plains, NY: Longman.

Harry, B. (1992). An ethnographic study of cross-cultural communication with Puerto Rican–American families in special education. *American Educational Research Journal, 29*(3), 471–494.

Johnston, P., Allington, R., & Afflerbach, P. (1985). The congruence of classroom and remedial reading instruction. *Elementary School Journal, 85,* 465–477.

McGill-Franzen, A., & Allington, R.L. (1991). The gridlock of low reading achievement: Perspectives on practice and policy. *Remedial and Special Education, 12*(3), 20–30.

Michelson, S.S. (1992). *Exploring the dynamic process of change in literacy curriculum and assessment in a collaborative relationship.* Paper presented at the 42nd Annual Meeting of the National Reading Conference, San Antonio, TX.

Patterson, J.L. (1993). *Leadership for tomorrow's schools.* Alexandria, VA: Association for Supervision and Curriculum Development.

Phillips, V., & McCullough, L. (1990). Consultation-based programming: Instituting the collaborative ethic in schools. *Exceptional Children, 56*(4), 291–304.

Pugach, M.C., & Warger, C.L. (1993). Curriculum considerations. In J.I. Goodlad & T.C. Lovitt (Eds.), *Integrating general and special education* (pp. 125–148). New York: Merrill/Macmillan.

Senge, P. (1990). *The fifth discipline: The art and practice of the learning organization.* New York: Doubleday/Currency.

Skrtic, T.M. (1991). *Behind special education: A critical analysis of professional culture and school organization.* Denver, CO: Love.

Thousand, J.S., & Villa, R.A. (1992). Collaborative teams: A powerful tool in school restructuring. In R.A. Villa, J.S. Thousand, W. Stainback, & S. Stainback (Eds.), *Restructuring for caring and effective education: An administrative guide to creating heterogeneous schools* (pp. 73–108). Baltimore: Paul H. Brookes Publishing Co.

Thousand, J.S., Villa, R.A., & Nevin, A.I. (Eds.) (1994). *Creativity and collaborative learning: A practical guide to empowering students and teachers.* Baltimore: Paul H. Brookes Publishing Co.

Turnbull, A.P., & Turnbull, H.R. (1986). *Families, professionals, and exceptionality: A special partnership.* Columbus, OH: Charles E. Merrill.

Vaughn, S., Bos, C.S., Harrell, J., & Lasky, B. (1988). Parent participation in the initial placement/IEP conference ten years after mandated involvement. *Journal of Learning Disabilities, 21*(2), 82–89.

Vaughn, S., Schumm, J.S., & Kouzekanani, K. (1993). What do students with learning disabilities think when their general education teachers make adaptations? *Journal of Learning Disabilities, 26*(8), 545–555.

Vaughn, S., Schumm, J.S., Niarhos, F., & Gordon, J. (1993). Students' perceptions of two hypothetical teachers' instructional adaptations for low achievers. *Elementary School Journal, 94*, 87–102.

ASSESSMENT STRATEGIES TO
DEVELOP APPROPRIATE CURRICULA
AND EDUCATIONAL PROGRAMS

SUSANN TERRY GAGE AND MARY A. FALVEY

This chapter delineates strategies for assessing the skill repertoires (i.e., the strengths and needs) of students, particularly those with significant disabilities. The assessment strategies emphasized are those that will assist educators and parents to develop *age-* and *grade-appropriate* curriculum and *functional* educational programs. "Formula" or "recipe" approaches to assessment do not adequately recognize the complex and unique abilities of individual students. Rigid formula or recipe approaches to assessment, such as a required and predetermined set of school district tools for all students, provides limited information about students. By considering the individual student and his or her needs and strengths, a more comprehensive assessment method can provide educators with a more authentic portfolio of information about their students' needs.

Alternative procedures and strategies should be considered, particularly when assessing students with disabilities who are attending their neighborhood school. This chapter discusses formal and informal assessments, authentic and performance-based assessments, ways to count and record target behaviors, methods to identify individual students' learning styles, steps to recognizing strengths and needs, and several other specific assessment procedures. In addition, using assessment in the context of developing individualized education programs (IEPs) is discussed.

Traditionally, the term *assessment* has been used to refer to the initial evaluation of a student's performance and the end-of-term or year evaluation. However, as presented and described in this book, assessment should be expanded to include ongoing and continuous evaluation of a student's performance throughout his or her educational career. Assessment should include an identification of the student's most critical educational needs and strengths, learning style, current performance level, and level of participation in various activities and environments.

Assessment is the process of gathering information to make an informed decision in developing a student's educational program. The information collected from a variety of sources should reflect the student's patterns of performance over a period of time. A collaborative team consists of parents and significant others, the student, student's friends, teachers (both general and special education), related service personnel (e.g., speech, language, and communication specialist, orientation and mobility trainer, physical therapist), job specialists (for postsecondary-age students), and others interested in the development of the student. The team gathers information that aids in determining the current level of performance based on the student's strengths and needs; this information then assists the team to determine the priority areas to target for instruction.

Assessment strategies and results need to be considered in the design and development of appropriate educational programs for several reasons. First, assessment allows the teacher to determine a student's abilities and levels of participation across a variety of activities and environments. Second, assessment provides the teacher with information about the effectiveness of ongoing instruction. Third, assessment can assist the teacher to determine the stimulus conditions that are present when the student engages in a specific behavior (e.g., measuring students' responses to cues delivered by peers across several different settings, such as home economics, history, and physical education). Fourth, assessment is mandated by federal law, originally in PL 94-142, the Education for All Handicapped Children Act of 1975 and later by its 1990 reauthorization, PL 101-476, the Individuals with Disabilities Education Act (IDEA). Specifically, IDEA requires that individualized education program (IEP) goals and objectives be based upon a student's current skill repertoire. In addition, IEP goals and objectives based upon assessment results must include performance criteria, written timelines, and statements that indicate how the student's current skill abilities will be periodically reviewed and evaluated to meet the specified objectives.

TYPES OF ASSESSMENT

The assessment process is the catalyst for the development of an instructional plan for a student. "Good assessment is an integral part of good instruction" (Herman, Aschbacher, & Winters, 1992, p. 5). In the following section, several types of assessment procedures and issues related to assessment are discussed: the importance of focusing on the students' strengths and needs; initial and ongoing assessment; formal and informal assessment; authentic assessment and sampling of behaviors; and the concept of multiple intelligences, as proposed by Gardner (1983).

Strengths and Needs Focus

In inclusive classrooms where students with and without disabilities are enrolled, differences in learning styles and abilities may seem more evident. *All* children, however, have diverse areas of both strengths and needs that the assessment process must recognize. Assessment must not merely identify a student's strengths and weaknesses, but also how a student uses those strengths to function within society. Thus, student needs are determined based on their strengths (Miller, 1990; Sapon-Shevin, 1992).

Assessment that focuses on students' strengths, or what students can do, is more likely to reflect student's educational needs because the learning experiences identified are more likely to be positive and motivating. Educators must design and implement educational programs from the perspective that all students are smart (Miller, 1990). Discovering students' strengths holds more essential information for a teacher than "seeking to identify their pathologies, impairments and disorders" (Miller, 1990, p. 4). For example, math assessment results indicate that 9-year-old Lisa's strengths are number recognition and simple addition. Therefore, her math needs can be met when working on two-digit addition problems instead of just copying numbers she already knows, even though other classmates are working on their multiplication tables.

Initial and Ongoing Assessment

The process of assessment must be used to determine students' needs. This process should be conducted both when a student is first referred for special education services and on an ongoing basis.

An *initial assessment* might be conducted when a student first enters a new school or classroom setting and is often used to determine whether a student is eligible for special education, especially identifying the level and type of support services needed. In addition, the initial assessment process can assist in the development of the IEP goals and objectives. During the initial assessment, some states and local school districts require that educators use specific formal assessment tools that yield a single score. These tools may measure students' ability to take tests rather than determine their overall educational strengths and needs. If such tools are used, educators should also use informal assessment procedures that yield more information about the student and his or her strengths and needs.

Ongoing assessment is conducted to evaluate students' progress, to assist with meeting instructional objectives, and to evaluate overall program effectiveness. It involves making decisions based upon objective, concrete, and specific information about the student, expected behavior(s), the educational setting, and other factors affecting student performance (Browder, 1991). Ongoing assessment is critical in determining what skills to teach and when to change instruction to improve student performance.

Formal and Informal Assessment Procedures

A variety of commercially available assessment tools exist that determine the current performance level of a student. Standardized tests are a type of formal assessment that is commercially available and measures samples of students' behaviors. Standardization means that students taking the test will respond to the same questions under the same conditions (e.g., amount of time) and that the exam will be scored the same way every time. Most of the standardized assessment tools that are available and provided to teaching staff in the United States have been commercially developed and distributed by nonschool testing companies, which are designed primarily to rank large numbers of students cheaply and efficiently (Darling-Hammond, 1991). Unfortunately, since the mid-1980s many American schools have increasingly focused on the use of standardized tests as measures of student achievement. In addition, the majority of students with disabilities have been subjected to numerous standardized tests throughout their school career.

If standardized assessments are used there are a number of reasons why their limitations should be recognized. They typically do not assess critical thinking or analysis processes that probe for understanding; they often simply tap into the process of rote memorization. In addition, they frequently do not measure what they propose to measure. Standardized tests often have a very narrow focus in their administration. For example, most standardized tests rely solely upon multiple choice or true/false questions to assess skills, rather than using a diverse range of responses such as short answer, essay, or oral responses to determine students' skills and knowledge. Finally, formal assessment tools are often unrelated to the curriculum or to real-life, practical experiences that are being taught (e.g., conducting science experiments using memorized scientific formulas instead of applying scientific information to everyday life skills) (Wolf, LeMahieu, & Eresh, 1992).

Informal assessment procedures are those that teachers, parents, and related service personnel design and develop themselves to obtain observations that cannot be obtained through formal assessment procedures. These procedures will yield results that more accurately reflect students' actual skill levels across the curriculum. Informal assessment procedures may include the following: authentic assessment, observations, teacher-made tests, checklists, language samples (see Chapter 9 for more information), interviews, Making Action Plans (MAPs), Planning Alternative Tomorrows with Hope (PATH), and ecological and student repertoire inventories. In addition, numerous data collection procedures; baseline data, event, duration, and latency recordings; and scoring by levels are types of informal assessment. These procedures are explored in more detail in later sections of this chapter, and in some instances in later chapters in this book.

When choosing either formal or informal assessment tools, the following characteristics should be considered:

- Procedures used to assess students must be free of linguistic, cultural, economic-circumstance, age, disability, sexual-orientation, and gender bias.
- A variety of test procedures (e.g., short-answer quizzes, writing samples, open-ended questions, essays, videos, exhibitions) should be used, not just one type/style, so as not to favor any particular group or preferred learning style (Miller, 1993).
- Concepts or ideas to be assessed should be real and valid; that is, the assessment tool should not test students' knowledge of artificial skills and activities, but rather skills and activities that are required in the students' everyday lives.
- Materials and the environment that are used should be conducive to obtaining a sample of behavior that is representative of the student; that is, the settings should not be so artificial and sterile as to make the student uncomfortable.
- Items that are selected for assessment should measure what the teacher intends them to measure (e.g., items selected to assess a student's writing skills reflect several writing samples, not a single response to a multiple choice question).

Authentic Assessment

Authentic assessments are composed of a variety of performance-based assessment instruments that require students to *generate* a response rather than *choose* a response, and the response that is generated can be demonstrated in a real-life context. In addition, the results of authentic assessments are based on an established set of criteria that frequently include multiple assessors as determined by both the student and teacher prior to the actual assessment (Dietz & Moon, 1992; Wiggins, 1989; Wolf et al., 1992).

Authentic assessment can be particularly meaningful for students because it provides information about their progress over time rather than capturing only a single moment of their learning (Brandt, 1992; Maeroff, 1991). In an authentic assessment, students are often asked to demonstrate a particular skill or behavior as part of their typical school routines (Meyer, 1992). When a student is engaged in routine activities, educators may observe and make a judgment about that student's skill repertoire based upon the observations.

While authentic assessments are performance based (i.e., requiring the student to generate a response, not merely guess or choose an answer), not all performance-based assessments are authentic. Consider, for example, a psychologist assessing a student's understanding and application of "object permanence," the concept that an object can continue to exist even though the student does not see or feel it. The psychologist hides two blocks under a scarf and waits for the student to search for these blocks. While this is an example of a performance assessment, it is not an authentic assessment since the context is contrived. An authentic assessment requires the student to demonstrate a desired skill in a real-life context (Meyer, 1992). To determine if this student had object permanence in his repertoire via an authentic assessment procedure, the psychologist would need to observe various activities where object permanence would naturally occur, such as during art when the scissors and crayons become naturally obscured under papers, or during recess when a ball rolls out of sight.

Authentic assessment often involves the development of students' portfolios, including samples of which include work such as essay examinations, research projects, behavior counts, scientific experiments, parent inventories, exhibits, video productions, student performances, student repertoire inventories, and/or debates.

Multiple Intelligences/Personal Learning Style

Howard Gardner (1983) has developed a model for thinking about and looking at one of the most frequently labeled personal attributes, intelligence. Instead of a traditional and narrow view of intelligence, where students who speak and write well are considered to be the most intelligent, Gardner designed a method for teachers to view their students from a broader perspective. The "multiple intelligences" perspective offers an alternative to our focus on IQ scores that typically identify students' deficits and ignore their strengths. Gardner's multiple intelligences perspective assumes that all students are intelligent, although not in the same way.

A traditional and narrow view of intelligence, using standardized measures, is often traced back to the work of Binet and Simon (1911, 1916). However, even Binet and Simon's (1905) work strongly opposed the practice of ranking students or discovering a student's innate potential from a test or series of tests. In their work, they specifically cautioned against labeling students based upon test scores for fear of the self-fulfilling prophecy inherent in the labels we assign students (Miller, 1993). A self-fulfilling prophecy occurs when an individual believes something about him- or herself so strongly that his or her actions play out that belief and it becomes true (e.g., if a student believes he or she is not strong in math, he or she might have difficulty with counting tasks).

Gardner (1983) and the subsequent work of Armstrong (1987, 1994) and Miller (1993) provide a framework of intelligence that requires a more comprehensive analysis of students' strengths and skills than was possible with a traditional view of intelligence. Specifically, Gardner proposes seven types of intelligence: linguistic, logical-mathematical, spatial, bodily-kinesthetic, musical, interpersonal, and intrapersonal. Table 1 presents a description of each form of intelligence. Specific strategies for assessing students using a multiple intelligences perspective is presented in a later section of this chapter.

DEVELOPMENT OF ASSESSMENT PROFILE

An assessment profile is the compilation of all relevant assessment information that is available regarding a particular student. A comprehensive assessment profile is

Table 1.   Multiple intelligences/personal learning style characteristics

Linguistic
- like to write
- spin tall tales or tell jokes and stories
- have a good memory for names, places, dates, or trivia
- enjoy reading books in spare time
- spell words accurately and easily
- appreciate nonsense rhymes and tongue twisters
- like doing crossword puzzles or playing games such as Scrabble or Anagrams

Logical-Mathematical
- compute math problems quickly in their heads
- enjoy using computers
- ask questions like, "Where does the universe end?" "What happens after we die?" and "When did life begin?"
- play chess, checkers, or other strategy games and win
- reason things out logically and clearly
- devise experiments to test out things they do not understand
- spend lots of time working on logic puzzles such as Rubik's cube

Spatial
- spend free time engaged in art activities
- report clear visual images when thinking about something
- easily read maps, charts, and diagrams
- draw accurate representations of people or things
- like the use of movies, slides, or photographs in educational context
- enjoy doing jigsaw puzzles or mazes
- daydream a lot

Musical
- play a musical instrument
- remember melodies of songs
- tell you when a musical note is off-key
- say they need to have music on in order to study
- collect records or tapes
- sing songs to themselves
- keep time rhythmically to music

Bodily-Kinesthetic
- do well in competitive sports
- move, twitch, tap, or fidget while sitting in a chair
- engage in physical activities such as swimming, biking, hiking, or skateboarding
- need to touch people when they talk to them
- enjoy scary amusement rides
- demonstrate skill in a craft like woodworking, sewing, or carving

Interpersonal
- have a lot of friends
- socialize a great deal at school or around the neighborhood

(continued)

Table 1. (continued)

- seem to be "street-smart"
- get involved in after-school group activities
- serve as the "family mediator" when disputes arise
- enjoy playing group games with other children
- have a lot of empathy for the feelings of others

Intrapersonal
- display a sense of independence or a strong will
- react with strong opinions when controversial topics are being discussed
- seem to live in their own world
- like to be alone to pursue some personal interest, hobby, or project
- seem to have a deep sense of self-confidence
- march to the beat of a different drummer in their style
- motivate themselves to do well on independent study projects

Adapted from Armstrong (1987).

required by IDEA for all students with disabilities, as part of the IEP. An IEP is a document prepared at least annually by the student and his or her family, teachers, friends, related service personnel (e.g., communication specialists, occupational therapists, physical therapists), and others as deemed appropriate. The IEP incorporates a statement regarding the student's present level of functioning, long-term goals, and short-term objectives, all of which are based upon comprehensive assessment results. In addition, the necessary supplementary aids and services, including specialized services, adaptations, and accommodations must be stated in the IEP.

Comprehensive assessment profiles ensure that the goals and objectives generated for students reflect their strengths and needs based on their current level of performance. This information is obtained by involving the family, collecting information from collaborative team members, reviewing pertinent data and records, and determining the student's current performance level using a variety of assessment strategies. The following are general guidelines that should at least be considered when developing an assessment profile for a student.

Family and Student Involvement

The family and significant others (e.g., friends, staff from after-school programs, child care providers) need to be actively involved in the development of a student's IEP. Family members and significant others have known the student longer than school staff, and their input is invaluable in determining priority areas to address in the assessment process. The student should also participate in the development of his or her own educational program. Students' involvement with their own IEPs assists the team in developing IEPs that reflect their choices and preferences. Involving students also facilitates their development of self-advocacy skills, which are essential and ensure that the students' educational program and future life plans reflect their personal wants and desires. For a more detailed discussion of self-advocacy, see Chapter 14.

Family Collaborative Meetings Family collaborative meetings facilitate the gathering of essential information about the student. These collaborative meetings should address perceived strengths and needs. Family and student conferences should not be conducted at just one setting, but rather considered an ongoing and regular process. Conferences should take place as often as necessary to maintain effective communication between the family and the school. The family or school personnel might request a meeting any time they feel the student's needs have changed, the educational programs previously developed for the student are not working well, or there is a need to share other information about the student's progress. It is recommended that the meetings be conducted in a friendly environment, preferably in the student's home environment if possible. The classroom teacher generally schedules and facilitates the meeting. There is a general guide (i.e., predetermined questions) that the facilitator follows to obtain the desired information. Listed below are key issues that should be addressed:

1. Student's strengths: What does the student like to do, show a preference for, or do well?
2. Student's needs with regard to increasing participation in family activities at home and increasing participation in community family activities.
3. Students friendships with neighbors, family members, school mates, including who they are and characteristics of their friendships (i.e., where they go, what they do, and how often).
4. If the student's friendships are limited, any ideas for facilitating friendships (e.g., potential neighborhood or school friends).
5. Medical information that would have an impact on teaching the student.
6. Strategies that the family uses to avoid or alleviate behavior challenges.
7. Student's means and modes of communication (receptive and expressive communication).
8. Future plans or dreams for the student.
9. The family's culture and implications for schooling.
10. Language(s) spoken at home.
11. Community service agencies that the family is connected to or is familiar with.

Structured Action Plans Formal action plans that have been designed to guide groups through the complex planning process for a student also can be helpful in gathering information.

MAPs Making Action Plans (MAPs; formerly called McGill Action Plans) (Falvey, Forest, Pearpoint, & Rosenberg, 1994; Forest & Lusthaus, 1989; Vandercook, York, & Forest, 1989) is the name given to a particular process for structuring day-by-day planning for students. A strategic planning/problem-solving team of student, peers, family members, friends, and school teaching staff work collaboratively to dream about creative schemes, plans, and outcomes for the student (Vandercook et al., 1989). During the MAPs process, participants are encouraged to interact informally as they address seven key questions. A facilitator and recorder are identified. The facilitator guides the group through the process, while the recorder writes down all the responses of the group (e.g., as in a large brainstorming session). During the MAPs session, each question is written on large pieces of paper in front of the group, and all the participants' responses are listed below each question. These MAPs questions should be addressed by the group (Falvey et al., 1994):

1. What is the student's history?
2. What is your dream for the student?
3. What is your nightmare for the student?
4. Who is the student?
5. What are the student's strengths, gifts, and abilities?
6. What are the student's needs?
7. What would the student's ideal day look like, and what must be done to make it happen?

Table 2 provides an example of Courtnee's MAPs process, held in the spring of her kindergarten year with Courtnee, her family, friends, and teachers. In addition, Chapter 11 provides information about the MAPs process.

   PATH   Planning Alternative Tomorrows with Hope (PATH) is another process for planning for the future (Pearpoint, O'Brien, & Forest, 1992). PATH provides an eight-step format for a group to plan for an individual student. There are three primary roles the team undertakes to create a PATH: 1) pathfinders, the group or team wishing to explore options for an individual; 2) a guide, an individual who facilitates the process; and 3) a graphic recorder, an individual who transcribes and summarizes words and images expressed by the group onto paper. The eight-step process requires that team members respond to the following (Falvey et al., 1994):

1. Touching the dream: Identify the dreams you have for this person.
2. Sensing the goal: Identify what could be accomplished in a year's time. Imagining that today is one year from now, identify what the focus person's life looks like.
3. Grounding in the now: Describe the focus person's present situation.
4. Identifying people to enroll: In order to "touch the dream," identify the people who can be enlisted to help.
5. Recognizing ways to build strength: In order to move along the path from what the focus person's life looks like now to the dreams for one year from now, identify the strategies for building the necessary strength to move along the path.
6. Charting action: Identify the most important actions that need to be accomplished within the next 3 months.
7. Planning the next month's work: In a very specific way, identify what people can do in the next month, who will do it, and when those actions will be accomplished.
8. Committing to the next step: As a participant, specify what you will do to contribute to making the dream become a reality.

Table 2. Six-year-old Courtnee's MAPs process (held in the spring of her kindergarten year with Courtnee, her family, friends, and teachers)

1. What is the student's history?

Courtnee is a 6½-year-old girl with Down syndrome.

She has a brother who is 9 years old, and he attends the neighborhood school.

Had formalized assessments conducted that stated she had a vision problem, as well as motor and cognitive delays in learning.

Psychologist recommended that Courtnee attend a special education preschool.

Family had to push to get help for Courtnee to attend neighborhood preschool.

Bussed to a special day class for kindergarten.

Family did not like her going away from neighborhood to attend school, but didn't know what else was available for her.

Family wants Courtnee to go to first grade at the same school as her brother.

She is on medication for seizures but hasn't had one for 2 years. She gets around well but appears clumsy at times.

She has difficulty playing with other children, although she plays well with her brother at home.

2. What is your dream for the student?

Family wants Courtnee to go to first grade at the school her brother attends.

Her vision is not a problem, but her learning style and rate of learning are different.

Family wants Courtnee to learn how to play with other children, have friends, make play dates, and go to birthday parties.

Want her to be happy and take care of herself.

To feel good about herself.

To participate in extracurricular activities (Brownies, gymnastics, or soccer).

3. What is your nightmare for the student?

That people will make fun of Courtnee and not accept her.

That she will not fit in.

Because she is strong willed, afraid no one will like her.

That she will be alone with only her family as friends to support her.

No one to play with; often physically pushes peers.

Not able to read or write.

No one understands her when she talks.

4. Who is the student?

Courtnee is a friendly little girl who likes to run, jump, and skip.

She likes to talk, although sometimes it is difficult to understand her.

She likes adult company more than her peers.

She is learning acceptable play behavior.

She knows how to push other people's buttons to get a reaction.

She smiles a lot.

She likes to get someone (usually an adult) to do things for her, rather than do it herself.

She can be very stubborn.

(continued)

Table 2.   (continued)

She like to dress herself and enjoys playing dress-up.

She is a people-pleaser.

She attempts to print her name.

Likes to color with crayons.

5.   What are the student's strengths, gifts, and abilities?

Courtnee loves to be outside.

She loves to play on the playground equipment.

She loves animals, especially cats.

She likes to listen to music.

She loves being with people.

She is very friendly, especially with adults.

Courtnee likes to look at books.

She likes to interact with people.

6.   What are the student's needs?

She needs to go to her neighborhood school with her brother and neighborhood kids.

Needs to learn not to push others when she doesn't get her way.

Needs to learn to share materials/toys.

Courtnee needs structure and consistency.

She needs help getting organized; she often forgets her school materials.

She needs her medication for seizures.

She needs to learn more appropriate ways to make and keep friends.

She needs some one-to-one attention, but not all the time.

She needs to learn her letters and numbers.

Needs to read simple sight words.

Needs to participate in more fine motor activities (prefers outside, gross motor activities).

She needs to be able to say, "I don't know," and "no."

She needs to learn not to rely on the adults around her.

She needs to have the support and reinforcement of peers.

She needs to have a contract for follow-through with tasks and activities.

Courtnee needs to assume more responsibility for herself.

She needs to get involved in after school activities (Brownies, soccer, gymnastics).

Needs help in the lunch line.

7.   What would the student's ideal day look like, and what must be done to make it happen?

Attend the neighborhood school for first grade.

Make new friends.

Play with peers on the playground.

Share toys with peers.

Schedule an IEP meeting to plan the specifics for instructional support based upon her strengths and needs in early September (see Appendix A for completed IEP and classroom schedule).

Schedule a class meeting early in September so that Courtnee can meet all the new kids and peer supports can be initiated.

Investigate after-school activities (e.g., Brownies, soccer teams, gymnastics).

For more detailed information and graphic displays of the PATH process, the reader is referred to Pearpoint et al. (1992).

Collaborative Team Input

Teachers, parents, students, and others should work in a collaborative team to obtain the necessary assessment data. A *collaborative* team generates information from a variety of perspectives across a multitude of disciplines (e.g., communication/speech-language specialists, general and special education teachers, parents, occupational therapists, physical education teachers). This teaming process assists in the collection of data that reflects all aspects of the student's skill repertoire. It is particularly critical to collaborate as a team when determining what assessments to use and when reporting assessment results, so that the student is viewed in a holistic manner rather than as a multiple set of unrelated parts. The collaborative team participants are determined based upon the student's needs, previous services provided, and anticipated services for the future. For a more detailed discussion of collaborative teams, see Chapter 3.

Review of Pertinent Data and Records

Collaborative team members should review pertinent data and records prior to the development of the IEP. Frequently, staff with specific areas of expertise will review their area of relevant data and records. Pertinent data and records such as confidential files, cumulative folders, formal and informal test results, data sheets and graphs, anecdotal records, and medical history should be included in the review. This will provide the team with information about different strategies and instructional techniques that have been employed prior to the development of the current IEP, and possibly with information about the student's strengths and needs. However, team members must be cautious when reviewing this information, so as not to let it bias their attitudes toward a student or influence a belief in a student's inability (e.g., if a student's records indicate a history of behavior problems the team should not assume these have continued).

Assessment of Current Performance Level

A student's current performance level should be determined using a variety of assessment instruments. Information from a variety of perspectives using performance-based, authentic assessment procedures should be obtained. The team should observe the student in numerous settings and over several days or weeks in order to determine his or her learning style. The following includes specific strategies for assessing students' individual skill level and learning styles. Educators should review these strategies and instruments and decide which are appropriate for each student.

Ecological Inventory Ecological inventories (EI) are surveys or observations that are used to identify skills within current and future settings in which the student functions (Brown et al., 1979). For example, teenagers must learn to function not only within secondary school settings but also within post-secondary settings such as jobs, colleges or universities, and technical schools. Skills are identified from an extensive inventory performed by peers without disabilities in the designated settings. The steps for conducting an ecological inventory include:

1. Divide the curriculum into subjects.
2. Delineate the environments that are available to peers without disabilities.
3. Delineate the subenvironments within each environment.
4. Delineate the activities within each subenvironment.
5. Delineate the specific skills expected or required in order to participate in each activity.

Figure 1 provides an example of an ecological inventory for obtaining lunch via the lunch line in a school cafeteria.

   Student Repertoire Inventories   Student repertoire inventories (SRI) are necessary after ecological inventories have been completed. An SRI is a way of measuring a student's existing performance against the skills identified in the ecological inventory as performed by peers without disabilities (Falvey, Brown, Lyon, Baumgart, & Schroeder, 1980). Steps for conducting student repertoire inventories are:

Curriculum Domain: Vocational
Environment: School cafeteria
Subenvironment: Lunch line

Activity: *Getting in lunch line*
Skills: Enter cafeteria doorway
            Scan for end of lunch line
            Go to end of lunch line

Activity: *Secure lunch*
Skills: Scan for lunch tray
            Pick up lunch tray
            Place on lunch counter
            Push tray along counter
            Scan selections
            State choices of food to cafeteria worker
            Pick up tray with two hands

Activity: *Locate a seat*
Skills: Scan lunch room for empty spot at a table/bench
            Go to empty spot
            Set tray down
            Sit down at empty spot on the bench

Figure 1.   Ecological inventory for obtaining lunch.

1. Delineate the skills performed by peers without disabilities for a given activity (same as Step 5 of the ecological inventory).
2. Observe and record the student's performance in these skill areas.
3. Conduct a discrepancy analysis of the student's performance against the performance of peers without disabilities.
4. If the student is unable to perform any of the skills, utilize one of the following three options: 1) teach the student the skill, 2) develop an adaptation and teach the student to use it, or 3) teach the student to perform a different but related skill.

Figure 2 provides an example of a student repertoire inventory for Courtnee obtaining her lunch via the lunch line in the school cafeteria.

Behavior Counts   The ecological and student repertoire inventories provide opportunities to use a variety of methods or approaches to record student behaviors or skills. Once the behaviors and conditions have been identified via the collaborative team input, data collection procedures need to be identified. A description of data collection procedures frequently used when measuring student behaviors follows.

Baseline Data   Baseline data are a recording of the behaviors exhibited by a student prior to any specific intervention. All behaviors, skills, and activities that make up a student's educational plan should include baseline data.

Event Recording   Event recordings measure the number of times a behavior occurs within a specified period of time (Brown & Snell, 1993). For example, during music class, which occurs for 35 minutes each day, the number of times a student raises his hand to respond to a teacher's question or the number of times a student lifts her head to look at someone else can be compared from one day to the next. This is considered event recording. Also used in this context are *interval recording* and *time sampling* procedures (Alberto & Troutman, 1982). These two procedures are particularly useful when determining the percentages of times a student engages in a specific behavior, especially when the timeframe for data collection varies from day-to-day. Interval recording and time sampling are data collection procedures that can be used when a teacher is unable to collect direct and continuous data regarding a student's behavior, particularly when the behavior occurs frequently. In interval recording, a teacher collects data only during predetermined time intervals. For example, a teacher might collect data on specific student behavior(s) during the first 5 minutes of class, the middle 5 minutes of that same class, and the final 5 minutes of the class.

In time sampling, the teacher predetermines different times throughout an activity or the entire day during which the specific student behavior(s) will be recorded if they are occurring. For example, a student who has demonstrated an extremely high rate of banging his head with his hand (over 100 times in a school day) might be observed every 30 minutes throughout the day after an intervention has been implemented. Every 30 minutes, the teacher notes whether the be-

NAME: Courtnee

CURRICULAR DOMAIN: Vocational

ENVIRONMENT: Cafeteria

SUBENVIRONMENT: Lunch line and counter

ACTIVITIES: 1. Locate lunch line   2. Secure lunch tray   3. Locate seat

Date	Inventory for student without disabilities	Student inventory	Discrepancy analysis	Adaptation hypothesis	What to do?
9/5	1. Locate lunch line				
	A. Enter cafeteria	+			
	B. Scan for end of line	–	Looks around	Pair with peer	Peer teaching
	C. Go to end of line	–	Walks to middle of line		Teach skill
9/5	2. Secure lunch tray				
	A. Scan for lunch tray	+			
	B. Pick up tray	+			
	C. Place on lunch counter	–	Holds to side		Teach skill
	D. Push along counter	–	Waits for others to push	Pair with peer	Peer teaching
	E. Scan selections	+			
	F. State choice	–	Grabs for items	Point to item	Teach to point and state choice
	G. Pick up tray at end of line	–	Waits for someone	Pair with peer	Peer teach to pick up
9/5	3. Locate seat				
	A. Scan for empty table/seat	+			
	B. Locate empty seat	–	Walks around	Sit with peer	Teach to find peer
	C. Set tray down	–	Stands at seat holding tray	Pair with peer	Teach to set down tray
	D. Sit at empty bench	+			

Figure 2. Student repertoire inventory for obtaining lunch.

74

havior is occurring. For further examples, see Figure 3 for an example of event recording, Figure 4 for an example of interval recording, and Figure 5 for an example of time sampling.

Duration Recording A duration recording identifies the length of time a student engages in a specific behavior. This data collection procedure is especially applicable when measuring, for example, the amount of time a student spends interacting with peers without disabilities in recreational activities (e.g.,

---

Event Recording: Number of times student is out of her seat.

Date	Frequency	Total #
8/23	✔ ✔ ✔ ✔ ✔ ✔ ✔ ✔	8
8/24	✔ ✔ ✔ ✔ ✔ ✔	6
8/25	✔ ✔ ✔	3

Code: ✔ = Number of times student is out of her seat inappropriately during the school day

Figure 3.   Sample event or frequency recording.

Interval recording: Number of times student initiates a communicative behavior and number of times student responds to others' communicative efforts.

Time: 9:15 A.M.– 9:30 A.M.

Environment: Free/play area   Activity: Playing with peers without disabilities

	Frequency	Total #
Initiations	✔ ✔ ✔ ✔ ✔ ✔	6
Responses	✔ ✔ ✔ ✔ ✔ ✔ ✔ ✔ ✔ ✔	10

Time: 12:00–12:15 P.M.

Environment: Cafeteria   Activity: Eating lunch with peers without disabilities

	Frequency	Total #
Initiations	✔ ✔ ✔ ✔ ✔ ✔ ✔ ✔	8
Responses	✔ ✔ ✔ ✔ ✔ ✔ ✔ ✔ ✔ ✔ ✔ ✔	12

Figure 4.   Sample interval recording.

Time Sampling: Number of times a student holds up her head across environments and samples of time

Setting	Homeroom	Math	English	Lunch	P.E.	History	Computers
Intervals	9–9:15	10–10:15	11–11:15	12–12:15	1–1:15	2–2:15	3–3:15
Frequencies	////////	////////////	/////////	////////	//////	////////	//////////////

Figure 5.   Sample time sampling.

Duration Recording: Amount of time student is on task when involved in Science Cooperative Learning Groups in Middle School Classroom								
	May 1	May 2	May 3	May 4	May 8	May 9	May 10	May 11
On task	15 min.	11 min.	12 min.	18 min.	15 min.	10 min.	13 min.	18 min.
Off task	15 min.	20 min.	11 min.	5 min.	9 min.	9 min.	4 min.	6 min.

Figure 6.   Sample duration recording.

swimming, playing basketball, or Nintendo). See Figure 6 for an example of duration recording.

Latency Recording   A latency recording determines the time between the presentation of the cue to perform the task and the student's actual initiation of the task (Alberto & Troutman, 1982). This procedure is particularly relevant when measuring, for example, the amount of time it takes a student to begin to input data into a computer terminal at a work-training site once a co-worker has given the directive to begin. See Figure 7 for an example of latency recording.

Scoring by Levels   Scoring by levels is a procedure for recording the levels of assistance or intervention necessary to facilitate the student's performance of a task. This system is particularly useful for scoring ecological and student repertoire inventories or for measuring a student's performance once teaching begins in natural environments. The levels of assistance a teacher might use to facilitate the student's performance of a skill are listed from the most to the least intense and are assigned a number value. The student is evaluated in terms of his or her ability to perform the given skills, and the level (number) of intervention that is necessary is recorded. These data are repeatedly recorded as the student continues to move closer to a level of independence. This procedure is also useful when recording the level of intervention that is necessary at designated intervals to en-

Latency Recording: Amount of time between when the teacher asks the class to get out their books for reading (cue issued) and the student (Sarah) takes out materials			
	Time		
Date	Cue issued	Sarah took out book	Total latency
1/17	10:15 1:12	10:17 1:15	2 min. 3 min.
1/20	10:05 1:15	10:06 1:15	1 min. 0 min.
1/21	10:12 1:12	10:14 1:15	2 min. 3 min.
1/25	10:13 1:15	10:13 1:17	0 min. 2 min.

Figure 7.   Sample latency recording.

sure a student's progress toward, or maintenance of, the independent performance of the skill. See Figure 8 for an example of scoring by levels.

Learning Style Assessment Gardner (1983) encourages the use of informal assessment strategies, such as observation and interviews with the student and significant others, in order to obtain information regarding a student's specific areas of intelligence and personal learning style. To determine a student's personal learning style, educators should observe student reactions to various activities both in and outside the classroom. In addition, input from the student and his or her family about what motivates the student and what he or she does well is essential. Once this information has been obtained, the teacher can analyze and categorize the data into the multiple intelligences as delineated by Gardner (1983). For example, Maria, a 10-year-old student, has been observed by her teachers, speech therapist, physical therapist, and her family as enjoying music and singing. She has also been observed choosing activities such as puzzles, and she frequently tries to "put things together," even things that were not designed to be put together. She touches others often and seems to need to touch when learning something new. Her collaborative team has concluded that she has musical and spatial intelligences and therefore must be provided with an instructional program that reflects the learning strategies specific to these two types of intelligences. First, because of her strengths and interests in music, she should be taught new skills and practice previously learned skills through rhythm and melody. Second, her spatial intelligence suggests that instruction should be pro-

Scoring by levels: Using a walker to move from classroom to office

Skills	Dates						
	9/2	9/3	9/4	9/5	9/6	9/9	9/10
1. Grasp handles	3	3	2	2	2	4	5
2. Raise self from wheelchair	6	6	6	6	6	6	6
3. Turn walker clear of wheelchair	1	2	2	2	4	2	4
4. Look up	1	2	4	4	4	5	5
5. Step with alternating feet	6	6	6	6	6	6	6
6. Walk straight	2	2	2	2	2	2	4
7. Make left turns	2	2	2	2	2	2	2
8. Make right turns	2	2	2	2	2	2	2
Student's Total	23	25	26	26	28	29	34
Independence level = 8 skills performed in response to natural cues (i.e., 6 × 8)	48	48	48	48	48	48	48
Percentage of independence (student's level ÷ independence level)	48%	52%	54%	54%	58%	60%	70%

Code: Physical guidance = 1; model = 2; direct verbal = 3; indirect verbal = 4; gestural = 5; natural cue = 6.

Figure 8.   Example of scoring by levels.

vided through images, shapes, colors, pictures, and the like. This information is extremely useful when designing IEPs for students. See Figure 9 for an example of a multiple intelligences assessment format.

Curriculum-Based Assessment   This assessment procedure refers to "assessment precisely based on what a student has been taught within a curriculum" (Salvia & Hughes, 1990, p. 15). There are several steps to conducting curriculum-based assessment (CBA), according to Salvia and Hughes (1990). The first step is to specify the reason for the assessment to ensure that the information will be useful in making decisions about what and how to teach a student. Second, the curriculum should be analyzed to determine its relevance and application to the individual student. Third, behavioral objectives need to be developed that are based upon the curriculum and are measurable, to ensure objectivity and accountability. Fourth, informal assessment procedures (e.g., behavior counts, ecological and student repertoire inventories) must be developed in order to measure each behavioral objective (i.e., the assessment plan). Fifth, the assessment data must be collected (i.e., implementing the assessment plan). The final step involves summarizing, displaying, and interpreting the assessment data collected in order to make curricular and instructional decisions. Table 3 provides a list of issues that should be considered when using CBA.

Portfolios   A student's portfolio includes work samples across a variety of subject or curricular areas. "Portfolios tell a story . . . put in anything that helps to tell the story" (Paulson & Paulson 1991, p. 1). Work compiled into portfolios includes the student's involvement in determining the topic, the time allocated to the task, the number of rough drafts, and the conditions under which the performance is to be generated (Meyer, 1992). Portfolios might also include projects that require experimentation; cooperation; analyses; investigation; and written, oral, or graphic presentations of the findings (O'Neil, 1992; Podl & Metzger, 1992). Portfolios focus more on a process over time than on content and provide authentic assessment data regarding students' progress. One particular model for portfolios, the Cognitive Model for Assessing Portfolios (CMAP) (Paulson & Paulson, 1991) includes a rationale for the portfolio, the identification of specific goals and set standards, and a determination of how the contents of the portfolio will be selected and evaluated.

Students actively participate in the selection of contents for the portfolio. They maintain portfolios throughout the year and meet frequently with teachers about their work-in-progress, additions, and/or deletions. At the end of the year, portfolios are stored in combination with past years' work in the school archives or storage facilities, thus serving as a permanent record of student progress. For example, Samantha, a student with significant disabilities enrolled in a home economics high school foods class, participates in a small group demonstrating their planning and food-preparation skills by compiling a pictorial step-by-step graphic display of a recipe. Samantha's portfolio would include a picture and/or

	Linguistic	Logical	Math	Spatial	Musical	Bodily/Kinesth	Intrapersonal	Interpersonal
Academic Strengths	• Likes to scribble • Enjoys looking at books • Likes to talk							
Needs	• To learn letters • To learn simple sight words • Print name	• Organizational skills • To obtain own classroom materials	• To learn simple addition (1+2)					
Social Strengths								• Smiles a lot • Very friendly, especially w/adults
Needs	• To ask for assistance					• To not push peers		• Initiate play w/peers • Investigate after-school activities
Personal care Strengths						• Dresses self		
Needs							• Obtain lunch tray	
Motor/sensory Strengths					• Enjoys listening to music		• Likes playground equipment	

Figure 9. Sample multiple intelligences assessment format.

(continued)

Figure 9. (continued)

	Linguistic	Logical	Math	Spatial	Musical	Bodily/Kinesth.	Intrapersonal	Interpersonal
							• Enjoys outdoor games • Likes to run	
Needs				• Participate in process art activities				
Behavior Strengths							• Strong willed	• People pleaser
Needs	• To ask for assistance when needed						• Initiate play with peers	• To work cooperatively with peers
Vocational Strengths						• Dresses self		
Needs								• To obtain lunch tray • Obtain own materials • Take responsibility for self

Summary of student characteristics. Courtnee's strong areas of intelligence and learning style preferences appear to be in the following areas: linguistic, bodily-kinesthetic, and interpersonal. She has a good memory for names and likes to color and listen to stories. She enjoys physical activities and demonstrates a definite preference for outdoor play, in particular on the swings and other playground equipment. She likes to talk with peers and adults and is frequently the first to initiate conversations with others. She displays a strong sense of self, which is often manifested by her strong will. Other areas that appear to be emerging as strengths are logical/mathematical and musical.

Instructional design considerations. The following are instructional design considerations promoting optimal learning situations and environments that will enhance learning for Courtnee.

Linguistic: Provide opportunities to say, hear, and see materials, instructions, and demonstrations. Encourage work in large and small groups with peers, including journal dictation, oral reading, taped stories, and access to typewriters/computers.

Bodily/kinesthetic: Provide opportunities to move around the classroom during activities and move, tap, or fidget while sitting in a chair. Access outdoor areas for learning centers or group work. Use computers.

Interpersonal: Provide group problem-solving activities. Oral reading with and by others. Encourage group games. Facilitate after-school activities.

Logical/mathematical: Use concrete materials. Allow for experimentation and exploration in group activities.

Musical: Encourage interest in musical instrument. Provide opportunities to work with music on in the background.

Table 3. Issues to consider when using curriculum-based assessment

Sample items should be selected from the curriculum.

The items should be arranged in order of difficulty.

A few selected items should be administered to the whole class.

The test should be repeated at least two times with different items.

Assessment should be conducted across curricular areas.

The performance of the class should be recorded.

Acceptable levels of student performance reflective of a classroom should be determined.

CBA should be conducted prior to instruction on that topic.

Results should be studied to determine which students already have the skills and which have not mastered them.

CBA should be readministered after instruction on the topic. This will yield information on which students have mastered the topic and which students require additional instruction.

Instruction should be modified or adjusted (i.e., do not reteach mastered areas, and give more assistance on unmastered areas).

Long-term retention should be assessed by periodically readministering CBA throughout the year.

photographs of the meals she had prepared and printed copies or graphics of her favorite recipes. A student in an English class may complete a required paper through the use of a pictorial display that would be included in a portfolio. This can be a particularly helpful tool for assessing the progress of students with disabilities. The student's portfolio can store the alternative modes that a student employs to complete the assignment (e.g., graphic representations, copies of taped performances/presentations, or a computer disc storing the work of a student) and continue to document a students' progress.

Portfolio assessments are useful organizers of students' performances and certain behaviors. As shown in this section a variety of procedures, tools, and strategies can be used to assess students' skills. The assessment procedures presented in this chapter are primarily quantitative. For a discussion of qualitative assessment, refer to Chapter 6.

Developing a comprehensive assessment plan using a collaborative approach results in the development of an appropriate assessment profile that accurately reflects the student's strengths and needs. Once a comprehensive assessment plan has been developed and executed, the next step is to formulate and state objectives and to develop and use monitoring and evaluation procedures appropriate for determining the student's acquisition of those stated objectives. Taken together, these steps constitute the IEP process. The following section provides a description of each of the essential components of the IEP.

COMPONENTS OF THE IEP

A comprehensive assessment process leads to the development of meaningful and relevant goals and objectives as well as identification of needed supplementary aids and services. The assessment data obtained becomes the driving force in the development of the student's IEP and its implementation through the student's classroom schedule.

The IEP provides the basic system for organizing the essential and relevant curricular content for a student. According to IDEA, this means a written document is individually developed for each student through an assessment process. This document is to be reviewed at least annually and must be prepared by the student, his or her family, teacher, and others as appropriate. Components of the IEP and recommended practices for implementing each component are provided below.

Component 1: A statement of the student's present levels of educational performance. This component should include the present chronological age of the student, the student's current level of independent functioning across all areas of the curriculum, the student's present level of performance of functional routines within general education settings, the student's current level of social and interactional skills, the student's present level of motor and mobility skills, the extent and existence of the student's network of friends, and the student's specific learning styles and needs (e.g., learning style, learning rate, ability to generalize, areas of difficulty). The information obtained from individual student assessments should be included in the IEP itself.

Component 2: A statement of annual goals for the student, including short-term instructional objectives. Based on the assessment results, a description of the specific skill sequences needed by the student, a rationale for the teaching of these sequences at this time, a delineation of comprehensive curricular areas and basic skills for teaching, a description of the instructional arrangements for teaching these skills (e.g., cooperative groupings, individual, or large group), specific performance criteria for each skill to be taught, and a description of strategies to be used to determine how to meet performance criteria. Again, this information can be included in the IEP.

Component 3: A delineation of needed supplementary aids and services. This component involves the identification of the needed supplementary aids and services to support students' participation in general education schools and classes. This assistance might include related services (e.g., communication/speech and language specialists, orientation and mobility specialists, psychologists, social workers, nurses, specialists in vision or hearing disabilities, physical or occupational therapists). These services might also include curricular or instructional adaptation and/or additional supports (e.g., instructional assistants, teachers, peers, volunteers). The determination of needed supplementary aids and services is based upon thorough and ongoing assessment.

Figure 10 provides an Assessment Profile Sequence that identifies the steps necessary to design a meaningful educational program for a student in an inclusive setting as well as the order in which the steps should occur. A case study for Courtnee is detailed in Appendix A, which illustrates her IEP using a multiple intelligences assessment, data collected in various areas, goals and objectives, and a matrix of the classroom schedule. The case study begins with the input at a MAPS meeting, which was included earlier in this chapter and designated as Table 2. A more detailed discussion for completing an IEP matrix can be found in Chapter 6.

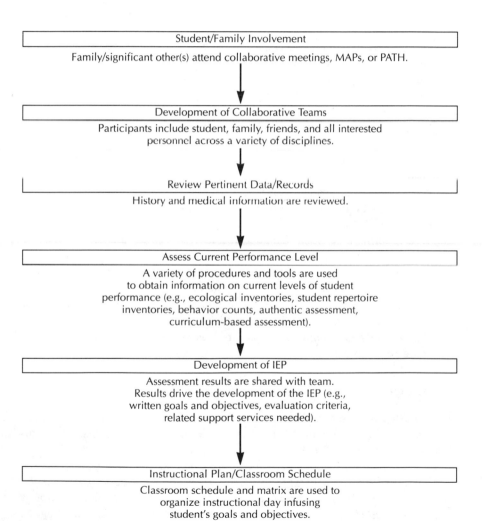

Figure 10.   Assessment profile sequence.

PROTECTION OF STUDENT RIGHTS

An important consideration in the assessment process is the protection of students' rights. If assessment is not performed and reported responsibly, students' needs and personalities can be misrepresented. Cultural, religious, gender, disability, and other biases have been reported in the assessment process. Care should be taken when interpreting and describing student performance based on assessment results. The following is a list of legal and ethical considerations that teachers should respect and practice (Browder, 1991):

1. Parental and, when possible, student consent must be obtained before initial assessment or evaluation is conducted.
2. Parents have the right to participate in the development of the IEP, and teachers should always encourage such participation.
3. Parents must have access to review all educational records, including assessment results and evaluations.
4. Only relevant and needed assessment information should be collected.
5. Information that has no educational relevance should not be collected or reported.
6. All assessment information must be kept confidential. Such information can only be shared by other agencies and/or individuals with written parental permission. Even posting assessment data on classroom bulletin boards can be in violation of the student's rights if not done with the student's and/or parents' permission.
7. When sharing assessment data and results with parents and students, do so with sensitivity and tact. Always indicate the student's strengths and needs when discussing assessment results. Never deny parents their right to have dreams and hopes for their son or daughter.
8. Parents have the right to obtain an independent assessment or evaluation of their son's or daughter's skills and needs.
9. Placement decisions must be based upon assessment results/evaluations and shared with parents.

SUMMARY

Assessment procedures need to be individualized for each student. The strategies employed by the collaborative team to secure information about a particular student should include information from the student, the family, and those who know the student well from a variety of school and nonschool perspectives. The tools and procedures identified in this chapter provide the necessary information via authentic, performance-based assessments. This assessment information is contextually based and taps into a range of personal learning styles (i.e., linguistic, spatial, musical, logical/mathematical, bodily/kinesthetic, interpersonal, and intrapersonal), as opposed to a one-shot true/false or multiple choice test format addressing a very narrow perspective of intelligence.

REFERENCES

Alberto, P., & Troutman, A. (1982). *Applied behavior analysis for teachers.* Columbus, OH: Charles E. Merrill.

Armstrong, T. (1987). *In their own way.* Los Angeles, CA: Jeremy P. Tarcher, Inc.

Armstrong, T. (1994). *Multiple intelligences in the classroom.* Alexandria, VA: Association for Supervision and Curriculum Development.

Baker, E.L. (1989). Mandated tests: Educational reform or quality indicator? In B.R. Gifford (Ed.), *Test policy and test performance: Education, language and culture* (pp. 3–23). Norwell, MA: Kluwer.

Binet, A., & Simon, T. (1905). Methods nouvelle pour le diagnostic du niveau intellectuel des anormaux. *L'Annee Psychologique, 11,* 191–244.

Binet, A., & Simon, T. (1911). *A method of measuring the development of the intelligence of young children.* Lincoln, IL: Courier.

Binet A., & Simon, T. (1916). The development of intelligence in children (The Binet-Simon scale), translated from articles in *L'Annee Psychologique* from 1905, 1908, and 1911 by Elizabeth S. Kite. Baltimore: Williams & Williams.

Brandt, R. (1992). On performance assessment: A conversation with Grant Wiggins. *Educational Leadership, 49*(8), 35–37.

Browder, D. (1991). Overview of educational assessment. In D. Browder, *Assessment of individuals with severe disabilities: An applied behavior approach to life skills assess ment* (2nd ed.) (pp. 1–26). Baltimore: Paul H. Brookes Publishing Co.

Brown, L., Branston, M.B., Hamre-Nietupski, S., Pumpian, I., Certo, N., & Gruenewald, L. (1979). A strategy for developing chronological age appropriate and functional curricular content for severely handicapped adolescents and young adults. *Journal of Special Education, 13*(1), 81–90.

Brown, F., & Snell, M. (1993). Measurement, analysis and evaluation. In M. Snell (Ed.), *Instruction of students with severe disabilities.* New York: Macmillan.

Darling-Hammond, L. (1991, November). The implications of testing policy for quality and equality. *Phi Delta Kappan, 73*(3), 220–224.

Dietz, M.E., & Moon, C.J. (1992). What do we want students to know? . . . and other important questions. *Educational Leadership, 49*(8), 38–41.

Education for All Handicapped Children Act of 1975, PL 94-142. (August 23, 1975). Title 20, U.S.C. 1401 et seq: *U.S. Statutes at Large, 89,* 773–796.

Falvey, M., Brown, L., Lyon, S., Baumgart, D., & Schroeder, J. (1980). Strategies for using cues and corrections procedures. In W. Sailor, B. Wilcox, & L. Brown (Eds.), *Methods of instruction for severely handicapped students* (pp. 109–133). Baltimore: Paul H. Brookes Publishing Co.

Falvey, M., Forest, M., Pearpoint, J., & Rosenberg, R. (1994). Building connections: All my life's a circle. In Thousand, J., Villa, R., & Nevin, A. (Eds.), *Creativity and collaborative learning: A practical guide to empowering students and teachers.* Baltimore: Paul H. Brookes Publishing Co.

Forest, M., & Lusthaus, E. (1989). Promoting educational equality for all students: Circles and maps. In S. Stainback, W. Stainback, & M. Forest (Eds.), *Educating all students in the mainstream of regular education* (pp. 43–57). Baltimore: Paul H. Brookes Publishing Co.

Gardner, H. (1983). *Frames of mind.* New York: Basic Books.

Herman, J.L., Aschbacher, P., & Winters, L. (1992). *A practical guide to alternative assessment*. Alexandria, VA: Association for Supervision and Curriculum Development.

Individuals with Disabilities Education Act of 1990 (IDEA), PL 101-476. (October 30, 1990). Title 20, U.S.C. 1400 et seq: *U.S. Statutes at Large, 104*, 1103–1151.

Maeroff, G.I. (1991, December). Assessing alternative assessment. *Phi Delta Kappan, 73*(4), 272–281.

Meyer, C. (1992). What's the difference between authentic and performance assessment? *Educational Leadership, 49*(8), 39–40.

Miller, L. (1990). *The smart profile: The qualitative approach for describing learners and designing instruction*. Austin, TX: Smart Alternatives.

Miller, L. (1993). *What we call smart*. San Diego, CA: Singular Publishing Group.

O'Neil, J. (1992). Putting performance assessment to the test. *Educational Leadership, 49*(8), 14–19.

Paulson, P.R., & Paulson, F.L. (1991). Portfolios: Stories of knowing. In P.H. Dreyer (Ed.), *Claremont reading conference 55th yearbook 1991. Knowing: The power of stories*. Claremont, CA: Center for Developmental Studies of the Claremont Graduate School.

Pearpoint, J., O'Brien, J., & Forest, M. (1992). *PATH: Planning alternative tomorrows with hope*. Toronto, Ontario, Canada: Inclusion Press.

Podl, J.B., & Metzger, M. (1992). *Anatomy of an exhibition. Studies on Exhibition, No. 6*. Providence, RI: Coalition of Essential Schools, Brown University.

Salvia, J., & Hughes, C. (1990). *Curriculum-based assessment: Testing what is tangible*. New York: Macmillan.

Sapon-Shevin, M. (1992). Celebrating diversity, creating community. In S. Stainback & W. Stainback (Eds.), *Curriculum considerations in inclusive classrooms: Facilitating learning for all students* (pp. 19–36). Baltimore: Paul H. Brookes Publishing Co.

Vandercook, T., York, J., & Forest, M. (1989). The McGill action planning system (MAPs): A strategy for building the vision. *Journal of The Association for Persons with Severe Handicaps, 14*, 205–215.

Wiggins, G. (1989, May) A true test: Toward more authentic and equitable assessment. *Phi Delta Kappan, 70*(9), 703–713.

Wise, A. (1988, June). *Restructuring school*. Paper presented at the Annual Georgia Leadership Institute, Athens.

Wolf, D.P., LeMahieu, P.G., & Eresh, J. (1992). Good measure: Assessment as a tool for educational reform. *Educational Leadership, 49*(8), 8–13.

APPENDIX A

Case Study of Courtnee

STUDENT PROFILE

Name: Courtnee
Age: 6.5 years
School Year: First grade; 1993–94

General Information:

Courtnee is 6½ years old and has Down syndrome. She lives with her mom and dad and 9-year-old brother in a middle class, ethnically diverse neighborhood. The family has lived here for 5 years. Courtnee was bussed to special day class/intensive preschool and kindergarten. For first grade, the family wants Courtnee to attend the neighborhood school, which is four blocks away, with her brother. She doesn't know or play with any neighborhood children, but does go to the park with her family. She likes to play outdoors and especially enjoys the playground equipment.

Strengths	Needs
Enjoys music	Initiate play request with peers
Dresses self	Interact cooperatively with peers
Likes to play outdoors	Share toys/material
Enjoys playground equipment	Print name
Strong willed	Build vocabulary
Likes to please others	Sight word recognition
Likes company of adults	Ask/seek assistance
Friendly	Obtain own class materials
Likes to color and scribble	Perform simple addition
	Obtain own lunch
	Participate in after-school activities
	(Brownies, soccer, gymnastics)

Additional Comments:

Does not currently attend neighborhood school
Family wants neighborhood school
Takes medication
Has difficulty asking peers to play; will physically push peers

Communication Data

Student: Courtnee

Date	Activity/Content	Communicative Mode	Frequency		Communication			Reinforcement/	Comments
			Initiation	Response	Message	Content		Consequence	
9/5	Recess on swings	verbal gestural	✓	✓	Push on swing No! No!	Would you swing me? Shook head/body "no"		Peer pushed her Stayed on swings	Difficult to understand Wouldn't take turns
9/6	Free choice Rug area Aladdin game	verbal	✓		I want it	I get it!		Got the game piece	Needs to ask nicely to share/play game
9/8	Story time on rug	verbal		✓	Let me sit here	No! No! Pushed peer		Had to sit at table for 3 minutes before returning to the rug area	Needs to learn how to ask to sit near a friend
9/8	Lunch line	verbal/gestural	✓		I want that	Dat! Dat!		Received lunch selection	Increase sentence length

Student Repertoire Inventory

Name: Courtnee

Domain: Motor/sensory

Environment: School

Subenvironment: 1st grade classroom

Activities: Participate in art activities (process, not product activities)

Date: 9/5

Recorder: STG

Inventory for Person without Disabilities	Inventory for Student with Disabilities	Discrepancy Analysis	Adaptation Hypothesis	What to Do?
Locate crayons	–	Does not get crayons		Teach location of crayons
Locate glue	–	Does not get glue		Teach location of glue
Color with crayons	–	Holds loosely	Provide fat crayons	Fade to thinner crayons
Squeeze on glue	–	Squeezed lightly	Provide different glue container	Teach to squeeze or pour glue
Spread with brush	–	Watches others	Peer assistance	
Shake on glitter	–	Did not shake bottle		Teach shaking bottle skills
Place on rack to dry	–	Needed verbal prompt		Teach placement of finished products
Wash off hands	+			

Student Repertoire Inventory

Name: Courtnee

Domain: Academic

Environment: Classroom

Subenvironment: Desk

Activities: Simple addition (2 + 4, 1 + 3)

Date: 9/5

Recorder: STG

Inventory for Student without Disabilities	Inventory for Student with Disabilities	Discrepancy Analysis	Adaptation Hypothesis	What to Do?
Locate math book	–	Took out wrong book	Peer assistance	Teach her to obtain own materials
Locate page	–	Could not do this	Tag with marker	Teach her to locate page marker
Locate pencil	–	Sat at desk	Provide pencil holder on desk	
Perform simple addition	–	Not sure what to do	Provide manipulatives in cooperative group	Teach use of manipulatives
Complete the page	–	Attempted to complete 2 out of 10	Provide more time	

Student Repertoire Inventory   *(continued)*

Name: Courtnee

Domain: Academic

Environment: Classroom

Subenvironment: Desk

Activities: Number identification (1–100)

Date: 9/5

Recorder: STG

Inventory for Student without Disabilities	Inventory for Student with Disabilities	Discrepancy Analysis	Adaptation Hypothesis	What to Do?
Identify numbers 1–5	+			
Identify numbers 1–10	+	Does not know 10		Teach number recognition
Identify numbers 10–20	–	Does not know	Provide model	Teach number recognition
Identify numbers 20–30	–	Does not know	Provide model and use the number line	Teach number recognition and use of number line
Identify numbers 30–40	–	Does not know	Provide model and use the number line	Teach number recognition and use of number line

Student Repertoire Inventory

Name: Courtnee

Domain: Vocational

Environment: Cafeteria

Subenvironment: Lunch line and counter

Activities: 1) Locate lunch line

2) Secure lunch tray

3) Locate seat

Date: 9/5

Recorder: STG

Inventory for Student without Disabilities	Inventory for Student with Disabilities	Discrepancy Analysis	Adaptation Hypothesis	What to Do?
1. Locate end of lunch line				
Enter cafeteria	+			
Scan for end of line	–	Looks around	Pair with peer	
Go to end of line	–	Walks to middle of line		Teach skill
2. Secure lunch tray				
Scan for lunch tray	+			
Pick up tray	+			

Inventory for Student without Disabilities	Inventory for Student with Disabilities	Discrepancy Analysis	Adaptation Hypothesis	What to Do?
Place it on lunch counter	–	Holds to side		Teach skill
Push it along counter	–	Waits for others to push		Teach skill
Scan selections	+			
State choice	–	Grabs for items	Point to item	Teach to point and state choice
Pick up tray at end of line	–	Waits for someone to do it		Teach to pick up
3. Locate seat				
Scan for empty table/seat	+			
Locate empty seat	–	Walks around	Sit with peer	Teach to find peer
Set tray down	–	Stands at seat		Teach to set it down
Sit at empty bench	+			

93

Scoring by Levels

Name: Courtnee

Domain: Academic

Environment: Classroom

Subenvironment: Desk

Activity: Print name

Recorder: STG

Date	9/4	9/5	9/6	9/7		
1. Sit at desk	6	6	6	6		
2. Hold pencil with pincer grasp	3	3	3	4		
3. Control movements to make letters	2	3	2	3		
4. Print "C"	1	1	3	2		
5. Print "O"	1	1	1	2		
6. Print "U"	1	1	1	1		
7. Print "R"	1	1	1	1		
8. Print "T"	1	1	1	1		
9. Print "N"	1	1	1	1		
10. Print "E"	1	1	1	1		
11. Print "E"	1	1	1	1		
Student's Total	19	20	21	23		
Performance	28%	30%	32%	34%		

Key: 1 - Physical guidance   2 - Partial physical prompt   3 - Modeling
       4 - Direct verbal cue   5 - Indirect verbal cue   6 - Natural

Independence Level = number of skills performed (11) in response to natural cues (6) (i.e., 11 × 6 = 66)

Percentage of Independence = student level totals (19) divided by independence level (66) (i.e., 19 ÷ 66 = 28%)

Anecdotal Record

Name: Courtnee

Target Behavior: To play cooperatively with peers

Curriculum Area: Behavioral/social/emotional

Recorder: STG

Date	Domain	Observation	Behavior
9/3	Motor/behavioral	Playing on playground during recess	Pushed peer to get the ball
9/3	Social/emotional/ behavioral	Choice time/free play	Threw game pieces and pushed peer
9/4	Social/emotional/ behavioral	P.M. recess/swings	Would not let another child have a turn
9/5	Social/emotional/ behavioral	A.M. recess/swings	Twisted the swings to spin around, legs hit another student while spinning
9/5	Social/emotional/ behavioral	P.M. recess/swings	Let another child have a turn on the swing

Anecdotal Record

Name: Courtnee

Target Behavior: Seek assistance when unsure of task demand

Curriculum Area: Social/emotional

Recorder: STG

Date	Domain	Observation	Behavior
9/4	Social/communication	Math time	Does not know what book to get
9/4	Social/communication	Art/music	Sits/observes; does not participate
9/5	Social/communication	Story time	Doesn't know where to sit; pushes peer
9/6	Social/communication	A.M. recess/playground	Throws large ball at peers
9/6	Social/communication	P.M. recess/playground	Asks playground aide for help getting on the swings

Frequency Record

Name: Courtnee

Target Behavior: Obtain own materials in classroom (pencil, book, crayons, glue)

Curriculum Area: Personal care

Recorder: STG

Date	Frequency	Total
9/5	√√	2
9/6	√√√	3
9/8	√	1

Code: √ = number of times Courtnee obtains own classroom materials independently during school day.

Frequency Record

Name: Courtnee

Target Behavior: Increase # of weekly spelling words correctly spelled

Curriculum Area: Academic

Recorder: STG

Date	No. of correct spelling words	Correct (%)
9/5	3	30%
9/6	5	50%
9/8	2	20%

Curriculum Area: Social/emotional
Recorder: STG
Date: 9/6; 9/7; 9/8

Target Behavior: Initiate play request with peers
Environment: School playground
Activity: Recess
Time: 9:45–10:00

Date	Activity	Frequency	Total #
9/6	Initiations	√√√	3
9/7	Initiations	√	1

Target Behavior: Initiate play request with peers
Environment: Classroom
Activity: Free choice time
Time: 1:35–2:15

Date	Activity	Frequency	Total #
9/6	Initiations	√√	2
9/8	Initiations	√	1

Name: Courtnee

Age: 6.5 years

Grade: First grade

School Year: 1993–94

Goals	Objectives	Interventions, Strategies, Modifications, and Accommodations	Evaluation Criteria (Expected date of achievement and criterion)	
Curriculum area: Vocational Obtain lunch tray and seat in cafeteria	In the cafeteria lunch area, Courtnee will obtain her own lunch tray and make her lunch selections 4 out of 5 days.	Pair with peer model, verbal prompt, gesture, fade	Observation	9/94
	After selecting her lunch, Courtnee will carry her tray to an empty spot at a lunch table to eat her lunch 4 out of 5 days.	Pair with peer model, verbal prompt, gesture, fade	Informal assessment (SRI)	9/94
Curriculum area: Sensory Motor Participate in art activity	During art activities, Courtnee will engage in a variety of art mediums, exploring multiple levels of process (not product) art activities without more than 2 verbal prompts, 4 out of 5 days.	Full physical assistance model, direct verbal, gesture, fade, small group instruction	Observation	6/94
Curriculum area: Personal Care Assume responsibility for materials needed in class activities	Throughout the school day, Courtnee will secure the materials (pencil, books, crayon, glue) required for each activity with no more than 1 verbal prompt, 9 out of 10 days.	Pictures of materials verbal prompt, indirect prompt, gesture, fade	Informal	9/94

(continued)

Goals	Objectives	Interventions, Strategies, Modifications, and Accommodations	Evaluation Criteria (Expected date of achievement and criterion)	
Curriculum area: Academics				
Build vocabulary	During language arts, Courtnee will correctly spell simple consonant-vowel-consonant (C-V-C) words taken from her basal level reader; C-V-C words will be determined by weekly pretest for 9 out of 10 consecutive weeks.	Small group instruction provide written model, verbal prompt, fade, pair oral with printed presentation	Informal	9/94
Read sight words	During reading groups, Courtnee will read 1–2 pages orally in her basal level reader with not more than 2 verbal prompts a day, 9 out of 10 days.	Whole word recognition model orally, verbal prompt, gesture, fade, pair with peer for oral reading, small group instruction	Informal	9/94
Improve printing skills	Throughout the school day, Courtnee will print her name on each of her worksheets with no more than 2 verbal reminders per work sheet, 4 out of 5 days.	Provide a printed model model, verbal prompt, fade	Observation	9/94
Improve addition skills	During math time, Courtnee will compute simple addition facts and identify numbers 1–100 with no more than 2 verbal prompts, 4 out of 5 days.	Model, direct verbal, fade	Informal	9/94
Curriculum area: Social/Emotional				
Seek assistance	Throughout the school day, Courtnee will seek assistance from peers when facing the unknown or requiring help with no more than 2 verbal prompts, 4 out of 5 days.	Model, direct verbal, indirect verbal, gesture, fade	Informal	9/94

Goal/Objective		Strategies/Supports	Evaluation	Date
Participate in extra-curricular activities (Brownies, soccer, or gymnastics)	No objective written. Not priority area at this time.	Parents to investigate options and supports needed		
Curriculum area: Communications				
Expand and refine personal interactions	During recess and free choice time, Courtnee will appropriately initiate a "play with me" request of her peers at least 2 times a day, 9 out of 10 days.	Pair with peer/buddy model, direct verbal, fade, small group instruction	Observation	9/94
	During recess and free choice time, Courtnee will play cooperatively with her peers with no more than 2 verbal reminders per day, 9 out of 10 days.	Peer/buddy model, direct verbal, fade, small group instruction	Observation	9/94

99

IEP Form

Student: Courtnee

Birthdate: 3/7/87

Date of meeting: 9/10/93

School of Attendance: Meadows Avenue

Summarization of collaborative assessment: All assessments were done in an informal format. Courtnee can identify the letters in her name and the numbers 1–9. She does not print her name. She's ready to increase her recognition of numbers and learn simple addition facts (1 + 1; 2 + 3). She enjoys music. She doesn't participate in process art activities. If unsure of what to do, she will sit and watch the teacher and other students.

She often relies on others to get her classroom materials. She enjoys the company of her peers, but is unsure of how to engage them in play. In the cafeteria, she needs assistance getting her lunch and finding a seat.

Recommendations: Team recommends that she attend her neighborhood school for first grade with the assistance of an inclusive facilitator for 2–3 weeks. She qualifies for speech services (in-classroom collaborative model): 2 times a week, 30 minutes, small group.

IEP Goals/Classroom Schedule and Matrix

√ = Opportunity to work on student's IEP goals

Courtnee   **Classroom Schedule**   1st grade

IEP Goals	8:30 Arrival/roll call	8:40 Flag salute/calendar	8:50–9:45 Language Arts, reading, spelling	9:45–10:00 Recess/snack	10:00–10:15 Journal writing	10:15–10:50 Math	10:50–11:30 Social studies	11:30–12:15 Lunch/recess	12:15–12:40 Story/sharing	12:45–1:20 Art/music	1:20–1:35 Recess	1:35–2:15 Physical education (T & Th) free choice (M, W, & F)
Print name			√		√		√			√		
Read sight words			√		√	√	√			√		
Build vocabulary		√	√		√	√	√		√	√		√
Simple addition						√						
Number recognition		√				√						
Obtain materials	√		√	√	√	√	√	√	√	√	√	√
Art activities (process art)										√		
Seek assistance	√	√	√	√	√	√	√	√	√	√	√	√
Initiate play requests			√					√			√	√
Play cooperatively			√					√		√	√	√
Secure lunch tray								√				
Locate seat	√		√	√	√	√	√	√	√	√		√

Appendix B

Sample Assessment Forms

STUDENT PROFILE
Name:
Age:
School Year:
General Information:
Strengths   **Needs**
Additional Comments:

Communication Data

Student: _____   Recorder: _____

Date	Activity/ Content	Communicative Mode	Frequency		Communication		Reinforcement/ Consequence	Comments
			Initiation	Response	Message	Content		

104

Student Repertoire Inventory

Name: _____

Domain: _____

Environment: _____

Subenvironment: _____

Activities: _____

Date: _____

Recorder: _____

Inventory for Person without Disabilities	Inventory for Student with Disabilities	Discrepancy Analysis	Adaptation Hypothesis	What to Do?

Scoring by Levels

Name: _____

Domain: _____

Environment: _____

Subenvironment: _____

Activity: _____

Recorder: _____

Date						
1.						
2.						
3.						
4.						
5.						
6.						
7.						
8.						
9.						
10.						
11.						
Student's Total						
Performance						

Key: 1 - Physical guidance   2 - Partial physical prompt   3 - Modeling
           4 - Direct verbal cue   5 - Indirect verbal cue   6 - Natural

Independence Level = number of skills performed _____ in response to natural cues _____

Percentage of Independence = student level totals _____ divided by independence level _____

Anecdotal Record

Name: _____

Target Behavior: _____

Curriculum Area: _____

Recorder: _____

Date	Domain	Observation	Behavior

Frequency Record

Name: _____

Target Behavior: _____

Curriculum Area: _____

Recorder: _____

Frequency Record

Date	Frequency	Total (%)

Code: √ = number of times _____

IEP

Name: _____
Age: _____
Grade: _____
School Year: _____

Goals	Objectives	Interventions, Strategies, Modifications, and Accommodations	Evaluation Criteria (Expected date of achievement and criterion)
Curriculum area:			
Curriculum area:			
Curriculum area:			

IEP Goals/Classroom Schedule and Matrix

√ = Opportunity to work on student's IEP goals

Student   **Classroom Schedule**   Grade

IEP Goals

CREATING A SUPPORTIVE CLASSROOM ENVIRONMENT

5

KIMBERLEE A. JUBALA, KATHRYN D. BISHOP, AND MARY A. FALVEY

To accommodate the diversity that exists in many schools today, educators must strive to provide learning environments that facilitate students' acquisition and performance of appropriate behaviors, accommodate individual strengths and needs, and create a sense of belonging for all students. In addressing challenging behaviors, a classroom teacher may need to rely on specific positive behavioral support procedures for one or two students in his or her classroom (see Chapter 7). There are, however, strategies that educators can use to enhance the overall climate of their classrooms to encourage and facilitate engaged learning behaviors for all their students. This chapter describes effective strategies for structuring a classroom in which all students can achieve academically, socially, and emotionally. In such an environment, students with disabilities have equal classroom membership with their peers. The goal is to provide opportunities for students with and without disabilities to be educated side-by-side in a supportive classroom. This chapter specifically examines strategies that increase the likelihood of appropriate and cooperative behaviors of students, through the creation of a supportive classroom and the use of a variety of instructional arrangements.

CREATING A SUPPORTIVE CLASSROOM

It is early on a Tuesday morning. The fifth graders have turned in their homework, hung up their backpacks, and spent a few minutes socializing and enjoying free time. At the sound of the hand chimes, they put away their comic books, science experiments, mystery novels, and baseball cards and gather in the front of the room.

"I'll get the rain stick," says one child, picking up the cylindrical noisemaker. "It's my turn to take minutes," announces another child as she retrieves

111

the classroom journal. "I have a problem to add to the agenda," comments a third student.

When everyone is seated quietly and comfortably on the floor, the teacher turns the rain stick on end, creating a series of rain-like sounds. Soon everyone settles and listens until the sound of "rain" fades away. "Welcome to today's community circle meeting in Room 14's caring community," recites a fifth grader.

"I'm glad that you are here with me today," begins the teacher. "And I am proud to see how well you are listening to each other and to me. Does anyone have anything to add to our agenda? If not, we will begin today by taking attendance. When I call your name, please complete the sentence, 'If I could have one wish it would be. . . .'"

The class meeting continues. The students gather together like this at the beginning of each week, for 10–20 minutes, depending on the agenda. This morning, for example, many things will be discussed. The upcoming unit on Native Americans will be announced, with the students' questions and suggestions woven into the discussion. Details on the culminating project on "ancestor detectors" are determined for the presentation to be made to parents. With his permission, Robert's problem with fighting on the playground will be examined, and his classmates will brainstorm potential solutions. Ideas will be presented on how to include Jayme—and her wheelchair—into the kickball game at recess. A vote will be taken to determine whether to use the money from the class recycling project to purchase an acre of rain forest or to fund and serve a meal at the downtown shelter. A sample of the books made for the class's Kindergarten Book Buddies will be passed around the circle. When there are no items remaining on the agenda, and after additional thoughts and feelings have been invited, the rain stick will be turned over once again to signal that the meeting is adjourned.

The class meeting is a weekly occurrence in this inner city elementary school. It is just one of the many strategies used to facilitate students' involvement in their classroom. The children described come from many different backgrounds; speak several different languages; and have varying strengths, needs, interests, and challenges. In the office, their files are peppered with labels such as "behavior problem," "average student," "learning disabled," "gifted," "severely handicapped," and "attention deficit disorder." During the class meeting and throughout the school day, however, these students are all equal and yet unique. Each student has an opportunity to contribute to the classroom and to be a part of this community. This environment helps to create a sense of inclusion that minimizes the occurrence of difficult or disruptive behavior.

There are many different ways to structure a classroom in order to be proactive and minimize behavior challenges. The class meeting described earlier reflects components that may be considered in providing a learning environment where a student's tendency to misbehave is reduced. These components include: 1) structuring the classroom environment to provide positive, cooperative relationships; 2) providing a democratic classroom; 3) developing communication and conflict-management skills; 4) encouraging whole-school community building and parent involvement; and 5) enhancing curriculum considerations. When problems do arise in this type of classroom, both the teacher and the students have a repertoire of strategies to help solve problems, heal hurt feelings, maintain order, and engender dignity and respect between adults and students.

Structuring the Classroom Environment

Research suggests that classrooms may be highly structured places dominated by authoritarian teachers, where students have few choices and limited opportunities to develop relationships with teachers or peers (Ames, 1987; Goodlad, 1984). Opportunities for students to feel like valued and accepted members of their classroom are not always prevalent in schools (Solomon, Schapps, Watson, & Battistich, 1990).

Yet, the need to belong and to be accepted can be seen as a basic goal of human behavior (Dreikurs, Grunwald, & Pepper, 1980; Kunc, 1992; Maslow, 1970). Applying this premise to the classroom, one can postulate that students will choose different behaviors to attain a sense of belonging. Most students will choose "appropriate," acceptable patterns of behavior. However, some students do not feel that they belong, or even that they can belong, through constructive, useful behavior. These students often resort to misbehaving. It is the teacher's responsibility to redirect and encourage all students and to provide opportunities for success and acceptance so that each student can feel significant and achieve a sense of belonging (Dinkmeyer, McKay, & Dinkmeyer, 1980). In doing so, students are more inclined to uphold the values and norms exemplified in the classroom setting, to feel better about themselves, and to have opportunities for greater success (Solomon et al., 1990).

It is possible that many of the problems inherent in our schools and society stem from a lack of belonging. Rather than concentrating on rigorous standards and academic demands, it may be more constructive to focus energies on building a sense of belonging in our schools (Kunc, 1992). In classroom settings that include students with disabilities, where all students (and teachers) have equal membership, there are many opportunities to learn with and from one another.

> For when we are able to rely on our peers' individual strengths rather than attempting to achieve complete mastery in all areas, then belonging begins to precede achievement, and we may be welcomed into community not because of our perfection, but because of our inherent natural and individual capabilities. (Kunc, 1992, p. 38)

Most importantly, students and teachers can learn that belonging is a right, not a status to be earned (Kunc, 1992).

As teachers, parents, and administrators encourage students to become thoughtful, self-directed, concerned about others, and committed to community, they are responsible for providing a learning environment that allows students to develop and practice these qualities (Solomon et al., 1990). The concept of "classroom community" or "caring community" embodies a place where these skills are practiced and where all students can experience a sense of belonging. This sense of community can impact students in many ways. Schaps and Solomon (1990) indicate that building community increases schools' effectiveness in fostering students' intellectual, social, and moral development. Peterson (1992) describes the influence of community in this way:

> When community exists, learning is strengthened—everyone is smarter, more ambitious, and productive. Well formed ideas and intentions amount to little without a community to being them to life. (p. 2)

Many resources exist enumerating the benefits of establishing a caring community in the classroom (Heller, 1993; Kohn, 1991; Noddings, 1992; Sapon-Shevin, 1990; Solomon et al., 1990). Still other sources describe activities that help to facilitate a sense of community among students and to improve self-esteem and belonging (Canfield & Wells, 1976; Gibbs, 1987; Hammond & Collins, 1993). For example, Gibbs (1987) delineates "Community Circle," cooperative drawing, and creative storytelling activities that encourage speaking and listening skills, develop cohesion, and build inclusion. Canfield and Wells (1976) describe journal writing, nickname research, and "student-of-the-week" displays as a means of improving self-awareness and positive support for class members. As discussed later in this chapter, many of these activities can be integrated into traditional content areas and may actually increase motivation to learn.

Providing a Democratic Classroom

The concept of a "democratic approach" to classroom management is most clearly delineated by Dinkmeyer et al. (1980). These authors describe a democratic classroom as a place where choices are clear, discipline is logical, self-discipline is encouraged, and the most positive components of a democratic society are mirrored. They suggest four plans of action to establish a democratic atmosphere in the classroom:

1. Establish a climate of mutuality and respect.
2. Encourage students.
3. Offer students roles in decision making.
4. Develop students' self-discipline through consistent, logical, fully understood guidelines for their behavior.

Establish a Climate of Mutuality and Respect   Integral to a climate of mutuality and respect is the understanding that all members of the classroom (including the teacher) are equal participants. A teacher should respect students' rights, and students should respect their teacher's rights (Dinkmeyer et al., 1980). Some teachers are uncomfortable with this concept, feeling that it undermines their authority. When the focus shifts to equality for all class members, it is easier to see that caring about each other and respecting one another crosses age, race, ability, gender, and other lines. As students learn to respect themselves, they may also learn to respect others (Isen, 1970).

"Developmental discipline" (Solomon et al., 1991) encourages all members of the classroom (adults and students) to be concerned about the well-being of the entire group. Each member has a responsibility to make meaningful contributions to the life and welfare of the group. The cornerstone of this model is that "teachers treat the students with respect—as capable people who can use and respond to reason" (Solomon et al., p. 48). Teachers help students by avoiding extrinsic rewards, trying instead to emphasize the inherent interest and importance of academic activities. When problems do arise, teachers make every effort to help the students learn from conflict and its resolution rather than relying on threats and punishments. By determining the source of the problem, thinking about alternative solutions, and examining the effects of the behavior on the other students, there is an opportunity to develop positive goodwill among all group members and reduce the need for problem behaviors.

Encourage Students By focusing on students' assets and strengths, teachers have the opportunity to influence overall classroom attitudes and climate. While this concept seems simplistic, it is often overlooked in a system that focuses solely on test scores and students' grades. By improving students' self-confidence, their academic skills may also improve (Purkey, 1970). The concept of multiple intelligences (see Chapters 3 and 6 for more detailed information) enables teachers to look at students in a new light. When approached from this perspective, all students can be seen as being "smart" in some way. By reevaluating a learner's potential, teaching skills and strategies can be refocused and other abilities honored and developed. As students' abilities are honored, the incentive for exhibiting positive behavior is enhanced.

Offer Students a Role in Decision Making From class rules to academic units to content-area tests, students can help to make decisions regarding their classroom and their education. Students will likely be more inclined to accept and follow classroom rules that they have helped to create than those that have been dictated to them (Dinkmeyer et al., 1980). Students will likely be more enthusiastic about participating in projects that they have helped to design (Solomon et al., 1990). When students assist in designing the tests that measure their learning, they are encouraged to look more closely at the material and to help determine the best way that they can learn new concepts. Offering students choices gives them an opportunity to shape the way they learn and the things that they learn about.

When students are allowed to make choices regarding behavior, they can be both positive and creative in their selection of options. The following example illustrates this point. A fourth-grade class was invited to participate in a month-long creative movement workshop led by a professional dancer. Before the activity began, the instructor emphasized that everyone was expected to participate and that being a "good dancer" was not a prerequisite. The goal was to have fun. One student adamantly refused to participate in the activity.

Traditional behavior management techniques might have prompted the teacher to say, "You will participate and if you do not, the consequences will be. . . ." Instead, the student was asked why he did not want to participate in the activity. He said it was because he was shy and did not like people watching him. When asked how he could participate as a class member without actually dancing, the student designed the following options: 1) keeping a journal about the weekly dance lesson, describing the dances and the funny things that happened; 2) using a stop watch to determine the amount of time spent on different dance steps and then writing story problems to be used as part of a math activity; and 3) drawing pictures and writing "directions" for the new dance steps to share with an absent classmate. Everyone benefited from this student's ingenuity. In the course of this process, he maintained his own dignity without sacrificing his status as a participating class member.

Develop Students' Self-Discipline   Self-discipline can be encouraged in students by offering them consistent, logical, fully understood guidelines for their behavior. Consistency is a critical component in a classroom behavior plan. Students have a right to know what to expect, and they should have confidence in the knowledge that the rules will not change from day to day or from situation to situation. Students also have a right to know that they will be treated fairly and that their thoughts and feelings will be considered. Among the disadvantages of a punishment-based behavior management program is that punishment in a classroom may actually teach the student to be punitive toward others, which, in turn may exacerbate behavior problems (Kohn, 1991). When a teacher attempts to manage behavior by raising his or her voice at or belittling a student, he or she is sending a message that these are appropriate ways to interact with other people. Based on modeling by the teacher, the likelihood of the student imitating these behaviors increases. More importantly, the use of punishment may, in some cases, teach the student what not to do, but it seldom serves to teach a student an appropriate alternative behavior (Carr, Robinson, & Palumbo, 1990; Kohn, 1991).

A democratic classroom emphasizes natural consequences that are predictable and logical rather than random. In this setting, teachers can no longer demand student actions "because I said so" or "because I am the teacher." To develop problem solving and critical thinking skills, students need to know the "why" behind the rules. Many current behavior management techniques emphasize teacher control (Bodenhammer, 1983; Canter & Canter, 1992). However, by relinquishing strict teacher control and encouraging a sense of community, students are encouraged to be responsible for the choices they make. It is a more laudable goal that students act responsibly because they understand it is right to do so than because the teacher told them to do so (Kohn, 1991).

The use of natural and logical consequences (Dreikurs, 1968) underscores the effects of behavior on other people and situations. Logical consequences are directly related to the nature of the behavior. For example, if a student breaks something in the classroom, the logical consequence is that he or she will be asked to repair or pay for it. If the class spends too much time getting focused and ready for an activity, they may lose the option of using the remaining minutes as free time following the completion of the activity. The use of logical consequences permits choice and arises from a willingness to let students experience and learn from the consequences of their behavior (Dinkmeyer et al., 1980).

Once classroom rules or expectations are established, it may be necessary to delineate further instruction for specific activities. Students may require a range of information before they can be successful in completing an activity. They may need to know who to ask for support, when they can be out of their seat, where to get materials, how much time is allotted, and what to do when they are finished. Reviewing this information in advance decreases the likelihood of behaviors that occur when students do not know what is expected of them. Verbal directions are helpful in guiding those students who rely on auditory cues. Writing notes, drawing picture cues on the board, or marking a reusable chart may provide reminders for students who depend on visual cues or for students who did not hear or understand the information when it was presented orally. Once instructions have been made clear, it is easy to draw students' attention to this written information if questions or problems arise. In time, many students develop self-monitoring strategies and will take the initiative to look at the board or chart to answer their questions.

Developing Communication and Conflict-Management Skills

Developing strong communication skills is essential in reducing the need for behavior problems. When students have opportunities to share their feelings and to discuss difficult situations, they can begin to develop acceptable problem-solving strategies. "Community Circle" activities (Gibbs, 1987) provide an open forum for the discussion of classroom problems and behavior issues.

In a classroom where time is designated for discussing issues, sharing feelings, and solving problems, students can develop and refine communication skills that are useful in circumventing the escalation of problems. Learning the language associated with conflict management helps to redirect problems before they happen or to redirect action once a conflict begins (Dinkmeyer et al., 1980; Kreidler, 1984).

While discussion is advantageous, some students are not comfortable sharing their feelings in a group or have difficulty talking with the teacher. It may be helpful to offer these students an opportunity to share their feelings using other forms, such as writing or drawing pictures. Writing or illustrating feelings may be a first step toward encouraging students to communicate about a problem and may also help some students clarify the components of a problem as well as possible solutions. This strategy is illustrated by a student's journal entry to her teacher discussing ways to solve problems:

> Me and you can get along just by thinking things out instead of arguing. I can try to calm down instead of getting a bad temper. In the first place, I wasn't mad at you, just angry. We can still be friends. We can work things out by calming down and talking to each other. I already know how much you care about me. When I get angry I say that you don't when I really know that you do and that you try to keep me knowing that you care. But after all that we can still be friends.

Students who lack verbal communication skills are encouraged to participate in these "discussions" as well. By providing relevant vocabulary choices on their augmentative systems, these students can express their own feelings in addition to commenting about issues involving other students. For example, a student may be given access to and instruction in signs and symbols for feelings, such as mad, hurt, scared, or bored. For other students, facial expressions or body posture may be used to express their feelings about a situation.

A teacher's willingness to listen should continue even when the messages are not positive. Students need to have permission to express the range of emotions—happiness, sadness, hope, fear, jealousy and compassion—in order to have a solid foundation for their later emotional life (Armstrong, 1987). After a disagreement with his teacher, one student wrote: "I think that I am disappointed in you. I wrote in one of my journals at home that you were a cool teacher. Now I am trying to decide if I should cross it out." This situation puts responsibility on the teacher to model problem-solving and communication skills in order to involve the student in working out a solution that is acceptable to both participants.

Unfortunately, teachers spend a lot of time trying to quell the emotions that are behind conflicts. In many situations, feelings can be used as an effective tool in facilitating learning (Armstrong, 1987). While it may not be acceptable for students to yell or hurt others, teachers often forget to remind students that it is okay to feel hurt, angry, or disappointed. Students need to learn alternative ways of expressing their emotions. And when emotions are under control, they can be used to augment the learning situation in various academic subjects. Initially, Armstrong (1987) acknowledges that this may be a little like "trying to catch a stampeding elephant with a butterfly net" (p. 108). With care, however, reading, writing, and art activities can reduce tension and channel energy while helping students share experiences and discover connections (Kohn, 1991; Warren, 1991).

The ability to resolve conflict is a skill that must actually be taught just like concepts in math or science.

> There is probably no elementary school in the country that does not have a rule against fights of the punching, hitting, kicking variety. On the other hand, there is probably no elementary school in the country that does not have fights. When we tell

students not to fight without giving them alternative ways to settle disputes, they fight. (Kreidler, 1984, p. 16)

Most students are inclined to bring conflicts to the teacher, expecting an adult to take control and mediate the dispute. When students have learned to work through their own problems, they are less likely to bring the conflict to the teacher and more likely to take on the responsibility of being peacemakers and solving their own conflicts (Kreidler, 1984).

Sources on conflict resolution and peacemaking offer lessons and activities that help teach students to think through their actions and resolve their differences (Drew, 1987; Kreidler, 1984; Prutzman, Stern, Burger, & Bodenhamer, 1988). Conflict in and of itself may not be all bad. Many positive effects have also been attributed to conflict, including stimulating creative problem solving; preventing stagnation; engendering personal, organizational, and societal change; and contributing to self-assessment and skill testing (Filley, 1975). Whether or not conflict is viewed as a dysfunctional element in a classroom is based upon how both students and teachers respond to it (Kreidler, 1984).

There are many different approaches to solving classroom conflicts. A key element is ensuring that students learn from the situation so that the lesson learned might guide their choices in the future. Conflict-management techniques need to be adjusted to meet the age of the students and the dynamics of the classroom. The choice of a conflict-resolution strategy should rest on its ability to provide a safe, structured way to air grievances, feelings, and differences of opinion so that conflict can serve a useful purpose with respect to the participants involved (Kreidler, 1984). There are many resources outlining conflict resolution skills, including storytelling (Kreidler, 1984), effective listening (Drew, 1987), role playing (Fry-Miller & Myers-Walls, 1988), "Peace Table" discussions (Hopkins & Winters, 1990), and activities aimed at reducing stereotypes and teaching tolerance of individual differences (Derman-Sparks and the ABC Task Force, 1989).

Encouraging Whole-School Community Building and Parent Involvement

When students have the opportunity to observe positive problem-solving approaches and caring, respectful attitudes in different environments and with different people, they begin to recognize the carry-over from the classroom to the school and, eventually, to the larger community. If the same components are used in the office, in the auditorium, and on the playground, students have multiple opportunities to observe the results of these efforts and to practice these skills. Some schools organize groups of students who serve as "conflict managers" and work toward solving problems on the playground and in other areas on the school campus. When students take on these roles, they have an opportunity to teach their peers how to use the language and strategies of conflict management.

When parents spend time in the classroom or at other school activities, they may have the opportunity to observe conflict-management skills in action. These same skills may be reinforced at home in solving problems that arise among family members. Sometimes homework can be structured to involve interaction between the student and family members through activities such as interviews, games, or role playing. In this way, homework can be a useful tool in reinforcing community building and problem-solving concepts learned at school in a nonthreatening manner (Solomon et al., 1990).

Communication between home and school may provide valuable information in helping to determine the cause of changes in behavior at school. Schools can be more effective as they become more sensitive to family needs and challenges. Whenever possible, teachers should be flexible in accommodating students' needs that arise from family issues. For example, one student asked if she could turn in her Wednesday homework assignments a day late each week, because her mother went to school and would not be available to help her on Wednesday nights. This student took pride in her school work and was looking for an amenable option in meeting the requirements of the assignment.

Students may spend time in environments outside of school where different principles of behavior management or conflict management are maintained. It is important to reinforce that a classroom reflective of a caring community is a place where children can feel safe, share feelings, and have someone listen. While it is not possible to change all of the environments in which students spend time, it is possible to structure the classroom so that students can experience acceptance and success.

Enhancing Curriculum Considerations

Behavior problems sometimes evolve because a student feels that he or she cannot be successful at academic tasks. In some situations, students will choose to act out in class because it draws attention away from the fact that they are involved in a task that is too difficult for them. Current trends toward recognizing multiple intelligences (Armstrong, 1987; Gardner, 1985), encouraging cooperative learning (Johnson, Johnson, & Holubeck, 1984), and creating reading/writing workshop settings (Routman, 1991) allow students to work at their own levels while maintaining their status as part of the class. A creative teacher can structure the learning environment and the curriculum itself to provide an opportunity for all students to experience success.

If the curriculum is meaningful and interesting, students are more likely to become engaged in learning. Kovalik (1993) suggests that providing a meaningful curriculum allows instruction to become "brain-compatible" and intrinsically motivating. If the curriculum provided to the student is rich and meaningful, "it digs deeply into the learner's intrinsic pool of motivation and provides focus for the ever active brain, harnessing its attention and channeling its power" (Kovalik, 1993, p. 40). In short, a meaningful curriculum makes it easier and more exciting to learn new material and, as a result, may reduce the need and opportunity to seek attention or belonging through inappropriate behavior.

If students are to internalize the concept that learning together and caring about each other are valuable characteristics, they will need opportunities to practice and experience this throughout the context of the school day. The more attention directed toward building community and acceptance, the more opportunities students have to build their prosocial self-concept and to minimize behavior problems (Kohn, 1991). Teachers have many opportunities to model problem solving, perspective taking, and caring in the classroom.

> The extent to which a teacher expresses concern about people in distress, and takes the initiative to help—which applies to both how the teacher treats the students themselves and how he or she refers to people outside the classroom—can set a powerful example and be even more effective than didactic instruction in promoting a sense of caring in students. (Kohn, 1991, p. 503)

In addition to day-to-day modeling, books and instructional units can be selected that reinforce the concepts addressed above. There are many opportunities in conventional subject areas that allow students to take a perspective and analyze solutions, whether the solutions relate to behavior choices or mathematical problems. A discussion of civil rights in the context of a social studies lesson, for example, allows students to reason through the importance of all people being treated fairly. Learning how people work through problems and resolve conflicts in the context of academic instruction provides additional "real-life" models of the skills being practiced in the classroom (Kohn, 1991). Opportunities for social justice activities can also be included as a part of the curriculum. Several sources (e.g., Hammond & Collins, 1993; Lewis, 1981) suggest ways of incorporating concern about the environment, community problems, and other issues into concrete activities that allow students to improve their understanding of the challenges that people in the world face today. This understanding enhances the potential for positive interactions and appreciation of diversity.

Literature offers an opportunity to help students develop their understanding of prosocial values and the ways in which these values are expressed in daily life (Solomon et al., 1991). Books can also be chosen that address characters learning about themselves and others. Many books written for children address a character's effort to search his or her feelings and change behavior. Books like *Heads, I Win* (Hermes, 1993), *The Great Gilly Hopkins* (Paterson, 1978), and *There's a Boy in the Girls' Bathroom* (Sachar, 1987) focus on children who choose inappropriate classroom behavior to disguise their feelings of hurt, anger, and disappointment. *Someone Called Me a Retard Today . . . and My Heart Felt Sad* (O'Shaughnessy, 1992) is a book that addresses the problem of name calling. Other books, such as *Josh, A Boy with Dyslexia* (Janover, 1988) and *My Friend Leslie* (Rosenberg, 1983), examine the difficulties that some students face in trying to cope with a disability that may make school work more challenging, while highlighting their strengths and talents as individuals. *Read It Again* (Vaughn &

Rothlein, 1994) describes books and activities designed to increase acceptance and awareness of children with a range of disabilities who are included in general education classrooms.

Exploring prosocial skill development, building community, and refining conflict-management skills do not have to be discrete entities sandwiched in between math and science in an already bursting schedule. These concepts and skills can be embedded into the curriculum, where students can discover their power in a nonthreatening way. These skills are less an element of the curriculum and more a way of learning and being.

INSTRUCTIONAL ARRANGEMENTS

The consideration of instructional arrangements can facilitate an environment where students with diverse needs and learning styles can be educated together and where the need for traditional management techniques is reduced. A discussion of instructional arrangements and groupings follows.

Individualistic Instruction

Instruction based on individual needs and diverse learning styles can allow each student to progress at his or her own rate toward established goals. This type of instruction also allows students to pursue interests in greater depth and to foster independence and responsibility for learning (Wiles & Bondi, 1989).

Historically, the heterogeneity of students receiving special education services influenced teachers to develop individualized programs. The traditional special education model has been based upon the assumption that instruction should be tailored to meet the needs of each individual student. This focus is readily apparent in the wording of PL 101-476, the Individuals with Disabilities Education Act (IDEA), where the term "individualized" is used frequently, particularly in relationship to the individualized education program (IEP).

The notion of individualizing curriculum has also been discussed in general education literature. Anderson (1977) suggests that the individualization of curriculum and instructional strategies remains an unfulfilled essential in the majority of general education classes. Some researchers even argue that the lack of individualization for students in the "mainstream" has been the major reason for the creation and maintenance of a separate service-delivery model (Pugach & Warger, 1993).

Consideration for individualizing instruction includes the following elements: identify what a student already knows; delineate what a student needs to learn; determine how a student learns best; and consider the student's interests and motivations for learning. Consequently, knowledge of assessment procedures, IEP development, and learning styles are critical components in the determination of appropriate instruction.

An example of individualizing instruction can be found in the general education literature regarding the "Writers Workshop" approach to language arts (Parry & Hornsby, 1985; Routman, 1991). This approach facilitates children working on different skills and activities at the same time, based on the objectives designated for each learner. In this model, the teacher circulates among the students, providing help as necessary. Conferences with individual students or with small groups allow the teacher to focus on specific skills targeted for instruction.

Individualized instruction is not synonymous with one-to-one instruction. Typically, one-to-one instruction involves a teacher and a learner working in isolation from the rest of the group. This type of service delivery has a number of inherent drawbacks. First, students often do not generalize what they learn in one-to-one settings to different situations in which others are present (Koegel & Rincover, 1974; Rincover & Koegel, 1975). Second, when working in one-to-one settings, students miss out on other activities and experiences presented to the rest of the class. Third, one-to-one instruction limits opportunities for interaction with other students, thereby limiting opportunities for socialization and language development, peer modeling, and skill sharing (Stainback, Stainback, & Slavin, 1989). Finally, the cost of providing one-to-one instruction is likely prohibitive.

While some activities (particularly those activities that focus on adaptive skills such as feeding and toileting) may require one-to-one instruction, teachers should be careful not to overuse this strategy. The effects of isolation, adult dependence, and stigma may outweigh the presumed benefit of intensified instruction. Instead, a program that has been individualized to meet a student's unique needs and interests can be implemented in a variety of instructional settings.

Group Instruction

Instruction can occur in a variety of groupings. While all types of grouping are appropriate in certain contexts, certain groupings facilitate the learning of all students.

Large-Group Instruction In many classrooms, the majority of the instruction has been provided in a large-group format. Often a teacher may open a lesson with a lecture or discussion on a specific skill or topic. Following this didactic instruction, students then begin work on an activity designed to reinforce the content. For example, a teacher may explain the process of multiplying decimals by using a lecture format and examples on the chalkboard. Following the demonstration, students might begin working on problems from the book or on a worksheet.

This type of instructional arrangement is likely to be more successful when most students are working at a similar ability level. When students with diverse abilities are included in this format, it may be necessary to adapt the materials or the assignment. The following examples illustrate some of the adaptations that might occur:

1. Some students may be required to complete only a portion of the problems assigned.
2. Some students may be working on the same assignment but instead might utilize enlarged print materials.
3. Some students may require additional materials, such as counting tools, a calculator, or a multiplication table.
4. Some students may be working on a different objective within the context of the activity, for example, copying numerals, matching and circling a specific numeral, or working on addition rather than multiplication.

Although large-group instruction time can be adapted somewhat to meet individual needs, it may not be the most effective strategy. Some students engage in undesirable behaviors during large group instruction. This may be due to factors such as reduced active participation, lack of interaction or attention, lack of motivation for content, or possibly just feeling lost in the crowd. To address some of these concerns, other grouping strategies may be more effective.

Small-Group Instruction   In small-group instruction, students may be divided into groups based on a number of factors, including instructional content, ability, interests, and learning styles. These small groups may be directed by an adult or by another student. This format allows for a reduced teacher:student ratio and may facilitate learning for those students who require additional assistance. In addition, students are provided with opportunities to interact and develop social and communication skills.

When properly designed, small-group instruction can be effective in meeting students' unique, personalized learning goals (Stainback et al., 1989). Examples of small-group instruction can range from students working on reinforcement of a math concept, to writing and practicing a play after reading a novel, to collecting and analyzing leaves from different plants around the school. Often the membership of small groups will vary throughout the day as students are involved in different content areas and activities. Instruction presented in the context of small groups can be described as either *competitive* or *cooperative* group learning.

Grouping for Competitive Learning   Competitive group learning can be described as organizing groups of students to work against one another to achieve a goal that only one or a few can obtain. In this situation, an individual can only achieve his or her goal if the students in other groups do not attain their goals. "Thus, individuals seek an outcome that is personally beneficial but detrimental to all others in the situation" (Johnson & Johnson, 1989, p. 4). Although competition may motivate high-achieving students, students with average or below-average skills may have fewer opportunities for success, and their motivation to learn may be diminished.

The following example illustrates some of the drawbacks to competitive grouping. Eight teams of four students each are ready to participate in a relay race. The goal is to hop to the marker and then to run back to the group. All eight teams are competing against one another. When the whistle blows, the students begin hopping. It is quickly apparent that some students are faster than the others. Not only does this focus negative attention on the participants with fewer skills, but it also discourages positive peer relationships. At the end of the race, there are 4 "winners" and 28 "losers." Many students who tried their best do not have an opportunity to experience feelings of success in this situation.

Grouping for Cooperative Learning   Cooperative group learning continues to receive attention as an effective strategy for instructing students with diverse needs and talents (Johnson & Johnson, 1989; Slavin, 1990). Cooperative learning is designed to teach students to work collaboratively and reach common goals (Putnam, 1993; Thousand, Villa, & Nevin, 1994). In addition to using cooperative learning groups to reach an academic or content-based goal, many cooperative learning groups work toward reaching a cooperation goal, such as praising one another or asking for help. Cooperative learning situations allow more students to feel successful. It provides opportunities for students to learn and practice positive interdependence, to participate in self-reflection and individual goal setting, to work in groups of varying membership, and to contribute to the success of the group while engaged in self-improvement (Putnam, 1993)

In revisiting the relay race, the same 32 students can be divided into four groups of eight. This time, however, one member from each "team" links arms with the person next to him or her to navigate to the marker. Each group of eight works as a cooperative group. At this point the goal is shifted away from competition and toward completing the task in a designated amount of time or simply having the entire group reach the marker and return. In this situation, interdependence is fostered; students actually work toward "helping" each other instead of "beating" each other. All students have the opportunity to feel successful, and peer relationships may be strengthened rather than hampered.

The benefits of cooperative learning groups have been well documented. Research demonstrates that for heterogeneous groups of students with varying levels of skills, cooperative learning arrangements:

1. Promote higher academic achievement (Slavin, 1990; Slavin & Karweit, 1984)
2. Improve self-esteem (Johnson & Johnson, 1989)
3. Promote active learning (Johnson & Johnson, 1989) and social-skill development (Putnam, Rynders, Johnson, & Johnson, 1989; Slavin, 1977)
4. Influence peer acceptance and friendships (Ballard, Corman, Gottlieb, & Kaufman, 1977; Johnson & Johnson, 1984, 1989; Johnson, Johnson, Deweerdt, Lyons, & Zaidman, 1983)

Sometimes within cooperative groups children may have goals that are different from other group members. For example, if students are making a chart of the events leading up to the Revolutionary War, a student with severe disabilities may be responsible for copying the names of all group members onto the chart. If the group is responsible for illustrating the events in a novel, a student with limited fine motor skills may be responsible for coloring the sky or the background, where there is more margin for error. Finally, it is important to note that students are an invaluable resource in helping to generate ways in which all team members with and without disabilities can be contributing and successful members of a cooperative group.

SUMMARY

In light of the acknowledged heterogeneity of school-age students, educators are being asked to move away from traditional curricular models, instructional strategies, and classroom arrangements. By creating a supportive classroom environment, students and staff alike work to accommodate and respect all members of the classroom. This chapter provides a foundation for building such classroom environments.

Designing a democratic classroom provides ways in which students and adults are considered equal members and where every member has a sense of value and belonging. In such classrooms, skills such as open communication and conflict management are emphasized. In addition, supportive classrooms play a vital role in encouraging whole-school community building and increasing parent involvement with their sons and daughters and the total school community. This broad base of involved, supportive community environments engenders a consistent message to students regarding respect for others and responsibility for their own behavior and interactions.

Finally, the area of instructional arrangements has been addressed. By understanding the unique strengths, interests, and needs of each student, educators are able to move away from traditional instructional arrangements. The value of large-group, teacher-directed instruction is questioned as educators discover arrangements more suited to meet the broad needs of learners in any given classroom. Individualizing curriculum and instruction in small, cooperative-group settings can provide academic and social benefits for learners of all ages and ability levels.

By focusing on supportive classroom environments and providing a variety of instructional strategies with relevant curricular content areas, educators are less likely to waste time on restrictive classroom-management plans. The goals of such educators are to enhance the academic achievements of all students while promoting the social and emotional well-being of individual students and the classroom/school community as a whole.

REFERENCES

Ames, C. (1987). The enhancement of student motivation. In M. Maehr & D. Klieber (Eds.), *Advances in motivation and achievemen. Vol 5: Enhancing motivation* (pp. 123–148). Greenwich, CT: JAI Press.

Anderson, R.H. (1977). Individualization—The unfulfilled goal. *Educational Leadership, 34*(5), 323–324.

Armstrong, T. (1987). *In their own way.* New York: Tarcher Press.

Ballard, M., Corman, L., Gottlieb, J., & Kaufman, M.J. (1977). Improving the social status of mainstreamed retarded children. *Journal of Educational Psychology, 69,* 605–611.

Bodenhammer, G. (1983). *Back in control: How to get your children to behave.* Englewood Cliffs, NJ: Prentice Hall.

Canfield, J., & Wells, H.G. (1976). *100 ways to enhance self-concept in the classroom.* Boston: Allyn & Bacon.

Canter, L., & Canter, M. (1992). *Assertive discipline.* Santa Monica, CA: Lee Canter and Associates.

Carr, E.G., Robinson, S., & Palumbo, L.W. (1990). The wrong issue: aversive vs. nonaversive treatment. The right issue: functional vs. nonfunctional treatment. In A. Repp & N. Singh *Perspectives on the use of nonaversive and aversive interventions for persons with developmental disabilities.* Sycamore, IL: Sycamore Publishing Co.

Derman-Sparks, L., & the ABC Task Force. (1989). *Anti-bias curriculum: Tools for empowering young children.* Washington, DC: National Association for the Education of Young Children.

Dinkmeyer, D., McKay, G., & Dinkmeyer, D., Jr. (1980). *Systematic training for effective teaching.* Circle Pines, MN: American Guidance Service.

Dreikurs, R. (1968). *Psychology in the classroom.* New York: Harper & Row.

Dreikurs, R., Grunwald, B., & Pepper, F. (1980). *Maintaining sanity in the classroom.* New York: Harper & Row.

Drew, N. (1987). *Learning the skills of peacemaking.* Rolling Hills Estates, CA: Jalmar Press.

Filley, A.C. (1975). *Interpersonal conflict resolution.* Glenview, IL: Scott, Foresman and Co.

Fry-Miller, K., & Myers-Walls, J. (1988). *Young peacemakers project book.* Elgin, IL: Brethren Press.

Gardner, H. (1985). *Frames of mind: Theory of multiple intelligences.* New York: Basic Books.

Gibbs, J. (1987) *Tribes: A process for social development and cooperative learning.* Santa Rosa, CA: Center Source Publications.

Goodlad, J. (1984). *A place called school: Prospects for the future.* New York: John Wiley and Sons.

Hammond, M., & Collins, R. (1993). *One world one earth: Educating children for social responsibility.* Philadelphia: New Society Publishers.

Heller, C. (1993, Spring). Equal play. *Teaching Tolerance,* 24–29.

Hermes, P. (1993). *Heads, I win.* San Diego: Harcourt Brace Jovanovich.

Hopkins, S., & Winters, J. (1990). Discover the world: Empowering children to value themselves, others, and the earth. Philadelphia: New Society Publishers.

Individuals with Disabilities Education Act of 1990 (IDEA), PL 101-476. (October 30, 1990). Title 20, U.S.C. 1400 et seq: *U.S. Statutes at Large, 105,* 587–608.

Isen, A. (1970). Success, failure, attention, and reactions to others: The warm glow of success. *Journal of Personality and Social Psychology, 15,* 294–301.

Janover, C. (1988). *Josh: A boy with dyslexia.* Burlington, VT: Waterfront Books.

Johnson, D.W., & Johnson, R.T. (1984). The effects of intergroup cooperation and intergroup competition on ingroup and outgroup cross-handicap relationships. *Journal of Social Psychology, 124,* 85–94.

Johnson, D.W., & Johnson, R.T. (1989). *Cooperation and competition: Theory and research.* Edina, MN: Interaction Books.

Johnson, D.W., Johnson, R.T., Deweerdt, N., Lyons, V., & Zaidman, B. (1983). Integrating severely handicapped seventh-grade students into constructive relationships with non-handicapped peers in science class. *American Journal of Mental Deficiency, 87,* 611–619.

Johnson, D., Johnson, R.T., & Holubeck, E. (1984). *Cooperation in the classroom* (rev. ed.). Edina, MN: Interaction Books.

Koegel, R.L., & Rincover, A. (1974). Treatment of psychotic children in a classroom environment: I. Lerning in a large group. *Journal of Applied Behavior Analysis, 7,* 45–59.

Kohn, A. (1991). Caring kids: The role of schools. *Phi Delta Kappan, 72,* 497–506.

Kovalik, S. (1993). *ITI (integrated thematic instruction): The model.* Village of Oak Creek, AZ: Susan Kovalik and Associates.

Kreidler, W.J. (1984). *Creative conflict resolution.* Glenview, IL: Scott, Foresman and Co.

Kunc, N. (1992). The need to belong: Rediscovering Maslow's hierarchy of needs. In R. Villa, J. Thousand, W. Stainback, & S. Stainback (Eds.), *Restructuring for caring and effective education* (pp. 25–40). Baltimore: Paul H. Brookes Publishing Co.

Lewis, B. (1981). *The kid's guide to social action: How to solve the social problems you choose—and turn creative thinking into positive action.* Minneapolis: Free Spirit Publications.

Maslow, A. (1970). *Motivation and personality.* New York: Harper & Row.

Noddings, N. (1992). *The challenge to care in schools.* New York: Teachers College Press.

O'Shaughnessy, E. (1992). *Somebody called me a retard today . . . and my heart felt sad.* New York: Walker and Co.

Parry, J., & Hornsby, D. (1985). *Write on: A conference approach to writing.* Portsmouth, NH: Heinemann.

Paterson, K. (1978). *The great Gilly Hopkins.* New York: Crowell.

Peterson, R. (1992). *Life in a crowded place: Making a learning community.* Portsmouth, NH: Heinemann.

Prutzman, P., Stern, L., Burger, M., & Bodenhamer, G. (1988). *The friendly classroom for a small planet.* Philadelphia: New Society Publishers.

Pugach, M.C., & Warger, C.L. (1993). Curriculum considerations. In J.I. Goodlad & T.C. Lovitt (Eds.), *Integrating general and special education* (pp. 125–148). New York: Macmillan.

Purkey, W. (1970). *Self concept and school achievement.* Englewood Cliffs, NJ: Prentice Hall.

Putnam, J.W. (Ed.). (1993). *Cooperative learning and strategies for inclusion: Celebrating diversity in the classroom.* Baltimore: Paul H. Brookes Publishing Co.

Putnam, J.W., Rynders, J., Johnson, R.T., & Johnson, D.W. (1989). Collaborative skill instruction for promoting positive interactions between mentally handicapped and non-handicapped children. *Exceptional Children, 55,* 550–558.

Rincover, A., & Koegel, R.L. (1975). Setting generality and stimulus control in autistic children. *Journal of Applied Behavior Analysis, 8,* 235–246.

Rosenberg, M. (1983). *My friend Leslie: The story of a handicapped child.* NY: Lothrop, Lee & Shepard Books.

Routman, R. (1991). *Invitations: Changing as teachers and learners K-12.* Portsmouth, NH: Heinemann.

Sachar, L. (1987). *There's a boy in the girls' bathroom.* New York: Knopf.

Sapon-Shevin, M. (1990). Initial steps for developing a caring school. In W. Stainback & S. Stainback (Eds.), *Support networks for inclusive schooling: Interdependent integrated education* (pp. 241–248). Baltimore Paul H. Brookes Publishing Co.

Schapps, E., & Solomon E. (1990). Schools and classrooms as caring communities. *Educational Leadership, 47,* 38–42.

Slavin, R.E. (1977). A student team approach to teaching adolescents with special emotional and behavioral needs. *Psychology in the Schools, 14*(1), 77–84.

Slavin, R.E. (1987). Cooperative learning and the cooperative school. *Educational Leadership, 45*(3), 7–13.

Slavin, R.E. (1990). *Cooperative learning: Theory, research and practice.* Englewood Cliffs, NJ: Prentice Hall.

Slavin, R.E., & Karweit, N.A. (1984). Mastery learning and student teams: A factorial experiment in urban general mathematics classes. *American Educational Research Journal, 21*(4), 725–736.

Slavin, R.E., & Karweit, N.A. (1985). Effects of whole class, ability grouped, and individualized instruction on mathematics achievement. *American Educational Research Journal, 22*(3), 351–367.

Solomon, D., Schapps, E., Watson, M., & Battistich, V. (1990). Creating caring school and classroom communities for all students. In R. Villa, J. Thousand, W. Stainback, & S. Stainback (Eds.), *Restructuring for caring and effective education: An administrative guide to creating heterogeneous schools* (pp. 41–60). Baltimore: Paul H. Brookes Publishing Co.

Stainback, W., Stainback, S., & Slavin, R. (1989). Classroom organization for diversity among students. In S. Stainback, W. Stainback, & M. Forest (Eds.), *Educating all students in the mainstream of regular education* (pp. 131–158). Baltimore: Paul H. Brookes Publishing Co.

Thousand, J.S., Villa, R.A., & Nevin, A. (Eds.). (1994). *Creativity and collaborative learning.* Baltimore: Paul H. Brookes Publishing Co.

Vaughn, S., & Rothlein, L. (1994) *Read it again!* Glenview, IL: Good Year Books.

Warren, M.L. (1991). Educating for global citizenship through children's art. *Educational Leadership, 49*(2), 53–57.

Wiles, J., & Bondi, J. (1989). *Curriculum development: A guide to practice* (3rd ed). New York: Merrill.

Zahn-Waxler, C. (1986). Conclusions: Lessons from the past and a look to the future. In C. Zahn-Waxler, E.M. Cummings, & R. Iannotti (Eds.), *Altruism and aggression: Biological and social origins.* Cambridge: Cambridge University Press.

6

INSTRUCTIONAL STRATEGIES

MARY A. FALVEY AND MARQUITA GRENOT-SCHEYER

An effective educator is able to utilize a variety of strategies to determine what skills to teach an individual student and how to teach those skills. The "how" of teaching includes finding ways to motivate individual students and to reinforce developing behaviors, determining individualized instructional strategies, and organizing and implementing instructional plans.

Educational recommended practices are grounded in solid research and humanistic values and are based, first, upon two important assumptions about learners with severe disabilities: 1) "learning is not only possible but probable"; and 2) "there are more similarities between these students [students with severe disabilities] and their typical peers than differences" (Snell & Brown, 1993, p. 99). A third assumption is also crucial: students should be given a voice in decision making. Through active participation they can learn to share roles and responsibilities to ensure that the class functions well, a basic lesson in democracy (Ford, Davern, & Schnorr, 1992). Through purposeful community building, students can learn that their actions, both individually and collectively, can have an influence on their environment and those within it (Ford et al., 1992).

To make it possible for educators to organize and deliver meaningful and individualized instruction for all students, Wiles and Bondi (1989) recommend that the following characteristics be present in schools, classrooms, and other teaching settings:

> The organization of the school should encourage individualized rates of student progress. That is, students should be allowed to participate in specific grade level curricular activities as well as activities that are of high interest to them that may occur in other classrooms. In addition, students should not be compared to other students, but only to themselves. Increases in an individual student's participation level is what constitutes progress.

The subject matter or content of the curriculum must have meaning for all students and be applicable to various aspects of the students' lives in and outside of school.

Administrative policies that govern progress and evaluation should be based upon a continuum of cumulative experiences along which students move at individual rates, and not solely be determined by developmental or grade level.

The instructional staff should be sufficiently large, knowledgeable, and reflective of the diversity present in the school community. Every student should be well known by at least one adult at any given time.

Social or recreation activities encouraged by the school should be available to all students, regardless of ability. That is, such activities should not exclude students who are not at a particular maturity level or who are different in some other way from their peers.

The human element in the teaching–learning process is critical. Teaching is most successful when students are treated as a surprise and a joy.

Teachers should use a variety of instructional arrangements including large group instruction, small and collaborative groups, and guided individual activities. Since students come from heterogeneous communities, teaching opportunities should reflect such diversity within instructional arrangements.

Evaluation procedures should convey a clear picture of student progress according to the student's individual development and growth.

Systematic and organized learning experiences are essential to student learning in any curriculum. This chapter describes teaching methods that have been successfully used with students identified as having severe disabilities as well as with students who do not have disabilities. These include motivation and reinforcement strategies, a variety of instructional strategies in which students are active participants in the learning process, personalized learning strategies based on students' multiple intelligences, specialized learning strategies, and strategies to assist students' access to curricula. Space allows only a basic introduction to each of these powerful teaching strategies, but references supplied throughout provide supplementary sources of information.

MOTIVATION

The learning process for all individuals begins with motivation. Motivation within an educational context may be defined as the strength of desire to engage and persist in achievement-related behaviors (Ruble & Boggiano, 1980). The correlation between motivation, on the one hand, and learning and achievement, on the other, has been explored for years by many researchers (Atkinson & Raynor, 1974; Ball, 1977; Hull, 1943; McClelland, Atkinson, Clark, & Lowell, 1953; Skinner, 1974; Tolman, 1959; Weiner, 1972). A variety of theories exist about how motivation affects people. Motivation has been shown to be influenced by individual differences in students' experiences and learning styles; by expectations about the likelihood of success or failure at a particular task; and by task incentives, both intrinsic and extrinsic. High levels of motivation, whatever the basis, generally result in high levels of performance, and even the best teaching strategies may fail to result in the desired achievement if the proper motivation is not considered and incorporated. Ensuring appropriate motivation for each student is an essential component of any instructional plan.

Using Maslow's (1987) concept of "self-actualization" can be a powerful tool to tap into students' motivation. Self-actualization can be defined as using one's abilities to the limit of one's potential. If students are convinced that they can and should fulfill their dreams and promises, they are on the path to achieving them. Maslow has identified a hierarchy of five needs: physiological, safety, love and belonging, esteem, and self-actualization.

When a student is not motivated and experiences repeated failures, that student becomes frustrated and often will not even try, a condition referred to as "learned helplessness" (Dweck, 1975; Dweck & Repucci, 1973; Seligman, 1975). Failing grades, sarcasm, ridicule, and general lack of confidence by significant adults such as teachers or parents are likely to result in a path of learned helplessness (Travers, Elliott, & Kratochwill, 1993). For students who have experienced learned helplessness, simply increasing the number of their successes will not be enough to change their outlook on learning. "Teaching students to realistically assess their failures and to focus on increasing their effort or motivation are necessary components in overcoming feelings of helplessness" (Travers et al., 1993, p. 304).

Motivation provides the incentive to perform the skills or behaviors being taught. In behavioral terms, motivation can be viewed as the specific consequence of engaging in a skill or activity. The consequence, or motivation, may be within the activity; that is, it may be intrinsic. (For example, a student learning to draw with colored markers may find the activity pleasurable and thus be highly motivated to develop skills necessary to participate in this activity.) Or the consequence or motivation may be extrinsic, such as a reward for the correct performance of a desired behavior. (For instance, the student who likes to draw might be given a set of colored markers as a reward for learning a difficult or disagreeable part of a task.)

Motivation is always important. School performance, for example, is affected by a wide variety of motivational variables. The single most essential motivational variable in schools involves the beliefs of educators. These people must have a strong belief in each of the students and in their potential for learning. Students are unlikely to succeed if they attend school where no one is committed to them as a person or learner.

Some students are more outer-directed, or more dependent on external and often artificial cues and rewards in their task orientation (Falvey, Brown, Lyon, Baumgart, & Schroeder, 1980; Yando & Zigler, 1971). Because of a forced dependence on others in meeting even a few basic needs, they often have significantly fewer experiences with initiating activities and with personal success. As a result, a major challenge for teachers is to develop and facilitate self-motivation. Carefully chosen and implemented motivational procedures can aid in teaching new behaviors, strengthening existing behaviors, and decreasing undesirable behaviors. Motivation is then an important first step in the development of instructional strategies.

The term *reinforcement* is often used to refer to motivation when discussing the selection of intervention strategies. The choice of effective reinforcement is a major element in an instructional program for all students. While this type of motivation is often extrinsic, developed and determined externally by someone other than the student himself or herself, this type of reward is the least desirable option in attempting to develop motivation. In fact, careless use of extrinsic reward can undermine students' intrinsic motivation (Green & Lepper, 1974). Educators must first determine specific skills and activities to be taught that are themselves interesting, relevant, and meaningful to the student; that is, the instructional activities should be highly motivating. Successful completion of such motivating activities would result in natural consequences that provide natural reinforcement to the student. Traditional, simple repetition of meaningless and nonfunctional educational tasks generally does not provide intrinsic reward and should not be used. When activities and skills themselves are functional and relevant but the student is unable to attain or maintain sufficient motivation, carefully developed external reinforcements may then be necessary. The development of appropriate external reinforcement and of a reinforcement schedule must be accompanied by a plan for phasing out the external reinforcement as soon as possible. The section following discusses different types of external reinforcement choices.

CLASSIFYING REINFORCEMENT CHOICES

Reinforcement may be defined as a specific stimulus that is awarded contingent upon the initiation of a particular behavior. There are two basic types of reinforcement: primary and secondary. Primary reinforcements are tangible reinforcers. If one is hungry, for example, food can be a primary reinforcer. Secondary reinforcers are those stimuli that are more social in nature, such as praise, a nod, or a smile following the student's performance of the desired behavior. Generally, reinforcement affects the action or response in some way, increasing it when the reinforcement is positive. Sailor and Guess (1983) have provided a useful model for classifying reinforcement choices (which they refer to as "motivational effects") into three categories: actions, events, and objects.

The *actions* category of reinforcement choices refers to the use of behaviors to reinforce other behaviors. In other words, actions engaged in by the student at a high frequency can often be considered motivating and may therefore be used as a reward for low frequency behaviors. This reinforcement category is based on the Premack principle: "Any response A will reinforce any other response B if and only if the independent rate of A is greater than that of B" (Premack, 1959, p. 220). This can be stated more simply as: "First, I must work on this skill that is not easy and pleasant; however, I can then do something I really like to do." For example, a student who enjoys listening to music using headphones may choose to spend 10 minutes engaging in that activity upon completing a math assignment. The action of listening to music reinforces the acquisition of the math skill being practiced.

Events can also provide reinforcement in learning situations. Some are social in form, such as a hug, or words, or praise. Pleasant sounds, a pat on the back, and other forms of sensory input also fall into this category. Events may serve as primary reinforcers that provide direct consequences for desired responses. For example, a student learning to turn on a tape recorder may be immediately rewarded by the sounds of his or her favorite music when the switch is in the "on" position. Events may also be secondary reinforcers when, paired with a tangible consequence such as food, they eventually become motivating in themselves. In this case, the reinforcing event is called a *conditioned reinforcer*.

A conditioned reinforcer is one that assumes its reinforcing properties through frequent pairings with strong unconditioned or previously conditioned reinforcers (LaVigna & Donnellan, 1984; Meyer & Evans, 1989). Praise, for example, may not be initially motivating to a student who is unaccustomed to it, but it may take on motivational properties when paired over time with something already meaningful to that student (e.g., playing a computer game). Initially, each time the student completes a desired activity, she can be rewarded with time on the computer paired with words of praise, as in: "What a great job, Sue!" Gradually, as praise becomes conditioned as reinforcing to her, the use of the computer games as a reinforcer can be reduced.

Objects include food or other tangible items (toys, tokens, etc.) that may be used as primary reinforcement under carefully controlled circumstances. Objects provide a direct and immediate external consequence for a specific response. The use of object reinforcement is illustrated by the following example.

Tom, a 3-year-old student, is learning to use signs for communication purposes. At snacktime in his preschool class, he is first given small amounts of his favorite foods (i.e., those foods previously observed by his teacher and parents to be his favorites). When he finishes eating, his teacher verbally asks him if he wants more, and uses the sign for "more." His response, initially an imitation of the sign MORE, is promptly rewarded with "seconds" of his favorite foods. Gradually, Tom begins to use the sign at snacktime, lunchtime, and mealtime at home without the model provided by the teacher, thus connecting the action (the sign for "more") with the object consequence (an additional serving of a favorite food).

REINFORCEMENT PROCEDURES

Reinforcement may be positive or negative and may be used to increase a desired behavior or to decrease an undesired behavior. Positive reinforcers strengthen the action they follow by providing a reward for those actions. When a stimulus—an object, event, or action—is made contingent upon a behavior and leads to an increase in that behavior, positive reinforcement occurs (LaVigna & Donnellan, 1984; Meyer & Evans, 1989; Snell & Brown, 1993). The careful use of positive reinforcement techniques provides the most effective and durable strategy for shaping student behaviors. Reinforcers that are individually determined, closely related to the desired behavior, and immediately and systematically administered are the most powerful.

Negative reinforcers can also increase behaviors if the removal of a negative stimulus is contingent upon that behavior. As a result, the likelihood of that specific behavior occurring again increases. For example, a student who has difficulty remaining on task during math and completing independent math problems might be told that if she completes three out of four problems correctly within 15 minutes, she will not be required to complete the fourth problem. Over time the goal is to increase her work rate while maintaining her quality. If this does not occur, this strategy should be discontinued since it might be inadvertently teaching her to "get out of work."

In cases where negative reinforcement has been used to develop a behavior, careful substitution of positive reinforcement must be planned to maintain that behavior. In the example of the student who needed assistance in motivating her to complete her math problems in a timely manner, that behavior (i.e., remaining on task) might initially diminish upon the removal of the negative reinforcer. The systematic substitution of positive reinforcement (e.g., praise from the teacher when remaining on task, opportunity to be singled out as the classroom monitor to collect completed papers) will be necessary. The negative reinforcer may have initially inhibited the undesired behavior, but the positive reinforcer will strengthen the desired behavior and thus ensure that it will become a part of the student's behavioral repertoire. It is generally unnecessary to use negative reinforcement, since positive reinforcement is more effective to sustain a behavior. The subsections that follow discuss the use and identification of reinforcers to increase behaviors.

Using Reinforcers to Increase Behaviors

Several important principles can be applied to the effective use of reinforcement procedures to increase behaviors. The first concerns the *immediacy* of the reinforcement. To be effective, reinforcement procedures must be individually and systematically developed, and delivered as close as possible to the actual performance of the desired behavior. The more immediately a reinforcer is presented following a desired behavior, the more likely that the reinforcer will be associated with the desired behavior. For example, a student who is being taught to use a communication board may not understand initially that pointing to a pictorial representation of an object will result in obtaining that object. However, if the behavior of pointing to the picture is immediately reinforced by the presentation of the object, the association will be reinforced.

The *frequency* with which the reinforcement is delivered is a second important consideration. A schedule for the delivery of a reinforcement may be *continuous* or *intermittent*; that is, a reinforcer may be administered each time the desired behavior occurs, or it may be administered after a specified number of occurrences of the desired behavior. The schedule of reinforcement frequency should be based upon the student's previous success with continuous or intermittent reinforcement schedules. When a new behavior is being introduced to a student, the frequency of reinforcement should be high enough to result in acquisition. As the behavior becomes more familiar, the frequency of reinforcement must be faded. It is also important to remember that constant and frequent reinforcement does not naturally occur in typical educational, community, and work settings. The frequency of reinforcement must be faded as quickly as possible to the type and frequency generally provided to persons in those settings, while still maintaining the skill performance. Too often students in special education programs have been artificially and externally reinforced. As a result, they have come to depend on this reinforcement for the performance of behaviors already in their repertoire. This over reliance on reinforcement, which may inhibit participation in inclusive settings, has created "reinforcement junkies" of students with disabilities.

A final important consideration in the choice and use of reinforcers is the *age appropriateness* of the object, event, or action chosen. For instance, an opportunity to play with a preferred sticker book when a classroom task has been completed may be an appropriate reward for a young child but not for a teenager. Likewise, a hug is a common consequence for work well done in a primary level classroom; for an older student, however, it can be inappropriate and stigmatizing, particularly in school and community settings. More appropriate choices must be made to reinforce students' completion of their work and/or participation in activities under those circumstances, especially in light of the natural consequences provided in inclusive school and community environments.

No reinforcer is effective in every situation; neither can something that is reinforcing for one student be assumed to be reinforcing for another student. Furthermore, even the best reinforcer loses effectiveness when made contingent upon multiple behaviors. Reinforcers must therefore be carefully selected for a specific individual and a specific target behavior. The most effective reinforcers are those that arise as a natural consequence to a given task or that have a logical relationship to that task (Wilcox & Bellamy, 1982). For example, a student being taught to use vending machines in the high school cafeteria may be naturally reinforced by what he or she is able to purchase from a vending machine. In this case, it would be important to select machines that carry items of interest to that student.

Occasionally, reinforcers natural to a given situation either are not motivating in themselves or fail initially to motivate a given student. Only when this happens should a gradual move toward more artificial reinforcement begin (LaVigna

& Donnellan, 1984; Meyer & Evans, 1989). The principle of using the most natural reinforcers serves a threefold purpose. First, natural reinforcers are less intrusive and thus are less likely to set the student apart from others in the "real world." Second, natural consequences have been shown to result in more efficient learning than arbitrary or generalized reinforcers (Wilcox & Bellamy, 1982). Natural consequences reinforce a more immediate connection between the task and the reinforcer. Finally, it is often difficult to develop a logical fading sequence of artificial reinforcers to natural reinforcers.

If the desired behavior itself lacks positive natural consequences, reinforcers that are natural and appropriate to the setting in which the desired behavior is being taught should be used to the maximum extent possible. For example, completing the science project related to the human skeleton may not be rewarding and intrinsically interesting for an individual student, but being able to study various forms of sea life once the project on the human skeleton is completed may be rewarding for that same student and is appropriate to the setting. Highly artificial reinforcers such as tokens, lavish praise, and physical displays of affection should be used only as last resorts. If they are used, they must be dispensed in nonstigmatizing and dignified ways and faded quickly (Ford & Miranda, 1984; LaVigna & Donnellan, 1984; Meyer & Evans, 1989).

Choosing Effective Reinforcers

To determine effective reinforcers for students, the following guidelines should be considered:

1. Identify consequences that are natural to the behavior itself and/or to the environment in which the behavior occurs.
2. Survey others familiar with the student's likes and dislikes, and record those that are reinforcing to the student and possibly relevant to the behavior/environment of interest.
3. Observe the student both on and off task in the natural setting, and record those naturally occurring consequences that appear to have particular salience for that student.
4. Observe peers to determine what is motivating and "in" with chronological age–appropriate peers
5. Offer the student paired choices from those potential reinforcers identified in Items 1, 2, and 3 and establish priority choices based on the student's responses.

Identify Natural Consequences   Many activities and skills involve consequences that may themselves provide sufficient reinforcement to promote the acquisition of those activities and skills. A strategy that can be used to identify natural consequences to an activity is to conduct a task analysis of that activity. Each step of the task analysis can be examined for potential naturally occurring consequences.

Not all behaviors contain easily identified natural consequences to serve as reinforcers of student performance. When a natural reinforcing consequence cannot be identified, a survey of the environment may identify other potential reinforcements. For example, Fred, a sixth-grade student, is learning to read, complete language arts worksheets, keep a journal, and pass the weekly spelling test, in spite of having difficulty remaining on task for more than a few minutes. Upon conducting an analysis of these activities, the teacher is initially unable to identify potential naturally occurring reinforcers.

A survey of the environment in which the language arts lessons occur, however, reveals that language arts activities require frequent opportunities to pass out papers and other materials. Passing out materials had been previously determined to be a reinforcing activity for this student. An inclusion facilitator might suggest to the classroom teacher that he arrange short breaks (contingent upon this student's on-task behaviors) for the student to pass out materials to the other students during the language arts activities. Gradually, the number of times this student is called on to pass out the materials can be decreased until Fred is working for periods of time similar to those of the other students in the class.

Survey Student Likes and Dislikes What is motivating to one student may not be motivating to another. A teacher must therefore be thoroughly familiar with a student's likes and dislikes when attempting to determine reinforcers for a given situation. The student should not just be allowed but encouraged to assist in the identification of desirable reinforcers. Family members and others familiar with the student should also be surveyed in order to determine their suggestions for desirable reinforcers. The teacher may wish to develop a series of questions to aid in gathering this information. The following areas, at a minimum, should be considered:

The student's favorite foods
The student's favorite activities, materials, and places at home
The student's favorite activities, materials, and places away from home
Rewards and consequences used at home to increase student behaviors

This information can be matched with activities and skills relevant to the environment of interest. For example, a home survey may identify that a first grade student's favorite activity is to listen to a storybook on cassette tape. By using this activity in the classroom environment, the teacher may establish a natural reinforcement for a desired classroom behavior for that student.

Observe the Student One of the most effective ways to determine what is motivating for a student in a given situation is to observe the student in that situation. Although an initial survey of the environment may produce a list of potential reinforcers, the teacher may overlook less obvious ones or those that have relevance only to the student in question. The following example illustrates this point.

John, a student with multiple disabilities, is working in a college bookstore as part of his transition program. His task is to dust. First, he empties a shelf of books. Then, using a cloth sprayed with cleaining fluid, he dusts the shelf, dusts each book, and then returns the books to the shelf. John is easily distracted and has a difficult time staying on task. He is not initially motivated by praise or the prospect of a break when the task is completed. His teacher, observing him on the job, notes that John really enjoys spraying his dusting cloth with the cleaning fluid. She restructures the activity so that John can re-spray the cloth each time he completes a small shelf of books. Getting to respray the cloth is an effective reinforcement for John, and ontask behavior increases significantly. Gradually, he is instructed to spray less often until he is spraying the dusting cloth only after dusting an entire bookshelf.

Offer Paired Choices   Occasionally, a situation will offer a number of potential reinforcers, and careful analysis by the teacher of the student's likes and dislikes may reveal many more. When this is the case, the student may be offered paired choices from the list of potential reinforcers. These can be ordered according to priority, based on the student's responses. The necessity of involving the student in the choice of reinforcement cannot be overstressed. To be effective, the reinforcement must be highly desirable to the student in the situation to which it is applied.

For example, a secondary student participating in a biology class has difficulty attending to the teacher when she is lecturing, which she does for about 10–15 minutes most days. After the student gives her attention to the lecture, she is offered the opportunity to look through an issue of *Science Digest* or to rinse out beakers, two activities previously identified as potential reinforcers. The student is not only provided with a preferred activity following appropriate behavior, but is also given a choice of a perferred activity.

To summarize this section on reinforcement procedures, naturally occurring consequences are the least obtrusive and often the most effective reinforcement choices. If systematic efforts to identify naturally occurring consequences fail, knowledge of student likes and dislikes across a variety of environments may provide educators with many potentially strong reinforcers with which to begin shaping the desired behavior. Gradually, natural consequences can be substituted for the more artificial ones. Information from parents and others who know the student well, in addition to systematic observation of the student, will assist in identifying potential reinforcers or motivators. In addition to using reinforcement as an effective instructional strategy, educators can also use generalized and specialized instructional procedures to facilitate students' learning. A discussion of such procedures follows.

GENERALIZED INSTRUCTIONAL PROCEDURES

To ensure effective instruction, educators must select instructional methods and provide learning opportunities that result in successful acquisition of skills as well as the use of these skills across time and settings (Snell & Brown, 1993).

Educators should examine the various environments and activities available in general education classrooms and schools, and design instructional programs that can be provided in these settings.

Activity-Based Instruction

Activity-based teaching facilitates students' learning within the context of functional and ongoing natural routines. For example, students are more likely to learn the routines and requirements associated with eating in the cafeteria by doing, observing, and getting feedback from others, rather than by a teacher giving only verbal explanations of routine and procedures. The context should define the materials and settings. In addition, other aspects of the activity, such as the time of day or week, the people present, and the typical noises and interruptions, should be kept natural or modified only when necessary to simplify the activity during initial instruction (Snell & Brown, 1993). The following activity-based instructional arrangements can facilitate learning.

Simulation These learning activities simulate or "copy," to the greatest degree possible, real-life experiences within a classroom or school setting. Since educators cannot always teach everything that needs to be taught in natural environments, simulation can be the next best strategy. For example, when a teacher teaches students about safety in the community, who might be a safe stranger (e.g., police officer) and who might be an unsafe stranger (e.g., a person luring a child into a car), simulation of the interactions can be an appropriate instructional method. While logistical and scheduling constraints may require that teachers use simulations to teach various skills and behaviors some of the time, caution should be used, since it is always "risky to teach through simulation and hope for generalization to real settings . . ." (Browder & Snell, 1993, pp. 484). Simulations should always be used in conjunction with teaching in real-life settings.

Role Play Learning activities that provide students and/or teachers with the opportunity to take on the behavior of a hypothetical or real personality in order to solve a problem or gain insight into a particular situation can be useful (Wiles & Bondi, 1989). Role play is particularly helpful for students to practice social and communicative skills, such as learning the approaches a student might use to greet a friend, parent, teacher, or prospective employer, or learning to say no to drugs.

Demonstration Opportunities for teachers to use examples, experiments, and/or other actual performance to illustrate a principle or demonstrate an action can also serve as important teaching tools (Wiles & Bondi, 1989). There are many concepts in science and social studies that are best taught when demonstrated to students. For example, students may better understand the physics concept of "force" through observing a pulley system (Wiles & Bondi, 1989).

Games Providing students with activities that allow them to learn by doing can be an effective tool. Games emphasize discovery through activity and are grounded in the belief that learning should be fun (Wiles & Bondi, 1989). "Games are useful because they represent activities with high appeal for children and because they can structure the environment for a brief period of time according to specific rules" (Sapon-Shevin, 1990, p. 73).

Community-Based Instruction   This instructional activity, also termed *field experiences* or *life skills*, is an opportunity to give students an early and accurate sense of the "real world." It entails teaching students how the world functions through active participation, thus empowering them for active roles as adults (Corbo, 1990). In addition to learning and applying academic skills in situations that closely approximate real life, a community-based instruction facilitates the development of "people" skills such as negotiation, communication, and problem solving (Falvey, 1989; Ford et al., 1992). Other such life skills might be learning to cross streets, shop in a grocery store, check out books from the library, and walk to school.

Throughout the 1980s, the primary emphasis of curriculum and instruction for students with severe disabilities was on community-based teaching. School inclusion of students with severe disabilities does not necessarily preclude students' participation in community-based educational experiences. However, students with disabilities should not be denied educational experiences in order to participate in community-based instruction. The involvement of students with and without disabilities in both school and community learning experiences merges the best from both general and special education. This merger involves combining resources and personnel in a service delivery model that provides opportunities for *all* students to learn about and from one another in natural settings.

Cooperative Groups   This instructional arrangement allows students to work and learn together in interdependent and heterogeneous groups to help one another learn academic content (Slavin, 1990). Cooperative learning groups provide opportunities for students to work together to accomplish goals while accommodating each other's differences (Sapon-Shevin, 1990). See Chapter 5 for a more detailed description of cooperative learning.

Computer-Assisted Instruction (CAI)   CAI involves the use of computers to present instruction to students. The interaction between the computer and the student is designed to assist students to learn new concepts or to improve upon their knowledge of concepts previously learned (Chan, 1984). CAI also provides opportunities for student-to-student interaction and cooperative learning experiences. See Chapter 9 for a more detailed discussion of CAI.

Instruction Based on Personal Learning Styles/Multiple Intelligences

In order to create an optimal learning environment for a heterogeneous group of students, educators must develop and use a variety of instructional approaches. As discussed in Chapter 4, Gardner's (1983) descriptions of seven different types of intelligence (linguistic, logical/mathematical, spatial, musical, bodily/kinesthetic, interpersonal, and intrapersonal) can be extremely useful to educators when developing approaches to accommodate individual learning styles. Gardner's work and the subsequent work of Armstrong (1987, 1994) and Miller (1993) have resulted in the identification of strategies for determining the most effective personal learning styles based upon students' areas of intelligence. Schools have typically responded to the learning needs of students who have linguistic and mathematical intelligence. However, large numbers of students are not particularly skilled in these two areas of intelligence; rather, they have strengths in one or a combination of other areas of intelligence. The information about a student's area(s) of intelligence, which all students possess, is extremely beneficial in determining a student's personal learning style. Personal learning styles refer to the strategies a student uses to acquire new skills successfully. For example, a student who has intelligence in both bodily/kinesthetic and intrapersonal areas should be given opportunities to acquire skills complementary to these areas of intelligence. Students talented in the bodily/kinesthetic area are likely to learn by touching, manipulating, and moving and by activities that are kinetic, dynamic, and visceral. They will do best when involved in physical and hands-on activities, such as fixing or building something, playing games, dramatic improvisation, and other creative movement activities. Students with intrapersonal strengths learn best when given some time to learn on their own. They require independent study opportunities as well as self-paced and individualized instructional projects and games (Armstrong, 1987). Educators must create learning atmospheres that offer opportunities to acquire skills across all seven types of intelligence, since heterogeneous classrooms will undoubtedly include students reflecting all seven areas. Table 1 provides a listing of each area of intelligence and suggested corresponding instructional approaches and strategies that could be used to teach students effectively with those strengths.

There is no single instructional approach that can be advocated for all types of learners (Wiles & Bondi, 1989). Instructional plans should begin with the student and build upon his or her strengths to facilitate student learning and success (Stainback, Stainback, & Moravec, 1992). In addition, instruction should also focus on teacher behaviors and how instruction is delivered. Finally, ongoing evaluation of the effect of teaching on learning must occur.

To promote learning, there are a series of instructional activities that teachers can use. Based upon the work of Popham and Baker (1963), teachers should provide the following:

1. *Appropriate practice:* Sufficient opportunity to practice target behaviors and skills should be provided for the student. The amount of time for practice will, of course, vary from student to student, and should be based upon the needs of the student as determined by a comprehensive assessment.
2. *Knowledge of results:* Through methods of discovery, the teacher should allow the student to determine whether his or her responses are adequate;

Table 1.   Instructional approaches and strategies for seven areas of intelligence

Linguistic
- saying, hearing, and seeing what needs to be learned
- telling or listening to tales and stories
- using tape recorders, taped stories, typewriters, word processors
- creating newsletters, journal writing
- using word problems
- reciting math problems
- using crossword puzzles or playing games that use words

Logical/mathematical
- using concrete objects for teaching
- using computers
- allowing for experimentation, exploration of new ideas, and time to answer
- using strategy games such as chess and checkers
- enlisting student's involvement in developing a behavior management plan
- using visual cues to teach, for example, a picture of a snake in the shape of an "S"

Spatial
- allowing student to be engaged in art activities, especially drawing and painting
- teaching through images, pictures, and colors
- using three-dimensional objects for teaching
- using jigsaw puzzles or mazes
- using students' "daydreaming" to create stories

Musical
- teaching to play musical instrument
- using rhythm and melodies
- working with music playing in the background
- using records or tapes
- singing songs, especially ones that have concepts or messages to teach

Bodily/kinesthetic
- using tactile images and interactions to teach
- moving, twitching, tapping, or fidgeting while sitting in a chair
- providing opportunities to engage in physical activities, such as jumping, skipping, crawling, somersaulting
- using patterns and computers
- using the outdoors to teach, with students working out math problems or reading

Interpersonal
- using mutual reading activities
- reading to others and/or teaching others to read
- using group problem-solving activities
- facilitating involvement in after-school group activities
- mediating when student disputes arise
- playing group games with other children
- using community volunteering to teach

Intrapersonal
- providing opportunity for independent work
- giving students answer sheets to do self-correcting
- using high-interest reading materials
- providing opportunity to be alone to pursue personal interest, hobby, or project
- providing cozy and private sections of the room
- respecting and honoring individual differences and learning approaches
- allowing for plenty of leisure reading time

Adapted from Armstrong (1987).

that is, the teacher should arrange for appropriate and consistent student feedback in the learning process.

3. *Analysis and sequence of student behavior:*   Using task-analytical methods (i.e., breaking the activity or skill into teachable steps), the teacher should identify and sequence of behaviors to be learned in the achievement of educational objectives.

4. *Perceived purpose:*   Teachers should arrange for and structure learning opportunities that allow students to discover and understand the value of what they are learning.

5. *Evaluation*:   Teachers must collect initial student assessment data, maintain ongoing evaluation of student progress, interpret their evaluation data, and reorganize learning situations as appropriate.

SPECIALIZED INSTRUCTIONAL PROCEDURES

As educators move toward more inclusive educational practices, instructional posture and strategies must change. Rather than teaching discrete skills in separate settings, student participation and learning should be facilitated through real-life projects and activities offering interaction and cooperation with typical peers (Stainback et al., 1992). That which is instructionally valid and effective must be maintained, but practices must be congruent with the general education classroom climate. Stainback et al. (1992) suggest a holistic or constructivistic perspective to curriculum and instruction. Such a perspective "must take into account the dynamic nature of what is needed to successfully live and work in a community" (p. 70). They also suggest that in order for information to be learned, used, and maintained, it must be meaningful and make sense for the student. Both general and special education teachers should rely on the instructional principles and strategies previously described in this chapter. However, when students with and without disabilities require additional instruction and learning experiences, a major challenge to the educational planning team may center upon how to provide such specialized instruction within the general education setting. That is, general and special education personnel must work collaboratively to provide individualized instruction to students in the least intrusive manner.

A variety of specialized instructional procedures are available to facilitate the acquisition of particular behaviors. One set of instructional procedures involves the use of selective reinforcement of behaviors that are already, in some way, part of the student's repertoire. This strengthens the existing behaviors and encourages their appearance under appropriate circumstances. Bringing existing behaviors under the control of the circumstances in which they should occur is known as stimulus control. Differential reinforcement, prompting, and fading are techniques used to develop stimulus control. Finally, more complex strategies such as shaping and chaining may be needed to develop new behaviors. The sections that follow define and illustrate the use of these strategies.

Bringing Existing Behaviors Under Stimulus Control

Stimulus control is defined as the predictable performance of a behavior under certain stimulus conditions (Wolery, Ault, & Doyle, 1992). This technique can be used to ensure that behaviors or skills that are part of an individual student's existing repertoire will be exhibited by that student under the appropriate conditions. The antecedent stimulus acts to cue or prompt the desired behavior at the specified time. For example, many students' skill repertoires include the ability to sit, but not all students will sit when told to do so. Sitting at one's desk is a desirable classroom behavior, yet some students have a difficult time settling down or staying seated. The action, sitting down, needs to be brought under the control of the antecedent stimulus, all students sitting down when the period begins (or when the teacher requests it). Stimulus control is generally accomplished by careful reinforcement of the desired behavior or skill when it is exhibited under the specified circumstances.

Before using stimulus control procedures, the educator must first determine that the desired behavior or skill is part of the student's repertoire of behaviors or skills. If it is not, more complex teaching procedures must be applied to develop the behavior or skill (these teaching procedures are discussed in detail in a later section of this chapter). Once it has been determined that the behavior or skill is present, the antecedent stimulus that will control the behavior under specified circumstances must be identified. Three types of stimuli can be used to control behaviors: instructional control, materials control, and setting control (Donnellan, Gossage, LaVigna, Schuler, & Traphagen, 1977). Instructional control involves the use of verbal or nonverbal prompts to initiate/request a desired student behavior. For example, a teacher might use an exaggerated form of putting his hands on his desk as a prompt designed to communicate to a student to do so and to stop masturbating during class time. Materials control exists when the specific resources to be used in performing the desired behavior serve to prompt the student to engage in that behavior. For example, when a teacher holds up her pencil and the Health workbook, the students are being instructed to put away other materials, get out their Health workbook and pencils, and prepare for Health class. Setting control exists when aspects of the environment in which the behavior is to take place trigger the behavior. For example, a student is physically guided to the sink area of a classroom following the completion of an art activity involving glue and paint. The setting, that is, the sink area, serves as the prompt for the student to begin using the sink to wash her hands.

Stimulus control is most effective when the antecedent stimulus used to cue a desired behavior is a natural part of the environment in which that behavior is to take place. For example, it is appropriate for a student to learn to sit down at a typing table for instruction when told to do so. Such a cue from the teacher is a natural part of the classroom environment, as in, "Students take your seats." To use that same verbal cue in the community to signal to the student that he or she has reached the place to sit and wait for the bus would be inappropriate because the student would be dependent upon an artificial cue that is not likely to exist when the student needs to sit and wait for a bus. A natural antecedent stimulus, or cue, in this instance, might be the bus stop sign or bench, or other commuters sitting on the bench.

When determining antecedent stimuli, educators must also be careful to identify all the relevant characteristics of potential antecedent stimuli (i.e., all the natural cues). Failure to identify all the natural cues might result in the student attending to the irrelevant aspects of antecedents and therefore engaging in the behavior at the wrong time or under inappropriate circumstances. For example, the relevant characteristics of a crosswalk include the white painted lines, the flashing signal, schoolmates crossing the street, and the presence of a street-crossing guard. All of these aspects may be important when trying to bring the student's behavior of crossing the street under the control of the critical antecedent stimulus, the presence of the crossing guard. If, for example, the student learns to attend to schoolmates only, he or she might incorrectly cross the street. Careful advance consideration of relevant characteristics and the use of numerous instructional trials under a variety of circumstances will facilitate bringing the behavior under the control of only the most relevant aspects of the antecedent stimuli.

A final step in the development of stimulus control for a particular behavior or skill is to determine reinforcement strategies. As discussed previously, this includes determining the rewards or consequences for the student when the desired behavior is exhibited under the specified circumstances and then fading to reinforcement that is naturally occurring. For instance, when the student crosses the street, the natural consequence is to arrive on the other side. Initially, however, other forms of reinforcement may need to be paired with the natural consequence to develop the desired behavior. The three steps, identifying the antecedent stimuli, determining the relevant characteristics of the stimuli, and establishing reinforcement strategies, are critical in the development of stimulus control procedures.

Differential Reinforcement Once the behavior has been specified, the antecedent stimuli described, and the reinforcement determined, stimulus control procedures can be used to teach the student to exhibit the behavior when the antecedent stimuli are presented. Differential reinforcement is one technique for developing this stimulus control. It involves the deliberate reinforcement of the specified behavior when, and only when, it occurs under the specified stimulus conditions. As students are continually reinforced for the behavior in the presence of a specified antecedent, they will come to associate the reinforcement with the antecedent. Gradually, the antecedent itself will trigger the desired behavior. For example, Sydney has a tendency to hum or sing to herself, which distracts the other students who are trying to complete their work. Humming and singing are appropriate behaviors under different circumstances, so the teacher, instead of attempting to extinguish the behavior, provides appropriate opportunities for Sydney to sing and hum, for example during school choir. Sydney is naturally reinforced for her singing and humming in this setting. However, when Sydney hums or sings in inappropriate settings, she is ignored. When she engages in the alternative appropriate behavior, that is, completing her work without humming or singing, she is rewarded through praise. This is an example of differential reinforcement, because the behavior is reinforced based upon the specific circumstances that occur.

Prompting   For some students, more specific guidance and instructional assistance may initially be necessary to acquire new skills. A range of instructional stimuli may need to be provided in order to direct the student toward a desired response. This technique is known as prompting. Prompts may take the form of cues, which are used to provide instructional information to a student before a skill is performed. Prompts may also be provided as corrections, which communicate to a student that a skill has already been performed inappropriately and/or needs to be attempted in a different way (Falvey et al., 1980).

Suppose, for example, that a teacher wanted to teach a student to wash her hands after painting. The natural cue that would indicate that the behavior was under stimulus control is the setting. In other words, when the student had finished painting, the presence of the sink would remind her to wash her hands. If this did not occur, the teacher might first gesture to the sink and/or the student's hands, providing a correction. The next level of prompt would be to ask, "Have you forgotten to do something?" At the most intense level, the teacher would actually physically guide the student through all or part of the whole cycle of hand washing.

The presentation of prompts must be carefully controlled to minimize student dependence, to provide maximum clarity, and to facilitate the student's learning of the desired behavior(s). A *discrete trial format* (DTF), also termed *antecedent prompt procedure* (Wolery et al., 1992), is an effective teaching procedure that enables educators to control the presentation of stimuli, prompts, and consequences. In DTF, prompts are used after the natural stimulus fails to control the desired behavior and prior to the end of the student's response. DTF is added to the stimulus to bring about a correct response and to thus provide immediate reinforcement to the student for correct performance of the behavior. The components of the DTF include the discriminative stimulus; the prompt (only if necessary); the desired response; and the reinforcement, or consequence, for a correct response. A trial is measured as a student's attempt to perform the desired behavior. One trial ends when the behavior is correctly performed and subsequently reinforced or when the student performs incorrectly. In the case of incorrect performance, the student is returned to the stimulus point, and a new opportunity to perform the skill is provided, perhaps using a more intensive level of prompt.

There are eight levels in the hierarchy of prompt usage. As indicated earlier, the highest level, level eight, is the natural cue or stimulus indicative of stimulus control. Level seven is the gestural prompt. This may include pointing; shaking one's head to indicate approval; or a facial cue, such as a frown. Level six is the indirect verbal prompt, or use of words to imply that some behavior needs to occur. At level five, a direct verbal prompt explicitly states the behavior that needs to happen. In the previous example, the teacher might have said directly, "Wash your hands." To prompt at level four is to actually model the desired behavior for the student, to encourage the student's imitation of that behavior. A minimal physical prompt is used at level three, that is, slight physical contact to guide a student toward a behavior. At level two, a partial physical prompt is applied; at this level, the teacher or other adult starts the student in the desired behavior, but then allows the student to complete the behavior independently. Finally, at level one, a full physical prompt may be used, in which the student is physically guided through the entire sequence of the activity.

Facilitation   Facilitation is a strategy most often used to assist in the performance of a communicative behavior (Biklen, 1990; Crossley & McDonald, 1984). While its use in this capacity is the source of significant controversy, facilitation as a general instructional strategy can be helpful for students who have difficulty focusing or making intentional motor or communicative responses. Based on the work of Biklen (1990), the key elements of facilitation are physical support, training, and focusing. Physical support involves the facilitator, who supports the forearm or hand of the student to help him or her isolate the index finger, make the selection, or perform an intentional behavior. Training occurs for both the facilitator (who learns how to provide enough, but not too much, support and how to gradually fade the support) and the student (who learns to isolate the index finger, point to letters, etc.). Focusing involves helping the student to reduce extraneous action like handflapping and to concentrate on pointing.

Fading   Just as the most effective reinforcers are those that are natural consequences of the skill to be developed, the most effective cues to use are those that are natural to the situation in which the desired behavior is to occur. Students must learn to respond to natural cues, as artificial prompts are not generally available in inclusive settings. A major consideration when using prompts is that they must eventually be faded or eliminated to promote learning (Browder & Snell, 1993). Students can quickly become dependent on artificial or intense levels of prompts. Therefore, the use of prompts must include a systematic plan to reduce the student's dependence on them until he or she is able to perform the behavior solely in response to the natural cues. The technique for reducing prompts is known as fading.

Fading procedures are necessary when artificial or intense levels of prompts have been used to facilitate a student's acquisition of skills. When fading procedures are properly employed, the student maintains existing high levels of performance of the behavior. This means that fading procedures must be gradually applied, reducing the degree and numbers of prompts provided. The following example illustrates this process.

Cecilia, a 7-year-old student with significant disabilities, is learning to use a "spork" (combination fork and spoon) at lunchtime at her elementary school. At first, physical prompts are needed for several steps. The occupational therapist provides a full physical prompt to assist her in scooping and piercing her food from the lunch tray. A partial physical prompt is needed to cue her to bring the food to her mouth. A verbal prompt reminds her to place the spork back in her tray. As these behaviors are established, the therapist begins to fade the levels of prompts provided. Rather than full physical guidance in scooping and piercing, a light guided touch prompts Cecilia to complete the movement. A gesture, the therapist motioning upward with her hand from the table toward Cecilia's mouth, encourages her to bring the food to her mouth. Eventually the verbal prompt is eliminated completely. This gradual fading process continues systematically until Cecilia reaches independence in eating with a "spork."

Fading should be done slowly so that the student maintains the desired behavior. If, as prompts are faded, the student begins to perform the behavior incorrectly or not at all, the fading sequence has been too rapid. At this point, it may be necessary for the teacher, or in the above example, the occupational therapist, to return to the last level of prompting at which the behavior was performed correctly and begin the fading sequence again.

Developing New Behaviors

The previous discussion focused on developing behaviors that were already a part of a student's repertoire of skills. Many important behaviors, however, are not likely to occur spontaneously and therefore cannot be increased by reinforcement and prompting. The development of new behaviors requires the more sophisticated use of the procedures described previously, paired with two major teaching strategies: shaping and chaining. The use of these procedures requires a specific delineation of the new behavior as well as of the circumstances under which that behavior should be exhibited.

Shaping   Reinforcing successive approximations or improved attempts at a target behavior is referred to as shaping. Shaping begins with reinforcement of the closest approximation of the target behavior that exists in the student's repertoire and systematically builds on slight changes in that behavior that lead toward the target behavior itself. Before beginning shaping procedures, the target behavior must be operationally defined; that is, the exact characteristics of acceptable performance must be specified. From this point, all possible steps in the direction of that target behavior must be outlined, and careful observations of the student must take place to determine the student's starting point toward that behavior. At first, the closest approximation that the student is able to make toward the target behavior is reinforced. The required level of performance is then gradually increased, and only responses that move in the direction of the target behavior are reinforced. In this way, the student's behavior is shaped toward the target behavior.

Many different behaviors can be developed using shaping procedures. For example, Carla can be taught to touch her peers only while playing tag on the playground, instead of touching them during instructional time in the classroom. At first, any touching on the playground would be reinforced by peers. The next step would be to make reinforcement contingent upon the children playing the game of tag.

Chaining   Another procedure that can be used to develop new behaviors and skills is chaining. Chaining involves breaking a target behavior down into its smallest component parts in order to teach the parts one at a time (Koegel & Schreiber, 1982). The first behavior in the chain is the first response taught. A chain should begin at the level at which the student is able to learn the first behavior successfully and should move in successive steps toward the target behavior.

Chaining begins with a task analysis of the target behavior. In task analysis, each component behavior of the target behavior is identified, and the sequence of those behaviors is defined. The analysis of the task should be linked to the student's ability level (Gold, 1980). For example, one student may learn to clean the chalkboard through a 3-step process, while another student may need the same activity broken down into a 10-step process in order to acquire the necessary skills. Each step in a task analysis should be clearly stated in order to measure the student's performance of the behavior objectively. There should be just enough steps in the task analysis to allow efficient and systematic teaching; each step itself can be broken down further if the student has particular difficulty in successfully performing that step. A task analysis should be individually developed and applied. Bellamy, Horner, and Inman (1979) suggest procedures for developing an effective and efficient task analysis. A modified version of their plan follows:

1. Watch an age-peer perform the task.
2. Break the task down into a logical number of parts based upon the previous performance.
3. Provide the opportunity for the student to complete the task, and prompt the student through the task if necessary.
4. Reanalyze the task based on student areas of need.

When an individualized task analysis has been developed, it can then be used as a teaching sequence to develop a desired target behavior.

A distinction can be made between forward, backward, or global chaining, depending on which step in the chain is taught first (Sulzer-Azaroff & Mayer, 1977). If *forward chaining* is being used, the student is taught to perform the first unlearned step in the chain. After this step is mastered, instruction proceeds to the next step, and so on. For example, a student learning to operate a copy machine in the school office must first learn to turn the machine on, place the document under the cover on the glass, bring down the cover, press the start button, and then follow each remaining step in the chain. Reinforcement is given as each step in the chain is successfully completed.

In *backward chaining*, the steps are taught in the reverse order. This method can be useful for linking the natural reinforcement inherent in the completion of the activity with the performance of the activity and also is beneficial when baseline assessment of the student indicates that he or she has mastered some of the steps at the end of a teaching chain. For example, when teaching a student to tie his or her shoe, the last step in the sequence, pulling the two loops tight in opposite directions, becomes the first step taught. Each subsequent step proceeding backward through the task analysis is taught, until the student had acquired all the skills to perform all the steps.

Global chaining entails identifying steps to teach based upon the specific characteristics of the steps. For example, when teaching a student to go through the cafeteria line to purchase lunch, the steps targeted for initial instruction might be those involving choice-making skills. In this case, the student might either have the skills to proceed through the other steps of the task analysis or be physically guided through the other steps. Until the student is able to demonstrate the required choice-making skills on the cafeteria line, the instruction continues to emphasize these skills. It is important to note that with backward and global chaining, the student actively participates in performing all the steps in the order they would naturally occur with the needed assistance.

As with shaping, prompts can be used to encourage the development of behaviors in a chain. Each step as it is introduced may first have to be prompted. In addition, most target behaviors are composed of component behaviors that are only meaningful in the context of the target behavior. They should not, therefore, be taught in isolation.

The preceding instructional strategies can facilitate students' successful learning in general education settings. In the following section, strategies for modifying the curriculum to ensure all students have access to the general education curriculum are described.

FACILITATING STUDENTS' ACCESS TO THE CURRICULUM

Snell and Brown (1993) suggest that once students with significant disabilities are assigned to age-appropriate general education classrooms, then shared planning, teaming, and teaching is possible between the special and general educators. Such planning must consider different ways to include the student with severe disabilities into the existing general education classroom and curriculum. As a starting point, the team should analyze the characteristics of the general education classroom and school to determine which, if any, curricular modifications are necessary. That is, teachers should not presume that a student's ability to participate in the general education curriculum, will of necessity, require modification of that curriculum. There are numerous learning and social activities that students with significant disabilities can participate in with their peers without disabilities that do not require modifications or adaptations. For example, Blair, a second-grade student with significant cognitive delays and limited communication skills, entered the class with her peers, organized her materials in her desk, removed materials when told to do so, and worked independently for approximately 5 minutes without any additional prompts or different levels of reinforcement. When she was uncertain of what to do next, or when she got "stuck" on a particular assignment, her peers assisted her (as they do other students in the class) without being told to do so. It is critical that educators allow these natural supports to emerge and avoid structuring artificial supports.

In order to provide adequate and appropriate access to the curriculum for all students, teachers can begin the process of analyzing the general education classroom by asking the following questions.

1. *What do students need to learn?* Teachers need to consider what the learning goals and objectives are for the student by examining general education curriculum content (academic) as well as specific skill acquisition (personal care, motor, communication, social).

2. *How do students need to learn?* As indicated previously, teachers should use both general and specialized instructional procedures to facilitate learning, but should always employ a "least intrusive support plan" (Jorgensen, 1992). That is, as teachers plan the supports a student will need during the school day they should "think first of using other students as supports; then using the classroom teacher or instructional assistant or volunteers; and finally using specialized supports such as an inclusion facilitator or related service personnel" (Jorgensen, 1992, p. 210). Such peer supports should not distract from or diminish learning, but should enhance and increase learning.

3. *What modifications or adaptations are necessary for student learning?* The literature suggests various ways to approach curricular modifications for students with disabilities (Ford et al., 1992; Giangreco & Putnam, 1991; Neary, 1992; Sapon-Shevin, 1990). Based upon this literature, Neary (1992) has developed a decision-making process to assist teachers and others to analyze the general education curriculum. Neary (1992) presents five choices that teachers can consider when analyzing the general education curriculum for specific student participation. First, teachers may decide to leave the curriculum as is, and not develop any modifications or changes. In many situations, students with disabilities may engage in the same lessons, use the same materials, and have the same objectives as their classmates without disabilities.

The second choice within this process involves the provision of *physical assistance.* Using this type of adaptation, the student participates in the same lessons, although he or she is provided with physical assistance to perform a part or all of the components of the lesson. This physical assistance can be provided by peers, older students, general education teachers, special education teachers, paraprofessionals or related services personnel (e.g., speech therapists).

Adapting materials is the third option. The student participates in the same activity with adapted materials. For example, during this math class, Charlie, who does not have the skills to multiply and divide, is given a calculator in order to participate in the class activities and to complete his assignments.

Providing a *multilevel curriculum* is the fourth choice and refers to the identification of different goals and objectives for different students within the same curricular domain. In addition, these objectives are taught within the same lesson or activity. For example, in a science lesson on temperature, one student might be learning to differentiate between hot and cold items, while another student learns the difference between Celsius and Fahrenheit.

Curriculum overlapping, a variation of multilevel curriculum, is a fifth choice teachers may consider. This strategy involves selecting individual goals and objectives from different curricular areas that are worked on within the context of a shared group activity (Giangreco & Putnam, 1991) and can also be considered a thematic approach to the curriculum. For example, during journal writing, Joey works on staying in his seat and arranging photos of his activities in an album, while his peers write a description of the previous day in their journals.

A final choice teachers may make is to provide a *substitute curriculum*. This decision should be made carefully and only as a last resort. This involves the student's participation in an alternative activity, that is, an activity other than the one in which classmates are engaged. This can be used when the general education curriculum does not provide the opportunity to teach skills that are essential to a student. Providing a substitute curriculum does not necessitate participating in an activity by oneself or only with peers with disabilities. Students without disabilities can also be successfully involved to meet their own needs. For example, Allison, a student with significant disabilities and Katie, her friend without disabilities, are responsible for collecting the lunch counts from all the classrooms in their elementary school (an objective on Allison's IEP) during math. Katie is reinforced for timely completion of her math work by the opportunity to accompany Allison.

To further assist teachers and others to modify general education curriculum for students, Neary (1992) suggests a *classroom activity analysis* process. This strategy assists teachers to analyze the specific components of a particular classroom activity and to develop adaptations and prioritize areas of instruction (see Figure 1).

SUMMARY

A variety of strategies exist to assist educators to teach all student effectively. This chapter has included a description of some of the most frequently used instructional strategies, especially those that have been used to facilitate the learning of students with a variety of educational challenges. An effective educator is one who is able to use this variety of teaching strategies to ensure students' success and progress in meaningful activities.

Classroom Activity Analysis Worksheet

Student name: Meagan **Month/year:** September–October, 1994

Activity	Student's objectives	Instructional strategies	Adaptations	Support
Good morning	Shake hands	Modeling of peers	None	None
Journals	"Own" writing	Review Meagan's previous writing and discuss areas of difficulty and corrections; reinforce correct formats	Computer	None
	Copy sentences	Verbal and gestural directions	Meagan dictates sentences to peer who writes her copy	Peer or adult
	Draw/color/stamps	Verbal and gestural directions	Large crayons or markers	Peer
	Magazine pictures	Verbal, gestural, and modeling	Magazines to cut	Independent
Reading circles	Books on tape	Verbal	Peer records books	Peer
	Partner reads to Meagan	Verbal	None	None
	Meagan "reads" to partner	Verbal and modeling	Picture cued books	None
Writer's workshop	Vocabulary cards	Verbal and gestural	Picture/work cards	Speech
	Computer	Pictorial	Sentences to copy	Speech
	Speech	Verbal and modeling	Materials as needed	Speech
	Generate "story" to peer	Verbal and modeling	None	Peer
	Performance of play for kindergartners	Verbal and gestural	Book, picture cues	Teacher

Figure 1. Sample third-grade classroom activity analysis.

Caring educators who use individualized instructional strategies can create classrooms and schools where students are excited about learning. Occasionally students need additional supports and strategies for learning. The following chapter includes those additional strategies that have been used successfully to educate students, particularly those with significant behavior challenges.

REFERENCES

Atkinson, J.W., & Raynor, J.O. (Eds.). (1974). *Motivation and achievement*. Washington, DC: Winston.

Armstrong, T. (1987). *In their own way*. Los Angeles: Jeremy P. Tarcher.

Armstrong, T. (1994). *Multiple intelligences in the classroom*. Alexandria, VA: Association for Supervision and Curriculum Development.

Ball, S. (1977). *Motivation in education*. New York: Academic Press.

Bellamy, G.T., Horner, R.H., & Inman, D.P. (1979). *Vocational habilitation of severely retarded adults: A direct service technology*. Baltimore: University Park Press.

Biklen, D. (1990). Communication unbound: Autism and praxis. *Harvard Educational Review*, *60*(3), 291–314.

Browder, D., & Snell, M. (1993). Daily living and community skills. In M.E. Snell (Ed.), *Instruction of students with severe disabilities* (4th ed.) (pp. 480–525). New York: Merrill.

Chan, Y. (1984). *Uses of microcomputers in schools*. Unpublished manuscript, Unified School District, Los Angeles.

Corbo, D. (Producer). (1990). *America's toughest assignment: Solving the education crisis*. New York: CBS News.

Crossley, R., & McDonald, A. (1984). *Annie's coming out*. Melbourne, Austraila: Penguin

Donnellan, A., Gossage, L.D., LaVigna, G.W., Schuler, A., & Traphagen, J.D. (1977). *Teaching makes a difference*. Sacramento: California State Department of Education.

Dweck, C. (1975). The role of expectations and attributions in the alleviation of learned helplessness. *Journal of Personality and Social Psychology*, *31*, 674–685.

Dweck, C., & Repucci, N.D. (1973). Learned helplessness and reinforcement of responsibility in children. *Journal of Personality and Social Psychology*, *25*, 109–116.

Falvey, M.A. (1989). *Community-based curriculum: Instructional strategies for students with severe disabilities*. Baltimore: Paul H. Brookes Publishing Co.

Falvey, M.A., Brown, L., Lyon, S., Baumgart, D., & Schroeder, J. (1980). Strategies for using cues and correction procedures. In W. Sailor, B. Wilcox, & L. Brown (Eds.), *Methods of instruction for severely handicapped students* (pp. 109–133). Baltimore: Paul H. Brookes Publishing Co.

Ford, A., Davern, L., & Schnorr, R. (1992). Inclusive education: "Making sense" of the curriculum. In S. Stainback & W. Stainback (Eds.), *Curriculum considerations in inclusive classrooms: Facilitating learning for all students* (pp. 37–61). Baltimore: Paul H. Brookes Publishing Co.

Ford, A., & Miranda, P. (1984). Community instruction: A natural cues and corrections decision model. *Journal of The Association for Persons with Severe Handicaps*, *9*(2), 79–87.

Gardner, H. (1983). *Frames of mind: The theory of multiple intelligences*. New York: Basic Books.

Giangreco, M.F., & Putnam, J.W. (1991). Supporting the education of students with severe disabilities in regular education environments. In L.H. Meyer, C.A. Peck, & L. Brown

(Eds.), *Critical issues in the lives of people with severe disabilities* (pp. 245–270). Baltimore: Paul H. Brookes Publishing Co.

Gold, M. (1980). *Try another way: Training manual.* Champaign, IL: Research Press.

Green, D., & Lepper, M.R. (1974, September). Intrinsic motivation: How to turn play into work. *Psychology Today, 8*, 49–54.

Hull, C.L. (1943). *Principles of behavior: An introduction to behavior theory.* New York: Appleton-Century Crofts.

Jorgensen, C.M. (1992). Natural supports in inclusive schools: Curricular and teaching strategies. In J. Nisbet (Ed.), *Natural supports in school, at work, and in the community for people with severe disabilities* (pp. 179–216). Baltimore: Paul H. Brookes Publishing Co.

Koegel, R.L., & Schreiber, L. (1982). *How to teach autistic and other severely handicapped children.* Lawrence, KS: H & H Enterprises.

LaVigna, G.W., & Donnellan, A.M. (1984). *Alternatives to punishment: Solving behavior problems with non-aversive strategies.* New York: Irvington.

Maslow, A. (1987). *Motivation and personality.* New York: Harper & Row.

McClelland, D.C., Atkinson, J.W., Clark, R.A., & Lowell, E.L. (1953). *The achievement motive.* New York: Appleton-Century Crofts.

Meyer, L.H., & Evans, I.M. (1989). *Nonaversive intervention for behavior problems: A manual for home and community.* Baltimore: Paul H. Brookes Publishing Co.

Miller, L. (1993). *What we call smart.* San Diego: Singular.

Neary, T. (1992). Student specific strategies: Designing an individualized program. In T. Neary, A. Halverson, R. Kronberg, & D. Kelly (Eds.), *Curriculum adaptations for inclusive classrooms* (pp. 56–125). San Francisco: San Francisco State University.

Popham, J., & Baker, E. (1963). *Planning an instructional sequence.* Englewood Cliffs, NJ: Prentice-Hall.

Premack, D. (1959). Toward empirical behavioral laws: I. Positive reinforcement. *Psychological Review, 66*, 219–233.

Ruble, E.N., & Boggiano, A.K. (1980). Optimizing motivation in an achievement context. In B.K. Keogh (Ed.), *Advances in special education. Vol. 1: Basic constructs and theoretical orientations.* Greenwich, CT: JAI Press.

Sailor, W., & Guess, D. (1983). *Severely handicapped students: An instructional design.* Boston: Houghton Mifflin.

Sapon-Shevin, M. (1990). Student support through cooperative learning. In W. Stainback & S. Stainback (Eds.), *Support networks for inclusive schooling: Interdependent integrated education* (pp. 65–79). Baltimore: Paul H. Brookes Publishing Co.

Seligman, M.E. (1975). *Helplessness: On depressions, development, and death.* San Francisco: Freeman.

Skinner, B.F. (1974). *About behaviorism.* New York: Random House.

Slavin, R.E. (1990). *Cooperative learning: Theory, research, and practice.* Englewood Cliffs, NJ: Prentice Hall.

Snell, M., & Brown, F. (1993). Instructional planning and implementation. In M.E. Snell (Ed.), *Instruction of students with severe disabilities* (4th ed.) (pp. 99–151). New York: Merrill.

Stainback, W., Stainback, S., & Moravec, J. (1992). Using curriculum to build inclusive classrooms. In S. Stainback & W. Stainback (Eds.), *Curriculum considerations in inclusive classrooms: Facilitating learning for all students* (pp. 65–84). Baltimore: Paul H. Brookes Publishing Co.

Sulzer-Azaroff, B., & Mayer, G.R. (1977). *Applying behavior-analysis procedures with children and youth.* New York: Holt, Rinehart & Winston.

Tolman, E.C. (1959). Principles of purposive behavior. In S. Koch (Ed.), *Psychology: A study of a science* (Vol. 2). New York: McGraw-Hill.

Travers, J.F., Elliott, S.N., & Kratochwill, T.R. (1993). *Educational psychology: Effective teaching, effective learning.* Madison, WI: WCB Brown & Benchmark Publishers.

Weiner, B. (1972). *Theories of motivation: From mechanism to cognition.* Chicago: Rand McNally.

Wilcox, B., & Bellamy, G.T. (1982). *Design of high school programs for severely handicapped students.* Baltimore: Paul H. Brookes Publishing Co.

Wiles, J., & Bondi, J. (1989). *Curriculum development: A guide to practice.* New York: Merrill.

Wolery, M., Ault, M.J., & Doyle, P.M. (1992). *Teaching students with moderate to severe disabilities.* New York: Longman

Yando, R., & Zigler, E. (1971). Outer directions in the problem-solving of institutionalized and non-institutional normal and retarded children. *Developmental Psychology, 4,* 277–288.

7

POSITIVE BEHAVIOR
SUPPORT STRATEGIES

KATHRYN D. BISHOP AND KIMBERLEE A. JUBALA

I've come to a frightening conclusion that I am the decisive element in the classroom. It is my personal approach that creates the climate. It is my daily mood that makes the weather. As a teacher, I possess a tremendous power to make a child's life miserable or joyous. I can be a tool of torture or an instrument of inspiration. I can humiliate or heal. In all situations, it is my response that decides whether a crisis will be escalated or de-escalated, and a student humanized or de-humanized.

(Ginott, 1972)

In the past, educators have often relied on tools of punishment to bring about changes in the behavior of students and adults with or without disabilities. The use of punishment techniques, including electric shock, cattle prods, water sprays, harmless bad tastes or smells (e.g., Tabasco sauce dripped onto the tongue or ammonia capsules broken under the nose), physical restraint, sensory deprivation, overcorrection, and any number of time-out techniques, have been employed in the attempt to change inappropriate behavior (Foxx, McMorrow, Bittle, & Bechtel, 1986; Singh, Dawson, & Gregory, 1980). General educators have relied on less drastic but still punishment-based techniques detailed in such well-known programs as *Assertive Discipline* (Canter & Canter, 1992) and *Back in Control* (Bodenhamer, 1983). Although each of these techniques and programs has demonstrated at least temporary change in behavior, the techniques may be missing the critical outcomes, such as increased choice, meaningful activity, positive relationships, and overall enhancement of quality of life, that are truly desired by students, parents, and educators. In addition, a person who implements these harsh techniques must feel like anything but an "instrument of inspiration."

The procedures described in this chapter have been developed, researched, and disseminated by the Rehabilitation Research and Training Center on Positive Behavior Supports funded by the U.S. Department of Education, National Institute on Disability and Rehabilitation Research.

A new technology has emerged that allows teachers to educate by supporting students with challenging behaviors to learn new skills and behaviors and attain a rich life of quality. This technology is often referred to as *nonaversive behavior management, positive behavior support,* or *comprehensive behavior support*. For the purposes of this chapter, the term *positive behavior support* is used to describe these techniques. Support techniques may require the assistance of an additional person or persons to help identify key factors that are maintaining the inappropriate behaviors. This person may be a teacher, parent, volunteer, counselor, aide, administrator, college fieldwork student, or anyone else who is available to support the classroom teacher during parts of this process. The term *support personnel* is used throughout the chapter to refer to any individual (teacher or other) who is involved in this process.

This chapter provides information that will enable educators to implement positive behavior support strategies for students who engage in challenging behaviors. Such behaviors range in severity from not completing tasks or not following directions to severe self-injurious or aggressive behavior that endangers others or damages property. Targeted behaviors may also vary in frequency from several times a minute to several times a year. A comprehensive range of strategies is presented that can be used to facilitate the needs of students with behavior challenges effectively and efficiently and that will provide these students with skills to lead a more satisfying life.

Perhaps the most important aspect of this new behavioral technology is a change in the way challenging behaviors are perceived. Historically, challenging behaviors have been viewed as isolated entities in and of themselves that were to be "eliminated" without consideration of other aspects of the student's life. Educators using a positive behavior support philosophy perceive behaviors as serving specific functions or purposes for the student. Certain needs have not been met for the individual through acceptable means of behavior, due to environmental problems or inherent skill deficits; thus, the individual is left to use unacceptable means to have those needs met. For example, a student who is nonverbal may repeatedly hit his or her own face in an attempt to communicate that he or she has a toothache. To broadly illustrate this notion, it is helpful to consider the concept of cycles of violence described by Camara (1984). Camara discusses the problems that some individuals in a society have because the society is not meeting their needs effectively. Figure 1 illustrates this concept.

In Figure 1, the top circle connotes the philosophical underpinnings of Western society. This foundation of democracy, capitalism, and so forth, creates a structure within which most of its members can exist successfully. The middle circle connotes societal members for whom that foundation is not working: criminals, gang members, people who are homeless, and so forth. The third circle connotes the strategies that the society uses to deal with those individuals in the middle circle, including jails, police forces, sophisticated weaponry, and de-

Figure 1. Cycles of violence: foundations of society, leading problems for individuals, and strategies by society. (Based on Camara, 1984.)

humanizing institutions. Figure 2, then, exemplifies a formidable challenge to society: as more people fall into the second circle, and as the members of the second circle have greater needs, most of the effort and energy of society becomes reactively focused on the third circle. The people and systems representing the third circle maintain order through greater control over and punishment of the people of the second circle. Continued efforts in the third circle prevent proactive society-building measures. Camara points out, sadly, that society is missing the point. The most effective strategy for supporting the people of the second circle is to focus effort and energy on the first circle. What is it about the foundation of a society that propels people into the second circle? By disrupting this pattern, there would be no need for a third circle (i.e., the most violent circle) to exist.

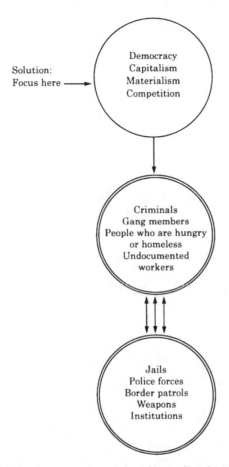

Figure 2.   Cycles of violence: current struggle and societal emphasis on reactive strategies. (Based on Camara, 1984.)

A parallel can be made between this concept and students in the classroom (see Figure 3). The first circle illustrates the foundation of the classroom, with rules and procedures, curricula, instructional strategies, and relationships. Although this foundation works for many students, there are some who will fall out and become labeled as having challenging behaviors. Traditional behavior management strategies become the third circle, and the struggle begins. As the challenging behaviors increase or become more severe, the methods that are used to "manage" them become more extreme. Positive behavior support strategies focus on the first circle, examining the foundation of the classroom and the student who functions within that foundation (see Figure 4). By considering these factors, the need for the second and third circles is eliminated.

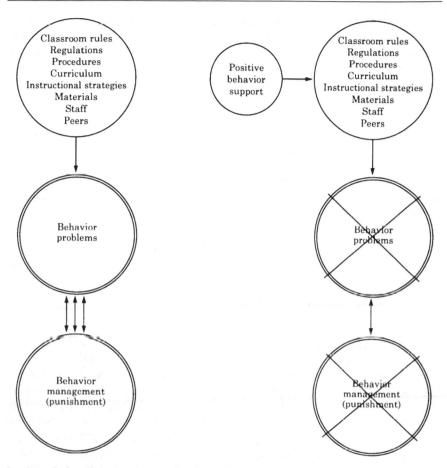

Figure 3.   Cycles of behavior: classroom foundations (left).
Figure 4.   Cycles of behavior: positive behavior support interventions (right).

OUTCOMES ACHIEVED THROUGH POSITIVE BEHAVIOR SUPPORT

For the most part, traditional behavior management strategies have focused on the objective of decreasing or eliminating inappropriate behaviors. The objective of positive behavior support is to increase the quality of life of the student. Quality is defined by a lifestyle with activities, environments, and relationships that are valued by all students and adults regardless of their strengths or needs with respect to their cultural background. Communication, social skills, exercising choices and control, relationships and interactions with peers, a variety of meaningful inclusive activities, productivity, health and safety, and a quality lifestyle should be the focus of instructional attention.

Traditionally, a student's IEP objectives in the area of behavior management have targeted things that the student *will not do*; for example, "Garret will stop hitting others," "Kristen will stop running away from adults," "Lauren will not throw objects in the classroom," "Morgan will not have tantrums on the playground," and "Adam will not touch inappropriate body parts during math group." In contrast, positive supports call for an "educative approach" to challenging behaviors (Evans & Meyer, 1985). As the support focuses on increasing skills, IEP objectives outline what a student *will do* to achieve the increased quality-of-life outcomes; for example, "Garret will ask for help when he needs assistance," "Kristen will use a communication board to select one of three activities offered by an adult," "Lauren will put away toys following a 2-minute warning that playtime is almost over," "Morgan will use two pieces of playground equipment with a peer at recess," and "Adam will use math manipulatives to actively participate in his math group." By increasing desired skills and behaviors, there will be a natural decrease in undesired behaviors, as the student will have a more appropriate means by which his or her needs can be met.

FUNCTIONAL ASSESSMENT AND ANALYSIS

In Chapter 4, a thorough discussion of assessment for student planning and programming is provided. However, in terms of providing support to students with behavior challenges, a functional assessment specific to behavioral needs is necessary. The purpose of a functional assessment of behavior is to gather information that will increase the quality and effectiveness of a behavior support plan (Horner, O'Neill, & Flannery, 1993). Until an understanding of the individual, the behavior, the environment, and the relationships between them is gained, it is difficult to determine what types of supportive interventions will be most successful. In other words, a functional assessment allows a determination of the relationship between events in a person's life and the occurrence of specific behaviors (Carr, Robinson, & Palumbo, 1990). A functional assessment also enables a prediction of when and where a specific behavior will be exhibited. It is believed that all behaviors serve a specific purpose or function for a student (Donnellan, LaVigna, Negri-Shoultz, & Fassbender, 1988); the process of functional assessment helps to determine what the purpose of a specific behavior is for a student. As such, functional assessment is perhaps the most important component of positive behavior support technology.

Know the Student

The initial step in completing a functional assessment is getting to know the student. For the purposes of functional assessment, gaining an understanding of the student involves more than gathering test scores and adaptive behavior scale information. The intent is to know the student as a person and to understand his or her daily routines and overall life circumstances. Gathering information about a student's current lifestyle includes gaining knowledge of issues such as the living situation; the activities that are engaged in during days, evenings, and weekends; leisure activities; relationships and interactions; opportunities for choice and control; medical history; and general preferences and dislikes.

Sometimes, just by gaining a better understanding of a student's relative quality of life, it becomes clear that the targeted behaviors occur for a very specific reason that can be easily remediated. For example, one girl with disabilities was fully included into a general education fourth grade classroom. This student needed support in a variety of ways throughout the day. In an attempt to provide support from other than a teacher or aide, the student was asked to share a table/desk with another student in the class. The student with disabilities always behaved aggressively toward (hit or kicked) her deskmate. Initially, it was suspected that she did not like that particular deskmate so they asked another student to share the desk with her. However, the aggression continued. Finally, she was allowed to have her own desk, like the other fourth graders in the class, with her own things in it just the way she wanted. The aggression was no longer an issue, so no elaborate behavior plans were needed.

Define the Behavior

Once information about the student as an individual has been gathered, the target behavior is defined. As with any behavior intervention effort, the targeted behavior is operationally defined; that is, it is described objectively in a way that can be clearly understood by all and avoids subjective terminology. For example, defining a problem behavior as a "tantrum" does not give a clear delineation of what is actually occurring. Defining a behavior as "lying on the floor, face down, pounding closed fists onto the floor while kicking feet up and down onto the floor, and screaming at a loud volume in a high-pitched tone" gives a more descriptive picture of the behavior that would be easily recognizable to others. In addition, the definition of the targeted behavior should include a description of the frequency, duration, and intensity of the behavior (Horner et al., 1993). To complete the description presented above, the target behavior might further be defined as occurring an average of three times a day (frequency), with each occurrence lasting an average of 20 minutes (duration); the intensity of this behavior is such that her fists become bright red, her feet are kicking forcefully with an audible sound as they hit the floor, and she screams at a volume that exceeds any normal conversational tones and prohibits normal classroom functioning for others.

Determining a precise definition of the target behavior or behaviors assures an understanding of that behavior by all those who interact with the student and those who will be involved in collecting and analyzing additional data related to the behavior. A clear and precise definition eliminates ambiguity and confusion as to whether the targeted behavior did or did not actually occur. In addition, by clarifying the definition one may also consider whether or not the behavior in and of itself is actually a problem, or whether the problem is instead when or where the behavior is exhibited. For example, chewing gum in and of itself is not a problem, but chewing gum within the classroom may be a problem. This clarification helps determine the focus of future intervention strategies.

Complete Traditional Behavior Assessment

Once the definition has been clarified and agreed upon, further data are collected for the functional assessment. Traditional assessment strategies are those strategies that have been commonly used in basic applied behavior analysis methods. Frequency and duration have already been mentioned. Interval recording requires the data collector to divide the observation periods into short equal intervals and then indicate in which intervals the behavior occurs. For example, a 1-hour observation period may be divided into four 15-minute observation periods. If the behavior occurs at any time during the 15-minute period, it is recorded and the observation may be discontinued for the duration of that period. Interval recording does not concern itself with frequency or duration of events, but simply with the existence of these events over time. Time sampling is an interval recording strategy that identifies specific recording periods within identified intervals. For example, data may be recorded only during the first and last 5 minutes of any given activity or during the last 10 minutes of every activity. The purpose is to identify whether the behavior occurs during identified periods. Although these quantitative methods of recording behavior have some useful applications (Alberto & Troutman 1990; Quilitich & Risely, 1973), the functional assessment process relies more heavily on qualitative assessment strategies.

Expanded Behavior Assessment

Expanded assessment strategies are concerned less with specific numbers per se, than with allowing the support personnel to gather richer, more descriptive information regarding the student and the behavior. A number of expanded assessment strategies are listed in Figure 5 and discussed in the following paragraphs.

    Stimulus–Response–Consequence   Stimulus–Response–Consequence (S-R-C; also known as Antecedent–Behavior–Consequence, A-B-C) data recording is a valuable first step in functional assessment data collection. The S-R-C allows support personnel to record events that occurred prior to the target behavior (stimulus), the behavior itself (response), and the reaction to the behavior (consequence). This information can be collected in narrative form on a three-column data sheet as follows:

Stimulus	*Response*	*Consequence*
Teacher asks students to line up for lunch	Juan crawls under his desk	Juan does not get lunch recess

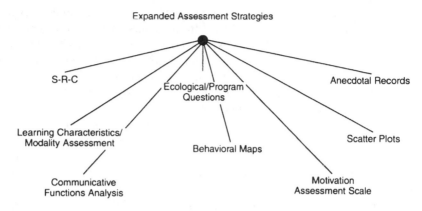

Figure 5. Expanded assessment strategies. (Adapted from Anderson, Mesaros, & Neary, 1991).

The data collected on an S-R-C form allow support personnel to identify those stimulus events in the student's environment that immediately precede and there fore may trigger (stimulus/antecedent) the target behavior and those events that follow and therefore may maintain (consequence) the target behavior. This information is helpful as support personnel begin to identify patterns in the occurrence of the target behavior. For example, if the stimulus column is filled with teacher demands that precede the target behavior and the consequence column consistently documents a reaction of removing the student from the room, it can be seen that the behavior may serve as a successful escape function. In some instances, the stimulus data may appear to have no consistent pattern, but if every time the behavior occurs it is followed with a consequence of giggling, crying, or other such peer reaction, it may be that the purpose of the behavior is to elicit the attention of peers.

Anecdotal Records Anecdotal records are another way of tracking information related to the occurrence or nonoccurrence of the behavior. These are narrative records kept by the observer documenting situations in which the student was involved. It is important to identify the conditions under which the behavior *does not* occur as well as the conditions under which the behavior does occur. Documentation that identifies a period of time when the behavior does not occur is valuable since it reinforces the notion that the behavior is under the student's control and serves a specific purpose. In addition, such information yields variables that can be analyzed to help identify that purpose. Anecdotal records provide descriptive accounts of events and behavior throughout the student's day.

Ecological/Program Questions An element frequently overlooked in traditional behavior interventions is that of examining environmental, or ecological, factors. Environmental factors may range from physical characteristics such as room temperature to psychological characteristics such as student expectations. A checklist of questions (adapted from Donnellan et al., 1988) regarding the student's interactions with the environmental setting and activities follows:

What Are the Student's Expectations of the Environment?   A group of fifth graders was asked this question on the first day of school and responded by saying that they expected to be safe, to be treated with respect, to learn new things, to make friends, to get work that was not too easy or too hard, to be listened to, to be given homework (but not too much), to find that the teacher would be nice, and so forth. One little boy said that he "expected the teacher to be the best she could be and to stay 'cool'!" If the student's expectations of the environment are not met or at least addressed with the student, inappropriate behaviors could result.

What Are the Expectations That Others Have of the Student?   The expectations of others can influence the behavior of students. On the one hand, if a student has been labeled as being difficult, adults typically expect that student to have challenging behaviors. If that is the expectation, the student is likely to live up to it. On the other hand, if there are no expectations of a student, it is also likely that inappropriate behaviors will occur. For example, one student in a class for students with significant disabilities was considered too disabled to participate in any structured activities. Being directed only to sit in the bean bag chair in the corner of the room, he began to exhibit the inappropriate behaviors of masturbation and head banging—he had access to no appropriate activities.

For some individuals with disabilities, the environmental or programmatic opportunity to be educated or employed alongside peers without disabilities is in itself enough to eliminate undesired behaviors. Edgerton and Kernan (1983) suggest that the way to predict the behavior of an individual is to first know where that individual is (e.g., in a library, he or she acts "library"; at the beach, he or she acts "beach"). It follows then that in a setting for people with behavior challenges, people will act behaviorally challenged. In a setting where behavior expectations and models are appropriate, it is more likely that individuals will act appropriately.

What Is the Interest Level of the Activity for the Student?   If an 11-year-old student is being asked to follow the old developmental curriculum of "put the blue bear on the blue square," one could expect some type of rebellion (perhaps blue bears being hurled across the room!). Activities of high interest to the student tend to be chronological age–appropriate and hold meaning, purpose, and/or fun for that student.

What Are the Materials Available to the Student?   Again, an examination of age appropriateness, interest, meaningfulness, and accessibility is in order. One adolescent was continually punished for stealing food from his classmates. It was soon learned that the student lived in a group home where the kitchen was kept locked. In addition, it was learned that the student's lunch was locked up at school, and he was required to "earn" the right to eat his lunch by sitting quietly at his desk throughout the morning. Giving access to snacks at home and to his lunch at the same time as his peers eliminated the need for stealing food.

Are There Any Environmental Pollutants Present? Fluorescent lights, loud noises, or temperature changes may all contribute to a student's discomfort. One boy became aggressive on days he suffered from allergies, which corresponded to the days the school lawns were mowed. The principal arranged for the lawns to be mowed after school hours, and the boy's aggressive behaviors no longer existed. Another young woman experienced extreme mood swings that were eventually found to be related to her consumption of a sweetener in diet sodas.

What Are the Physical Constraints of the Environment? Students who are diabetic may need to eat at times other than scheduled lunch hours. Students may have bathroom needs that do not match the designated break times of the classroom. One teacher was adamant about students remaining in their seats during the academic periods of the day. For one particular student who seemed unable to stay in any one place for very long, the most successful strategy was to designate several seats in the room for her and to give her freedom to select and change between a number of seats as she needed. This strategy can be appropriate because it is critical that all students learn that everyone's needs are different and that we all need to learn to respond to others' needs. For example, when a student with diabetes needs to eat a snack more often than other students or when a student with a bladder infection or smaller bladder needs to use the restroom more often, generally schools, classrooms, teachers, and students adjust and accommodate.

Additional considerations include the following:

- What choices are available to the student?
- When is the behavior most likely to occur? When is it least likely to occur?
- What are the student's interaction opportunities/patterns?
- What are the medications and schedules for medications? Are there other health-related issues?
- What are the typical eating/sleeping routines?
- What are the reinforcers available to the student, and when are they available?
- What previous behavior interventions have been tried? What was the result?

This information can be helpful in designing a more complete picture of the student and the relationship between environmental considerations and the occurrence of behaviors.

Communicative Functions Analysis Nearly all behavior serves some communicative function (Carr & Durand, 1985; Donnellan, Mirenda, Mesaros, & Fassbender, 1984; Durand & Crimmins, 1990). People use their behavior to get a message across to someone or to respond to a message given by someone. A great danger with using punishment to eliminate behaviors is that it tells the student exhibiting the behavior to stop communicating. Positive behavior support strategies provide the student with more appropriate behaviors with which to communicate.

Systematically observing the behaviors and attempting to interpret their communicative meanings is another component of functional assessment. Students with severe disabilities are often unable to communicate through verbal means and have not been provided with appropriate augmentative communication methods. These students have no choice but to try to get their needs met through their behavior. Frequently, inappropriate behaviors are much more effective for getting needs met than are appropriate behaviors! For example, the student who shouts out an answer in class is often attended to more frequently (either positively or negatively) than the student who quietly raises his or her hand. Extensive tools for analyzing the communicative function of behavior have been developed to more clearly identify how a student might be using behavior to communicate wants or needs (Donnellan et al., 1984; Schuler, Peck, Tomlinson, & Theimer, 1984).

It is important to recognize, however, that even people with good verbal skills may not be competent communicators. Many marital relationships are destroyed due to lack of communication. Verbal communication attempts may be overlooked or misunderstood, thereby causing a student to rely on behavioral communication attempts. Gaining an understanding of the communicative functions of the behavior will assist in determining the appropriate support plans.

Scatter Plots   One tool often used in functional assessments is the scatter plot (Touchette, MacDonald, & Langer, 1985). The scatter plot (see Figure 6 for a version adapted by Anderson, Mesaros, & Neary, 1991) is a data collection instrument that simplifies efforts to determine when the behavior does and does not occur. This instrument is one that is easy for teachers to use and provides an important baseline of information from which further analysis can be developed. The scatter plot is completed by documenting time periods and activities down the left hand column of the data sheet. Specific dates are labeled across the top of the sheet. Notations are made in each box any time the behavior occurs.

A completed scatter plot allows a more precise pinpointing of behaviors. For example, in Figure 7, the behavior consistently occurs between 10:00 A.M. to 10:30 A.M. and never between 2:00 and 2:30 P.M. An analysis of the differences between activities, choices, level of participation, medication schedule, and peer interaction during those times can be conducted. In addition, the second half of social studies should be examined, as the scatter plot demonstrates that to be a more difficult period of time than the first half of social studies. Further analysis can also consist of breaking the time slots into smaller increments (similar to time sampling) to determine more specific triggers for the behavior. Information

Student: _____   Starting Date: _____

☐ = No occurrence   / = 1 occurrence   ■ = More than 1 occurrence

Time of day	Activity	M	T	W	Th	F	M	T	W	Th	F	M	T	W	Th

Figure 6.   Scatter plot. (Adapted from Anderson, Mesaros, & Neary, 1991.)

Student: _____   Starting Date: _____

□ = No occurrence   / = 1 occurrence   ■ = More than 1 occurrence

Time of day	Activity	M	T	W	Th	F	M	T	W	Th	F	M	T	W	Th
8:30–9:00	Opening			/											
9:00–9:30	Journals							/							
9:30–10:00	Reading Groups														
10:00–10:30	Math	■	/	/	■	/	■	■	/	■	/	/	■	■	■
10:30–11:00	Recess					/									
11:00–11:30	Social Studies	/						/							
11:30–12:00	Social Studies		■	/	/		■				/	■		■	
12:00–12:30	Lunch												■		
12:30–1:00	Silent Reading	/	■		/			■		/	/	■		■	
1:00–1:30	Science							/							■
1:30–2:00	P.E.			/											
2:00–2:30	Music														
2:30–3:00	Health			■				/							
3:00–3:30	Jobs				/				■		/				

Figure 7.   Sample of completed scatter plot. (Adapted from Anderson, Mesaros, & Neary, 1991.)

gathered in a scatter plot can yield hypotheses regarding the function of the behavior that may relate to specific activities, times of day, environments/settings, task demands, peers, choice and social opportunities, and so forth.

Behavioral Maps   A behavioral map (Ittelson, Rivlin, & Prochansky, 1976) is another way of collecting data on the occurrence of target behaviors. The behavioral map adapted from Anderson et al. (1991) (see Figure 8) graphically delineates the configuration of a particular setting or settings. Each time the target behavior occurs, a mark is made on the map in the spot representative of the place and time in which the behavior occurred. An analysis of the places and times in which the behavior occurs can yield information from which more specific data can be collected or may suggest hypotheses as to the function of the behavior. One classroom teacher used the behavioral map tool and realized that the inappropriate behavior of a young girl occurred primarily at the girl's desk, when

Behavioral Map

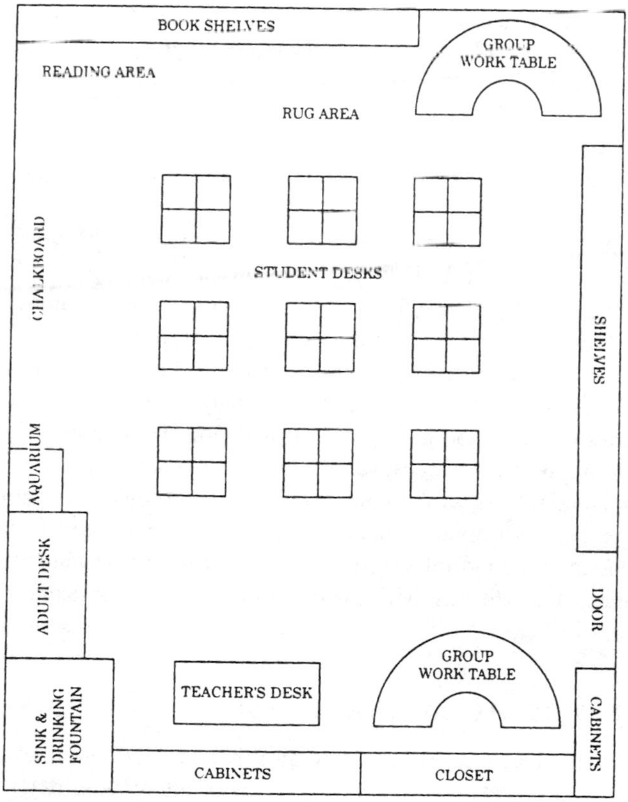

Figure 8.   Behavioral Map. (Adapted from Anderson, Mesaros, & Neary, 1991.)

the class lined up, and during physical education warm-up exercises. An analysis of these specific settings led to the awareness that she sat between two particular boys at her desk, was assigned to line up between them, and was also assigned to the row next to them in physical education. A change in seating placements, along with supervised positive interactions with these two boys, resulted in a significant decrease in the behaviors.

Motivation Assessment Scale   Durand and Crimmins (1990) developed a standardized rating scale that aids in the classification of potential functions of a behavior. The 16-question scale sorts potential functions of behavior into four major categories: sensory reinforcement (essentially things that feel good), escape/avoidance (attempts to get away from settings, tasks, situations, specific people), social attention (either positive or negative), and obtaining tangible rewards (food, objects, etc.). Although the Motivation Assessment Scale can provide some key information for determining the function of specific behaviors, further observation and additional data collection instruments are necessary to develop hypotheses as to why the student is choosing to escape or avoid certain situations, or what tangibles the student is attempting to secure.

Learning Characteristics/Modality Assessment   Another piece of information that is an important element of a functional assessment is a determination of learning characteristics. Traditionally, learning characteristics have focused on three modalities: visual (learns by seeing, demonstration), kinesthetic (learns by doing), and auditory (learns by hearing information and instructions from self or others).

Determining the learning characteristics of a student provides valuable information regarding a student's reaction to the presentation of information and can assist in generating strategies and suggestions for presenting information in the future. One such analysis determined that a particular student learned best through visual information. He became so frustrated and upset by cues, information, and demands constantly given to him verbally that he frequently became aggressive toward the person giving the information. He had also destroyed televisions, radios, and stereos because of their auditory messages. After completing the district's modality assessment instrument and thereby determining his need to learn and process information visually, his teacher was able to support him by providing instruction and information through primarily visual means (pictures, notes, objects, etc.). He was then less frustrated, which eliminated his need to be so aggressive.

HYPOTHESIS DEVELOPMENT AND TESTING

After the functional assessment information is compiled, an analysis of that information is conducted. This analysis consists of attempts to determine the specific functions or purposes that the target behaviors serve for the student. In reviewing the functional assessment information, support personnel look for patterns in specific events that seem to trigger the behavior or consequences that appear to maintain the behavior. From these patterns, hypotheses can be developed as to when and why the student is exhibiting the behaviors (Carr, Robinson, Taylor, & Carlson, 1990; Durand, 1990). In other words, support personnel begin to assign meaning to the behaviors. An example of hypothesis development follows.

Lucas, a preschooler with autism, hits and kicks adult staff when they attempt to take him to the bathroom. The functional assessment revealed that Lucas does not use verbal communication skills and has no augmentative communication method but does know sign language for BATHROOM. The assessment also indicated that every time Lucas used the sign for bathroom, a staff person attempted to accompany him to the bathroom, at which time he behaved aggressively toward that person. Scatter plots and behavioral maps were completed to examine his use of a signed request for the bathroom. These tools identified that Lucas used the sign during many different times of the day, at many different locations in the classroom, and on the playground. A hypothesis was developed that perhaps Lucas was using the only sign he knew (BATHROOM) for all of his request and denial functions. For example, if Lucas wanted to play with the blocks, he would sign BATHROOM. If he wanted to leave the music group, he would sign BATHROOM. In each of these situations, a staff member would take Lucas to the bathroom, which would anger him because he had no desire to use the bathroom yet had no other communication method.

A second hypothesis for Lucas might be that he indeed needed to use the bathroom but he did not want any adults to escort him. Therefore, when he signed BATHROOM and a staff person moved to take him, he became angry and aggressive toward the staff person because he wanted to be independent in this activity.

A third hypothesis is that Lucas was displaying aggressive behavior in order to obtain physical contact with an adult. Through an analysis of what occurred following the aggressive behavior (consequence), it was learned that the staff had been physically restraining Lucas by holding him tightly against their bodies so that he would not be able to hit or kick them.

Once the hypothesis or hypotheses have been generated, the next step in the process is hypothesis testing, which helps to determine if the assumptions made regarding the functions of the behaviors are correct. Hypothesis testing requires that the support personnel manipulate variables in the student's environment and measure the effect of those manipulations on the behavior. Hypothesis testing typically focuses on changing stimulus/antecedent variables (things that happen prior to the occurrence of the behavior) or on changing consequence variables (things that happen after the occurrence of the behavior).

Using the three hypotheses related to Lucas, both stimulus and consequence manipulations are necessary to test the hypotheses. The first hypothesis (Lucas uses the sign for bathroom for other purposes) requires a test through stimulus/antecedent manipulation. For a designated period of time, when Lucas uses the sign for bathroom, staff will not take him to the bathroom but will instead attempt to determine what else he might be saying and act upon those possible communicative messages. For example, if Lucas signs BATHROOM while in the play area, staff will offer him the blocks or a number of other toys that he might be requesting. If Lucas proceeds to be aggressive, then this hypothesis is unlikely to be correct. If Lucas does not become aggressive, there is some likelihood that this is a correct hypothesis.

In the second hypothesis (Lucas wants to use the bathroom, but he wants to do so independently), stimulus/antecedent manipulation is also used for testing the hypothesis. In this case, every time Lucas signs BATHROOM, a staff member hands him the bathroom pass and does not intervene further, allowing him to walk to the restroom on his own. If Lucas behaves aggressively in spite of these changes, this is likely to be an incorrect hypothesis.

The third hypothesis (Lucas desires physical contact with staff) requires a test using consequence manipulation. Once Lucas signs BATHROOM, staff are instructed to take him to the bathroom. If Lucas begins to hit and kick, the staff person does not restrain him but moves away, preventing physical contact and essentially ignoring the behavior. If the hypothesis is correct, in this situation the aggressive behavior is likely to immediately increase because Lucas will be trying even harder to obtain the physical contact. If the behavior decreases within a short period of time, the physical contact hypothesis is probably incorrect.

It is important to realize that there may be more than one function for any given behavior or class of behaviors (e.g., hitting and kicking are two different behaviors but may be considered a behavior class, meaning that they are often exhibited together and serve the same function). If a student has a small repertoire of behaviors that are successful, he or she may use the behavior or behaviors to serve many purposes. It is possible then that more than one hypothesis may prove to be correct. If this is the case, support plans and intervention strategies need to be developed to address each of the functions of the behavior.

Hypothesis testing should be done with caution, as there are some practical and ethical issues to consider (Durand & Crimmins, 1990). Using manipulations that cause dangerous behaviors to increase and consequently may cause harm to the student or others should be avoided. Testing hypotheses may also require time and effort from staff and therefore interrupt the normal routines of the classroom or other environment. However, this expenditure of time and effort in the short run may pay off greatly as behavior support plans are implemented and significant changes in behavior do occur.

If none of the hypotheses are supported by the tests, two factors need to be considered. First, the testing situation should be reexamined. Do the testing manipulations really reflect the hypothesis, and are they being clearly and consistently implemented? Second, if the procedures are accurate, it may mean that the hypotheses themselves are incorrect. In this case, support personnel will need to reanalyze the assessment data, and they may also need to collect further information to determine more accurate hypotheses.

IDENTIFYING AND ENCOURAGING ALTERNATIVE BEHAVIORS

Once there is an understanding of the purpose or function that a behavior serves (through hypothesis development and testing), support personnel can begin to identify options for addressing the function. In some cases, the function of a behavior may be addressed by simply changing environmental conditions. For example, if the function of a behavior is a reaction to a new medication, then a physician should be consulted to change the medication, the dosage, or the times of ingestion. Lighting, noise pollution, seating arrangements, social opportunities, schedules, curriculum activities, choice-making opportunities, and other ecological and contextual variables may all be adapted to meet the needs of the student (Brown, 1991; Dunlap, Kern-Dunlap, Clarke, & Robbins, 1991; Favell & Reid, 1988; Haring & Kennedy, 1990; Meyer & Evans, 1989), thereby reducing the presence of the target behaviors.

One important difference in positive behavior support strategies, however, is that simply eliminating the presence of target behaviors is not enough. A major component of this process is to provide a student with an increased skill repertoire so that he or she can address needs in an appropriate manner even if the contextual variables have not been addressed. This process, also referred to as positive programming (LaVigna & Donnellan, 1986; LaVigna, Willis, & Donnellan, 1989) or an educative approach (Evans & Meyer, 1985), provides a student with specific skills or alternative behaviors that will allow him or her to get needs met effectively.

As support personnel begin to identify alternative behaviors for the student, several factors are important to consider. First, the skills and behaviors already in the student's repertoire should be determined. It is often easier to increase a skill already in the current repertoire (or at least a related skill) than it is to teach a new skill. Other considerations are the likelihood that the student will master the new skill and how long that process will take. If it is believed that skill mastery will take a long period of time, some intermediary reinforcement strategies or skills may need to be developed. Perhaps most important, support personnel should consider the functional equivalence of the alternative behavior.

Functional Equivalence

Functional equivalence refers to an alternative behavior meeting the same needs as the target behavior, and meeting those needs as effectively and as efficiently (Carr, 1988; Carr et al., 1994). In order for a student to progress from the old inappropriate behavior (which was very successful for getting needs met) to an alternative behavior, the alternative behavior must be as powerful in achieving the purpose of the behavior (the reinforcer) and must be as easy or easier for the student to perform. For example, Maria has successfully obtained the attention of adults in her environment by hitting them forcefully with a closed fist. If Maria is taught to type, letter by letter, on her communication board, "Excuse me, may I please ask you a question?", she will soon realize that it is much faster and easier to hit someone than it is to spell out her request. In addition, if she is taught to tap a person on the shoulder as an appropriate way to get attention, and that person does not attend to her or tells her to wait a minute and not interrupt, Maria will return to her more successful strategy of hitting forcefully. Therefore, a strategy that allows Maria's shoulder tap to be attended to immediately might succeed for initially reducing the hitting. After she has enjoyed success with this strategy, she can be taught to wait appropriately when someone responds with, "I'll be with you in a minute," or other such remarks.

Instructional Strategies and Reinforcement

Identifying Reinforcers   To support the success of the alternative behavior, support personnel must carefully consider the instructional strategies that will be used in teaching the new skill and must determine powerful reinforcers for the demonstration of that new behavior. The obvious reinforcer for the new behavior is the reinforcer or consequence that maintained the old behavior. In order to support the acquisition of the alternative behavior or skill, therefore, it may be necessary to provide additional or more powerful reinforcers to strengthen the student's desire to perform the new skill.

In addition, diverse reinforcers are important for behaviors that naturally elicit a consequence that is undesirable given the time and place of the behavior. For example, if a target behavior such as shooting spit wads occurs for the purpose of eliciting a negative reaction from a peer or the teacher, it is not appropriate to teach a new behavior that will continue to elicit such a reaction. Therefore, it may be necessary to determine a reinforcer for that individual that is even more powerful than the negative attention reaction. Reinforcers and reinforcement power differ from individual to individual. One student may be very motivated by teacher praise, while another might be embarrassed by such overt attention.

One strategy for determining reinforcers for a particular student is to complete a reinforcement inventory, which is a compilation of potential reinforcers for a person as determined through interviews with that student, peers, parents, and significant others. In addition, direct observation of the student's activity preferences also provides valuable information. If a student frequently draws pictures, then that may be considered a reinforcer for that student. If he or she often chooses to sit on the couch and do nothing, then perhaps sitting on the couch and doing nothing may be reinforcing. By completing a reinforcement inventory, we can be more confident in the power of the reinforcers that are being used to support alternative behavior acquisition. It is helpful to remember, however, that as individuals gain more skills and have more opportunities and experiences their reinforcement preferences will change and evolve, thereby requiring the use of reinforcers to change as well (see Chapter 6 for additional discussion of reinforcers).

Specific Positive Procedures Some students will exhibit inappropriate behaviors at such high frequency rates that it almost seems impossible for any instruction to occur. Other behaviors have such levels of intensity or duration that they create very dangerous situations, and teaching seems secondary to crisis management. For example, continuous head banging, which causes tissue or structural damage to a student, must be immediately and directly addressed (however, even situations that are this extreme do not warrant the use of punishing procedures). In these situations, it may be necessary to rely on specific positive procedures, like those described by Donnellan et al. (1988). Basic strategies and definitions of these procedures provided are these:

- Differential reinforcement of other behavior (DRO): reinforcement for engaging in any behavior other than the target behavior for a specified interval of time
- Differential reinforcement of low rates of responding (DRL): reinforcement if the rate of the targeted behavior is lower than an established criterion within a given time period
- Differential reinforcement of alternative behaviors (DRA): selective reinforcement of behaviors that are topographically different from the target behavior
- Stimulus control: reinforcement of a behavior exhibited in the presence of specific stimuli, thereby increasing the likelihood of the behavior's occurrence
- Instructional control: an example of stimulus control in which a desired behavior occurs in the presence of or following the presentation of an explicitly communicated direction, request, or cue/prompt
- Stimulus change: the sudden introduction of a new stimulus or a dramatic alteration of the existing or expected stimulus conditions, which results in a temporary reduction of the target behavior
- Stimulus satiation: providing the reinforcer, which has been identified as maintaining the target behavior, in a continuous and noncontingent manner such that the effectiveness of the reinforcer is weakened, thereby reducing the rate of the target behavior

These procedures have been highly successful in the reduction of inappropriate behavior through differentially reinforcing appropriate behaviors, or in some instances, reinforcing the nonexistence of the inappropriate behaviors (Carr, Robinson, & Taylor, 1990).

Categories of Alternative Behaviors

Alternative behaviors often fall into one of several broad categories: communication skills, social skills and assertiveness training, coping strategies and relaxation, and choice- and decision-making strategies.

Communication Skills   Frequently, inappropriate behaviors can be assigned communicative functions; therefore, communication is perhaps the most common area targeted for alternative behaviors (Carr & Durand, 1985; Donnellan et al., 1984; Doss & Reichle, 1991; Durand & Carr, 1991). This category consists of improving verbal skills and competence, or it may mean the development and implementation of augmentative communication methods, such as the use of sign language, picture symbols, or an electronic communication device. Chapter 9 provides a more detailed discussion of communication issues and strategies.

Social Skills and Assertiveness Training   Social skills and assertiveness training relate to the communication category as a functional outcome of communication. Inclusive settings support the opportunity for social interaction; however, at the same time plans for specific instruction for an increased array of social skills must be developed and implemented. Opportunities for students to participate with peers in educational, employment, recreation, leisure, and other community settings should be supported with instruction in the skills necessary for students to participate as fully as possible. Specific training in assertiveness and self-advocacy may also reduce the need for inappropriate behavior.

Coping Strategies and Relaxation Techniques   In addition to tangible skill development, some students may benefit from learning coping strategies and/or relaxation techniques (Cautella & Grodin, 1978; Zipkin, 1985). For example, Pam is a young woman who, when asked to wait in long lines at the high school cafeteria, would begin slapping herself in the face and rocking back and forth. One strategy for supporting Pam was to prevent her from having to wait in long lines by manipulating her schedule. She could go to the cafeteria before or after the other students were there. Even if manipulating the contextual variables were a helpful strategy, however, it was not possible to assure that Pam would never have to wait in line. Therefore, it was necessary to teach her coping strategies to utilize while waiting in lines. Pam was taught coping strategies that most people use when waiting in lines: she learned to look at the lunch choices, read the menu, talk to others in line, count her money, file her fingernails, and so forth. Although Pam still did not enjoy waiting in line, this range of options at least provided her with the opportunity to participate in some type of appropriate activity.

Relaxation strategies are important skills in many situations as well. The ability to recognize that tension is building and then have options for easing that tension is a valuable skill. Deep breathing, muscle relaxation, getting a drink of water, or going for a short walk are all appropriate strategies that can often prevent the need for aggressive or explosive behavior incidents.

Choice- and Decision-Making Strategies   The importance of choice making, particularly for persons with significant disabilities, is often overlooked. However, there has been some demonstration that increasing choice-making skills and opportunities can reduce the need for inappropriate behavior (Dyer,

Dunlap, & Winterling, 1990; Zeph, 1986). Choice-making encompasses activities and environments directly and indirectly related to the student, such as choice of food and drink, times to eat, daily schedule and activities within that schedule, choice of clothing, whom to sit next to, Halloween costumes, and so forth. This type of empowerment provides an acceptable alternative to the power of inappropriate behavior.

Adjusting contextual variables, identifying and teaching functionally equivalent alternative behaviors, and providing opportunities and reinforcement for the use of those behaviors allow a student access to a quality lifestyle. By enhancing and supporting this lifestyle, support personnel can reduce the need for more traditional techniques for "managing" behaviors.

CRISIS MANAGEMENT

There will be occasions when a behavior occurs unexpectedly that is potentially dangerous to a student or to those around him or her. Such behavior requires the use of crisis management procedures to prevent any serious injury or property damage from occurring. Severe behavior challenges do not warrant the use of aversive (punishing) interventions. Willis and LaVigna (1989) delineate the following steps of crisis management:

1. Eliminate precipitating events:

    Remove seductive objects
    Relocate people
    Remove unnecessary demands/requests
    Change the location or time of activities
    Rearrange the environment

2. Interrupt the behavior chain (e.g., some behaviors begin with pacing followed by swearing, followed by aggression; the intent is to intervene and interrupt at the stage of pacing, thereby proactively preventing the aggression):

    Control proximity (simply being near the student)
    Inject humor (breaking the tension)
    Control instruction (get the person involved in a favored activity or redirect him or her in some way)
    Support communication attempts
    Facilitate relaxation
    Provide a stimulus change (introduce a novel request, interaction, activity)

3. Geographical containment (using the immediate environment to prevent potential harm; e.g., positioning yourself behind a table while working to calm the person down)

4. Emergency physical containment—to be used as a last resort in emergency situations only:

   If there is a likelihood that such an emergency may present itself, all staff should be trained in the appropriate use of physical restraint techniques.

   Support personnel need to understand that *crisis management techniques are not considered positive behavior support techniques.* If a crisis management procedure is used with a student on more than two occasions, support personnel are relying on these techniques as behavior management strategies and must begin the positive behavior support process. Again, a crisis management procedure only serves the purpose of preventing injury during the time of the emergency. Positive behavior support procedures focus on teaching adaptive skills and enhancing the environment so that dangerous situations are prevented.

DEVELOPING BEHAVIOR SUPPORT PLANS

The purpose of a behavior support plan is to delineate the positive behavior support process for a specific student as described in this chapter, and to do so in a clear manner so that all staff members, family members, and others can participate knowledgeably in its implementation. The components of a behavior support plan (adapted from Anderson et al., 1991) are as follows:

1. Concise description of the target behavior and the conditions under which it is likely to occur
2. Summary statement of the findings from a functional assessment (with actual data attached to the plan)
3. Hypotheses as to the function of the behavior and the method and results of the hypothesis testing
4. Suggested lifestyle enhancements (supported living situations, inclusive neighborhood school placement, supported employment, increased variety of environments and activities, etc.)
5. Environmental or contextual changes (curriculum, instructional strategies, classroom arrangements, environmental pollutants, materials adaptations, schedules, choices, etc.)
6. Specific positive procedures (DRO, DRL, DRA, stimulus control, stimulus satiation, stimulus change, etc.), if necessary.
7. Alternative behaviors with instructional strategies and plans (communication skills, social skills and assertiveness training, coping skills and relaxation, choice- and decision-making, other functionally equivalent skills)
8. Crisis management procedures (nonaversive, nonintrusive procedures)

Figure 9 consists of a completed behavior support plan.

Behavior Support Plan

Plan developed for: Jamshid

Developed by: Jamshid's father, Ms. Newbury (5th-grade teacher), Mrs. Priest (special education support teacher), Mr. Shirai (classroom aide), Ms. Chavez (vice principal)

Date of plan approval: July 27, 1994

Description of target behavior: Jamshid will squeal at a loud sharp pitch then hit and/or push his peers without disabilities during academic periods of the day.

Functional assessment findings: Anecdotal records indicate that behavior is most likely to occur during academic activities, whether during individual work or cooperative groups. Adapted scatter plot reveals behavior occurs near the end of each activity period. A specific S-R-C chart indicates that the trigger appears to be peers attempting to collect his work, build upon his work, or edit his work.

Hypothesis and test information: Last year in his Special Day Class, many of the tasks Jamshid completed were given to another group to sort into recycling bins or to take apart to be reused as an activity the following day. The function of Jamshid's behavior seems to be to protect his tangible work from destruction. This was tested by allowing Jamshid to keep his own work after completing it individually or within groups. On those days, Jamshid did not hit or push peers.

Lifestyle enhancements: Maintain his full inclusion with same age peers. At home Jamshid will be given his own toy chest to keep his things separate from his siblings and share when he wants to.

Environmental changes: Jamshid will be allowed to initially put his completed work in a folder in his desk to be checked by the teacher and returned to the folder after school each day. Jamshid will be allowed to collect work from others throughout the day and will also return checked work to others. The next step will be for him to collect his own work and turn it in with the other students' work, at which time the aide will check it and return it to him immediately. In cooperative groups, he will participate in reporting by holding up or pointing to his contribution to the project. He will be allowed to keep the product at his desk as soon as the group is over and then after a 10-minute period he will be assisted in taking the project to the work display table with the other group projects. This will eventually be faded to the same procedure the rest of the class follows.

Specific positive procedures: Not necessary; however, the reinforcement inventory suggests that Jamshid likes to look at books in the reading corner, likes orange soda, and likes playing with toy figures such as space creatures.

Alternative behaviors and instructional strategies: Jamshid will be taught to improve his interactions with peers by increasing the number and type of symbols in his communication wallet. Existing symbols consist of objects and people he is interested in. New symbols will represent requests, denials, and feelings. New symbols will be taught by systematically pairing symbol use with teacher verbalization of the symbol and peer support by immediately responding to the interaction. Specific instructional strategies will be delineated on an attached sheet.

Crisis management procedures: If Jamshid squeals, he is likely to follow with hitting or punching a peer. Should Jamshid begin to squeal, an adult will quickly intervene by physically standing between Jamshid and the peer and facilitating Jamshid's communication, asking peers to respond. Should Jamshid follow through with a hit or push, the adult will deflect the attempt with his or her arm and follow through with communication symbols.

Figure 9.   Sample behavior support plan.

SUMMARY

Traditional behavior management practices have focused on attempting to control the behavior of students through consequence manipulation. For example, if a student behaved appropriately, he or she would receive some type of reward for good behavior. If a student behaved inappropriately, he or she would be punished for that behavior. The intent was that, over time, the rewards would win out and the inappropriate behavior would disappear. The process focused solely on eliminating behaviors.

The intent of positive behavior support procedures is to take a proactive, skill building, life enhancement approach to behavior change. Although consequence manipulation through the use of differential reinforcement may be a component of positive behavior support, the process is far more comprehensive in nature. By gaining an understanding of the student as an individual, assigning meaning to the functions of behaviors, analyzing those functions, and providing students with functionally equivalent skills to meet their needs, positive behavior support practices prevent the need for inappropriate behaviors. Regardless of the severity of the behavior, once the function is determined, environmental issues addressed, and alternative behaviors taught, there is no longer a reason for the student to exhibit such behaviors. A further intent of this process is to facilitate an increased quality of life for students so that their lifestyle reflects that which is culturally valued and appreciated within the context of the community in which they live.

REFERENCES

Alberto, P.A., & Troutman, A.C. (1990). *Applied behavior analysis for teachers* (3rd ed.). New York: Merrill/Macmillan.

Anderson, J.L., Mesaros, R.A., & Neary, T. (1991). *Community referenced non-aversive behavior management trainer's manual*, Vol. 1. Washington, DC: National Institute on Disability and Rehabilitation Research.

Bodenhamer, G. (1983). *Back in control*. Englewood Cliffs, NJ: Prentice Hall.

Brown, F. (1991). Creative daily scheduling: A nonintrusive approach to challenging behaviors in community residences. *Journal of The Association for Persons with Severe Handicaps, 16*, 75–84.

Camara, D.H. (1984). *It's midnight, Lord*. Washington, DC: The Pastoral Press.

Canter, L., & Canter, M. (1992). *Assertive discipline*. Santa Monica, CA: Lee Canter & Associates.

Carr, E.G. (1988). Functional equivalence as a mechanism of response generalization. In R.H. Horner, G. Dunlap, & R.L. Koegel (Eds.), *Generalization and maintenance: Lifestyle changes in applied settings* (pp. 22–41). Baltimore: Paul H. Brookes Publishing Co.

Carr, E.G., & Durand, V.M. (1985). Reducing behavior problems through functional communication training. *Journal of Applied Behavior Analysis, 18*, 111–126.

Carr, E.G., Levin, L., McConnachie, G., Carlson, J.I., Kemp, D.C., & Smith, C.E. (1994). *Communication-based intervention for problem behavior: A user's guide for producing positive change*. Baltimore: Paul H. Brookes Publishing Co.

Carr, E.G., Robinson, S., & Palumbo, L.W. (1990). The wrong issues: Aversive vs. non-aversive treatment. The right issues: Functional vs. nonfunctional treatment. In A. Repp & N. Singh (Eds.), *Perspectives on the use of nonaversive and aversive interventions for persons with developmental disabilities* (pp. 361–379). Sycamore, IL: Sycamore Press.

Carr, E.G., Robinson, S., Taylor, J.C., & Carlson, J.I. (1990). *Positive approaches to the treatment of severe behavior problems in persons with developmental disabilities: A review and analysis of reinforcement and stimulus-based procedures* (Monograph No. 4). Seattle, WA: The Association for Persons with Severe Handicaps.

Cautela, J.R., & Grodin, J. (1978). *Relaxation: A comprehensive manual for adults, children, and children with special needs.* Champaign, IL: Research Press.

Donnellan, A.M., LaVigna, G.W., Negri-Shoultz, N., & Fassbender, L.L. (1988). *Progress without punishment; Effective approaches for learners with behavior problems.* New York: Teachers College Press.

Donnellan, A.M., Mirenda, P.L., Mesaros, R.A., & Fassbender, L.L. (1984). Analyzing the communicative functions of aberrant behavior. *Journal of The Association for Persons with Severe Handicaps, 9,* 201–212.

Doss, S., & Reichle, J. (1991). Replacing excess behavior with an initial communication repertoire. In J. Reichle, J. York, & J. Sigafoos, *Implementing augmentative and alternative communication: Strategies for learners with severe disabilities* (pp. 215–237). Baltimore: Paul H. Brookes Publishing Co.

Dunlap, G., Kern-Dunlap, L., Clarke, S., & Robbins, F.R. (1991). Functional assessment, curricular revision, and severe behavior problems. *Journal of Applied Behavior Analysis, 24,* 387–397.

Durand, V.M. (1990). *Severe behavior problems: A functional communication approach.* New York: Guilford Press.

Durand, V.M., & Carr, E.G. (1991). Functional communication training to reduce challenging behavior: Maintenance and application in new settings. *Journal of Applied Behavior Analysis, 24,* 251–264.

Durand, V.M., & Crimmins, D.B. (1990). Assessment. In V.M. Durand (Ed.), *Severe behavior problems: A functional communication training approach* (pp. 31–82). New York: Guilford Press.

Dyer, K., Dunlap, G., & Winterling, V. (1990). Effects of choicemaking on the serious problem behaviors of students with severe handicaps. *Journal of Applied Behavior Analysis, 23,* 515–524.

Edgerton, R.B., & Kernan, K.T. (1983). Introduction. In K. Kernan, M. Begab, & R. Edgerton (Eds.), *Environments and behavior: The adaptation of mentally retarded persons.* Baltimore: University Park Press.

Evans, I.M., & Meyer, L.H. (1985). *An educative approach to behavior problems: A practical decision model for intervention with severely handicapped learners.* Baltimore: Paul H. Brookes Publishing Co.

Favell, J.E., & Reid, D.H. (1988). Generalizing and maintaining improvement in problem behavior. In R.H. Horner, G. Dunlap, & R.L. Koegel (Eds.), *Generalization and maintenance: Life-style changes in applied settings* (pp. 171–196). Baltimore: Paul H. Brookes Publishing Co.

Foxx, R.M., McMorrow, M., Bittle, R., & Bechtel, S. (1986). The successful treatment of a dually diagnosed deaf man's aggression with a program that included contingent electric shock. *Behavior Therapy, 17,* 170–186.

Ginott, H.G. (1972). *Teacher and child.* New York: Macmillan.

Haring, T.G., & Kennedy, C.H. (1990). Contextual control of problem behavior in students with severe disabilities. *Journal of Applied Behavior Analysis, 23,* 235–243.

Horner, R.H., O'Neill, R.E., & Flannery, K.B. (1993). Effective behavior support plans. In M. Snell (Ed.), *Instruction of students with severe disabilities* (4th ed.). New York: Macmillan.

Ittelson, W.H., Rivlin, L.G., & Prochansky, H.M. (1976). The use of behavioral maps in environmental psychology. In H.M. Prochansky, L.G. Rivlin, & W.H. Ittleson (Eds.), *Environmental psychology: People and their physical setting.* New York: Holt, Rinehart, & Winston.

LaVigna, G.W., & Donnellan, A.M. (1986). *Alternatives to punishment: Solving behavior problems with non-aversive strategies.* New York: John Wiley & Sons.

LaVigna, G.W., Willis, T.J., & Donnellan, A.M. (1989). The role of positive programming in behavioral treatment. In E. Cipani (Ed.), *The treatment of severe behavior disorders: Behavior analysis approaches* (Monograph No. 12) (pp. 59–83). Washington, DC: American Association on Mental Retardation.

Meyer, L.H., & Evans, I.M. (1989). *Nonaversive intervention for behavior problems: A manual for home and community.* Baltimore: Paul H. Brookes Publishing Co.

Quilitich, R.H., & Risely, T.R. (1973). The effects of play materials on social play. *Journal of Applied Behavior Analysis, 6*, 573–578.

Schuler, A.L., Peck, C.A., Tomlinson, C., & Theimer, R.K. (1984). Communication interview. In C.A. Peck, A.L. Schuler, C. Tomlinson, R.K. Theimer, T. Haring, & M. Semmel (Eds.), *The social competence curriculum project: A guide to instructional programming for social and communicative interactions* (pp. 43–52). Santa Barbara: University of California–Santa Barbara.

Singh, N.N., Dawson, M.J., & Gregory, P.R. (1980). Suppression of chronic hyperventilation using response-contingent aromatic ammonia. *Behavior Therapy, 11*, 561–566.

Touchette, P.E., MacDonald, R.F., & Langer, S.M. (1985). A scatter plot for identifying stimulus control of problem behavior. *Journal of Applied Behavior Analysis, 18*, 343–351.

Willis, T.J., & LaVigna, G.W. (1989). *Emergency management guidelines.* Los Angeles: Institute for Applied Behavior Analysis.

Zeph, L.A. (1986, November). *The CHOICE curriculum model: A positive programming and intervention strategy for students with severe behavior problems.* Paper presented at the 1986 Annual Conference of The Association for Persons with Severe Handicaps, San Francisco.

Zipkin, D. (1985). Relaxation techniques for handicapped children: A review of the literature. *Journal of Special Education, 19*(3), 283–288.

8

MOTOR AND PERSONAL CARE SKILLS

CHRISTINA H. KIMM, MARY A. FALVEY,
KATHRYN D. BISHOP, AND RICHARD L. ROSENBERG

Progess in the development of technology and other adaptations has increased the accessibility of a variety of classrooms, schools, and community settings and allowed children and adults with significant disabilities to participate in a wider range of inclusive activities (Helle, 1988; Howard & Williams, 1991; Lahm, 1989; Schery & O'Connor, 1992). As students with disabilities take part in general education classrooms, educators, including related services professionals, recognize the importance of collaboration and the need for integrated approaches to providing services (Rainforth, York, & Macdonald, 1992). Through collaboration among physical therapists, occupational therapists, and teachers in conjunction with parents and students, students' motor and personal care skill needs can be met more effectively within general education classrooms than in a segregated therapy room (Giangreco, 1986).

All individuals, including those who may require full or partial assistance, have the right to attend neighborhood schools, live with a family as a child or in a home of their choice as an adult, and be an active part of their home and neighborhood communities. The basic goal of education should be to prepare students to handle the rights and responsibilities of adult life and to help them develop the skills that support a life of high quality. This preparation can be facilitated through instructional strategies focusing on motor and personal care skills. All students can increase their motor skills and care for their personal needs as independently as possible in general education settings so that they function as an active part of a larger familial and societal unit.

This chapter provides educators and parents with a practical guide to working together to assess and implement instruction in the functional aspects of motor and personal care skills for students with significant disabilities in inclusive settings. Personal care skills, such as hygiene and appearance as well as motor skills, are important to increase self-esteem, promote positive social interaction, and maintain physical health and well-being. This information is based upon the premise that instructing students in inclusive settings is the most effective means for increasing motor and personal care skills to facilitate increased independence and interdependence in all areas of life.

MOTOR SKILLS

Knowledge of the physical conditions affecting each student enables the educator to provide a comprehensive instructional program facilitating that student's maximum independence and interdependence in society. *Independence* refers to the ability to perform certain activities by oneself without assistance from others. For example, if a child can walk to the cafeteria independently, it means that he or she can do so without the supervision or assistance of others. *Interdependence* refers to the ability to perform certain activities with the cooperation of others. For example, while completing a home economics class project about preparing a meal, every student takes an active part in the project: some make a menu and a shopping list, others go grocery shopping, another prepares the meal, another sets the table, and so on. Finally, they finish the lunch and clean up successfully because everyone completed a part of the project. All the students in this home economics class project depend on one another to be successful. Too often education has overemphasized the need to increase students' independence and de-emphasized the need for students to develop interdependence. This chapter, as well as other chapters in this book, is designed to provide a better balance between the need for students to develop independent and interdependent skills.

To obtain information about a student's physical characteristics, it is essential that educators become familiar with each student as a complete individual, as opposed to focusing solely on a student's physical disabilities. Therefore, information should be gathered on an individual's functional abilities in various learning environments such as home, classrooms, schools, and communities. To assist families and educators in understanding information provided by medical experts and others, brief and nontechnical definitions of the most common terms used to discuss and describe physical disabilities and their related manifestations are provided in Table 1. Physical therapists, occupational therapists, and physicians also use a number of terms to denote specific techniques and procedures related to positioning or movement.

Full inclusion of students with severe disabilities means their involvement in all school activities with their peers without disabilities, placement in general education classrooms, and participation in extracurricular activities. Students should be attending schools that are accessible for all students. School officials must ensure that schools, classrooms, and extracurricular activities are accessible for all students, including those with physical challenges. For example, a tennis class should include opportunities for students who walk and run, as well as those

Table 1. Common terms related to the description of physical disabilities

Physical manifestation

Abduction	Movement of limbs away from the midline of the body
Adduction	Movement of limbs toward the midline of the body
Apraxia	Inability to perform specific movements, although there is no muscle or sensory impairment
Atrophy	Deterioration of muscles or nerve cells through nonuse
Clonic	Shaking movements of muscles; repetitive contractions; often resulting from stretching a spastic muscle
Contracture	Permanently tight or frozen muscles and joints that can cause deformities
Hypertonia	Increased muscle tension and tone resulting in stiffness and often the inability to initiate movement. If not treated, it can result in increased contractures
Hypotonia	Decreased muscle tension and tone resulting in floppiness and often the inability to initiate movement
Reflexes	Positions or movements that are beyond one's control. Primitive reflexes are those that normally occur during infancy. As the normally developing infant gets older, primitive reflexes either fade or become integrated into more complex positions or movements
Spasm	Sudden tensing of a muscle or muscles

Characteristics of physical conditions

Asymmetrical	One side of the body is in a different position from the other
Symmetrical	Both sides of the body are in the same position
Extension	Straightening of muscle(s) at the joint
Flexion	Bending of muscle(s) at the joint
Prone	Lying on stomach
Supine	Lying on back
Righting	When in uncomfortable or abnormal positions, being able to position head and body in a correct, or right, position
Midline	Toward the center or middle of the body
Tonicity	A measure of the tension in the muscles

who use manual and/or motorized wheelchairs. When school officials provide activities equally accessible for all students, inclusion will be achieved. Inclusion does not mean merely physically placing students with disabilities in general education settings with other students without disabilities. Inclusive education provides the opportunities for all students to learn to function in a diverse society, to cooperate, and to build self-esteem. Examples of successful inclusive educational opportunities are increasing in the United States and Canada (*IMPACT*, 1988, 1991; Villa, Thousand, Stainback, & Stainback, 1992; York, Vandercook, Macdonald, & Wolff, 1989). When former President Bush signed the Americans with Disabilities Act in 1989, he said, "Let the shameful walls of segregation come tumbling down." As a society, we can no longer tolerate settings and programs that are inaccessible to any individual.

Assessment of Motor Skills

In order to determine appropriate goals and objectives, the individualized education program (IEP) team must develop strategies and procedures for acquiring critical and accurate information regarding a student's motor skills. Assessment procedures that take place in isolated, clinical settings cannot provide a comprehensive picture of a student's functional motor abilities. Formal and informal assessments must be conducted in students' natural environments (home, school, and community), settings that more accurately portray the students' abilities and needs. See Chapter 4 for more specific information about informal and formal assessment procedures and techniques.

Conducting an assessment in the student's natural environments with familiar activities enables educators, parents, and therapists to use the natural materials and cues that are already part of a student's life. For example, a student may discover a way to independently climb the three steps leading to the cafeteria at lunch time but appear unable to climb the three steps artificially positioned in the middle of a therapy room. Students often create their own way of adapting in order to accomplish tasks in their daily routines. For example, a student who uses a walker walks up the stairs backward, moving her legs up leaning on the walker and then pulling the walker up for the next step.

Assessing a student across environments provides more complete information than an assessment limited to one environment. Behaviors change as the environment changes, requiring observation of the student's actions in the presence of a variety of people and in a variety of settings. People who are interacting with the student or the setting in which the student is present may affect that student's motivation, comfort, confidence, and performance. Specific motor skill abilities and disabilities must be determined, as well as the student's overall daily functioning. Following is a discussion of motor behaviors to be assessed in natural environments that can be used to determine a student's functional motor skill abilities.

Mobility   The extent of the student's independent mobility must be determined. If a student lacks or has limited mobility, educators, therapists, and parents, as a team, assess his or her current mobility skills in various learning environments. Traditional methods of mobility such as walking and running are assessed, as well as alternative methods, such as rolling, creeping, and crawling. The MOVE program (Bidabe & Lollar, 1990) assesses 16 components of a student's mobility: 1) maintains a sitting position, 2) moves while sitting, 3) stands, 4) makes the transition from sitting to standing, 5) makes the transition from standing to sitting, 6) pivots while standing, 7) walks forward, 8) makes the transition from standing to walking, 9) makes the transition from walking to standing, 10) walks backward, 11) turns while walking, 12) walks up steps, 13) walks down steps, 14) walks on uneven ground, 15) walks up slopes, and 16) walks down slopes. Once independent mobility is determined, the appropriate mode of aided mobility is also determined. Devices such as scooter boards, braces or crutches, walkers, standers, and wheelchairs can significantly increase a student's mobility. Independent or aided mobility provides the student with opportunities to initiate movement, move to desired locations, obtain desired materials, and so forth. Although this information is extremely useful in designing mobility intervention and supports for students, the MOVE program is presented as an isolated set of mobility activities. Independence of movement should be demonstrated and evaluated by participation in activities within general education classrooms and schools and the community. The MOVE program emphasizes segregated mobility intervention for students who need such intensive mobility training; however, such intervention should never occur in isolation.

The various modes of aided mobility should be used to support a student with disabilities to have appropriate movement and positions for specific educational activities and settings. For example, a student might use braces and crutches to walk to and from school and in the community, a scooter board for physical education activities in the gym, and a wheelchair for ball games on the playground. In the general education classroom, a student might use a wooden chair with roller wheels to move or be moved from one group to another for class projects or from one station to another for different activities. The chair with wheels may be equipped with seat belts or other supports according to the student's needs.

Upright Positioning   Since learning generally occurs when people are in stable, upright sitting or standing positions, the student's ability to obtain and maintain such positions must be assessed. If the student is unable to obtain such a position independently, the amount of assistance and adaptation necessary for that student to sit or stand must be determined. The student's ability to sit or stand in a stabilized manner for a reasonable amount of time must be determined, as well as the amount of assistance and adaptation necessary to maintain that stable position. For example, a student with weak trunk control might stand on a chariot (i.e., a prone stander) to participate in a group project using one or both hands. Educators evaluate the amount of time that the student can sustain standing without fatigue or exhaustion and note, in addition, how much assistance he or she needs to be transferred to different positions.

Range of Motion   The extent of the student's range of motion in all joints should be assessed, not only to determine the student's ability to perform specific skills but also to prevent contractures. A contracture is a shrinkage or shortening of muscle or scar tissue that decreases the range of motion in the joints or decreases the flexibility in the muscles due to the lack of use or exercise. Range of motion can be evaluated more meaningfully in the inclusive classroom than in an isolated testing situation. The purposes of the movement in the meaningful situation will motivate the student to move with extra effort, demonstrating actual functional range of motion. Educators can observe a student's performance of functional activities and assess his or her available range of motion. Students participate in meaningful activities using range of motion throughout the day, such as reaching for the radio, opening books and turning the pages, turning their heads when their names are called, bending down to pick up a pencil, walking to the cafeteria, using their hands to activate an electronic wheelchair, and raising their hands to answer a question.

Reflexive Involvement   Reflexes are the motor movements that everyone demonstrates in initial encounters with the external world. Some reflexes have distinct survival values such as breathing, blinking, rooting, sucking, swallowing, vomiting, coughing, and sneezing. Several other reflexes (such as the Moro reflex, Babinski reflex [when the toes spread out following stimulation of the sole of the foot], and swimming reflex [paddle-like movements of the arms and legs made by infants when placed in water]) do not have clear purposes, although they are useful in evaluating typical development during infancy. As infants develop integrated movements, several earlier reflexes will disappear. For example, the Moro reflex, which is a reaction to sudden disruptive stimulation by flinging the head and four extremities out and bringing them to the middle of the body, disappears after the first few months of life. The Moro reflex exhibited by a school-age student would be an atypical motor reflex and would affect that student's learning activities. Therefore, any reflexes not typical of age-peers should be identified, and strategies should be designed to inhibit such reflexes. For example, a student with cerebral palsy might exhibit reflexes that prevent him from speaking. If the reflex occurs when the student's name is called suddenly, a teacher might try to obtain that student's attention by eye contact or gestures before calling his or her name. Inhibiting reflexes that prevent the student from performing functional motor skills is an important goal for students with physical disabilities.

Structural Disorders   Any structural disorders that a student has, such as scoliosis, dislocated hip, or cleft palate, should be determined. In addition, all interventions and functional motor programs should consider any structural disorders that are present to ensure appropriate positioning and handling. Structural disorders should be accommodated to the maximum extent possible so as not to cause more difficulty for the student in controlling his or her movement. For example, a student who has a tendency to turn her head to the left and not to the right should be shown books or talked to from the right side, not the left side. In addition, her teacher and peers can provide most of the school activities from the student's right side so that turning to the left can be discouraged and avoided naturally.

Tonal Qualities   The quality of the student's muscle tone should be assessed to determine normal tone, hypertonia, hypotonia, or combinations of tone (see Table 1 for definitions). Attention should be given to the student's tonal quality changes, so that information can be used when teaching and facilitating functional motor skills. For example, a student who exhibits hypotonia might require supports in the form of safety belts around her sides to maintain an upright sitting position during classroom activities. However, when she is excited that same student might demonstrate signs of hypertension, which would require some relaxation procedures.

Intervention

Once the goals, objectives, skills, and activities have been targeted, intervention strategies to enhance movement are implemented. To facilitate efficient and effective movement, it is often necessary to inhibit abnormal tone, patterns, and/or reflexes. Educators can consult with physical and/or occupational therapists so that they can provide the student with postural tone and positions that are as normalized as possible in order for the student to acquire the functional movements necessary to participate in activities involving motor skills (Campbell, 1993; Cicirello, Hylton, Reed, & Hall, 1989; Trefler, 1988). When hypertonicity is involved, postural tone can be stabilized by inhibiting specific reflexes and patterns. To inhibit abnormal patterns and facilitate controlled motor movements, support can be given at the key points of the neck and spine, the shoulder girdle, and the pelvic area (Bobath, 1969). To inhibit rigid muscle tonal quality specifically, flexion should be encouraged and supported. Students' levels of tonicity vary and tend to change or fluctuate in different situations (Campbell, 1993; Cicirello et al., 1989; Trefler, 1988). Such factors as noise levels, familiarity of a task and surroundings, and day-to-day mood changes may affect tonal quality. Educators must engage in a "give and take" approach when physically interacting with students, which requires sensitivity to those tonal changes (Utley, 1982). Although many techniques for intervention may be similar, students will have differing needs and are entitled to receive intervention with specific regard to their individuality.

Overall body stability is crucial to the learning process. Students who experience excessive, uncontrolled movement (e.g., athetoid cerebral palsy) rarely see stimuli in a consistent manner. Excessive, uncontrolled movements need to be inhibited as much as possible so that objects appear constant and consistent. Students whose movements have been stabilized are likely to learn more rapidly and efficiently (Bergen, Presperin, & Tallman, 1990; Brady, Martin, Williams, & Burta, 1991). Increased stability will instill a sense of security as well as provide a base from which movement can be initiated. To accomplish this, educators and therapists should implement good physical management techniques and utilize proper equipment.

Motor skills development involves setting appropriate and realistic goals that promote necessary and sufficient movement in educational environments. For example, a child can have a goal of holding a pen as a fine motor skill, while another child can have a fine motor goal of touching the keyboard for writing in a class. To facilitate motor independence, it is important to determine the function of a particular behavior, rather than focus strictly on the form of the behavior (Campbell, 1993; Campbell & Forsyth, 1990; Cicirello et al., 1989; Trefler, 1988). Motor skills development should be facilitated in functional motor activities for its acquisition. Necessary and sufficient movement should be facilitated in functional motor activities with active student participation. Table 2 provides examples of age-appropriate and functional motor activities for motor skills acquisition.

Students should be provided with various positions in inclusive classrooms to encourage participation and active involvement. For example, students who need assistance to use their wheelchairs must be positioned so that they can view and participate in activities going on in the classroom, on the playground, in the gym, in the cafeteria, and all other settings. During a small group discussion, a student might sit in his or her wheelchair. However, that student may need to be transferred to a prone stander in order to use his or her hands during an art project. At the gym, a scooter board can be used to move around the floor with other students. To secure active student involvement, educators must ensure that each student has equal opportunity to access to activities. In addition, teachers need to promote active involvement of all their students throughout the lessons.

Students must be active rather than passive learners in their educational programs. In order for students to increase their motor and mobility skills as well as to inhibit abnormal motor patterns, educators must offer opportunities for students to be active participants in all activities. For example, a student who has cerebral palsy might show improvement in his articulation during a class discussion on Native American Indians when feeling relaxed. However, that student might exhibit difficulty speaking in front of the class when he is the only speaker, because of increased tension in his neck muscles. After this student has had frequent opportunities to speak in the group, he will learn to relax this tension and demonstrate increased voluntary muscle control. It is not enough for students with significant physical challenges to merely observe other students performing activities in classes; they must have the opportunity to be directly and actively involved. Procedures must be developed and implemented to provide methods for all students' active involvement. For example, in a science lab, students with limited use of their arms can touch a bird to feel the feather and report orally, while other students hold a bird and then write a report.

The motor skill objectives for individual students should be taught within the framework of ongoing activities that occur in general education classrooms, throughout the school or within the community. Students are more likely to retain skills if they are taught within the context of meaningful and functional activities (Bergen et al., 1990; Donnellan & Mirenda, 1984). For example, a student whose objective states that she will increase her head control from 45 to 60 seconds may be specifically encouraged and taught to do so while having lunch in the cafeteria with all the noise level and activity that typically occurs at this time. The opportunity to participate in interesting activities in inclusive settings will likely provide natural motivation to increase head control.

Students should receive information on how to interact effectively with all of their peers, including those who require adaptive equipment (e.g., wheelchairs, computers, augmentative communication equipment, tracheotomies, catheters).

Table 2.   Functional, age-appropriate motor skills activities

Motor skills	Preschool-age activities
Range of motion	
Upper extremities	Dressing
Lower extremities	Playing language-experience activities
Neck and spine	Playing "Simon Says"
Locomotor	
Crawling	Playing "Duck-Duck-Goose"
Standing	Using drinking fountain
Walking	Walking to dinner table
Climbing stairs	Climbing up slides
Manipulative skills	
Pushing	Punching bags
Pulling	Popping toys on strings or poles
Twisting/turning	Turning faucets on and off
Carrying objects	Carrying food to table, toys to bath
Zipping/buttoning	Fastening clothes
Fine motor	
Reaching	Taking toys off shelves
Grasping	Holding toys, foods, parent's hand
Hand to mouth	Eating; brushing teeth
Coordinating both hands/arms	Doing finger plays
Gross motor	
Sitting/trunk control	Eating; playing games
Head control	Activating toys with mercury switch
Righting	Doing movements to songs

Motor skills	Elementary-age activities
Range of motion	
Upper extremities	Manipulating wheelchairs
Lower extremities	Kicking balls; learning karate
Neck and spine	Playing "Simon Says"
Locomotor	
Crawling	Moving to different classroom areas
Standing	Standing for flag salute
Walking	Walking to playground equipment
Climbing stairs	Climbing stairs around school, home, and friend's house
Manipulative skills	
Pushing	Opening doors; pushing in chairs
Pulling	Getting clothes from closet, food from refrigerator
Twisting/turning	Using different doorknobs; opening containers and cabinets
Carrying objects	Taking cafeteria tray to table
Zipping/buttoning	Fastening gym bags, clothes
Fine motor	
Reaching	Pushing doorbells; getting food from shelves
Grasping	Holding pencils; using sports equipment or toys
Hand to mouth	Eating; using napkins; brushing teeth
Coordinating both hands/arms	Playing catch; manipulating wheelchairs
Gross motor	
Sitting/trunk control	Reading; talking with friends
Head control	Activating equipment with a special switch
Righting	Dancing; balancing on bicycles

(continued)

Table 2.   *(continued)*

Motor skills	Secondary-age activities
Range of motion	
Upper extremities	Sweeping; washing windows; mixing batter
Lower extremities	Riding bicycle (stationary, two or three wheels)
Neck and spine	Doing exercise or other relaxation techniques
Locomotor	
Crawling	Transferring self to and from wheelchair
Standing	Singing in school choir
Walking	Moving from school bus to classroom; walking from one class to another
Climbing stairs	Going to library, gym, music room, and auditorium
Manipulative skills	
Pushing	Pushing a chair under the desk; sweeping with a push broom
Pulling	Opening doors; pulling a lever on the machine in the woodshop
Twisting/turning	Turning volume of personal cassette tape recorder; turning a lock on the locker
Carrying objects	Carrying books, a drawing pad, and gym bags
Zipping/buttoning	Fastening a zipper on a jacket; opening and closing a backpack
Fine motor	
Reaching	Picking up food in the cafeteria; turning lights on and off
Grasping	Holding racquet and playing sports; holding workshop tools
Hand to mouth	Shaving; eating in the cafeteria
Coordinating both hands/arms	Carrying a ball for PE class; manipulating wheelchairs
Gross motor	
Sitting/trunk control	Sitting in the class; watching a movie
Head control	Activating equipment with a special switch; using a head pointer; looking at a friend while listening
Righting	Doing aerobic exercises; looking at own body in a mirror while exercise walking

For example, peers of students who use wheelchairs can be given basic information on the use of wheelchairs, including putting on and taking off brakes, pushing wheelchairs up an incline and guiding wheelchairs down an incline, requesting permission to move a student's wheelchair, giving students information about where they are going before they are moved, and so forth. This can include information on how to effectively and safely use or facilitate the students' own use of the equipment. For example, a student will learn and practice how to use a head pointer to type in a computer more efficiently, to push a micro-switch activating a tape recorder, and to maneuver an electrical wheelchair around classrooms, a school, and communities.

Occasionally, peers and adults have a tendency to do things for students with significant physical disabilities, making them passive recipients in life with little or no control over their environment. This lack of control fosters a sense of learned helplessness (Williams & Barber, 1992). Learned helplessness is defined and described in more detail in Chapter 6. Active participation by each student, to the greatest extent possible, helps the student to maintain a sense of control over his or her environment, usually resulting in increased motivation and a greater awareness of self in relationship to the surroundings. Active participation may be expressed through body movements, facial expressions, eye movements, and/or vocalizations (Ford et al., 1982).

Educational settings should reflect natural environmental proportions. Natural proportion in the public schools reflects the diversity and proportion of individuals in the larger community in race, ethnicity, culture, values, religion, disabilities, gender, sexual orientation, and so forth. General education classrooms that include "clustering" or "centralizing" a large number of students with disabilities, as well as special education segregated classrooms for students with disabilities, are not natural. They are artificial environments where students cannot learn to value the differences among people with various abilities. The educational environments and all the conditions within those environments should reflect environments utilized by all people in the community.

The development and provision of appropriate student/staff ratios is an important factor to consider for both students and educators. Some students with physical disabilities may initially or continually require additional assistance within general education classrooms, especially to accommodate physical and/or personal care needs. Creating heterogeneous groupings of students so that all the students with significant physical disabilities are not forced into segregated settings is one of the most important planning measures. In collaboration, general and special education teachers, paraprofessionals, and related services personnel can provide the support needed for students with severe disabilities within general education settings. For example, educators, peers, or bus personnel might be assigned to push a student's wheelchair or guide a person with a visual impairment from the classroom to the auditorium. In addition, friends can serve as appropriate social models, providing opportunities for social interaction and giving students support for getting around campus.

When providing education in general education classrooms and throughout the school, the image of each student should be positive, healthy, and chronological age appropriate. Involvement in activities should be unobtrusive, allowing students to learn independent and interdependent skills without drawing undue negative attention. For example, Betsy, a 10-year-old student with cerebral palsy, is learning to walk independently by using a walker. To enhance her self-image and provide unobtrusive instruction, she can practice walking around campus with her peers rather than walking alone while a physical therapist supervises. The actual teaching environments are also taken into account. Betsy can naturally practice walking using her walker when she goes to the cafeteria with her friends at lunch time or when she goes from one classroom to another.

Finally, for the image of each student, careful evaluation of the appearance of any special equipment is necessary—for example, cleanliness and odor of wheelchairs or parts of wheelchairs is very important. Wheelchairs and tray tables should be clear of outdated and age-inappropriate bumper stickers and decals that would portray a "square or nerdy" image. In addition, clothing may be worn on the outside of braces. In effect, students with physical disabilities not only have the right to be educated in inclusive settings but they have the right to be taught in a dignified manner.

Integrated versus Isolated Therapy Models Most students with significant physical disabilities have a need for several types of educational and therapy-based services. In most cases, the educator is responsible for coordinating all of the resources available to a student. As a result, educators should have a broad understanding of the issues involved in providing direct instruction and in securing necessary additional resources to meet the variety of needs related to motor skills and development; services of professionals who have diverse areas of expertise (e.g., communication, physical, and occupational therapists) are often necessary.

Students with physical disabilities are typically provided with one of two service delivery models: isolated or integrated therapy (Sternat, Messina, Nietupski, Lyon, & Brown, 1977). In the isolated therapy model, the therapist determines the student's current motor functioning utilizing specialized equipment, materials, and environments. This determination is made through formal and informal testing. In collaboration with the physician, the therapist develops a program that progresses through typical developmental stages. A schedule for therapy is then established (e.g., 20 minutes twice a week) for motor training. This training is generally conducted in a "therapy room" or other environment separate from the student's classroom or other natural settings. Often with such an isolated therapy model, parents and educators are unaware of the student's progression or of his or her motor needs. Similarly, therapists are frequently unaware of the educational goals established by the parents and teachers. Then, due to the slow progress exhibited by many students with severe disabilities, therapists tend to discontinue therapy or provide maintenance therapy only, without informing the parents or educator. Clearly, the isolated therapy model has serious drawbacks in terms of its ability to support students with significant physical disabilities in the most comprehensive manner possible.

An alternative is the integrated therapy model, in which the therapist observes the student in the classroom, school yard, home, community, and other natural settings (Giangreco, 1986). The therapist observes the student engaging in familiar activities. In addition, the therapist assesses the student in the presence of peers and teachers and in the student's natural environments. From the information gathered, the therapist determines the student's primary motor needs and works with parents, educators, and peers to develop motor goals and objectives that can be incorporated into an inclusive educational program within the general education classroom, school, and community.

Therapy is integrated into a general education schedule, which results in more opportunities for students to learn and use the motor skills in functional and natural situations (Rainforth et al., 1992). In the integrated therapy model, direct intervention occurs within the classroom, other school and/or home settings, and is provided by the educator, instructional assistants, peers, and/or parents under the supervision of the therapist. The therapist trains the parents, educators, peers, and other support personnel to implement the program at home and at school on a regular basis. At regular intervals, they meet to collaborate about the student's progress and design changes to maximize the effectiveness of programs.

A pilot study by Giangreco (1986) compared the effectiveness of isolated therapy with techniques that were incorporated into a functional activity in the regular teaching plan (i.e., integrated therapy). The study resulted in students' significantly improved performance of activities with integrated therapy, although there was minimal learning when isolated direct therapy was used. In order for students to acquire maximum support service benefits, the concept of integrated therapy should be utilized. This model facilitates a team approach to the development of motor goals, objectives, and strategies.

To maximize the effectiveness of the team approach, the team members must share relevant information regarding each student. Following are some of the most important areas of information to share:

1. Medical information (past and present)
2. Home living environment, including information related to cultural and linguistic characteristics of the family
3. Behavior support plans
4. Effective reinforcers
5. Mode(s) of communication
6. Optimal and naturally occurring times for the student to work on specific goals and objectives
7. Amount of time in the classroom for mobility/movement
8. Any relevant changes that might affect the student's demeanor

In summary, the integrated therapy model provides program support and training throughout a student's daily routine by those regularly involved with the student. The model relies on communication and a team orientation to deliver the most effective programming. Furthermore, Orelove and Sobsey (1991) suggest that, to be most effective, each member of the collaborative team must be able to broaden the perspective of his or her discipline enough to consider the holistic being of the student. Collaborative team approaches in integrated settings challenge each contributor to use the vantage point of his or her discipline and at the same time interface with and bridge the gaps between the structural frameworks of each discipline. The educator can play a key role in facilitating this teamwork to provide a holistic model of intervention for each student within general education classrooms and in schools and communities. Chapter 3, this volume, provides more details on strategies for collaboration.

Physical Management Techniques   Students with physical disabilities may temporarily or permanently require assistance with positioning and mobility. Physical management techniques such as positioning, transferring, and carrying of students must be provided in an effective manner for both the student and the person providing the services. Physical management techniques have been widely reviewed in the literature (Finnie, 1975; Fraser, Hensinger, & Phelps, 1990; Rainforth & York, 1991).

When providing physical support to a student, educators and others must consider the following factors:

1. Students' preferences for their own positions and the positions of staff and peers when interacting with them should be accommodated whenever possible.
2. Students should give permission before being moved and be told when they are going to be moved, where they will be moved, and what their next activity will be.
3. Students' positions should be changed regularly to allow for more comfort and prevent sores or stiffness.
4. Students should be positioned so that they are able to view other people in the room and are in proximity to classroom activities and peers.
5. Positions must be changed to facilitate various skill training tasks (e.g., the student may be placed on a wedge to participate in an activity on the floor such as putting together a puzzle, and then be positioned upright with a head brace to participate in science and math manipulative activities requiring reaching skills).
6. Students should be positioned in a manner that will not indirectly encourage negative patterns (e.g., if a student with a strong extension pattern is placed with her back to a screen when the class is viewing a film, the extension may occur because to view the screen she has to turn her head and body).

Effective physical management techniques involve attending to the student's overall well-being in addition to the safety of the person providing the support (Bleck, 1991). Whenever a student is transferred or moved from one situation to another, a systematic, well-planned approach should be used. Educators should anticipate how the movement will be done and where the student will be moved. Following are some important points to consider when preparing to move a student:

1. Request students' permission to be moved before moving them.
2. Communicate movement intentions to the student.
3. Encourage the student to help in any way possible.
4. Obtain help from others when necessary. Undertaking a task that is too difficult may result in injury to the person lifting as well as to the student.

5. Bend knees when lifting a student. Lifting should be done with the entire body, as opposed to using just the back.
6. Establish a broad base of support by keeping one's feet apart (approximately shoulder width) when bending or lifting.
7. Avoid reaching, instead positioning oneself near the student.
8. Take small steps in order to turn or rotate while moving a student. Do not rely on twisting or turning at the trunk while lifting or carrying.
9. Anticipate the path of movement, to be sure there are no obstacles and the student will end up in the most ideal position possible.
10. If additional support is necessary, use a support belt and/or additional support person to make the move with the student.

Proper physical management techniques provide the safest and most effective method of moving and otherwise physically supporting students. Positioning and handling techniques can facilitate movement that supports active inclusion. A student with physical disabilities might be properly positioned at his desk and given a computer assignment, which would be functional and age-appropriate in an inclusive setting.

Emergency Procedures   It is recommended that educators and parents be trained in basic first aid and cardiopulmonary resuscitation (CPR). Classes are frequently offered by the American Red Cross at convenient sites such as hospitals, YMCAs/YWCAs, college campuses, and elsewhere. The classes usually are inexpensive, demand little time, and offer extremely valuable information.

Educators working with students with significant disabilities may need to respond to a student's seizures. Students who have seizures should have accompanying records indicating the type, length, and severity of their "typical" seizures. Anticipatory signs of seizures and the length of recovery time should also be noted, as well as any special emergency procedures. Many individuals who have seizures are treated with medication. It is important that educators are aware of the type of medication used and possible side effects (including toxic effects). These basic procedures can be used to aid a student who is having a seizure in class (Lechtenberg, 1990):

1. If the student is likely to fall, assist him or her to lie down.
2. Clear the area of furniture and/or other harmful objects.
3. If the student is lying down, roll the student on his or her side to prevent choking, and loosen any restrictive clothing.
4. Do not try to restrain the student or attempt to stop the seizure.
5. Do not force anything into his or her mouth.
6. Record the incident as accurately as possible (e.g., school incident report form).
7. Notify the parents, physician, and school nurse.
8. Allow for appropriate recovery time. Once the student is awake, do not assume that he or she can get back to work right away.

These procedures can be used by teachers without training. However, it is advised for special education teachers to be trained in basic community first aid classes offered by the American Red Cross.

Adaptations   The principle of *partial participation* (Baumgart et al., 1982; Ferguson & Baumgart, 1991; York & Rainforth, 1991; York, Rainforth, & Wiemann, 1988) refers to the assumption that a person has a right to participate in any and all activities to any extent possible. This principle states that it is better for students to participate partially than to be denied access to activities. Often, persons with severe disabilities are denied activity-oriented opportunities because of their inability to fully perform all of the skills required. Instead of excluding students from activities, individualized adaptations can be developed and provided for those students to facilitate participation in a variety of natural environments. Adaptations should be developed as necessary to facilitate students' active participation in all aspects of their educational program, since there are times when some students do not yet possess the skills necessary to participate in a particular curricular activity.

Adaptations include the design and utilization of materials and devices as well as other actions. Following is a list of adaptations that can be used to facilitate students' participation in inclusive settings (York & Rainforth, 1991).

1. Adapting skill and activity sequences—rearranging the typical order of steps within a task
2. Adapting rules—changing certain rules to allow more participation
3. Utilizing personal assistance—providing aides, peer tutors, buddy systems, crew labor, and so forth, to accomplish tasks
4. Fostering social/attitudinal changes—changing assumptions and beliefs of the student, family, professionals, and/or community members
5. Creating or using materials and devices to meet specific needs of individual students—microswitches, mechanical devices, calculators, computers, communication devices, special handles, lifts, and so on

Table 3 includes examples of adaptations to facilitate independence for a variety of skills across ages.

When determining whether or not to use an adaptation and what adaptation should be used, several factors should be considered. Listed below is a decision-making process for determining the use of adaptations (York & Rainforth, 1991).

1. Select an environment for instruction; select natural environments in which a student will function.
2. Delineate the activities and skills required in the environment (i.e., design a task analysis).
3. Assess the performance of the student with disabilities.
4. Identify performance discrepancies.
5. Develop an instructional solution (e.g., designing adaptations through team collaboration).

Table 3. Examples of adaptations to facilitate independence

Student	Task	Adaptation
Adapting Skill Sequences		
Needs pureed food	Eating with peers in cafeteria	Pick up lunch tray early; prepare in classroom; take to cafeteria
Five-year-old student has ataxic cerebral palsy; has no mobility; unable to crawl	Being independently mobile in all events	Student may pass over crawling stage and learn to be mobile by walking
Fatigues extremely easily	Cleaning classroom	Clean one part of a classroom instead of cleaning whole classroom in one day
Has short attention span	Playing table games	Provide reinforcement throughout the game instead of just at the end
Has difficulty with balance	Using toilet independently	Sit on toilet, then remove pants
Is unable to maintain balance while bending and reaching	Picking up puzzle pieces from the classroom floor	Sit down on the floor, then pick up pieces into a box
Adapting Rules		
Has difficulty eating quickly	Eating with peers in cafeteria	Allow a longer lunch period for this student by starting earlier
Is unable to locate bus-stop landmarks	Riding the bus independently	Student asks bus driver to tell him or her when they are at the right stop
Has difficulty bending and maintaining balance	Sweeping floors	Sweeps dirt out the door instead of using a dustpan
Is unable to write name	Writing names on personal belongings	Write name with assistance or have a rubber stamp made
Cannot discriminate between written numbers	Doing math problems	Uses objects to count and solve math problems
Uses a wheelchair	Going to gym where there are stairs	Student goes around the gym to use a ramp
Uses crutches	Using school cafeteria	Ask peer to carry tray of food
Has limited cooking skills	Eating a complete meal	Have a team meal where each person prepares one course in a home economics class
Has poor fine motor skills	Using shop class appliances	Ask a friend or a teacher to plug in appliance
Has low reading ability	Reading directions for a group assignment	Peer reads all questions while student and peer take turns answering

(continued)

Table 3.   (continued)

Student	Task	Adaptation
Utilizing Personal Assistance		
Has poor fine motor skills	Turning book pages	Ask a friend to assist with turning pages
Uses a wheelchair	Riding in an elevator	Ask someone to push button for correct floor if button is out of reach
Materials and Devices		
Is unable to add or subtract amounts	Doing math assignment	Use calculator to add and subtract
Has low reading ability	Identifying home phone number	Use color-coded numbers
Uses a wheelchair	Cleaning classroom	Use long-handled brushes/ sponges
Has difficulty matching colors	Dressing independently	Tag clothes that match with coded labels
Has poor fine motor skills	Playing table games	Use enlarged pieces and adapting switches
Has difficulty with balance	Walking to the classroom	Use a cane, handrails, or wheelchair

For example, a student with physical disabilities who uses a cassette tape player to listen to a taped story during silent reading needs motor skills to operate a cassette tape player. The teacher assesses the skills and activities needed to operate the tape recorder by analyzing its operation by a classmate without disabilities (see Figure 1). Then, the same operating process will be evaluated for a student with disabilities. If that student has difficulty pushing the PLAY button due to limited fine motor skill, a microswitch might be selected as an appropriate adaptation.

Microswitches are control devices that allow access to electrical or battery-operated equipment by students who cannot activate the equipment in the manner most frequently used. Types of microswitches include: mercury tilt switch, pillow switch, pedal switch, chin switch, push on/off switch, or puff switch (Levin & Scherfenberg, 1987). Microswitches are used with a relay or battery adapter that functions as a remote control unit so that the equipment can be controlled by the microswitch. Developing a microswitch allows a student with physical disabilities access to equipment, which increases that student's independence and interdependence in functional activities. In determining the use of adaptations, including the use of microswitches, several considerations should be reviewed.

The first consideration is establishing the validity of the educational activity. The goal should not be the successful development of an adaptation, or even its

Assessment of Motor Skill
(Turning on a tape player)

Student name:
Skill:
Setting:
Teacher:

Skills	Dates				Adaptation
	/ /	/ /	/ /	/ /	
Turning on a tape player					
Choose a tape to play					
Reach for the OPEN button					
Push the OPEN button					
Check which side of the tape goes in first					
Put the tape in the recorder					
Close the door					
Push the PLAY button					

Response codes: + = performed the skill; − = did not perform the skill.

Figure 1. Template for assessment of functional motor skills needed to turn on a cassette tape player.

use. The goal for the student is to gain functional movement or control over the environment that leads to greater learning, experiences, interdependence, and independence. If it is an activity a student will participate in daily (e.g., dressing), developing needed adaptations seems appropriate. However, if the activity occurs infrequently (e.g., changing a light bulb) it may be a waste of valuable instructional time to develop and teach the student to use a large number of adaptations to complete the task.

The second consideration is whether the activity in question can be taught directly without the use of an adaptation. There is no need to develop an elaborate adaptation if the skill can be taught without it. Students with significant physical disabilities need to be encouraged to use as many of their motor skills and muscles as possible. Adaptations may be challenging for educators to create and fun for students to use. It is important, though, not to overuse or foster dependence on nonfunctional or unnecessary devices. The goal for the student is active participation in activities in the most unobtrusive and appropriate manner.

The third consideration is determining what adaptation is appropriate. As mentioned earlier, there are many possible types of adaptations. The ideal adaptation allows for greater participation, control over one's environment, and compensation for any motor disabilities. A student's current skills, strengths, needs, and motivation also contribute to determining the appropriate adaptations.

Whether an adaptation will be permanent or temporary also influences decisions regarding the kind of adaptation used. If it will take longer to teach the student to use an adaptation than to recover from a temporary condition that is preventing the student from participating in a certain activity, the adaptation should not be developed. For example, it is not necessary to develop mechanical bathing devices for a student who has an arm cast for a month. If, however, the adaptation can be used to teach other skills, it would be more appropriate to develop and teach the student to use the adaptation. For example, the student with an arm cast can learn to use a computer for his or her writing assignment because those skills can be used in the future. Permanent adaptations must be expanded or adjusted as students become older and more skilled (e.g., instead of continuing to push a student in a wheelchair, the student can learn to independently operate a motorized wheelchair). The care and maintenance of long-term adaptations must be considered, and students should be taught to perform the maintenance to the maximum extent possible. Accessibility, convenience, and reliability of the adaptation is also important. For instance, a microswitch that works sporadically is of no value. Similarly, there is little worth in an adaptation that restricts use to a limited area or to a limited number of people (e.g., the use of a nonportable computer as a primary means of communicating with others).

The fourth consideration is the development of the educational program around the use of the adaptation(s) selected. A program should reflect the appropriate instructional position and dominant motor movement(s) of the student. The most appropriate environments and materials for instruction, the specific instructional procedure (e.g., teaching sequences, natural cues, a system for fading), and a data-based measurement system must be determined.

The final consideration is ensuring the safety of all students using adaptations. This is especially important when using electrical adaptations and equipment. There are several "how-to" manuals (e.g., Burkhart, 1980, 1982, 1987; Levin & Scherfenberg, 1987; Wright & Nomura, 1988) that provide information on the construction of microswitches. Although they are quite simple, it is important to follow safety tips such as those recommended by York, Nietupski, and Hamre-Nietupski (1985):

1. Always seek expert advice from an electrician, an electrical engineer, or a qualified radio/electronic technician when questions arise or when equipment is malfunctioning.
2. When using microswitches to activate plug-in devices, use either an optical isolator or a power relay (also called a voltage regulator) in the circuit to decrease the 110V from a household electrical outlet to a safe level for the microswitch. The amount of voltage that typically goes to the microswitches is 6V. Caution should be taken when using devices with heating elements, such as a hair dryer or popcorn popper; a power relay that can handle a higher number of watts must be used.

3. Always check frayed and exposed wires and replace or repair them as necessary.
4. Be careful that wires and cords are positioned such that they do not become wet and students cannot become tangled in them. If there is a possibility of exposure to water, precautions should be taken so that wires and cords remain waterproof.
5. Use tin solder, not lead solder, when assembling microswitches.
6. Secure small microswitches so they cannot be inhaled or swallowed.
7. Batteries contain acid, so be sure damaged or used batteries are disposed of properly.
8. Mercury is a poison. Encase mercury microswitches in plastic tubing or glue. Use caution when handling mercury switches, and keep them safely stored when not in use.
9. Check to be sure that microswitches and other equipment are free of rough and sharp edges to avoid abrasions and puncture wounds.
10. Check with a physician prior to using any electrical devices with students who have heart problems or use electrical medical equipment.

Equipment and adaptations are selected to achieve the goals of facilitating or inhibiting movement, supporting posture, and aiding independence and interdependence in motor tasks across all areas of the curriculum. Educators, parents, and therapists should work closely with physicians and orthotists to ensure that the student's equipment is appropriate. (Orthotists are professionals who are concerned with the design and use of mechanical devices to support or supplement weakened joints or limbs.)

The fit and function of any equipment or adaptation must be continually reevaluated (York & Rainforth, 1991). The major purpose of reevaluation is to determine whether the equipment or adaptation can or should be discontinued. Fading the use of special equipment as soon as possible leads to a more typical appearance for the individual and more convenient functioning in daily tasks. With the help of special equipment and creative adaptations, students with significant physical disabilities are often able to accomplish the same tasks as their peers. Table 4 contains a list of some of the most commonly used equipment. For more detailed information, refer to Burkhart (1980, 1982, 1987), Church and Glennen (1992), Finnie (1975), Fraser et al. (1990), Levin and Scherfenberg (1987), Lindsey (1992), and Male (1994).

It is essential that all students be given the opportunity to participate in inclusive school, community, and work settings, including those students who need support to move or perform personal care skills. Adaptations for and sensitivity toward these students will facilitate their full inclusion in school, community, and work settings. In addition to the mobility and motor movement issues that need to be considered when designing and implementing inclusive educational programs for students with severe disabilities, attention should also be given to their personal care skills and needs.

Table 4.   Common equipment to facilitate various motor skills

Positioning

Bolsters/sand bags	Pillow-like objects used to support desired positions
Triangle/corner chairs	Provide three-sided support in upright position; can also be used with table
Bean bags	Allow comfortable positioning; adjust to individual
Wedges	Wedge-shaped foam pads used in prone position; allow work on head control, use of hands/arms
Car seats	Provide safety and appropriate positioning
Wheelchairs/inserts	Upright positioning and mobility inserts, individually designed and fitted
Prone boards	Standing positioning, allowing use of hands/arms

Mobility

Scooters	Used by young children from many positions
Walkers	Style varies with need
Crutches	Style varies with need
Bicycles (two or three wheels)	Can have adapted seats, handlebars, or pedals, as necessary
Wheelchairs (power and regular)	Standard: with specific equipment such as footrests, neckrests, headrests, side supports, and inserts
	Travel chairs: serve as both therapeutic chairs and car seats (rear wheels are collapsible)

Isolated Support

Braces	Plastic, fiberglass, or cloth; are removable support for scoliosis or joint strengthening; metal braces are being used less frequently
Splints	Used on hands, wrists, arms, knees, and ankles, for support or to help inhibit contractures

Activity-Oriented

Mercury switches	Devices worn on part of student's body where movement is desired; attached to radio or device that switches on when body part moves; other switches controlled by hands, feet, cheeks, voice, breath
Battery-operated devices	Toys, wheelchairs, communication systems adapted with special switches
Computer aids	Communication, leisure/recreation, calculators for shopping, and so forth
Toy modifications	Larger handles, switches, controls, adapted to be operated by different modalities (e.g., by voice)
Radio-controlled devices	Door openers, telephone answering machines, toys
Mobility devices	Battery-operated riding toys, power wheelchairs, scooters

PERSONAL CARE SKILLS

Special education services for students with significant disabilities have often included personal care skills training as a major focus of the overall curricula. The specific skills of eating, controlling bowel and bladder, grooming, dressing, and simple household chores have been the major emphasis of personal care curricula and traditionally have been considered as beginnings for the development of independence. Although these personal care skills are essential for developing independence for persons with severe disabilities, curricula in this area have traditionally been used to teach only a small portion of the skills needed to function within a variety of inclusive settings. For example, students with physical disabilities have been taught how to put on and take off clothes and how to practice chewing and swallowing food. However, it is inappropriate to assume that mastery of the skill mechanics is equivalent to independence. The personal care skills needed to enable students with significant disabilities to function independently and interdependently within their living environments go beyond the mechanics of physical appearance and hygiene. Personal care skills involve the total physical well-being of individuals, including an understanding of the need for task performance as well as an awareness of the choice and options involved.

Preparing students to actively participate in inclusive classroom activities and to become contributing members of the society requires that families and educators work together to develop appropriate and systematic educational programs. A team approach should be utilized to determine which strategies are most effective for a given student. Support personnel (e.g., communication therapists, occupational therapists, physical therapists) can cooperate to utilize effective personal care skills programs within general education classrooms. This approach makes the activities more relevant for the student and minimizes problems of generalization. For example, a physical therapist works cooperatively with a physical education teacher to provide personal care skill lessons to a student in the locker room while peers model independent dressing skills after the physical education class. It is more natural to learn and practice dressing in the locker room than to learn to dress alone in the isolated therapy room.

Personal care skills involve not only independence and interdependence but also a positive self-concept and acceptance by others. Objectives must reflect parental and student needs. The role played by parents and families in developing and implementing the curriculum, for cultural and familial relevance, is a critical component of teaching personal care skills. The selection of objectives also takes into consideration the students' adulthood by anticipating the living skills and support needed. The teaching of these personal care skills begins early in a student's life, and the sequencing of these skills is developed systematically in response to the changing needs of the student, home, and school environments. Most important, objectives reflect the student's choices of priority areas for skill development and his or her plans for the future. In addition, factors such as the student's age, motivation, type and degree of disability, and amount of present independence, as well as the obtrusiveness of the intervention, should be considered.

Teaching students to perform personal care skills within their home, classrooms, schools, and community is critical for several reasons. First, students' self-esteem is likely to increase as they become more independent in those environments. Their self-esteem also increases as they realize the rights and power they have for making decisions that affect their lives. Second, since students' abilities to perform independent personal care skills will likely create more acceptance and interaction within general education classrooms and the community, teaching students to perform these skills independently is important and will also result in decreased reliance on care providers. Finally, the acquisition, maintenance, and generalization of personal care skills can be developed into vocational or career opportunities (e.g., becoming a chambermaid, custodian, flight attendant, hairdresser, dishwasher, receptionist, computer operator, graphic designer). Strategies for assessing and teaching specific self-help skills in the inclusive classroom are described below.

Eating Skills

Eating is critical for health, education, well-being, and happiness. Eating provides nutrition for energy and growth; food offers various tastes, aromas, and textures; and dining provides opportunities to learn about culture and socialize with others. Children with severe physical disabilities, however, find eating to be stressful and unpleasant due to poor oral muscle coordination, which impedes typical eating patterns, and interventions that are provided in a disrespectful manner.

Assessment   Assessment of eating skills must include nutritional concerns, oral muscle/motor aspects, and functional eating skills to determine specific eating techniques that can be used to inhibit abnormal patterns and to ensure an appropriate intake of nutrients. Students with physical disabilities often have nutritional deficits related to eating difficulties. For students with specific nutritional deficits, nutrition information is collected by carefully recording daily food intake and by assessing daily calories needed. These data can be collected cooperatively among parents, classroom teachers, teaching assistants, school nurses, peers, and the student.

Oral muscle/motor aspects of eating include sucking, sipping, biting, chewing, swallowing, and bringing the hand to the mouth. The physical aspects of eating can be assessed primarily by a doctor, physical therapist, speech therapist, and other related services professionals including parents and educators. This assessment will determine the most appropriate types of foods the student can eat and the most appropriate utensils for the student to use, such as pureed foods or finger foods and eating with spoon, fork, or knife.

However, it is very important to assess functional eating skills in the inclusive educational setting (see Figure 2). Assessment of functional eating skills in the school cafeteria or during snacktime in the classroom will reveal a student's current abilities in eating skills: making choices, communicating what he/she wants, carrying trays, paying for food, finding a table, eating, and cleaning up a table. This assessment enables a teacher to determine the level of assistance and the amount of adaptation for a student to eat in the inclusive settings.

Intervention   Strategies for facilitating eating include, among others, proper positioning for chewing and swallowing (Utley, 1982); the Mueller (1975) techniques for mouth opening; and jaw control, lip closure, swallowing, and tongue exercises that will increase tone (Bigge, 1991). However, there are also issues to consider beyond specific intervention techniques. Learning to eat independently includes not only the specific mechanical skills of eating, but also the ability to make choices about what and when to eat, to develop good nutritional habits, and to understand social norms associated with eating. Foods should be chosen in accordance with student preference, family food and cultural norms, nutritional value, texture, and specific eating goals (e.g., peanut butter can be used to encourage tongue lateralization).

Eating patterns often deteriorate while students are learning to eat independently (Utley, 1982). Consideration of a student's age and motivation and the application of ideas such as Campbell's (1993) theory of independence (i.e., providing the least amount of assistance that will result in a sufficient level of independent skill performance), as well as the concept of least intrusive interventions, are important to consider when teaching a student to eat independently. For example, proper lip closure may be sacrificed for independent eating, particularly for older students. Facilitating independent eating in the cafeteria at lunch time with peers without disabilities to the maximum extent possible allows for greater independence, less invasion of personal space, greater chance of socialization, and increased self-concept.

However, specific skill intervention also can be provided in an inclusive educational setting that secures more privacy than a cafeteria (e.g., snacktime in the classroom for younger students, or the school nurse's office for taking medication or supplementary diet food). Skills and behaviors are best taught in the inclusive settings and at the times at which students will naturally be required to perform them. Using inclusive settings ensures that a student will receive natural and relevant prompts and reinforcements to learn appropriate ways to use the skills being learned. During the snacktime preschoolers will, for example, practice eating skills, learn how to interact with peers, and be given opportunities to make a choice (e.g., What kind of fruit do you want?).

For students who require assistance at lunchtime in the cafeteria, it is important to remember that assistance should be offered with dignity and respect for the student. Regardless of age, considerations should be made as to the student's choice of foods and when he or she is full. It is also important to sit naturally be-

Assessment of Personal Care Skills
(Eating)

Student name:
Skill:
Setting:
Teacher:

Skills	Dates					
	/ /	/ /	/ /	/ /	/ /	/ /
Getting Food						
Stays in the line						
Takes a tray						
Picks up utensils and napkins						
Puts the tray on the rail						
Pushes the tray						
Looks at a server						
Listen for the choices						
Makes a choice						
Tells what he or she wants						
Takes a plate						
Puts a plate on the tray						
Carries the tray						
Locates a table						
Walks to a table						
Eating Food						
Picks up a fork						
Picks up food						
Brings food to mouth						
Chews and swallows food						
Wipes mouth with a napkin						
Cleaning						
Cleans the table						
Picks up the tray						
Throws garbage in the trash						
Takes the tray to the window						

Response codes: + = performed the skill; − = did not perform the skill.

Figure 2.   Template for assessment of functional eating skills needed in the cafeteria.

side the student rather than facing him or her as one would do with an infant, to use one's dominant hand in feeding so as to demonstrate good control, to pace eating according to the student's needs for chewing and swallowing, and to bring food to the student at an appropriate level (not swooping down as if the food were an airplane). In inclusive educational settings, peers may, after receiving appropriate instruction, assist their friend eating in the cafeteria. Other personal dignity, social acceptance, and hygienic considerations to be aware of include: not blowing or tasting for the temperature of a student's food; using a napkin rather than a bib, towel, or spoon to wipe around a student's mouth; wiping gently around the mouth and not the whole face; getting a wet napkin rather than spitting on a napkin to clean dried food; and not mashing the foods or mixing foods together so that they lose their appeal. Again, the dignity of each student should be the uppermost consideration for determining whether assisted eating, independent eating, and/or social integration are the appropriate mealtime objectives.

Bowel and Bladder Control Skills

Lack of independent bowel and bladder control skills is often the reason students with significant disabilities have been excluded from general education classrooms, home, recreation/leisure, and work settings. These skills are very important for a student to master because they are needed for a lifetime, and if he or she cannot perform them, someone always has to assist. Going to the restroom independently will assist a student to feel competent and maintain personal privacy.

Assessment   Students with significant physical disabilities may have difficulty in going to the restroom independently because of their disabilities. In the case of a student who cannot signal when he or she needs necessary assistance going to the restroom, assessment of bowel and bladder control skills should determine a student's stable pattern of elimination using a bowel and bladder control schedule such as that provided in Figure 3. Based on the assessment data, a teacher can schedule the restroom break at the arrival to class and regularly throughout the day.

Bowel and bladder control skills are not only related to the ability to voluntarily constrict or relax muscles, but also to locate the appropriate restroom, manage clothes, sit on the toilet, and clean oneself after using the toilet. Figure 4 provides an assessment of functional bowel and bladder control skills using a task analysis format. These sample assessment tools provide educators with the ability to assess a student's bowel and bladder control skills, ability to use the restroom, ability to dress and to undress, and his or her needs for assistance.

Intervention   Bowel and bladder control training programs developed for persons with severe disabilities have proven highly successful within the last 15 years (Azrin, 1989; Azrin & Foxx, 1971; Copeland, Ford, & Solon, 1976; Fraser et al., 1990; Fredericks et al., 1975). Goals for bladder and bowel care must include cleanliness and comfort, prevention of urinary tract or bowel infections,

Toileting Schedule

Student name:
Skill:
Setting:
Teacher:

Time	Monday	Tuesday	Wednesday	Thursday	Friday
8:30 A.M.					
9:00					
9:30					
10:00					
10:30					
11:00					
11:30					
12:00 P.M.					
12:30					
1:00					
1:30					
2:00					

Codes: UT, UP, BT, BP (U = urine, B = bowel movement, T = went in toilet, P = wet in pants)

Figure 3.   Toileting schedule form.

prevention of skin irritation, social acceptance, and maximum independence (McCubbin, 1983). However, for some students with significant physical disabilities, the issue is not always one of implementing programs to teach control; it is physically impossible for some students to have bladder and/or bowel control. Incontinence should not exclude a student from participation in general education classes. When incontinence is an issue, students should be given support to use the restrooms before, during, and after the class or according to the result of the bowel and bladder control schedule assessment. It is critical that educators work with the physician, parent, and student in determining the most appropriate means of bladder and bowel care.

Some students can regulate their bowel movements so that they make it a habit to go to the bathroom at home in the morning before going to school. They can reduce the amount of water intake in the morning so that they need fewer restroom breaks. The student's age, degree of control, and movement capabilities are all important considerations when deciding the most appropriate method of care. A student, during the break, who is learning bowel and bladder control skills can be prompted to go to the restroom and to practice bowel and bladder control skills with assistance from teachers, paraprofessionals, or peers. After using the

Assessment of Personal Care Skills
(Toileting)

Student name:
Skill:
Setting:
Teacher:

Skills	Dates					
	/ /	/ /	/ /	/ /	/ /	/ /
Going to Restroom						
Signals wanting to go to restroom						
Walks to restroom						
Using Toilet						
Finds available stall						
Enters stall						
Pulls pants down						
Sits on toilet						
Voids						
Uses toilet paper						
Stands up						
Pulls pants up						
Using Sink						
Goes to the sink						
Turns on faucet						
Washes hands						
Turns off faucet						
Dries hands						

Response codes: + = performed the skill; − = did not perform the skill.

Figure 4.   Template for assessment of skills needed to use the restroom.

toilet, he or she will have opportunities to practice dressing and washing hands through modeling and other natural prompts provided by the peers.

Self-catheterization, ostomies, and other techniques can also be used to aid in healthy, socially appropriate means of bladder and bowel control (Bigge, 1991; McCubbin, 1983; Taylor, 1990). Such technical assistance can be provided by a school nurse, teachers, or other paraprofessionals in a private area. It is important to have a specialist provide training for those who need specific skills to assist a student using these adaptations. If a student requires changing the underpant during class, he or she must be changed in a private area of a restroom. If a student needs access to a table for changing, then the school nurse's office or a private room should be arranged at school. At no time should a student be changed on the floor of a classroom or in any area that is neither private nor clean.

Hygiene, Grooming, and Dressing Skills

Personal care skills such as hygiene, grooming, and dressing are necessary for maintaining a healthy body, positive self-image, and social acceptance. Cleanliness is an important health factor as well as a critical aspect in developing and maintaining social relationships. Generally, grooming skills include hand and face washing, showering and bathing, and hair washing and care. These skills are also important for a student's independence and social acceptance. One of the most important areas of personal hygiene for girls and young women is menstrual care.

Assessment   Assessment of dressing skills should consist of gathering general information related to skills involved in removing and putting on various items of clothing (e.g., socks, pants or skirts, shirts, sweaters, shoes). See Figure 5 for a sample of a dressing assessment tool. Besides this general dressing skill assessment, ongoing assessment on the skills necessary for a particular clothing item should be administered for instructional planning. Figure 6 provides an assessment of dressing skills using a task analysis format. Dressing may be easier for students who have proper positioning based upon their muscle tone and movement patterns. Therefore, consultation with physical and occupational therapists may be essential. Parents may provide useful information and suggestions in this area, since they have more opportunities to see their son or daughter practice these skills at home.

Hygiene, grooming, and dressing skills, as with all skills, should be assessed at naturally occurring times and in natural environments. For example, middle and high school students' dressing and grooming skills might be assessed in the locker room before and after physical education class when students are expected to perform these skills. Preschoolers and kindergarten-age students might be assessed during "dress-up" time. Assessment of these skills for elementary-age students might be conducted when setting up for and cleaning up from art activities (e.g., putting on smocks, washing hands).

Intervention   Students should be taught skills that will lead to the greatest independence, whether that means the use of adaptive equipment or opting for the simplest care (e.g., an adolescent male may choose to grow a beard rather than struggle with shaving). A student with significant disabilities has numerous opportunities to practice dressing skills in the inclusive educational setting. Dressing skills can be practiced daily when students arrive at the classroom in the morning, when they are ready to leave school, when they go to the restroom, and when they change T-shirts after physical education class. For students who have a difficult time learning a sequence of the class schedule, these natural learning opportunities will prompt them to understand the routine and perform dressing skills. For example, at the gym, students will change their clothes. After the physical education class, there is a natural opportunity to teach a student showering

Assessment of Personal Care Skills
(Dressing)

Student name:
Skill:
Setting:
Teacher:

Activities	Responses		Assistance needed
Puts on shoes			
Takes off shoes			
Puts on socks			
Takes off socks			
Puts on underwear			
Takes off underwear			
Puts on pants/skirt			
Takes off pants/skirt			
Puts on shirt			
Takes off shirt			
Puts on jacket			
Takes off jacket			
Buttons			
Unbuttons			
Snap on			
Snap off			
Zipper up			
Zipper down			
Tie			
Untie			
Hook			
Unhook			
Fasten Velcro			
Unfasten Velcro			

Response codes: + = performed the skill; − = did not perform the skill

Figure 5. Template for assessment of general dressing skills.

and grooming skills as well as dressing skills while peers are doing the same activities. According to the level of a student's dressing skills, a teacher or peers
can provide assistance with dressing.

Mastery of the mechanical skills necessary for dressing oneself (e.g., putting
on clothing items, using fasteners) does not imply that the student has achieved

Assessment of Personal Care Skills
(Dressing—taking off a jacket)

Student name:
Skill:
Setting:
Teacher:

Skills	Dates					
	/ /	/ /	/ /	/ /	/ /	/ /
Taking Off a Jacket						
Grabs the zipper						
Unzips it						
Opens a jacket						
Lets go						
Grabs the cuff						
Pulls one arm out						
Grabs the other cuff						
Pulls the other arm out						
Grabs the collar						
Hangs it on the hook						

Response codes: + = performed the skill; − = did not perform the skill.

Figure 6.   Template for assessment of skills needed to take off a jacket.

independence in dressing. Students should be taught to select their own clothing, with instruction being provided when necessary regarding ease of dressing, correct peer styles, seasons/weather, comfort, fit (with special equipment such as braces or casts), appropriateness for specific occasions, and how and when to care for one's clothing. A student with disabilities in general education classrooms will also learn to make age-appropriate choices about what to wear by watching other students in the classroom. At home, parents can help students select what to wear to school according to their preference in color, style, and material for the day. At school, teachers and peers can reinforce their choices. Again, the main goal is maximal independence and interdependence, with a healthy and positive self-image.

Obtaining specific skills in the areas of dressing are not prerequisites for being provided the opportunity to learn other important skills related to dressing, such as making choices about what to wear for a certain occasion and weather. In fact, the specific skills may be the least important skills to focus on for individuals with severe physical disabilities, or for students where other skills are more important at this time. For example, a student who has significant disabilities will learn to signal bowel movement and to use a toilet before working on specific dressing skills. All students, however, should be provided continual opportunities to practice their skills in decision and choice making concerning the selection of the clothing they wear, the color and design of their clothing, and so on.

Grooming skills can also be introduced in general education classrooms. Students are often required to wash their hands after using the restroom, wash their face or take a shower after a physical education class, or brush their teeth after lunch. With careful planning, a student with significant disabilities can practice grooming skills within the general education class schedule. Students can receive assistance from adults, special education teachers, physical education teachers, or other paraprofessional staff when necessary, especially at the beginning of teaching specific grooming skills. Peers can also learn how to assist.

Menstrual care is one of the most important areas of personal hygiene for girls and young women. The first day of the period should be recorded every month in the student's private calendar. In the home economics or physical education classes, a teacher can instruct students how to select and use personal hygiene products. During the menstrual period, if necessary the educator can remind and assist a student to check and/or change her product.

An important consideration when teaching hygiene skills as well as grooming and dressing skills is the issue of privacy. All students should learn to participate in caring for their personal needs as independently as possible and with respect to their privacy when assistance is necessary. For example, when assisting a secondary-age student who uses disposable underpants, caution should be taken to assist this student in a private setting where other students are not able to observe the activity, such as the school nurse's office or an empty locker room.

In addition, when performing a health-related procedure such as suctioning, changing catheters, or providing nutrition through a student's feeding tube, educators and health care professionals should perform these procedures in a healthy and safe manner as well as in a private setting. The issue of privacy should include age-appropriate and normalized use of bathing, showering, dressing, and the restroom areas in the environment. For example, secondary students typically do not dress or undress in their classrooms, and the dressing area in a school gym is generally less private than a private stall in a small school restroom.

Home Management Skills

Home management is used here to refer to teaching the mechanics of money, time, and mobility skills. It includes the development of responsibility and of decision-making skills. Incorporating time management into personal care skills provides the student with experiences that lead to making personal choices regarding schedules and routines and becoming an active member of a household. These skills will provide students access to a rich quality of life.

Assessment   Money skills are needed for buying lunch in school cafeterias, shopping, approximating the amount of tax on purchases, determining bus fares, selecting coins needed for a vending machine or telephone call, and so on.

Assessment should be conducted to the greatest extent possible in the settings where skills naturally occur. For example, students in a program designed to assist them to make a successful transition from high school to adult lives might be assessed when they take a bus to go to a job site, dine in a restaurant for lunch, go to a grocery store or department store for shopping, and so on. Elementary-age students might be assessed while purchasing school supplies at the school office, on a field trip, and when they choose and pay for what they want to eat at the school cafeteria. Soliciting input from the family can assist in developing educational interventions in this area. Figure 7 provides a questionnaire for parents about home management skills. Figure 8 (pp. 223–224) provides a personal care skills priority checklist that can also aid in developing educational interventions in this area. The family and the student work in collaboration with the educators to complete this checklist. For example, team members will brainstorm to list several personal care skills that are needed by the student to perform; complete the personal care skills priority checklist for each skill that team members identified; and compare the total scores of each skill and start teaching the skill with the highest total scores.

Intervention   The basic home management skills, which include time management, money management, and mobility, are often taught in isolation or as individual, unrelated sequences. Home management skills include all of the activities that contribute to the student's daily routine. They reflect the participation of the student in cooperative activities with classmates, family members, co-workers, and/or friends. Students can learn these home management skills in inclusive school settings while participating in group projects such as shopping for decorating the classroom, taking a bus for a field trip or to work, and making a personal time management schedule for daily school activities. Sharing responsibilities with peers in the group and cooperative skills will assist the development of home management skills, which are all important to learn.

At home, meal preparation for some families is a time for getting together and sharing the day's experiences. Each family member may have an individual role in the preparation of the meal, and participating in family interactions during mealtime is equally important. When approaching a family, sensitivity to the family's cultural background is necessary. The specific strategies and/or the specific materials used when teaching personal care skills should not cause the family any conflict. For example, when teaching students eating skills, educators should consider using some of the same types of foods and utensils (e.g., forks, knives, spoons, chopsticks, fingers) that the family is likely to use. In addition, teaching the student to cook without teaching him or her to participate in interactions with others results in incomplete training.

This more comprehensive approach necessitates the inclusion of specific skills in cooperative learning environments that facilitate a sense of personal and family organization. Basic personal care and home management skills should not be taught in isolated, discrete activity units. Instead, these skills should be placed in the larger context in which they occur, including the social context. Skill sequences should be developed that allow the student to more fully participate in

Parent Questionnaire:
Home Management Skills

1. What types of jobs does your son or daughter perform at home? (For example: making the bed, setting the table, watering the lawn, preparing a meal, raking leaves)

2. Does your son or daughter have any jobs outside the home?

3. What jobs do the siblings without disabilities perform at home?

4. Does your son or daughter have any special hobbies or interests?

5. What types of responsibilities at home would you like your son or daughter to be able to perform?

6. In terms of eating by himself or herself, are there any skills you would like your son or daughter to learn? (For example: using a knife, cooking)

7. What dressing skills would you like your son or daughter to learn? (For example: buttoning, caring for clothing)

8. In terms of personal hygiene, what are the skills your son or daughter has now and what would you like him or her to learn?

9. What types of home recreational and leisure activities would you like your son or daughter to learn?

10. How does your son or daughter get along with other family members?

11. What skills would enable him or her to participate more in family activities?

12. To what places do you think your son or daughter might go when he or she is older?

13. In the future, where do you see your son or daughter living? (For example: supervised apartment, group home)

Figure 7. Sample parent questionnaire for developing a basic living skills curriculum in the domestic environment.

(continued)

Figure 7.   *(continued)*

Parent Questionnaire:
Home Management Skills

14. What type of work do you think your son or daughter might do when he or she is older?

15. What activities does your son or daughter now enjoy that might lead to vocational preparation?

16. What skills and/or activities not already mentioned would you like your son or daughter to learn so that you don't always have to do them for him or her?

---

the inclusive educational living environments, rather than to merely perform separate tasks within "therapy" periods.

SUMMARY

A number of issues associated with the development of an appropriate curriculum for motor and personal care skills within inclusive educational settings were presented in this chapter. The development of a comprehensive motor skills program for persons with physical disabilities should include the following components: an understanding of the physical disability and the related terms; assessment of functional skills in natural environments; determination of functional chronological age–appropriate goals; consideration of related issues, such as integrated therapy models and interdisciplinary team approaches; and implementation of teaching strategies, which may include adaptations. Motor skills programming is integrated into all aspects of the student's daily routine by educators and therapists, with input from the students and parents. As support is integrated, a student's motor functioning will enhance his or her potential for independent functioning across all activities in the curricula and across various environments.

The focus of teaching personal care is to prepare students to function within their present and future environments: classroom, home, and community. Starting early in life, students with severe disabilities must begin to acquire skills that will allow them an active level of participation in activities and that will lead to fuller participation and interaction with others in inclusive settings. Skills chosen for development must reflect student and parental preferences in terms of existing routines, priorities, culture, and possible future living and working options. Students' needs and preferences must also be considered by providing a curriculum that allows for individual choice and decision making.

The traditional self-help curriculum has been expanded in this chapter to include the often neglected aspects of family interactions, neighborhood integration, and inclusion in general education classrooms. Inclusive educational oppor-

Personal Care Skills Priority Checklist

Student name:
Date:
Skill:
Teacher:

1. Family input:
   Is this a skill the student routinely needs at home?   1   2   3   4
   Is this a skill the family considers critical?   1   2   3   4
   Will this skill increase the student's participation
      in family routines?   1   2   3   4
   Is this skill relevant to the student's home culture?   1   2   3   4

   Average score for this item: _____

2. Functional nature:
   Is this a skill that someone else must now perform
      for the student?   1   2   3   4
   Is this a skill the student must use often?   1   2   3   4
   Is this a skill that will continue to be useful in
      the future?   1   2   3   4

   Average score for this item: _____

3. Current and subsequent settings:
   Is this a skill that can be used in a number of
      settings other than home?
   For example: In classroom   1   2   3   4
                  In community   1   2   3   4
                  In a job site   1   2   3   4
                  In recreational setting   1   2   3   4

   Average score for this item: _____

4. Number of uses:
   Is this a frequently occurring activity at home?   1   2   3   4

   Average score for this item: _____

5. Social significance:
   Will performing this skill increase the student's
      social acceptance?   1   2   3   4
   Will this skill enhance the student's interpersonal
      skills?   1   2   3   4

   Average score for this item: _____

Figure 8.   Personal care skills priority checklist.

(continued)

Figure 8.   *(continued)*

Personal Care Skills Priority Checklist

Student name:
Date:
Skill:
Teacher:

---

6. Physical harm:
   Will learning this skill increase the student's
      personal safety?   1   2   3   4
   Is the skill safe for the student to perform by
      himself or herself?   1   2   3   4
   Can the skill be performed without
      adult supervision?   1   2   3   4
          Average score for this item:_____

7. Logistics:
   Can this skill be taught or practiced in an
      inclusive classroom?   1   2   3   4
   Is this a skill that will increase the student's
      independent participation in an inclusive
      classroom?   1   2   3   4
          Average score for this item:_____

8. Age appropriateness:
   Is this a personal care skill a peer without
      disabilities is likely to perform?   1   2   3   4
   Is this a skill preferred by peers without disabilities?   1   2   3   4
   Is this a skill expected of siblings in the home?   1   2   3   4
          Average score for this item:_____

   Total skill score (*add average scores*):   _____

Codes: 1 = No
         2 = Somewhat
         3 = Average
         4 = Very much

---

tunities are now available for students with significant disabilities. All students need to learn skills to participate as individuals, as family members, and as members of a larger society. Teaching motor and personal care skills in a comprehensive and systematic manner will lead to independence, interdependence, and participation by individuals with severe disabilities in the full range of natural living environments.

REFERENCES

Azrin, N.H. (1989). *Toilet training in less than a day.* New York: Simon & Schuster.

Azrin, N.H., & Foxx, R. (1971). A rapid method of toilet training the institutionalized retarded. *Journal of Applied Behavior Analysis, 4,* 89–99.

Baumgart, D., Brown, L., Pumpian, I., Nisbet, J., Ford, A., Sweet, M., Messina, R., & Schroeder, J. (1982). Principle of partial participation and individualized adaptations in educational programs for severely handicapped students. *Journal of The Association for the Severely Handicapped, 7*(2), 12–27.

Bergen, A., Presperin, J., & Tallman, T. (1990). *Positioning for function: Wheelchairs and other assistive technologies.* Valhalla, NY: Valhalla Rehabilitation Publication.

Bidabe, L., & Lollar, J. (1990). *Mobility Opportunities Via Education* (MOVE). Office of Kelly F. Blanton, Kern County Superintendent of Schools. Bakersfield, CA.

Bigge, J.L. (1991). *Teaching individuals with physical and multiple disabilities* (3rd ed.). Columbus, OH: Charles E. Merrill.

Bleck, E.E. (1991). *Orthopedic management of cerebral palsy* (2nd ed.). New York: Cambridge University Press.

Bobath, B. (1969). The treatment of neuromuscular disorders by improving patterns of coordination. *Physiotherapy, 55,* 18–22.

Brady, M.P., Martin, S., Williams, R.E., & Burta, M. (1991). The effects of fifth grader's socially directed behavior on motor and social responses of children with severe multiple handicaps. *Research in Developmental Disabilities, 12*(1), 1–16.

Burkhart, L.J. (1980). *Homemade battery powered toys and educational devices for severely handicapped children.* Millville, PA: Author.

Burkhart, L.J. (1982). *More homemade battery devices for severely handicapped children, with suggested activities.* Millville, PA: Author.

Burkhart, L.J. (1987). *Using computers and speech synthesis to facilitate communicative interaction with young and/or severely handicapped children.* College Park, MD: Author.

Campbell, P.H. (1993). Physical management and handling procedures. In M. Snell (Ed.), *Instruction of students with severe disabilities* (4th ed.) (pp. 248–261). Columbus, OH: Charles E. Merrill.

Campbell, P.H., & Forsyth, S. (1990). *A system for classifying impaired or delayed posture and movement skill development.* Unpublished manuscript, Family and Child Learning Center, Children's Hospital Medical Center of Akron.

Church, G., & Glennen, S. (1992). *The handbook of assistive technology.* San Diego: Singular.

Cicirello, N.R., Hylton, J., Reed, P., & Hall, S. (1989). Teaching nontherapists to do positioning and handling in educational settings. *TIES: Therapy in Educational Settings.* Portland, OR: Health Sciences University.

Copeland, M., Ford, L., & Solon, N. (1976). *Occupational therapy for mentally retarded children.* Baltimore: University Park Press.

Donnellan, A.M., & Mirenda, P.L. (1984). Issues related to professional involvement with families of individuals with autism and other severe handicaps. *Journal of The Association for Persons with Severe Handicaps, 9,* 16–25.

Ferguson, D.L., & Baumgart, D. (1991). Partial participation revisited. *Journal of The Association for Persons with Severe Handicaps, 16*(4), 218–227.

Finnie, N.R. (1975). *Handling the young cerebral palsied child at home.* New York: E.P. Dutton.

Ford, A., Davis, J., Messina, R., Ranieri, L., Nisbet, J., & Sweet, M. (1982). Arranging instruction to ensure the active participation of severely multihandicapped students. In

L. Brown, J. Nisbet, A. Ford, M. Sweet, B. Shiraga, & L. Gruenewald (Eds.), *Educational programs for severely handicapped students* (Vol. 12, pp. 31–80). Madison, WI: Madison Metropolitan School District.

Fraser, B.A., Hensinger, R.N., & Phelps, J.A. (1990). *Physical management of multiple handicaps: A professional's guide* (2nd ed.). Baltimore: Paul H. Brookes Publishing Co.

Fredericks, H.D., Baldwin, V.L., Grove, D.N., Riggs, C., Furey, V., Moore, W., Jordan, E., Gage, M.A., Levak, L., Alrick, G., & Wadlow, P. (1975). *A data-based classroom for the moderately and severely handicapped.* Monmouth, OR: Instructional Development Corp.

Giangreco, M.F. (1986). Effects of integrated therapy: A pilot study. *Journal of The Association for Persons with Severe Handicaps, 11(3),* 205–208.

Helle, K.M. (1988). Modern technology in the rehabilitation process. *International Journal of Rehabilitation, 11*(3), 243–249.

Howard, V.F., & Williams, R.L. (1991). Advances in education for persons with severe handicaps. *Psychology in the Schools, 28*(2), 123–138.

IMPACT: Feature issue on Inclusive education (K–12). (1991). Institute on Community Integration, University of Minnesota, Minneapolis.

IMPACT: Feature issue on Integrated education. (1988). Institute on Community Integration, University of Minnesota, Minneapolis.

Lahm, E.A. (1989, June). *Technology with low incidence populations: Promoting access to education and learning.* Paper presented at The Advancing the Use of Technology: The Research/Practice Connection FY89 Invitational Technology Symposium, Washington, DC.

Lechtenberg, R. (1990). *Seizure recognition and treatment.* New York: Churchill Livingstone, Inc.

Levin, J., & Scherfenberg, L. (1987). *Selection and use of simple technology in home, school, work, and community settings.* Minneapolis: ABLENET.

Lindsey, J.D. (Ed.). (1992). *Computers and exceptional individuals* (2nd ed.). Austin, TX: PRO-ED.

Male, M. (1994). *Technology for inclusion: Meeting the special needs of all students.* Boston: Allyn and Bacon.

McCubbin, T. (1983). Routine and emergency medical procedures. In M. Snell (Ed.), *Systematic instruction of people with severe handicaps* (2nd ed.). Columbus, OH: Charles E. Merrill.

Mueller, H. (1975). Feeding. In N. Finnie, (Ed.), *Handling the young cerebral palsied child at home.* New York: E.P. Dutton.

Orelove, F.P., & Sobsey, D. (1991). *Educating children with multiple disabilities: A transdisciplinary approach* (2nd ed.). Baltimore: Paul H. Brookes Publishing Co.

Rainforth, B., & York, J. (1991). Handling and positioning. In F.P. Orelove, & D. Sobsey, *Educating children with multiple disabilities: A transdisciplinary approach* (2nd ed.) (pp. 79–117). Baltimore: Paul H. Brookes Publishing Co.

Rainforth, B., York, J., & Macdonald, C. (1992). *Collaborative teams for students with severe disabilities.* Baltimore: Paul H. Brookes Publishing Co.

Schery, T.K., & O'Connor, L.C. (1992). The effectiveness of school-based computer language intervention with severely handicapped children. *Language, Speech, and Hearing Services in Schools, 23*(3), 43–47.

Sternat, J., Messina, R., Nietupski, J., Lyon, S., & Brown, L. (1977). In E. Sontag (Ed.), *Educational programming for the severely and profoundly handicapped* (pp. 263–278). Reston, VA: Council for Exceptional Children, Division on Mental Retardation.

Taylor, M. (1990). Clean intermittent catheterization. In J.C. Graff, M.M. Ault, D. Guess, M. Taylor, & B. Thompson, *Health care for students with disabilities: An illustrated medical guide for the classroom* (pp. 241–252). Baltimore: Paul H. Brookes Publishing Co.

Trefler, E. (1988). Positioning: Concepts and technology. *Exceptional Parents, 18*(5), 28–33.

Utley, B. (1982). Motor skills and adaptation. In L. Sternberg & G. Adams (Eds.), *Educating severely and profoundly handicapped students* (pp. 163–204). Rockville, MD: Aspen.

Villa, R.A., Thousand, J.S., Stainback, W., & Stainback, S. (Eds.). (1992). *Restructuring for caring and effective education.* Baltimore: Paul H. Brookes Publishing Co.

Williams, M.V., & Barber, W.H. (1992). The relationship of lòcus of control and learned helplessness in special education students. *Journal of Special Education, 16*(1), 1–12.

Wright, C., & Nomura, M. (1988). *From toys to computers: Access for the physically disabled.* San Jose, CA: Christine Wright.

York, J., Nietupski, J., & Hamre-Nietupski, S. (1985). A decision-making process for using microswitches. *Journal of The Association for Persons with Severe Handicaps, 10*(4), 214–223.

York, J., & Rainforth, B. (1991). Developing instructional adaptation. In F.P. Orelove & D. Sobsey, *Educating children with multiple disabilities: A transdisciplinary approach* (2nd ed.) (pp. 259–295). Baltimore: Paul H. Brookes Publishing Co.

York, J., Rainforth, B., & Wiemann, G. (1988). An integrated approach to therapy for school-aged learners with developmental disabilities. *Totline, 14*(3), 36–40.

York, J., Vandercook, T., Macdonald, C., & Wolff, S. (Eds.). (1989). *Strategies for full inclusion.* Minneapolis: University of Minnesota, Institute on Community Integration.

9 COMMUNICATION SKILLS

MARY A. FALVEY

One of the most basic quality-of-life requisites is individual choice- and decision-making opportunities. The freedom to have choices and personally make decisions is cherished by people in all stages of life, yet it is also a freedom that has been typically denied to persons with disabilities. To perform these essential skills, one must have a means to communicate that is respected as well as listened to and responded to by others. The ability to communicate has often been used as a measure of intelligence and worth (Mirenda, Iacono, & Williams, 1990).

Williams (1991) called for a *communication imperative* that would result in every person, regardless of the severity of his or her disabilities, having the right to communicate. He further stated that everyone has the ability to communicate and therefore "should be given the chance, training, technology, respect, and encouragement to do so" (p. 543). Educators, service providers, and others must have a strong belief in everyone's innate communication abilities, or persons with significant communication difficulties and/or delays will continue to be ignored and disregarded (Mirenda et al., 1990). It is not enough, however, to have such a belief; specific interventions, opportunities, and technologies must be made available to meet individual student's needs.

For school and community inclusion to be effective, educators and communication specialists must work in collaboration with the student and his or her peers and parents to design communication systems, methods, modes, and technologies that will facilitate that student's communicative interactions. The purpose of this chapter is to present a framework and a set of strategies that can be used to facilitate students' effective communication with others.

ELEMENTS OF COMMUNICATION

Communication involves certain elements. First, the use of a *system* is essential (e.g., spoken language, manual signs, pictures, objects). Second, the communicator must be able to employ a *mode(s)* for delivering a message with these symbols (e.g., speech, pointing, gesturing, blinking). Third, *social interaction skills* are necessary for the message to be understood by the listener and for comprehension of the rules that dictate the reciprocal nature of interacting. Finally, vocabulary or *communicative content* is necessary to communicate. Communication can involve speech and language, although it is not dependent upon these components. Rather, communication is defined as "occurring when people interact in some way (verbally or nonverbally) so that a message passes from one person to another and a response is given in return" (Musselwhite & St. Louis, 1982, p. 48). The strategies emphasized in this chapter are those that teach students with disabilities to communicate and interact with others within a variety of inclusive school, home, and community settings.

PAST RESEARCH IN COMMUNICATION INTERVENTION

Students with severe disabilities often exhibit significant difficulties and delays in the area of communication skills. Students with autism, for example, experience major problems in the use of language, both in being understood and in comprehending the communications of others (Kanner, 1943; Prizant, 1983; Schuler, 1979; Wing, 1981). Students with severe cognitive delays exhibit substantial delays in communication and are often unable to verbally express even simple thoughts. Other students with cognitive delays are characterized by prompt dependency, passivity, or learned helplessness (Calculator, 1988; Seligman, 1975). Students with physical disabilities may have difficulty producing the sounds necessary to communicate verbally. In addition, some students exhibit communication difficulties associated with several or all three of the disabilities just mentioned.

Traditionally, speech and communication have been viewed as synonymous (Calculator, 1988). This has led to isolated intervention efforts that focused on drill, comprehension, and articulation skills within continued and artificial adult–child interactions (Bedrosian, 1988). In addition, intervention has traditionally focused on teaching students to label objects, feelings, and materials rather than to encourage spontaneous use of language. Teachers have also reported that this focus on the development and refinement of "speech" led to the exclusion of many students from speech and language services. Students with severe disabilities were often described as not being ready for speech services due to their delay.

Another practice that has interfered with the development of students' communicative skills and interactions has been an overreliance on and narrow interpretation of the developmental skills of typical children. The majority of students with significant disabilities demonstrate a delay or difficulties in communicating their thoughts and feelings. Although a developmental perspective is critical to teaching all students, at times professionals have used this orientation to limit the possibilities of students with significant disabilities simply because their skills were not developing at the same rate or even in the same order as those of children without disabilities. For example, using traditional assessments, one communication specialist concluded that because a certain student did not use words to communicate, he must not understand concepts either. These kinds of assumptions and conclusions can have a tremendously detrimental effect on a student's development of communicative skills and behaviors.

PRESENT TRENDS IN COMMUNICATION INTERVENTION

In the past, communication intervention services for students with disabilities were limited for many reasons. Recent research into language development has led to an expanded focus of communication intervention, in terms of both intervention targets and intervention style. This research has suggested that pragmatic communication, or control of the environment through communication, intentional or not, occurs much earlier than the use of language (Halliday, 1975; Keogh & Reichle, 1985). Current intervention programs for students with communication delays are therefore targeting speech and language skills as well as these early prelinguistic and presymbolic forms of communication (Owens & Rogerson, 1988; Siegel-Causey & Downing, 1987). In addition, studies of language development have suggested a style of intervention characterized by the following components: contingent, responsive student-centered interactions that maximize the student's attention to the task at hand; active interactions within routines and joint activities involving the student and someone else; scaffolding, which assists a student's performance by using prompts that are finely tuned to the student present ability; assigned meaning to communicative attempts; and use of varied stimuli (Ainsworth, 1973; Hart, 1985; MacDonald, 1985; Snow, 1972; Snow & Ferguson, 1978; Vygotsky, 1978). Communication intervention no longer targets speech alone in isolated instructional settings; rather, effective communication intervention targets teaching the functions, forms, and content that will have the greatest impact on the person's life within natural, normalized, and inclusive environments and activities (Falvey, Bishop, Grenot-Scheyer, & Coots, 1988; McLean & Snyder-McLean, 1978).

A trend in the area of communication that has attracted much attention in the 1990s and has significantly altered approaches to and attitudes about intervention is facilitated communication. Facilitated communication has been defined as an "alternative means of communication where students are given physical and emotional support to type on an electronic keyboard or point at letters on an alphabet board" (Biklen & Schubert, 1991, p. 46). Although not without controversy and doubts concerning its legitimacy (Cummins & Prior, 1992; Prior &

Cummins, 1992), facilitated communication has had a dramatic effect on the lives of thousands of people previously thought to have no or extremely limited communication and cognitive abilities. Facilitated communication's relationship to traditional aspects of communication intervention continues to be researched. Specific strategies for using facilitated communication appear later in this chapter.

Requisites to Communication

Traditionally, such behaviors as attending, imitating, and following simple directions have been viewed as prerequisites to communication (Kent, 1974). While such behaviors are important for communication, insistence upon mastering a skill such as imitation as a prerequisite may delay the teaching of functional communication behaviors. These skills must instead be taught concurrently with specific communication skills and, in such a context, have been referred to as "requisites" for communication (Gruenewald, Schroeder, & Yoder, 1982). These requisites are described below.

Reasons for Communicating   Unfortunately, students with disabilities are often inadvertently discouraged from producing appropriate communicative behaviors. Well-meaning educators and families anticipate the needs and wants of students to such an extent that the students find little or no reason to communicate. In addition, traditional programs that emphasize speech production in isolation of communication frequently produce the perception by the students that there is no purpose for those speech behaviors. Because students are all too often given little control over their lives, they may also develop "learned helplessness" resulting in a lack of motivation to control their environment by communicating. Finally, students exhibiting such behaviors as temper tantrums or abuse of self, others, or property are frequently placed on strict programs to eliminate such behaviors. Research has demonstrated that such inappropriate behaviors might serve as the student's only attempts at communicating and should therefore be shaped into more appropriate responses rather than extinguished (Donnellan, Mirenda, Mesaros, & Fassbender, 1984; Prizant & Duchan, 1981; Rein, 1984; Schuler & Goetz, 1983). Educators and parents must determine what motivates a student in order to provide that student with reasons to communicate (Gruenewald et al., 1982).

Communicative Content   Once there is a reason to communicate, there must be something to communicate, known as *communicative content*. To determine the communicative content to be taught, ecological inventories, parent and significant other interviews, and systematic observation of the students should be considered. Content should reflect vocabulary that will have the greatest impact upon the individual student's life. The communicative content should reflect a student's primary language and the family's cultural values and perspectives. The content should allow the student to exhibit control over what occurs in his or her life and should reflect the ideas the student most wants to communicate.

Emphasis must be placed on communicative content that will assist the student to become as independent as possible in a variety of environments (Gruenewald et al., 1982). In addition, the communicative content taught to a student must focus on messages necessary to interact with peers both with and without disabilities, family members, community members, neighbors, co-workers, and employers (Wulz, Myers, Klein, Hall, & Waldo, 1982). Moreover, too much emphasis has often been placed upon teaching students to respond to someone else's initiation. Emphasis must instead be placed on teaching students the content needed to initiate interactions as well.

Communication Methods Since many students with severe disabilities may not develop intelligible speech, providing an augmentative or alternative means to communicate is essential. When possible, speech should always be the first choice, as it is the most convenient and adaptable mode of communication available. However, it is also highly abstract and requires strong temporal processing abilities; for many students, other more concrete methods of communication are therefore essential. Others may require alternative methods of communication because they are unable to acquire enough intelligible speech to allow it to serve as a functional communication system (Gruenewald et al., 1982).

Communication Environments As with all instruction for students with disabilities, it is best if communicative behaviors are assessed and taught in the environments most natural for individual students. This allows for efficiency in instruction and learning. Varying environments dictate varying expectations in communicative behaviors and can serve as a prompt for students displaying appropriate communicative behaviors (Gruenewald et al., 1982). In addition, communication instruction should be infused throughout activities within a student's daily routine. For example, the communication specialist can come to the second-grade class attended by a student with severe disabilities and teach her to signal during the morning calendar and sharing time. The specialist can consult with the second-grade teacher regarding strategies for teaching choice-making skills during lunch for this same student. The specialist can also consult with the parents so that they can teach the same skills during play, dressing, and mealtimes at home. If generalized communicative competence is the goal of intervention, then natural, inclusive settings provide the most appropriate environments in which to assess, instruct, and evaluate a student's skills and behaviors (Falvey, McLean, & Rosenberg, 1988).

Communication Partners Since communication implies interaction, a second person must be involved in communicating with the student. That person can be the one who initiates or the one who responds. In either case, the second person can serve as a prompt, as can the environment (Gruenewald et al., 1982). Systematic instruction must be provided in such a way that students have opportunities to learn to interact with others, particularly with nonspecialized staff persons and peers. Communication intervention should facilitate interactions and relationships with others, particularly with family members, peers without disabilities, and community members. In addition, training must emphasize teaching the student to initiate interactions with familiar and unfamiliar people at appropriate times.

An unfortunate result of traditional service delivery models has been the placement of students with disabilities into segregated educational environments. These students then had limited access to appropriate communicative models and persons with whom to interact effectively. Therefore, social interaction and communication behaviors may have been extinguished or inhibited. As stated by Schuler (1981), a segregated situation in which students with disabilities are communicating and interacting solely with one another will not be conducive to behavior change, nor to the maintenance or generalization of communication skills. Access to peers without disabilities who are competent communicators is therefore essential to the development of effective communication skills.

COMMUNICATION ASSESSMENT PROCEDURES AND TECHNIQUES

In the past, assessments have been limited to group or individual standardized measures conducted in artificial environments and at the beginning of a program. Assessments should be modified to emphasize the use of various measures and techniques in order to determine critical needs for individual students and their present levels of performance in those areas. A comprehensive assessment (discussed in Chapter 4) is essential. Specifically, assessment of the student's current communication ability is undertaken so that present abilities can be built upon. Communication assessment strategies have been broadened to include critical information with regard to when, where, what, and how assessments should be conducted.

When to Assess

Detailed and thorough assessments must be conducted in order to determine relevant and functional programs that will facilitate the student's acquisition and performance of communicative behaviors. These behaviors should enhance interactions and interaction opportunities and should provide students with appropriate ways to control their environments. Assessment is the first component in developing and determining programs, but assessments must continue to be conducted in order to verify that the student is acquiring skills and that the skills are still functional for that student as time passes.

Where to Assess

A critical part of the assessment process is determining the environments that will be used for assessment and instruction. In order to determine how the student is currently communicating, what the student is communicating, and what the student needs to communicate, assessment of those behaviors must be conducted in the student's natural environments (e.g., home, school playground, classroom, school cafeteria, neighborhood, community recreation center). It is essential to assess a student across a variety of environments to determine the conditions that exist when the student is exhibiting communicative behaviors. Assessment is also essential for evaluating the student's ability to generalize communicative behaviors across environments, persons, cues, and other stimulus dimensions.

What to Assess

Needless to say, determining what to assess in order to develop a comprehensive communication program for a student must be done prior to the actual assessment. Several areas that should be addressed in order to develop such a communication program follow.

   1. Receptive Understanding   The student's understanding of the critical communicative concepts and terms that occur in his or her environments must be assessed. This should involve presenting communicative concepts and terms in familiar and functional ways for the student. For students who have had little to no exposure to English, assessment must occur in their own language.

   2. Expressive Communicative Behaviors   The student's attempts at communicating, verbally and nonverbally, must be assessed. Differences in frequency and type should be noted; assessment should also determine when the student is responding and when the student is initiating the interaction. Emphasis should be placed upon identifying as many different communicative behaviors as the student is able to produce (e.g., signing, talking, pointing, smiling, blinking, grunting). The primary language(s) spoken in a student's surroundings at home and in the community should be made available during assessment and, if used by the student, noted. In addition, attempts to communicate through inappropriate behavior must be carefully examined (Donnellan et al., 1984). For many students with severe disabilities, assessment of communicative behaviors needs to target the initial presymbolic level of increasing or decreasing participation within activities with regard to seeing or touching an interesting object, using a differentiated cry, and/or vocalizing to indicate states such as fear, contentment, and anger. Table 1 (Siegel-Causey & Guess, 1987) provides a listing of nonsymbolic communications that should be assessed when analyzing a student's expressive communication behaviors.

   3. Cognitive Understanding   The student's understanding of cognitive concepts must be assessed. Specifically, assessment must be conducted to determine the student's abilities with regard to paralinguistic skills such as memory, perceptual discrimination, and attending. Similarly, symbolic and representational skills, understanding of cause and effect and anticipation of events, and imitative skills should be assessed. This information becomes essential in the selection of the appropriate symbol set, method, and content for communication.

Table 1.　Forms of learner nonsymbolic communications

Generalized movements and changes in muscle tone
　Excitement in response to stimulation or in anticipation of an event
　Squirms and resists physical contact
　Changes in muscle tone in response to soothing touch or voice, in reaction to sudden stimuli, or in preparation to act

Vocalizations
　Calls to attract or direct another's attention
　Laughs or coos in response to pleasurable stimulation
　Cries in reaction to discomfort

Facial expressions
　Smiles in response to familiar person, object, or event
　Grimaces in reaction to unpleasant or unexpected sensation

Orientation
　Looks toward or points to person or object to seek or direct attention
　Looks away from person or object to indicate disinterest or refusal
　Looks toward suddenly appearing familiar or novel person, object, or event

Pause
　Ceases moving in anticipation of coming event
　Pauses to await service provider's instruction or to allow service provider to take turn

Touching, manipulating, or moving with another person
　Holds or grabs another for comfort
　Takes or directs another's hand to something
　Manipulates service provider into position to start an activity or interactive "game"
　Touches or pulls to gain attention
　Pushes away or lets go to terminate an interaction
　Moves with or follows the movements of another person

Acting on objects and using objects to interact with others
　Reaches toward, leans toward, touches, gets, picks up, activates, drops, or pushes away object to indicate interest or disinterest
　Extends, touches, or places object to show to another or to request another's action
　Holds out hands to prepare to receive object

Assuming positions and going to places
　Holds up arms to be picked up, holds out hands to initiate "game," leans back on swing to be pushed
　Stands by sink to request drink, goes to cabinet to request material stored there

Conventional gestures
　Waves to greet
　Nods to indicate assent or refusal

Depictive actions
　Pantomimes throwing to indicate, "throw ball"
　Sniffs to indicate smelling flowers
　Makes sounds similar to those made by animals and objects to make reference to them
　Draws picture to describe or request activity

(continued)

Table 1.   (*continued*)

Withdrawal
   Pulls away or moves away to avoid interaction or activity
   Curls up, lies on floor to avoid interaction or activity

Aggressive and self-injurious behavior
   Hits, scratches, bites, or spits at service provider to protest action or in response to frustration
   Throws or destroys objects to protest action or in response to frustration
   Hits, bites, or otherwise harms self or threatens to harm self to protest action, in response to frustration, or in reaction to pain or discomfort

From Siegel-Causey, E., & Guess, D. (1989). *Enhancing nonsymbolic communication interactions among learners with severe disabilities* (p. 7). Baltimore: Paul H. Brookes Publishing Co.; reprinted by permission.

4.   *Communicative Functions*   The student's understanding of the functions of communication must be evaluated. Determining for what purposes the student uses communication is an important part of the assessment. Chapman (1981) describes several functions of communication that should be assessed, including the student's ability to: give information; get information; describe an ongoing activity; get the listener to do something, believe something, or feel something; express his or her own intentions, beliefs, or feelings; indicate readiness for further communication; solve problems; and entertain. Request, refusal, and recurrence (e.g., requesting "more") are additional initial functions of communication (Keogh & Reichle, 1985; Reichle, Piche-Cragoe, Sigafoos, & Doss, 1988; Reichle, Rogers, & Barret, 1984).

5.   *Interaction Skills*   The frequencies and types of interactions that the student exhibits across settings with others must be assessed. Specifically, the following questions must be addressed:

Does the student attempt to interact?
How often does the student interact?
What communication modes does the student use to interact?
With whom does the student interact (e.g., siblings, familiar and unfamiliar peers, adults)?
In what contexts (e.g., what materials and persons are present, what environments) does the student interact?
What content does the student use in interacting?

6.   *Mobility and Manipulation*   The student's overall mobility must be assessed, particularly when considering augmentative communication systems and when teaching interaction skills. The following mobility and manipulation skills should be assessed:

Fine motor skills and coordination (e.g., reaching, pointing, grasping)
Degree of control over head, arms, legs, and shoulders
Mobility skills (e.g., crawls, walks, uses wheelchair)
Overall positioning (both optimal and usual position)

Range of motion in all joints
Amount and type of motor exploring, interacting, and/or manipulating

7. Sensory and Perceptual Students' ability to use their sensory skills, both auditory and visual, are essential to assess in order to develop augmentative communication systems. A list of the sensory and perceptual skills that should be assessed follows:

Tracking and scanning
Visual acuity and discrimination abilities
Hearing acuity and discrimination abilities

How to Assess

Several methods must be considered when assessing students' communicative behaviors and abilities. These methods should be used in combination rather than in isolation. The major question that needs to be answered by the assessment process is, "What does the student usually do with regard to communicating?" so that those skills can serve as the basis for intervention. A discussion of these methods follows.

Developmental Measures First, the use of developmental measures must be considered. Developmental sequences of communication contain critical information for assessment. Determining the typical developmental sequence of communication skills can assist educators in assessing and understanding the student's levels and abilities.

Some cautionary remarks must be delineated concerning the appropriate use of developmental measures. First, developmental measures often ignore the variation that occurs among individuals in the acquisition of skills (Hecht, 1986). Second, much attention has been placed on the correlation between cognitive development and language development. The term *cognitive hypothesis* has been used to refer to the supposition that a particular conceptual achievement or mental age is necessary to a specific linguistic achievement (Bloom, 1970; Brown, 1973; Chapman & Miller, 1980; Cromer, 1974, 1976). Recent developments in the study and acquisition of communication behaviors have demonstrated that language acquisition cannot be adequately understood apart from achievements in the areas of cognitive, social, and motor skills. However, the difficulties involved in measuring cognitive level makes the discussion concerning the relationship between language, cognition, and other areas of development problematic. The use of developmental assessments in determining communicative performance and needs may therefore be problematic. The recent controversy surrounding facilitated communication (Biklen, 1993) raises significant questions about our traditional methods of assessing such skills, particularly cognitive skills. Often students assessed prior to the provision of facilitated communication were determined, based upon traditional assessment methods, to have low or very low cognitive skills compared to their chronological age peers. However, when provided with facilitated communication, these same students demonstrate cognitive abilities close to, at, or above their chronological-age peers in cognitive skills. In order to increase accuracy and validity in determining the most functional communication program for a given student, developmental assessment should be used in conjunction with other assessment procedures, particularly the results from informal measures.

Systematic Observational Procedures The second type of assessment that should be used is that of systematic observational procedures. Gruenewald et al. (1982) stated that the major purpose of using observational techniques is to determine the relationship of a predetermined set of expectations to a student's skill proficiency, rather than comparing that student to other students or groups of students. This procedure is designed to tell educators how the student learns best and what the student should be learning.

Observations should be conducted in the student's natural environments (e.g., home, classroom, playground, after-school programs). Materials, cues, and familiar and unfamiliar people should be present. The data that are collected should reflect environments, familiar and unfamiliar persons and materials, natural cues used, and any other stimulus dimensions. Observation should initially be conducted in the student's natural environments without manipulation of those environments. Assuming additional assessment information is necessary, manipulation of the stimulus dimensions within those environments should take place in order to determine the extent of the student's communicative behaviors and abilities. Figure 1 provides an example of a communication and social skills survey that can be used to obtain the necessary information about the conditions present when students communicate.

Language sampling is a technique involving the observation of the student in his or her own natural environments and the recording of a sample of that student's spontaneous use of language. Each utterance is recorded along with the context in which it is made. The sample is then analyzed for the communicative function and intent. Syntactic and semantic categories, vocabulary, and the mean length of utterance (MLU) (which refers to the average length of a student's utterances) are also examined.

Ecological and Student Repertoire Inventories The third type of assessment that can be used is ecological and student repertoire inventories. These inventories are used to identify functional communicative content for students. They are also used to determine the student's understanding and skill proficiency with regard to communication in his or her current and subsequent natural environments. Ecological and student repertoire inventories are discussed in Chapter 4 of this volume. An ecological inventory is conducted within the student's current and subsequent natural environments to determine the communicative content and expectations within those environments.

Utterances	Initiated	Responses	Persons present	Materials present	Time of day
"Want more"	✓		Mom	Cookies and milk	3:30 P.M.
"Boo" (for book)		✓	Older sibling asked student, "What do you want?"	Book, doll, and radio	7:30 P.M.
"Night"		✓	Dad said, "Goodnight."	Bed, toys, bed sheets, and light	8:45 P.M.

Figure 1.   Example of a communication and social skills survey.

Once information collected from an ecological inventory has been determined, the student repertoire inventory must be conducted. The student repertoire inventory is conducted by taking the student to those environments that have been inventoried and comparing his or her communicative performance to those delineated in the ecological inventory of same-age peers without disabilities. This information is analyzed with regard to the student's abilities to perform the specific communicative behaviors expected within the natural environments, and to utilize the communicative content present in those environments. The discrepancies that exist in behaviors and content between the performance of the student with disabilities and peers without disabilities are then targeted for instruction.

Interviews and Questionnaires   The fourth assessment method, interviews and questionnaires, must be employed with parents and significant others. Although observation and other forms of direct assessment can yield critical information, parents and significant others can be an essential source of information concerning the student's critical needs and present level of performance (Klein et al., 1981). A sample survey is presented in Figure 2.

Parents can be initially surveyed or called upon to assist in the determination of who else would be appropriate to complete the questionnaire. This questionnaire should be completed by parents and by anyone else who is significant to the student—for example, those who interact with, have responsibility for, or have a special relationship with the student. Siblings, grandparents, other relatives, neighbors, friends, respite care workers, and tutors could all be significant others for a student.

Before a program is instituted, data should be collected using the various methods of assessment just described. Once a program has started, continual data collection must occur in order to determine program effectiveness on a consistent and regular basis.

COMMUNICATION MODES

The most commonly used mode of communication among the general population is speech, although all persons augment their use of speech with nonverbal communication modes (e.g., gestures, body language, expressions, writing) (Vanderheiden & Yoder, 1986). Speech is often impossible for a large number of students with severe disabilities because they lack the motor, linguistic, and/or cognitive skills necessary to produce sounds in a manner that can be understood by others. This section therefore begins with a brief overview of speech as a communication mode, followed by a more detailed description of augmentative and/or alternative methods of communication.

Speech

For those students who are developing speech or who already have speech, several issues should be considered. First, speech must not be assessed and analyzed

1. Describe the way your son/daughter communicates.

2. Which do you see as being your son's/daughter's preference?

3. Does your son/daughter exhibit the following behaviors when communicating: smiling, frowning, eye blinking, looking at objects/persons, gesturing/pointing, signing, touching, pulling person, banging objects, laughing, crying/whining, screaming, making sounds, words, other?

4. Describe conditions, including times, events, people, places, and materials present when your son/daughter communicates.

5. Does your son/daughter respond to commands? If yes, give examples.

6. Does your son/daughter answer questions? If yes, give examples.

7. Does your son/daughter functionally use objects? If yes, give examples.

8. List the objects, persons, places, activities, and emotions that you wish your son/daughter to be able to communicate.

9. What objects, food, toys, materials, music, expressions, persons, and so forth, are positively reinforcing to your son/daughter?

10. What body parts does your son/daughter use voluntarily when participating in activities and/or manipulating objects?

11. List adaptive equipment and/or physical assistance needed by your son/daughter. Describe his or her preferred position(s).

12. Does your son/daughter have visual or auditory difficulties? If yes, describe.

13. What language(s) are spoken at home?

Figure 2.   Sample parent survey questionnaire to determine student's communication repertoire and skills.

apart from the context in which it is produced. Some students, particularly those with autism, exhibit speech with reasonable to good articulation skills but produce the speech only in an echoic form, that is, modeling someone else's speech. This form of speech is referred to as *echolalia*. Schuler (1979) has contributed extensively to our understanding of echolalia, classifying it into several categories along a continuum, from noncommunicative to communicative. Schuler identified "delayed noncommunicative echolalia" as the least functional echolalia. Echolalia can also be classified as "delayed," "immediate," and "mitigated," and as having communicative functions. The results of Schuler's work and that of others (Prizant, 1983; Prizant & Duchan, 1981; Rein, 1984) strongly suggest that intervention strategies for students who exhibit echolalia should be based upon careful analysis of the communicative functions of the student's speech. Additionally, shaping and other procedures should be used to facilitate their production of appropriate communicative speech.

The second issue that needs to be considered in speech assessment is that of the *student's primary language*. Students who are non–English speaking, use English as a second language, or whose families do not speak English or speak it as a second language should be assessed in their primary language. Intervention programs should reflect the student's most familiar language, as well as the language(s) used in their home, neighborhood, school, and work environments.

Augmentative and Alternative Communication Modes

Once a student has been identified as having significant communication difficulties, he or she may be considered to be at risk for not developing intelligible speech. Educators and parents must consider developing and teaching augmentative and/or alternative communication modes to students. An augmentative and alternative communication system is "an integrated group of components, including the symbols, aids, strategies, and techniques used by individuals to enhance communication" (American Speech-Language-Hearing Association, 1991, p. 10).

In order to determine and develop appropriate augmentative or alternative communication modes for students who do not have intelligible speech, educators and parents must be familiar with the variety of modes available. A discussion of some of the most commonly used modes follows.

Gestures Gesturing is a common form of nonverbal communication among the general population; therefore, it is a commonly understood augmentative mode of communication that may be useful for persons with disabilities. Generally understood gestures refer to motor movements that are topographically similar to the object or action they represent (e.g., motioning someone to go in a different direction by pointing in that direction). In addition, gestures might consist of body language that is generally understood within a cultural group or across several cultural groups (e.g., smiling when happy or content). Hamre-Nietupski et al. (1977) delineated over 150 generally understood gestures that are used by persons with and without disabilities to communicate. Gestures should be taught within the context in which they will be used—that is, the student should be taught how, with whom, and when to use what gestures. Several limitations must be considered when teaching the use of gestures. First of all, not all concepts, feelings, and other information that a student might want to communicate can be communicated with a gesture; therefore, using gestures as the only communicative mode would limit the student's available communicative content. Second, although many gestures are widely understood, many others are ambiguous and do not clearly communicate a message. Third, certain gestures may be understood only by a specific group and not by the general population.

Manual Signing   Manual signing refers to the use of fingers, hands, and arms to communicate. There are various forms of manual signing; the most frequently used system is American Sign Language (ASL) (Wilbur, 1976), and Signing Exact English (SEE) (Mayberry, 1976) is used less frequently. Students can be facilitated to develop speech skills through the introduction of sign language paired with the spoken referent (i.e., total communication). Several issues need to be considered when teaching students to use manual signs as a form of communication. First, manual signing is not understood or used by the general population. Therefore, caution should be used when teaching students to use manual signing as the sole form of communication, as it limits the number of people with whom the student can communicate. Second, students with significant motor difficulties might not be able to produce all of the signs. Third, since manual signing involves the use of fingers, hands, and arms, students will need to limit the use of their fingers, hands, and arms in other communicative manners when signing. Fourth, although signing has been successfully used as an augmentative mode for some persons with severe disabilities, one must not assume that signing is the best, most efficient mode of communication in every case. For young children with severe disabilities (especially those with Down syndrome), signing is sometimes best used as a temporary form of language (Hobson & Duncan, 1979); as these children develop the skills to communicate verbally, their reliance on manual signs can be reduced and even eliminated.

System Displays   A variety of system displays (i.e., methods for organizing and presenting the augmentative communication referents) are available. In order to determine, design, and develop appropriate functional system displays for students with severe communication disabilities, several categories of information must be considered. First, the symbol system that will be used must be determined—that is, whether it will involve objects, photos, black-and-white line drawings, abstract symbols, or traditional orthography. Second, the selecting/activating response (e.g., pointing, gazing, head movement, or switch activation) must be determined. Third, the form of the system display (e.g., single cards, wallet displays, books, manual boards, or electronic aids) must be determined. Each of these issues is discussed in the following paragraphs.

Symbol System   The most concrete form of communication is to use *actual objects*. This form eliminates ambiguity and requires little or no abstract cognitive ability on the part of the student. Therefore, this form of communication can be used initially to assess the student's receptive understanding and object preferences and as a beginning method of communication. However, objects can be cumbersome, and if they are not in sight (i.e., if they are in the other room, outside, or across town), they cannot be discussed or used to communicate. In addition, if objects are used as the only form of communication, the student has no way of communicating abstract concepts such as feelings. As a result, objects should be used only when other more abstract forms of communication are unsuccessful or impossible. In addition, as the student becomes proficient at using objects to communicate, those objects should be paired with more abstract forms (e.g., miniature objects, pictures, words). The objects should then be gradually faded so that the student is able to use a more expandable, abstract, and flexible system.

Photographs, line drawings, and other pictures of objects, actions, and places can be used for students who require a nonverbal form of communication. One of the advantages of using photographs of actual objects, actions, and places is that they can be used to reduce ambiguity and to individualize for each student (e.g., using an actual photograph of the student's jacket). A number of issues should be considered when using pictures. First, when using actual photographs versus line drawings, when determining the appropriate size of the pictures, and when determining the location and placement of pictures on a display, educators must determine the student's preferences and visual discrimination skills. Second, because unnecessary and irrelevant stimuli within photographs may be confusing to some students and/or message receivers, the actual pictures must be carefully selected for individual students. For example, when using a photograph of a woman holding an apple to represent "apple," the student or the message receiver might attend to the woman, to the type of clothing she is wearing, or to other irrelevant stimulus dimensions. In this instance, a picture featuring only an apple would be preferable. Third, pictures should be paired with words so that the message receiver is able to interpret the communicative referent for each picture and the student can recieve additional input for developing literacy skills.

Abstract symbols such as Blissymbols (Vanderheiden & Grilley, 1976) and non–SLIP (non–Speech Language Initiation Program) symbols (Carrier, 1976) have been taught to students who require a nonverbal form of communication. The term "abstract symbols" refers to symbols that represent objects, actions, feelings, or concepts. Several issues need to be considered when using abstract symbols. First, because these symbol systems do not resemble their actual referents, they may be confusing and too visually complex to the student or the message receiver. Second, if the student is able to understand and use an abstract symbol system, educators should consider a more commonly used form of abstract symbols, such as traditional orthography.

The term *traditional orthography* refers to the use of written words for communication. Because this form of communication is used among the general population, it should be encouraged and taught if the student has the capacity to use this form. Several factors must be considered when using traditional orthography as a nonverbal form of communication. First, traditional orthography cannot be used as a communication system with message receivers who are nonreaders within the language being used. This might eliminate communicating with young siblings or peers who have not acquired reading skills, or with family members, neighbors, and friends who are nonreaders of the language being used. This concern is addressed when words are written in the language the family/community understands. Second, traditional orthography involves using specific materials (e.g., pencils, pens, paper, typewriters, computers, memory writers); some environments may not contain those materials or may not be conducive to the use of those materials.

Selecting/Activating Response   "Selecting responses" is a term that refers to the action the student makes when using an augmentative and/or alternative communication system. There are two choices for students who communicate through the use of symbol systems—direct selection or scanning. *Direct selection* occurs when a student points directly to the desired symbol. *Scanning* refers to the student indicating his or her choice by performing a predetermined behavior that can function as a signal. Scanning is typically used by students who have significant difficulty making intentional motor responses using direct selection techniques. A student's skills must be assessed in order to determine the most appropriate response that he or she can voluntarily control. Following is a list of the most common selecting responses used in order to communicate:

Pointing (using a finger, wrist, hand, elbow, foot, knee, hip, shoulder, tongue)
Head movements
Eyegazing

In addition to the choice of selecting responses to communicate, educators and parents must consider the possibility of a student using an activating switch that can interface with a scanning device or direct selection device. Vanderheiden and Grilley (1976) delineated some of the more common switch-activating devices as follows:

1. Mechanical switches for the extremities, such as buttons or keys on keyboards, paddles and levers, pillow switches, wobblesticks, joysticks, sliding or trolley switches, poke switches, and tip or tilt switches
2. Mechanical switches for specific body parts, such as the head, chin, eyebrow, knee, palate, splint (finger), tongue, thumb, or wrist
3. Pneumatic (air or breath) switches, such as suck and puff switch or air paddles
4. Touch switches requiring contact by no physical pressure, such as touchplates or cybergloves and cyberplates
5. Moisture-sensitive switches
6. Proximity switches sensitive to the body or to a special trigger element (e.g., metal, magnet, circuit) when brought within a certain range of the switch
7. Optical switches, such as a lightspot (a light source attached to a head pointer or some other body part) or interrupted-beam switches
8. Sonic switches that are activated by sound
9. Bioelectric switches that are activated by the electric impulses generated in nerves and muscles of the body

System Display Forms   Several of the forms of communication already described require the use of devices or materials to display available symbols.

Following is a discussion of some of the most commonly used devices and materials.

Pictures, symbols, and/or words can be used in *single-card* or *wallet-display* augmentative communication systems. Single cards and wallet displays can contain pictures, symbols, or words that students carry in their pockets, handbags, knapsacks, or the like. Single cards and wallet displays can be used by the student in order to nonverbally communicate about a specific object, action, place, feeling, or concept. The single card can be smaller than a credit card or as large as needed for an individual student. The specific size of the single card should be determined on the basis of the student's visual discrimination skills. The finer the student's skills, the smaller the single card should be. The student's motor abilities should also be considered when selecting the size of the card and the type of display (e.g., book, wallet). Wallet display pictures, symbols, and words are generally credit card size and allow for communication about several ideas. Additional credit-card holders can be added as the student's abilities and vocabulary needs increase.

Communication books can be used to allow for a large number of ideas. Communication books can contain one or more pages, each page allowing for one or several referents. Pictures, symbols, and/or words are used to represent objects, actions, places, feelings, or concepts and can be displayed in a communication book. Such books can be carried by the student in his or her arms, bookbag, handbag, or knapsack, or on a wheelchair tray. They can also be placed on revolving hooks attached to the front of a walker. The student's ability to turn pages and hold the book so that someone else can see it must be assessed before a communication book is selected as the appropriate augmentative system. Students using communication books need to be taught to locate the desired referent as quickly as possible and to indicate through pointing or gesturing in order for the message receiver to get the message. (See Beukelman & Mirenda, 1992, for a complete description of issues to consider in selecting and designing pictorial display systems.)

Manual communication boards can be designed to fit on wheelchair trays or can be part of the actual wheelchair tray. Pictures, symbols, and/or words can be displayed on a communication board so that the student can, through pointing or gesturing, communicate with others. The student's range of motion, ability to cross midline, and visual discriminative abilities must be assessed before determining if and how a manual communication board can meet a student's communicative needs. Boards must also be designed in order to facilitate interactions with other students.

The most sophisticated nonverbal communication systems available are *electronic communication aids*. These aids can be designed to fit on a communication tray (e.g., Zygo communicator), to be carried in a pocket (e.g., Canon communicator), or to be carried in one's arms, bookbag, knapsack, or handbag. These electronic communication aids can allow a student to communicate simple and complex messages expediently. Some of the most commonly used devices are described in Table 2.

In addition, *computer technology* continues to be refined and the use of voice synthesizers and switches has made computers easier to use as augmentative communication devices for persons with disabilities. Students who are unable to talk, unable to hold a pencil, or whose cognitive or thinking process prevents them from constructing written language may benefit from the use of computer technology. Computers that are equipped with speech synthesizers produce messages that are heard and understood by everyone and can produce a written text (Male, 1994). Alternative and custom-made keyboards, touch screens, and "mouse" emulators can provide students access to computer technology. Devices can be programmed with words and phrases for particular situations. Technology teams made up of the student, his or her parents, educators, communication specialists, and someone knowledgeable about computers can meet to explore the options that would be appropriate for an individual student. A growing number of various types of powerful computers and computer technology, both hardware and software, can be used to facilitate a student's communication and participation. Educators should remain abreast of the latest advances in technology so that the needs of students can be met in the most efficient manner possible.

DECISION-MAKING CRITERIA

Decision-making criteria have been developed in order to determine candidacy for augmentative system use and to select systems of augmentative communication for students with disabilities (Chapman & Miller, 1980; Nietupski & Hamre-Nietupski, 1979; Reichle, York & Sigafoos, 1991; Shane, 1980). Unfortunately, some of these decision-making criteria eliminate persons with significant disabilities from candidacy for the use of an augmentative system (Reichle & Karlan, 1985). The Participation Model of assessment (Beukelman & Mirenda, 1987) differs from those previously developed, in that the model's goal is to meet the communication needs of any person. The Participation Model involves assessing communicative needs by means of an activity inventory, including an inventory for peers without disabilities and a student repertoire inventory, and then assessing the communicative barriers to participation in the targeted environments. The communicative barriers are divided into opportunity and access barriers. Opportunity barriers include such factors as the lack of competent communication partners due to placement in a segregated educational placement, or the lack of communicative partners knowledgeable concerning adaptations necessary to communicate with an augmentative communication device user. Each of these barriers interferes with participation in identified activities and with successful use of augmentative devices. Access barriers might include student difficulty with mobility, manipulation, communication, or cognitive/linguistic and sensory/

Table 2.   Sample electronic communication devices

Supplier	Name
ADAMLAB 33500 Van Born Road Wayne, MI 48202	AIPS Wolf
ADAMLAB	Mega Wolf
Adaptive Communication University of Washington Department of Speech and Hearing Science, JG-15 Seattle, WA 98195	Acs Eval PAC with Real Voice
Adaptive Communication	Systems ACs Samy
Adaptive Communication	Acs Scan PAC with Real Voice
Adaptive Communication	Digital Augmentative Communication Systems
Adaptive Communication	Real Voice Systems
Adaptive Communication	Real Voice with Small Membrane Keyboard
American Printing House for the Blind P.O. Box 6085 Louisville, KY 40206	Speakqualizer
ADAMLAB 33500 Van Born Road Wayne, MI 48202	AIPS Wolf
ADAMLAB	Mega Wolf
Canon, Inc. Sahura Nagata, Director Audio Visual Aids Department P.O. Box 50 Tokyo Airport JAPAN	Canon Communicator
Consultants for Communication Technology 508 Bellvue Terrace Pittsburgh, PA 15202	Handy Speech Communication Aid
Detroit Institute for Children 5447 Woodward Avenue Detroit, MI 48202	AudioScan
Don Johnson Developmental Equipment 1000 N. Rand Building 115 Wauconda, IL 60084	Dial Scan
EKEG Electronics Co., Ltd. P.O. Box 46199, Station G Vancouver, BC V6R 4G5 CANADA	Expanded Keyboards for Learning Aids
Enabling Technologies Co. 3102 S.E. Jay Street Stuart, FL 34997	Info Touch 20 and 40

(continued)

Table 2. (continued)

HC Electronics, Inc. 250 Camino Alto Mill Valley, CA 94941	Phonic Mirror
HC Electronics, Inc.	Handivoice
Innocomp 33195 Wagon Wheel Drive Solon, OH 44139	Say It All Plus
Innocomp	Say It Simple Plus
Innocomp	Talk-O
Prentke Romich Co. 1022 Heyl Road Wooster, OH 44691	Intro Talker
Prentke Romich Co.	Liberator
Prentke Romich Co.	Light Talker
Prentke Romich Co.	Touch Talker
Royal Data Systems Route 14, Box 230 Morganton, NC 28655	RIDS Speech & Learning Center System
Sentiment Systems Technology 5001 Baum Boulevard Pittsburgh, PA 15213	Dyna Vox
Sentiment Systems Technology	Eye Typer
Speller Teller Communications 3234 S. Villa Circle West Alis, WI 53227	Speller Teller Communicator
Tiger Communication System 155 E. Broad Street #325 Rochester, NY 14604	Peacekeeper
Voice Connection 17835 Skypark Circle, Suite C Irvine, CA 92714	Portable Transaction Voice Computer
Zygo Industries, Inc. P.O. Box 1008 Portland, OR 97207	Lightwriter
Zygo Industries, Inc.	Parrot
Zygo Industries, Inc.	Polycom/Polytalk
Zygo Industries, Inc.	QED Scribe
Zygo Industries, Inc.	Scan Writer
Zygo Industries, Inc.	Steeper Communication Teaching Aid
Zygo Industries, Inc.	Switchboard

perceptual abilities. Potential intervention options are examined so as to meet the abilities and needs of the student and to decrease the barriers to the student's participation in the identified activities. Decision-making criteria and models concerning appropriate augmentative communication systems for students with disabilities should meet all of the student's needs in the most effective manner possible.

Another decision-making factor involves selecting the components of an augmentative communication system. In the past, the focus has been on the selection of a single best augmentative device for an individual; currently, the multimodal approach (providing students with opportunities to develop several modes of communication—typical of the general population) is applied to augmentative device users. Multimodal systems of communication can include: a communication board, gestures, grunts, and/or vocalizations. Multimodal systems become critical when considering, for instance, an augmentative system user whose system of communication includes a communication board. This person must have a method for getting the attention of others (e.g., by grunting or by using a buzzer). In this manner, communicators are urged to use whichever mode "gets the message across" in the most efficient manner in each environment and activity, rather than using a single mode that may not be efficient in all environments. Although probably no communication system can be effective all the time, Vanderheiden and Lloyd (1986) contributed the following list of characteristics that should be considered when evaluating the systems of individual students:

Provides a full range of communicative functions
Is compatible with other aspects of the individual's life
Facilitates interactions with peers
Facilitates students' participation in all aspects of the curriculum
Does not restrict communication partners
Is usable in all environments and physical positions
Does not restrict topic or scope of communication
Is effective
Allows and fosters growth and change
Is acceptable and motivating to user and others
Is affordable

INTERVENTION

As mentioned earlier in this chapter, recent research has suggested that the optimal environment for acquisition of communication is interactive, active, student centered, and contingent upon what is of interest to the student. In addition, the optimal environment is characterized as being responsive, nondidactic, nondirective, varied in stimuli, fine tuned to provide sufficient prompts to the learner while allowing for maximal independence, and involving the assignment of meaning to early communicative attempts (Ainsworth, 1974; Hart, 1985; MacDonald, 1985; Snow, 1972; Snow & Ferguson, 1978; Vygotsky, 1978). Language intervention strategies should reflect these characteristics, while at the same time providing systematic instruction in the identified areas and environments needed. Natural cues, corrections, and prompts help to determine those areas of need.

While general instructional strategies such as shaping and chaining are discussed in Chapter 6 of this volume, the present chapter delineates systematic instructional strategies that can be used in developing the communication competencies of students with disabilities.

Nonsymbolic Communication

Siegel-Causey and Downing (1987) suggest that beginning communicators must first acquire physical and social control over their environments in order to learn the purpose of communication. Some of the specific strategies to develop such skills that these authors describe include responding consistently to the possible communicative purpose of any intentional behavior of the student (such as change in muscle tone) while positioning and providing the student with an activity or item that is not preferred to allow him or her the opportunity to develop refusal skills. Mirenda (1987) suggests using gestural dictionaries to allow all interactive partners involved with the beginning communicator to respond to idiosyncratic gestures in a consistent manner. A board can be posted on the wall that lists the gestures, the communicative intent, and the appropriate response for each gesture made by the particular student. Over time, all significant others, including parents, siblings, friends, peers, and teachers, can shape the gestures by responding to more specific and refined gestures by the individual.

Mirenda (1988) also suggests using scripted routines with beginning communicators. This strategy can be implemented by first teaching a student a regular routine for an activity such as eating or participating in a cooperative group activity. Once the script for the routine is established, pauses can be inserted into the routine at specific points to allow the student to communicate by a change in body tone, vocalization, or gesture that they expect or want the activity to continue. Whatever behavior the student engages in should be assigned a communicative meaning by the interactive partner. This allows the student the opportunity to develop the ability to anticipate activities and/or events and to communicate acceptance or refusal of those events.

Choice- and decision-making skills are also important for beginning communicators to develop, in order for them to learn that they can control events occurring around them (Guess, Benson, & Siegel-Causey, 1985; Shevin & Klein, 1984; West & Parent, 1992; Williams, 1991). In the course of any given day, most people will make hundreds, possibly thousands, of choices. These choices can range from a major life issue such as a job change, purchasing a new car or house, or starting a family, to minor day-to-day decisions such as what to eat, wear, watch on television, or when, where, and with whom to participate in any number of activities. Typically, individuals with severe disabilities have been limited in their choice-making opportunities. This limited opportunity stems from uninformed beliefs by educators and others that individuals with disabilities do not have preferences, are unable to make appropriate choices, or are unable to express their choices.

The importance of facilitating greater skills and enhancing opportunities for people with disabilities in choice and decision making is now becoming more apparent to educators. As with other skill areas for many students with disabilities, choice making must be taught directly and systematically. Choice making involves having preferences, expressing preferences, and selecting from among alternatives. In general education, choice making, also referred to as critical thinking, is receiving more attention (Kovalik, 1993; Paul, 1990).

Choosing among alternatives is an integral component of communication and is an expression of autonomy and dignity. The power of choosing gives us the freedom to define ourselves and our values. Denying the power of choice leads to the phenomenon of learned helplessness, a belief that nothing that we do will make a difference. Educators must also make a distinction between noncompliance, misunderstanding or lacking skills to complete a task, and choosing not to participate in a given task. In order to distinguish between what may be subtle differences, educators must know the student's experience base and history, affective discriminations, and overall skill levels.

Curricular and instructional strategies used for teaching these skills are effective only to the degree that educators are willing to listen to or watch for the expression of choices and then, more important, respond to what is chosen. Facilitating a student's choice-making skills and enhancing the opportunities to do so may at times create a dilemma for teachers and others involved in the student's life. Professional responsibilities, safety issues, and other limitations based upon age and setting appropriateness must be considered and respected in balance with efforts to foster independence.

There are times when students should be allowed to choose *not* to do something or to make a "wrong" choice (e.g., buying baseball cards with lunch money). Such opportunities teach the important concept of logical consequences (in the above example, not having money to buy lunch and therefore being hungry). One component of choice making is understanding of the consequences of a choice, and often the concept can be learned only through experience. Obviously, allowing a student to experience natural consequences is appropriate only if the actions are not safety risks (e.g., it is not appropriate to allow a student to choose to cross the street at the wrong time and experience the natural consequence of being hit by a car!).

Similarly, limitations according to the chronological age of the student, the standards of a particular setting, and the professional responsibilities of an educator are to be considered. These standards need to be based on factors that do not relate to whether a student has a disability or not. A 21-year-old, for example, can legally make a choice between water or a glass of wine with dinner; a 10-year-old does not have that same choice. Yelling at a football game is expected, but choosing to yell in the school library is unacceptable. Mixing different flavors of soda into a cup at a soft drink fountain is a common choice of teenagers, whereas mixing chemical cleaning supplies in the storage shed could prove to be a dangerous choice and is not tolerated by adults in a position of responsibility. The fact that a student has a severe disability should not limit his or her opportunity to make choices; it does, however, usually increase the need for educators to conscientiously teach, facilitate, and evaluate the choice-making process.

Moving to Symbolic Communication

As students develop the skills to use symbols to communicate, a variety of teaching strategies can be used.

Incidental Teaching Strategies   Incidental teaching procedures (Hart & Risley, 1975; Peck, 1985) make use of naturally occurring environments, activities, and initiations of activities by beginning communicators. While incidental teaching strategies can also be used in developing nonsymbolic communication skills, teachers can use these strategies to develop the use of symbols as well by looking for opportunities to teach, model, or prompt the use of previously identified symbols within ongoing activities. Teachers can also arrange environments and activities in order to facilitate the use of incidental teaching strategies. For example, teachers can give the student the wrong book or materials when a request is made, perform a routine activity incorrectly or in a nonroutine fashion, place a desired item within sight but just out of reach, or provide a symbol when a student communicates nonsymbolically that he or she would like a different item when choosing foods at a high school cafeteria. Each of these examples sets up an opportunity for a student to use a symbol or other communicative behavior.

Time Delay Procedures   Time delay procedures have proven effective with students who have become dependent upon prompts to communicate (Halle, Baer, & Spradlin, 1981; Halle, Marshall, & Spradlin, 1979). When using this strategy, the teacher pauses rather than prompts when the student has an opportunity to request or respond. For example, while a student turns on a computer, the teacher may pause rather than ask "What do you want?" when the student is ready to request assistance for a desired computer program. The teacher can prompt the request by showing the toy, but he or she should not verbally or physically prompt the request, as the goal is to develop spontaneous requesting skills.

Verbal Prompt-Free Strategies   Verbal prompt-free strategies have also proven effective with students who are beginning symbol users and who are either prompt dependent or are at risk for developing prompt dependency (Mirenda & Dattilo, 1987; Mirenda & Santogrossi, 1985). This strategy is implemented by presenting a symbol of a desired item to the student and waiting until he or she intentionally or unintentionally touches the symbol. Once the student touches the symbol, he or she may be given the item. A physical prompt may be required initially, but over time the student should be reinforced only for intentional touches, and the number of choices should be increased.

Interrupted Behavior Chain Strategy   An interrupted behavior chain strategy has also been effective in teaching initial symbol users (Goetz, Gee, & Sailor, 1985; Hunt, Goetz, Alwell, & Sailor, 1986). The first step in this strategy is to identify and teach a routine activity to a student. Once the student has learned the routine or the chain of steps, the teacher attempts to identify appropriate steps for interruption by rating the student's level of distress and desire to complete the activity at possible points of interruption. Once a point of interruption is identified that does not cause undue distress but that reflects a point at which the student desires to complete the activity, the chain of steps is implemented. The teacher interrupts at the predetermined point, and a symbol for the next step is presented. For example, once a student in a home economics class has learned to wash dishes, the activity is interrupted at the point at which he or she is to obtain the dish soap, and a picture of the dish soap is presented. The teacher then models or prompts the student to select the symbol and obtains the requested item, and the chain continues. If the student does not touch the symbol with assistance, the chain is either stopped, or in some instances, the student is assisted in completing the activity. The researchers involved in developing the interrupted chain strategy have found that acquisition of symbol use is attained within four to five trials when used with chains that occur several times per day.

Second Language Acquisition   A growing number of students in the United States are limited or not proficient in English but are instead proficient in or at least more familiar with another language (Gollnick & Chinn, 1990). In addition, it is projected that by the end of the twentieth century, the numbers of students whose first language is other than English will increase by 35% (Council for Chief State School Officers, 1987). For these students, there are several strategies that can be used. The most commonly used strategies for teaching students who have limited or no proficiency in English are listed below.

Bilingual Instruction   Providing initial instruction in a student's first language while teaching previously learned content areas in English is referred to as bilingual education (Cummins, 1984). Although this approach has been designed to teach the student to become a proficient English communicator while maintaining his or her own language, culture, and customs, this approach requires the provision of teachers who are bilingual themselves. This is not always feasible in a country that has not and does not emphasize second languages in elementary and secondary schools.

English as a Second Language (ESL) Instruction   Although some of the major goals of bilingual education and ESL instruction are similar, maintaining the students' first language, culture, and customs is not emphasized in most ESL programs as compared to bilingual programs. In addition, the student may be instructed in English using a variety of approaches such as *sheltered English* and *total physical response*. Sheltered English is an approach where the student is learning new content in English; however, the teacher is presenting the material in ways that make it more understandable to students with less proficiency in English. Specifically, the techniques used in sheltered English include: speaking more slowly than usual; articulating clearly; limiting vocabulary array; avoiding the use of idiomatic expressions, syntactic complexity, and long sentences; using visual aids, objects, and body language to supplement the meaning of the words; emphasizing key words, phrases, or concepts; repeating key ideas; giving concrete examples of abstractions; and previewing material for students before lessons, lectures, or assignments (Richard-Amato & Snow, 1992).

Total physical response is based upon the principle that second language is most effectively learned through a motor activity medium. Students listen and respond to commands by imitating behaviors modeled by the teacher. Students listen to and watch the teacher describe and model an activity in the second language the students are learning. After listening and watching, they are encouraged to respond by imitating the teacher or other students. This strategy is based upon the principles of natural patterns of first language learning, which are listening and speaking (Genesee, 1987).

Two-Way Immersion Education   A growing number of schools and school districts are recognizing that children learn second languages more easily than adults, especially if the learning is done naturally; as a result, some schools are establishing immersion programs. Immersion programs were originally designed to teach students a second language other than English. However, the success of teaching students second languages (Genesee, 1987) has led to the development of two-way immersion programs. These programs include students who are proficient in the second language and not in English and those who are not proficient in the second language but are proficient in English. These students learn together with teachers who use both English and the second language for instruction along with some of the techniques described above (i.e., sheltered English and total physical response).

For years, students not proficient in English and also having a disability have had their second language needs overlooked. The strategies described above are those most frequently used with students without disabilities; however, with growing frequency they have also been used to effectively teach students with disabilities. Specifically, strategies have been identified to effectively teach students with disabilities who also are learning a second language (for examples, the reader is referred to Baca & Amato, 1989; Cegelka, Lewis, & Rodriquez, 1987; Ortiz & Wilkinson, 1991).

Facilitated Communication   Facilitated communication has been described as a way to physically or emotionally support an individual's intentional behavior via the assisted use of a keyboard or alphabet-like board. Facilitators physically support the student's hand, wrist, arm, or shoulder and also angle letters, boards, or other materials to maximize access. In facilitated communication, the goal is to fade the physical support provided to the student, so that the student can be taught to communicate eventually with little or no support.

While providing support and assessing communicative content, the facilitators should ask themselves the following questions: What do other students the same age do? What is the student already doing? What are the printed and written words already used during the day? What kinds of activities will help build mutual trust? What activities will be interactive and natural? Regularly scheduled retraining and evaluations should be implemented to ensure that the students are communicating, and not the facilitators.

When facilitating communication, the goal is to fade the physical support provided by the facilitator. Initially a student might require very intense amount and type of support; however, with careful fading, that same student can be taught to communicate with minimal support or no support at all (Sabin & Donnellan, 1993).

While both debate and research about facilitated communication continues, reports of its impact on people's lives cannot be ignored. In the interest of providing students with whatever means of communication works for them, all of the strategies discussed in the previous subsections, including facilitated communication, should be considered.

Dimensions to Consider

When developing and implementing a communication program, a number of additional dimensions should be considered. Reichle (1991) offers a decision-making model for determining which augmentative communication methods would be appropriate for a student (see Figure 3). In addition, the following elements should be considered when developing communication interventions (Horner & Budd, 1985; Stremel-Campbell & Campbell, 1985):

1. The communication program, including the determination of an augmentative and/or alternative communicative system, should be based upon individualized needs across all of the student's natural environments.
2. The communicative program, including the determination of a communication mode, should facilitate interactions with friends, peers, nonspecialized staff, and community members.
3. The communicative content, symbol set, mode, and instructional program should reflect a student's primary language and cultural values.
4. The communicative behaviors should be taught directly in all the student's environments.
5. The communicative content to be taught should be relevant and functional to the student.
6. Communication intervention should focus on developing the skills of both initiating and responding.
7. The most efficient mode(s) and systems possible for a given student should be taught.
8. The communication program, including the determination of a communication mode, should reflect the student's and his or her family's preferences.

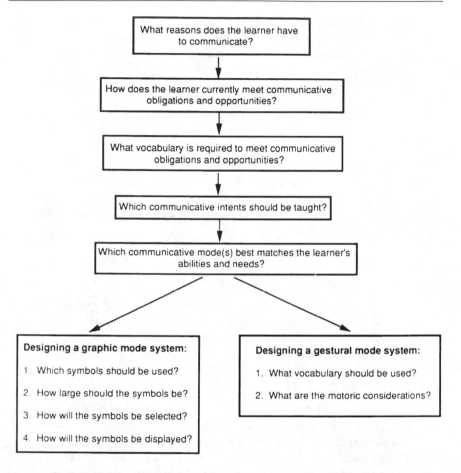

Figure 3. Decisions involved in designing augmentative or alternative communication systems. (From Reichle, J. [1991]. Defining the decisions involved in designing and implementing augmentative and alternative communication systems. In J. Reichle, J. York, & J. Sigafoos, *Implementing augmentative and alternative communication: Strategies for learners with severe disabilities* [pp. 39–60]. Baltimore: Paul H. Brookes Publishing Co.; reprinted with permission.)

9. Communication modes should be developed that are flexible enough for "add-ons"; if appropriate, they should allow for communicating simple as well as complex messages.

10. Directions to the message receiver should be included for all augmentative and alternative communicative modes.

11. Pictures, symbols, and words should be self-explanatory to the message receiver.
12. Communication programs should be developed that facilitate generalized communicative competence. This is achieved by loosely training and by training multiple exemplars and behaviors with multiple trainers in multiple settings with natural contingencies.
13. When unsure of a student's ability to comprehend, assume that he or she can.

Issues involved in training to facilitate generalization of skills are discussed in more detail in Chapter 5 of this volume.

EVALUATION

Data need to be collected over time in order to determine the effectiveness of a communication training program and the appropriateness of augmentative and/or alternative communication systems for a student. Several types of data should be collected:

1. The modes used to communicate a message
2. The frequency of the communicative behaviors
3. The frequency of communicative behaviors that were initiations and responses
4. The communicative intent
5. The conditions present when the communicative response was made (e.g., location, number of people, structured/unstructured environment)
6. The exact and the intended message
7. The reinforcers/consequences that were provided after the response

Figure 4 provides a sample of a data sheet that can be used to collect data.

SUMMARY

This chapter reviews issues and strategies related to the determination, development, implementation, and evaluation of educational programs designed to facilitate the acquisition and maintenance of communicative behaviors in natural environments. Specific procedures for assessing students' present communicative repertoires and preferences, as well as the effectiveness of communication programs, are delineated. Since students with severe disabilities are at risk for not developing intelligible speech, this chapter emphasizes developing augmentative and alternative communicative modes. Finally, procedures for teaching communicative behaviors are described.

Communicative mode	Frequency		Communicative intent	Conditions present	Exact message	Reinforcement consequence
	Initiated	Responses				
Verbal and gestural	✓		Wanted the towel	In kitchen with sister	"Wa ta" and pointed to towel	Got the towel
Gestured using communication booklet		✓	To indicate desire to go outside	In classroom; recess bell has rung	Pointed to picture of "outside"	Positive reinforcement; got to go outside
Blinked eye		✓	To indicate desire to eat carrots	In school cafeteria with students without disabilities and teacher	Blinked eyes once after teacher asked, "Do you want your carrots?"	Positive reinforcement; got the carrots

Figure 4.   Sample data sheet for determining communicative competence.

REFERENCES

Ainsworth, M.O.S. (1973). The development of infant-mother attachment. In B.M. Caldwell & H.N. Ricutti (Eds.), *Review of child development research* (Vol. 3, pp. 1–94). Chicago: University of Chicago Press.

American Speech-Language-Hearing Association. (1991). Report: Augmentative and alternative communication. *Asha, 33*(Suppl. 5), 9–12.

Baca, L., & Amato, C. (1989). Bilingual special education: Training issues. *Exceptional Children, 56*(2), 168–173.

Bedrosian, J.L. (1988). Adults who are mildly to moderately mentally retarded: Communicative performance, assessment and intervention. In S.N. Calculator & J.L. Bedrosian (Eds.), *Communication assessment and intervention for adults with mental retardation* (pp. 265–307). Boston: College-Hill Press.

Beukelman, D., & Mirenda, P. (1987). Communication options for persons who cannot speak: Assessment and evaluation. *Proceedings of the National Planners Conference of Assistive Device Service Delivery.* Columbus, OH: Great Lakes Area Regional Resource Center.

Beukelman, D.R., & Mirenda, P. (1992). *Augmentative and alternative communication: Management of severe communication disorders in children and adults.* Baltimore: Paul H. Brookes Publishing Co.

Biklen, D. (1993). *Communication unbound: How facilitated communication is challenging traditional views of autism and ability/disability.* New York: Teachers College Press.

Biklen, D., & Schubert, A. (1991). New words: The communication of students with autism. *Remedial and Special Education, 12*(6), 46–57.

Bloom, L. (1970). *Language development: Form and function of emerging grammars.* Cambridge, MA: Massachusetts Institute of Technology Press.

Brown, R. (1973). *A first language.* Cambridge, MA: Harvard University Press.

Calculator, S.N. (1988). Exploring the language of adults with mental retardation. In S.N. Calculator & J.L. Bedrosian (Eds.), *Communication assessment and intervention for adults with mental retardation* (pp. 95–106). Boston: College-Hill Press.

Carrier, J. (1976). Application of a nonspeech language system with the severely language handicapped. In L.L. Lloyd (Ed.), *Communication assessment and intervention strategies* (pp. 523–547). Baltimore: University Park Press.

Cegelka, P.T., Lewis, R., & Rodriquez, A.M. (1987). Status of educational services to handicapped students with limited English proficiency: Report of a statewide study in California. *Exceptional Children, 54*(3), 220–227.

Chapman, R. (1981). Exploring children's communicative intents. In J.F. Miller (Ed.), *Assessing language production in children: Experimental procedures.* Baltimore: University Park Press.

Chapman, R., & Miller, J. (1980). Analyzing language and communication in the child. In R.L. Schiefelbusch (Ed.), *Nonspeech language intervention* (pp. 159–196). Baltimore: University Park Press.

Council for Chief State School Officers. (1987, December). *Model interdepartmental state education agency strategies to meet the educational needs of limited English proficient students: Project summary.* Participant's notebook for the conference on "Improving the Educational Achievement of Limited English Proficient Students."

Cromer, R.F. (1974). The development of language and cognition: The cognition hypothesis. In B.M. Foss (Ed.), *New perspectives in child development* (pp. 184–252). Harmondsworth, England: Penguin Books.

Cromer, R. (1976). The cognitive hypothesis of language acquisition and its implication for child language deficiency. In D. Morehead & A. Morehead (Eds.), *Normal and deficient child language* (pp. 283–333). Baltimore: University Park Press.

Cummins, J. (1984). *Bilingualism and special education: Issues in assessment and pedagogy*. San Diego, CA: College-Hill Press.

Donnellan, A.M., Mirenda, P.L., Mesaros, R.A., & Fassbender, L.L. (1984). Analyzing the communicative functions of aberrant behavior. *Journal of The Association for Persons with Severe Handicaps, 9,* 201–202.

Falvey, M.A., Bishop, K.B., Grenot-Scheyer, M., & Coots, J.J. (1988). Issues and trends in mental retardation. In S.N. Calculator & J.L. Bedrosian (Eds.), *Communication assessment and intervention for adults with mental retardation* (pp. 45–65). Boston: College-Hill Press.

Falvey, M.A., McLean, D., & Rosenberg, R. (1988). Transition from school to adult life: Communication strategies. *Topics in Language Disorders, 9*(1), 82–86.

Genesee, F. (1987). *Learning through two languages*. New York: Harper & Row.

Goetz, L., Gee, K., & Sailor, W. (1985). Using a behavior chain interruption strategy to teach communication skills to students with severe disabilities. *Journal of The Association for Persons with Severe Handicaps, 10,* 21–30.

Gollnick, D.M., & Chinn, P.C. (1990). *Multicultural education in a pluralistic society* (3rd ed.). Columbus, OH: Charles E. Merrill.

Gruenewald, L., Schroeder, J., & Yoder, D. (1982). Considerations for curriculum development and implementation. In B. Campbell & V. Baldwin (Eds.), *Severely handicapped/hearing impaired students* (pp. 163–180). Baltimore: Paul H. Brookes Publishing Co.

Guess, D., Benson, H.A., & Siegel-Causey, E. (1985). Concepts and issues related to choice-making and autonomy among persons with severe disabilities. *Journal of The Association for Persons with Severe Handicaps, 10,* 79–86.

Halle, J., Baer, D., & Spradlin, J. (1981). Teachers' generalized use of delay as a stimulus control procedure to increase language use by handicapped children. *Journal of Applied Behavior Analysis, 14,* 389–409.

Halle, J., Marshall, A., & Spradlin, J. (1979). Time delay: A technique to increase language use and facilitate generalization in retarded children. *Journal of Applied Behavior Analysis, 12,* 431–439.

Halliday, M. (1975). *Learning how to mean: Explorations in the development of language*. New York: Elsevier/North Holland.

Hamre-Nietupski, S., Stoll, A., Holtz, K., Fullerton, P., Flottum-Ryan, M., & Brown, L. (1977). Curricular strategies for teaching nonverbal communication skills to verbal and nonverbal severely handicapped students. In L. Brown, J. Nietupski, S. Lyon, S. Hamre-Nietupski, T. Crowner, & L. Gruenewald (Eds.), *Curricular strategies for teaching functional object use, nonverbal communication, problem solving and mealtime skills to severely handicapped students* (Vol. 8, pp. 95–250). Madison, WI: Madison Metropolitan School District.

Hart, B. (1985). Naturalistic language training techniques. In S.F. Warren & A.K. Rogers-Warren (Eds.), *Teaching functional language* (pp. 63–88). Baltimore: University Park Press.

Hart, B., & Risley, T. (1975). Incidental teaching of language in the preschool. *Journal of Applied Behavior Analysis, 8,* 411–420.

Hecht, B.F. (1986). Language disorders in preschool children. *Advances in Special Education, 5,* 95–119.

Hobson, P., & Duncan, P. (1979). Sign learning and profoundly retarded people. *Mental Retardation, 17*, 33–37.

Horner, R.M., & Budd, C.M. (1985). Acquisition of manual sign use: Collateral reduction of maladaptive behavior and factors limiting generalization. *Education and Training in Mental Retardation, 20*, 39–47.

Hunt, P., Goetz, L., Alwell, M., & Sailor, W. (1986). Using an interrupted behavior chain strategy to teach generalized communication responses. *Journal of The Association for Persons with Severe Handicaps, 11*, 196–204.

Kanner, L. (1943). Autistic disturbances of affective contact. *Nervous Child, 2*, 217–250.

Kent, L. (1974). *Language acquisition program for the severely retarded.* Champaign, IL: Research Press.

Keogh, W.J., & Reichle, J. (1985). Communication intervention for the "difficult-to-teach" severely handicapped. In S.F. Warren & A.K. Rogers-Warren (Eds.), *Teaching functional language* (pp. 157–194). Baltimore: University Park Press.

Klein, M.D., Myers, S.P., Hogue, B., Waldo, L.J., Marshall, A.M., & Hall, M.K. (1981). *Parent's guide: Classroom involvement, communication training resources.* Lawrence, KS: Early Childhood Institute, Comprehensive Communication Curriculum.

Kovalik, S. (1993). *Integrated thematic instruction: The model* (2nd ed.). Oak Creek, AZ: Books for Educators.

MacDonald, J.D. (1985). Language through conversation: A model of intervention with language-delayed persons. In S.F. Warren & A.K. Rogers-Warren (Eds.), *Teaching functional language* (pp. 89–122). Baltimore: University Park Press.

Male, M. (1994). *Technology for inclusion: Meeting the special needs of all students.* Boston,: Allyn & Bacon.

Mayberry, R. (1976). If a chimp can learn sign language, surely my nonverbal client can too. *Asha, 18*, 228–233.

McLean, J.E., & Snyder-McLean, L.K. (1978). *A transactional approach to early language training.* Columbus, OH: Charles E. Merrill.

Mirenda, P. (1987, November). *Facilitating augmentative communication: A public school model.* Paper presented at the Annual Conference of The Association for Persons with Severe Handicaps, Chicago.

Mirenda, P. (1988, August). *Instructional techniques for communication.* Paper presented at the Augmentative and Alternative Communication for Students with Severe Disabilities Special Education Innovative Institute, Fremont, CA.

Mirenda, P., & Dattilo, J. (1987). Instructional techniques in alternative communication for students with severe intellectual disabilities. *Augmentative and Alternative Communication, 3*, 143–152.

Mirenda, P., Iacono, T., & Williams, R. (1990). Communication options for persons with severe and profound disabilities: State of the art and future directions. *Journal of The Association for Persons with Severe Handicaps, 15*, 3–21.

Mirenda, P., & Santogrossi, J. (1985). A prompt-free strategy to teach pictoral communication system use. *Augmentative and Alternative Communication, 1*, 143–150.

Musselwhite, C.R., & St. Louis, K.W. (1982). *Communication programming for severely handicapped: Vocal and non-vocal strategies.* Houston: College-Hill Press.

Nietupski, J., & Hamre-Nietupski, S. (1979). Teaching auxiliary communication skills to severely handicapped learners. *AAESPH Review, 4*, 107–124.

Ortiz, A.A., & Wilkinson, C.Y. (1991). Assessment and intervention model for the bilingual exceptional student (AIM for the BESt). *Teacher Education and Special Education, 14*(1), 35–42.

Owens, R.E., & Rogerson, B.S. (1988). Adults at the presymbolic level. In S.N. Calculator & J.L. Bedrosian (Eds.), *Communication assessment and intervention for adults with mental retardation* (pp. 189–238). Boston: College-Hill Press.

Paul, R. (1990). *Critical thinking: What every person needs to survive in a rapidly changing world.* Rohnert Park, CA: Center for Critical Thinking and Moral Critique, Sonoma State University.

Peck, C.A. (1985). Increasing opportunities for social control by children with autism and severe handicaps: Effects of student behavior and perceived classroom climate. *Journal of The Association for Persons with Severe Handicaps, 10,* 183–193.

Prior, M., & Cummins, R. (1992). Questions about facilitated communication and autism. *Journal of Autism and Developmental Disorders, 22,* 331–337.

Prizant, B.M. (1983). Echolalia in autism: Assessment and intervention. *Seminars in Speech and Language, 4,* 63–77.

Prizant, B.M., & Duchan, J.F. (1981). The functions of immediate echolalia in autistic children. *Journal of Speech and Hearing Disorders, 46,* 241–249.

Reichle, J. (1991). Defining the decisions involved in designing and implementing augmentative and alternative communication systems. In J. Reichle, J. York, & J. Sigafoos, *Implementing augmentative and alternative communication: Strategies for learners with severe disabilities* (pp. 39–60). Baltimore: Paul H. Brookes Publishing Co.

Reichle, J., & Karlan, G. (1985). The selection of an augmentative system in communication intervention: A critique of decision rules. *Journal of The Association for Persons with Severe Disabilities, 10,* 146–156.

Reichle, J., Piche-Cragoe, L., Sigafoos, J., & Doss, S. (1988). Optimizing functional communication for persons with severe handicaps. In S.N. Calculator & J.L. Bedrosian (Eds.), *Communication assessment and intervention for adults with mental retardation* (pp. 239–264). Boston: College-Hill Press.

Reichle, J., Rogers, N., & Barret, C. (1984). Establishing pragmatic discriminations among the communicative functions of requesting, rejecting and commenting in an adolescent. *Journal of The Association for Persons with Severe Handicaps, 9,* 31–36.

Reichle, J., York, J., & Sigafoos, J. (1991). *Implementing augmentative and alternative communication: Strategies for learners with severe disabilities.* Baltimore: Paul H. Brookes Publishing Co.

Rein, R.L. (1984). *Observational study of the use of verbal perservations by persons with autism.* Unpublished doctoral dissertation, University of California, Los Angeles, and California State University, Los Angeles.

Richard-Amato, P.A., & Snow, M.A. (1992). Strategies for content-area teachers. In P.A. Richard-Amato & M.A. Snow (Eds.), *Readings for content-area teachers* (pp. 145–163). New York: Longman.

Sabin, L.A., & Donnellan, A.M. (1993). A qualitative study of the process of facilitated communication. *Journal for The Association for Persons with Severe Handicaps, 18*(3), 200–211.

Schuler, A.L. (1979). Echolalia: Issues and clinical applications. *Journal of Speech and Hearing Disorders, 4,* 411–434.

Schuler, A.L. (1981). Teaching functional language. In B. Wilcox & A. Thompson (Eds.), *Educating autistic children and youth* (pp. 154–178). Washington, DC: U.S. Department of Education.

Schuler, A.L., & Goetz, L. (1983). Toward communicative competence: Matters of method, content, and mode of instruction. *Seminars in Speech and Language, 4,* 79–91.

Seligman, M. (1975). *Helplessness: On depression, development, and death.* San Francisco: W.H. Freeman.

Shane, H. (1980). Approaches to assessing the communication of nonoral persons. In R.L. Schiefelbusch (Ed.), *Nonspeech language and communication* (pp. 197–224). Baltimore: University Park Press.

Shevin, M., & Klein, D.K. (1984). The importance of choice-making skills for students with severe disabilities. *Journal of The Association for Persons with Severe Handicaps, 9*, 159–166.

Siegel-Causey, E., & Downing, J. (1989). Nonsymbolic communication development: Theoretical concepts and educational strategies. In L. Goetz, D. Guess, & K. Stremel-Campbell (Eds.), *Innovative program design for individuals with dual sensory impairments* (pp. 15–48). Baltimore: Paul H. Brookes Publishing Co.

Siegel-Causey, E., & Guess, D. (1987). *Enhancing nonsymbolic communication interactions among learners with severe disabilities.* Baltimore: Paul H. Brookes Publishing Co.

Snow, C. (1972). Mother's speech to children learning language. *Child Development, 43*, 549–565.

Snow, C., & Ferguson, C. (1978). *Talking to children.* London: Cambridge University Press.

Stremel-Campbell, K., & Campbell, C.R. (1985). Training techniques that may facilitate generalization. In S.F. Warren & A.K. Rogers-Warren (Eds.), *Teaching functional language* (pp. 251–285). Baltimore: University Park Press.

Vanderheiden, G., & Grilley, K. (Eds.). (1976). *Non-vocal communication techniques and aids for the severely physically handicapped.* Baltimore: University Park Press.

Vanderheiden, G.C., & Lloyd, L.L. (1986). Communication systems and their components. In S.W. Blackstone & D.M. Bruskin (Eds.), *Augmentative communication: An introduction* (pp. 49–162). Rockville, MD: American Speech-Language-Hearing Association.

Vanderheiden, G.C., & Yoder, D.E. (1986). Overview. In S.W. Blackstone & D.W. Bruskin (Eds.), *Augmentative communication: An introduction.* Rockville, MD: American Speech-Language-Hearing Association.

Vygotsky, L.S. (1978). *Mind in society.* Cambridge, MA: Harvard University Press.

West, M.D., & Parent, W. (1992). Consumer choice and empowerment in supported employment services: Issues and strategies. *Journal of The Association for Persons with Severe Handicaps, 17*(1), 47–52.

Wilbur, R.B. (1976). The linguistics of manual languages and manual systems. In L.L. Lloyd (Ed.), *Communication assessment and intervention strategies* (pp. 423–500). Baltimore: University Park Press.

Williams, R. (1991). Choices, communication, and control: A call for expanding them in the lives of people with severe disabilities. In L.H. Meyer, C.A. Peck, & L. Brown (Eds.), *Critical issues in the lives of people with severe disabilities* (pp. 543–545). Baltimore: Paul H. Brookes Publishing Co.

Wing, L. (1981). Language, social, and cognitive impairments in autism and severe mental retardation. *Journal of Autism and Developmental Disorders, 11*, 31–44.

Wulz, S.V., Myers, S.P., Klein, M.D., Hall, M.K., & Waldo, L.J. (1982). Unobtrusive training: A home-centered model for communication training. *Journal of The Association for the Severely Handicapped, 7*, 36–47.

DEVELOPING AND FOSTERING FRIENDSHIPS

10

MARY A. FALVEY AND RICHARD L. ROSENBERG

The need for positive relationships and friendships is universal (Schaffner & Buswell, 1992). The importance of peer relationships and building a sense of community have emerged as important themes both within special and general education (A.N. Amado, 1993; Falvey, Forest, Pearpoint, & Rosenberg, 1994; Noddings, 1992).

The purpose of this chapter is to provide an overview of the process whereby friendships are developed and supported among students with and without disabilities. As more and more students with significant disabilities move into their neighborhood schools, and as increasing numbers of adults live and work in their own communities, the importance of social relationships, and in particular, friendships, becomes increasingly clear to professionals and families who organize and deliver such services (A.N. Amado, 1993; Stainback, Stainback, & Forest, 1989).

FRIENDSHIP DEFINED

Friendship has been defined in a number of ways. The concept of friendship is elusive yet familiar to all (Perske, 1989). Friendship, according to Wieck (1993), is characterized by "interdependence, connectedness, equality, symmetry, give and take, support, and unity" (p. ix). Friendship means different things to different people at different times and at different ages (Stainback & Stainback, 1987). Depending upon one's age, a friend may be someone with whom to play or share lunch (Hayes, 1978; Howes, 1983), someone with whom to share secrets, or someone to be trusted and someone with whom one may be intimate (Berndt, 1982).

267

Perske (1989) included the following descriptors of friends: friends can stretch us beyond our families; friends help people beyond human services goals; friends help people rehearse adult roles; friends serve as fresh role models; and friends are no big deal. He also identifies several aspects of friendships: friendships become a haven from stress; many aspects of friendships are mysterious; friendships are reciprocal; good friendships generate their own energy; a good friendship is noticeable; a good friendship can be attractive; and each friendship is unique and unrepeatable. Often the terms friendship and popularity are used interchangeably when in fact their meanings are very different. Popularity, usually measured by ratings of sociometric status, indicates whether one is liked or accepted by a number of peers (Hartup, 1970). Popularity differs from friendship, in that there are popular children who do not have friends (Hymel & Asher, 1977) and children who have friends who are not necessarily popular (Masters & Furman, 1981). The definition of friendship that seems most useful for educators and researchers is that it is a bond between two individuals characterized by mutual preference for one another, a positive affective style, and sustained social interactions (Hartup, 1975, 1983; Howes, 1983).

Friendships are characterized by a wide range of social interactions. Friends engage not only in reciprocal interactions (i.e., give-and-take), but also in helping (i.e., voluntary assistance) and proximal interactions (i.e., interactions during which only sensory contact is made between two or more people). For example, Ryan, a 10-year-old boy with significant multiple disabilities and his friend without disabilities, Sam, enjoy playing games on the adapted computer, which is considered a reciprocal interaction. In addition, they sit together at lunch, and Sam sometimes helps Ryan with his straw and milk, which is considered a helping interaction. Ryan and Sam are often observed just "hanging out" together, which would be considered a proximal interaction. As this example illustrates, friends engage various types of interactions, including give-and-take, helping, and sometimes just being together. All of these types of interactions are essential, and no single type is more important than another.

When interactions between two individuals involve helping or proximal interactions exclusively, the relationship in not likely to be a friendship where each partner equally gives and receives. All types of interactions exist in most friendships, and educators should foster the expression of a range of interactions among their students.

Conditions Essential for Friendships to Develop

Several key conditions have been identified by Lutfiyya (1988) as essential to the development of friendships. These conditions are not characteristics of an individual student, but rather are reflected in his or her surrounding opportunities, the people with whom he or she interacts, and the expectations of others. The first condition, *opportunity,* is composed of proximity and frequency, which allows peers to practice and elaborate upon skills (Lewis & Rosenblaum, 1975); to get to know one another (Asher, Oden, & Gottman, 1977); and, subsequently, to develop friendships (Hartup, 1975; Howes, 1983). Educators need to remember that friendship opportunities increase as interaction opportunities increase. Clearly, one of the greatest barriers to friendships for individuals with and without disabilities has been the lack of opportunity to interact with one another. Although opportunities for students with significant disabilities to attend the same school as their neighbors and siblings have increased, significant numbers of students with significant disabilities continue to be denied such opportunities (Shapiro, 1993).

The second condition, *support,* is defined as the provision of necessary assistance to ensure opportunities for friendship to develop. For example, a high school student might need someone to provide transportation so that she can attend a Friday evening football game. Such a need might be met by arranging a ride with another student who attends the same high school and is planning to go to the game.

The third condition is *diversity.* Over the past 15 years, much of the literature has emphasized the need for students with disabilities to develop relationships and friendships with students without disabilities (e.g., Brown et al., 1979; Falvey, 1989; Stainback & Stainback, 1985). This emphasis arose from an effort to change the service delivery model to an inclusive model from a segregated model, where students with disabilities had opportunities to interact with and relate only to other students with disabilities. With the growing number of inclusive educational opportunities for students with disabilities, diverse friendships of choice must be emphasized. All students must have opportunities to develop friendships with people of diverse ability levels, backgrounds, interests, jobs, education levels, and so forth.

A fourth condition is providing *continuity* in people and settings. Students who attend the same schools as their neighbors are more likely to develop friendships than those who are relegated to centralized programs or to those programs where students with disabilities "come and go" and there is no continuity of participation and involvement in the general education classroom (Schnorr, 1990). The people with whom a student comes in contact must be the same over time to establish relationships and eventually friendships. Most students without disabilities go to school in the same neighborhood or community where they go to the grocery store, movie theater, doctors' offices, banks, and so forth. Continuity is essential to build friendships and social networks.

The fifth condition is opportunities to develop relationships that are *freely given and chosen.* Friendships are only "real" if the choice is reciprocal. Unfortunately, people with significant disabilities often find themselves in the company of those who are paid to be with them (Lutfiyya, 1988; Strully & Bartholomew-Lorimer, 1988). It is critical that everyone have people in their lives who are there because they want to be in a relationship, not because they are obligated to do so.

The final condition is that *intimacy opportunities* must be provided. Too often in the past, it has been assumed by teachers, caregivers and sometimes parents that students with significant disabilities could not develop intimate relationships. Unfortunately, this has resulted in students with significant disabilities having limited opportunities to develop such intimate relationships. Students with significant disabilities, especially those in secondary programs, must have the opportunity to develop friendships that could result in short-term and/or ongoing intimate relationships.

BENEFITS OF FRIENDSHIP

Families have asked, challenged, and compelled professionals to realize the importance of friendships to their sons and daughters. Parents have urged professionals to facilitate the development and maintenance of friendships between their children and their peers. Numerous studies have been conducted to measure various aspects of social relationships and friendships of students with significant disabilities (e.g., Guralnick, 1980; Haring, Breen, Pitts-Conway, Lee, & Gaylord-Ross, 1987; Haring et al., 1992; Hartup, 1983; Howes, 1983, 1987; Rubin, 1982; Rynders, Johnson, Johnson, & Schmidt, 1980; Storey & Gaylord-Ross, 1987; Strain, 1983; Weiss, 1974). These studies support the notion that students with significant disabilities can and do have friends. In addition, the determining factors about who does and does not have friends are not related as much to students' characteristics, such as disabilities, as much as the opportunities they have to build social relationships and friendships.

There are numerous developmental, psychological, and sociological reasons for fostering social relationships, particularly friendships between individuals with and without disabilities. First, friendships provide the opportunity to develop, practice, and maintain a variety of communicative, cognitive, and social-emotional skills (Field, 1984; Guralnick, 1980; Hartup, 1983; Howes, 1983; Rubin, 1982). This is not to suggest that these skills are prerequisite to the development of friendships, but rather that these skills can best be learned and practiced within the context of friendship. Second, friendships can provide individuals with nurturance and support (Berndt & Perry, 1986; Howes & Mueller, 1980; Rubin, 1982; Weiss, 1974). Third, lack of friendships in the early years is correlated with difficulty in adjustment for individuals in later years (Buhrmester & Furman, 1986; Cowen, Pederson, Babigian, Izzo, & Trost, 1973; Robins, 1966; Roff, Sells, & Golden, 1972; Sullivan, 1953).

Friendships may be at the base of a network of relationships that allow individuals with disabilities to grow up, go to school, live, work, and recreate within their own neighborhoods and communities (Strully & Bartholomew-Lorimer, 1988; Strully & Strully, 1985; Taylor, Biklen, & Knoll, 1987; Weiss, 1974). Friendships are useful to examine within the context of building community. Widely held prejudices against people with disabilities will change only with an increasing amount of personal contact between individuals with and without disabilities. The community connections that children with disabilities develop while in school can serve as a guide and support for building such connections as adults. Such connections facilitate students' attachment to other people who are emotionally important, opportunities to engage in shared activities, and opportunities to play a variety of roles in community life (O'Brien & O'Brien, 1992). While many more students with disabilities are included in schools and classrooms, and more adults are employed and living in the community, they may in fact be very lonely and without support networks (Bishop, 1991). Loneliness, although a complex phenomenon, must be examined in the context of friendship development. Those who do not have friends often experience a sense of isolation and loneliness. Loneliness and being lonely have been extensively researched in the population at large (e.g., Hojat & Crandall, 1989; Weiss, 1982). To decrease the probability of loneliness, the rules, regulations, and practices that contribute to people's "isolation must be changed immediately and replaced with designs, practices, and policies that support the building of social networks" (Amado, 1993, p. 82).

Recently, the concept of facilitating "natural supports" has received tremendous attention (Nisbet, 1992). Natural supports involve providing people with needed support(s) by using human resources typically available to those without disabilities. Too often we have "over-bureaucratized" the system of supports for persons with disabilities, resulting in segregation. For example, instead of exclusively relying on a paid adult (e.g., instructional assistant) for a student who needs help performing the fine motor components involved in completing an art project, peers might provide the needed support. In addition, adults with disabilities often do not live in homes located in neighborhoods where they receive natural supports from neighbors. Instead they live in group homes, owned and operated by people who have control over their lives. They receive support only from paid staff who do not live in the neighborhood. Friendships lead to the development of support networks and can replace many of the impersonal bureaucratic structures in schools, housing, and employment. Educators and service providers must continue to develop more opportunities to facilitate students' friendships, which result in the opportunities for natural support(s).

Friendships between students with disabilities and their peers without disabilities may be the best illustration of a true sense of community. Although individuals with significant disabilities may have increased dependency and vulnerability, individuals without disabilities can come to recognize such vulnerability as a characteristic shared in one way or another by everyone at various times in our lives, rather than as something that divides people (Strully & Bartholomew-Lorimer, 1988). Given the opportunity to become acquainted, to interact with one another, and subsequently to develop friendships, individuals with significant disabilities and their peers can grow past acceptance of each other and begin to cherish one another for their unique contributions. Table 1 provides the words to

Table 1.   Words to Bob Blue's song, *Courage*

A small thing once happened at school
That brought up a question for me,
And somehow, it forced me to see
The price that I pay to be cool.
Diane is a girl that I know.
She's strange, like she doesn't belong.
I don't mean to say that's wrong
We don't like to be with her, though.
And so, when we all made a plan
To have this big party at Sue's,
Most kids in the school got the news,
But no one invited Diane.

The thing about Taft Junior High,
Is, secrets don't last very long.
I acted like nothing was wrong
When I saw Diane start to cry.
I know you may think that I'm cruel.
It doesn't make me very proud.
I just went along with the crowd.
It's sad, but you have to at school.
You can't pick the friends you prefer.
You fit in as well as you can.
I couldn't be friends with Diane,
'Cause then they would treat me like her.

In one class at Taft Junior High,
We study what people have done
With gas chamber, bomber, and gun
In Auschwitz, Japan, and My Lai.
I don't understand all I learn,
Sometimes I just sit there and cry.
The whole world stood idly by
To watch as the innocent burned
Like robots obeying some rule
Atrocities done by the mob
All innocent, doing their job.
What was it for? Was it cool?

The world was aware of this hell,
But how many cried out in shame?
What heroes, and who was to blame?
A story that no one dared tell.
I promise to do what I can.
To not let it happen again
To care for all women and men.
I'll start by inviting Diane.

By Bob Blue, Amherst, Massachusetts; reprinted by permission.

a song entitled *Courage* which summarizes that need for all students to feel a sense of connections.

Given the complex needs of individuals with significant disabilities, one may question the importance of examining peer relationships, and friendships in particular, for these individuals. As stated by Strain (1984), "While the case has been made by others of the developmental significance of friendships for normally developing children, it may be argued that friendships are even more important for handicapped children's language, cognitive, sexual, and academic development" (p. 193). Furthermore, Taylor et al. (1987) have suggested that if there has been one thing lacking in the lives of individuals with significant disabilities, it is the opportunity for close, mutual, and ongoing relationships with other individuals.

FOSTERING FRIENDSHIPS

In spite of all the technology available to human services professionals, professionals cannot "program" friendships. Friendships are neither easy to achieve nor guided by an exact path. Educators can, however, build connections to foster and support friendships between students with and without disabilities, and variables can be manipulated in such a manner as to allow for the opportunity for individuals to become friends (Perske, 1987). Acquaintances or family members might introduce the person to some potential friends; the individual might enroll in a variety of activities that could lead to the development of friendships (e.g., Scouts, sports, clubs, churches); or the individual might seek the formal support of professionals (e.g., dating service personnel, inclusion facilitators, counselor). Several specific curricular, instructional, and community strategies that educators and service providers can employ to facilitate friendships follow.

Curricular Considerations

Defining and building curricula to facilitate friendships is an important and complex process. No "cookbook" approaches are recommended. Curricula must be built upon the strengths and diverse needs of the students, considering the age, gender, and culture of the students' classroom and school (Schaffner & Buswell, 1992).

Integrate Friendships into the Core Curriculum   When classrooms and schools intentionally build friendship into the curriculum, students are more likely to learn about the complex nature of the relationship between friendship, respecting others, treating others with dignity, and so forth. For example, elementary-age students might be instructed to write about and pictorially present the characteristics of their friends after reading several children's stories about friendships (i.e., language arts). The students, using their art, math, and science skills, could construct their pictorial presentation. After studying about several world leaders during the early 1900s, secondary students in a history class could develop a relationship diagram demonstrating the conflicts and allies that existed at that time. This activity could be expanded in a social studies class where the students might be asked to develop a similar diagram of their own relationships identifying their conflicts and allies.

Develop an Anti-bias Curriculum   The curriculum should be free from bias or stereotyping of any individual or group. An anti-bias curriculum is based upon the value that differences are good and that we should teach students about appreciating differences among people (Derman-Sparks & the ABC Task Force, 1989). Conflict can arise when students are not given accurate and respectful information about their own characteristics as well as those of others. An anti-bias curriculum is not an activity for 15 or 45 minutes once or twice a week, but rather is integral to all aspects of the school day and year. With a curriculum that is free of bias against people with disabilities and other characteristics, students are more likely to develop the attitudes and skills necessary to respect, interact, and ultimately develop social relationships and friendships with students who reflect diverse characteristics such as varying abilities, cultural backgrounds, religious associations, sexual preferences, and so forth.

Highlight and Emphasize Students' Similarities   Educators should de-emphasize the "special-ness" of programs and highlight and emphasize the similarities of individuals with and without disabilities. It has been suggested that friendships are based upon the similarities and compatibility between individuals (Asher et al., 1977). Factual information regarding disabilities can be provided as appropriate, but natural opportunities within the curriculum for peers to learn about each other should be encouraged. As the relationships evolve, information regarding an individual student's disability may need to be provided to friends, such as, "This is what we need to do in case Yolanda has a seizure." However, a curriculum that overemphasizes students' disabilities and weaknesses is counter-productive to facilitating friendships.

Social Skills and Friendship   There is an emerging literature base that documents the positive effects of students' social interactions and inclusion on students with and without disabilities (Evans, Salisbury, Palombaro, Berryman, & Hollywood, 1992; Hunt et al., 1993; Schnorr, 1990; York, Vandercook, MacDonald, Heise-Neff, & Caughey, 1992). Even though one cannot teach friendship, there are a number of social skills that educators can teach that are associated with having friends. Skills associated with friendship can be practiced and enhanced like any other skill (Stainback & Stainback, 1987). Table 2 provides a listing of skills often demonstrated by children and adolescents interacting with a friend. If a student lacks one more of these skills, educators can and should facilitate their development. These skills are not prerequisites to the development of a friendship; however, the use of these skills can facilitate the development of friendships.

Social-Sexual Skills and Friendships   As a result of increased emphasis on facilitating social interaction for students with disabilities, there is growing recognition of the importance of social and sexual relationships. Although it is generally accepted that human sexual relationships increase the quality of life for all persons, that is an area where persons with disabilities have often been excluded (Edwards, 1988; Monat-Haller, 1992). When social behaviors, social skills, and human sexuality have been addressed in relation to students with significant disabilities, the emphasis has generally been on providing rudimentary

Table 2. Social skills displayed when interacting with friends

Displays Positive Interaction Style Positive interactions are those that are enjoyed by others and make others feel good to be around you. Positive interactions can include a smile, a laugh, a soft touch, or a special gaze in a friend's direction.

Gets the Message Across An intended message can be communicated to a friend utilizing verbal, nonverbal, gestural, pictorial, or other means. A smile or eye gaze as greeting and as a way to say, "I like you," are examples of communicating a message.

Is Reinforcing to Others Friends demonstrate a positive affective style that reflects their enjoyment of being with one another.

Initiates Thoughtful Actions Thoughtful actions are important within friendships. Such actions remind someone that a friend is thinking about him or her and is concerned about his or her welfare. Examples of such actions include sending a greeting card, calling a friend to send a birthday wish, or calling just to say, "hi."

Is a Good Listener Critical to a friendship is attentiveness and responsiveness to the other person's needs.

Shares Belongings and Feelings Friends often share a variety of belongings and feelings. Depending upon their ages, friends can share, among other things, toys, food, feelings, and secrets.

Has Similar Likes and Dislikes Friends are often described as having similar likes and dislikes.

Takes the Perspectives of Others Being able to see the joys and challenges of life through the eyes of a friend is a unique characteristic of friendship.

Is Trustworthy and Loyal A friend is someone to count on and who will be there when needed.

knowledge because of myths, prejudices, and limited expectations for students with significant disabilities. However, there is a need to teach all students about relationships, sexuality, and the responsibilities of parenting (Edwards, 1988). The curriculum taught should vary according to the age of the students but might include the following concepts:

Appropriate/inappropriate dress, grooming, touching of self and others, social behaviors, and language

Private/public clothing, body parts, places, conversation, voice level, touching, and thoughts

Assertive/passive-aggressive behavior, language, and voice tone

Respect for self, privacy, and taking ownership of one's body

Respect for others/making friends by allowing for others' privacy, discriminating between strangers, acquaintances, and friends

Initiating appropriate social interaction and sharing places/interests, activities, thought, and feelings.

Developing and implementing such curricula requires the close participation and involvement of parents, teachers, students, and school district personnel. Parental support and consent is required when providing sex education to students who are minors. As with other basic skills, social-sexual skills should not be taught in isolated, discrete activity units, but should be incorporated throughout the curriculum so that they have relevance to the student's total life.

Instructional Approaches

There are a number of instructional approaches that have been described in detail in Chapter 6 of this book. As previously noted, friendships are highly complex and unique relationships and do not lend themselves to systematic task analyses and traditional instructional strategies. With this cautionary note, professionals may utilize instructional approaches to assist students with and without disabilities to engage in the social skills usually expressed by friends. These approaches include shaping, modeling, and coaching.

Shaping   Shaping involves the systematic reinforcement of a desirable behavior; students with disabilities can be systematically reinforced for engaging in those social skills used by friends. For example, when a student approaches another student, the teacher or that student can reinforce the approaching student for initiating an interaction, even if the approaching student has not communicated anything verbally. Over time, the approaching student's behavior would need to become more complex and explicitly indicate a desire to interact in order to be reinforced.

Modeling   Modeling is a way to teach some of the complex skills that can facilitate the development of friendships; modeling might consist of demonstrating a behavior for the student to imitate. Teachers can serve as models of respectful and friendly interactions when interacting with students, teaching colleagues, administrators, parents, and others. In addition, students who interact with their friends can also serve as excellent role models.

Coaching   Coaching may assist some students to practice the social skills important to facilitate the development of friendships. Coaching typically involves direct instruction, opportunities to practice the skill(s) with peers, and a "post review" session to discuss effects of the instruction (Gottlieb & Leyser, 1981; Oden & Asher, 1977). Coaching is a beneficial strategy in that specific social skills or behaviors can be targeted for improvement (Gottlieb & Leyser, 1981). For example, a counselor utilized coaching strategies to teach Brian, a young man with significant disabilities, the finer nuances of asking someone to dance at a school dance. Specifically, Brian and his counselor practiced what Brian would say and do, then Brian tried the suggestions; afterward, they reviewed how the interaction went.

Establishing Social Opportunities

Varied, Frequent, and Regular Opportunities   Students with significant disabilities and their peers need varied, frequent, and regular opportunities to be with one another and develop friendships. Educators can develop and structure such opportunities in a variety of ways. For example, teachers of children and adolescents can facilitate the development of friendships during school activities and at after-school events. Community recreation leaders can assist students to develop friendships during after-school and weekend recreation activities. Job coaches can assist adults to develop friendships at their job sites by such activities as joining baseball leagues and attending after-work functions. It is important that professionals identify and analyze the age-appropriate social activities in which individuals without disabilities participate, in order to best utilize naturally occurring opportunities.

Making Action Plans (MAPs)   MAPs are tools designed to assist students with disabilities to become better connected with their peers, co-workers, and other associates. In addition, the MAPs process is designed to facilitate student inclusion in schools and communities.

Specifically, the MAPs process facilitates the collection of information about a particular student through a meeting involving the student and his or her significant others (Falvey et al., 1994; Forest & Lusthaus, 1990; Vandercook, York, & Forest, 1989). The meeting typically includes the student's friends, or acquaintances who are potential friends, family members, teachers, therapists, administrators, neighbors, and so forth. For further discussion and an example of a completed MAPs process, readers are referred to Chapter 4.

Circles   A circle of friends process involves gathering a group of students together. Each student considers his or her own circle of friends and then reflects on each other's circles (Sherwood, 1990). The members of a circle usually agree to meet on an ongoing basis. Figure 1 provides a list of the steps involved in conducting a circle of friends process.

A facilitator is identified to encourage the participants' involvement. In the beginning the facilitator is often an adult, such as a teacher. However, the adult should be replaced as quickly as possible by one of the peers or by the student him- or herself. Frequently, the facilitator role rotates among the participants. In addition, although the circle may originally be formed around the needs of the student with disabilities, the needs of other participants often become the focus during subsequent meetings. Eventually the circle becomes a network of support for all those participating. The initial meetings might be more formal (i.e., people might wear name tags, an agenda might be prepared, and so forth) until the members of the circle become comfortable with each other. Meetings then typically become more informal, like a group of friends getting together.

A circle of friends provides a network of support from family and friends and is available when one needs someone to listen, to give loving advice, and/or to provide support (Perske, 1989). A circle of friends is something that many of us take for granted—that is, unless it is something we do not have. In the absence of a naturally formed circle of friends, educators can facilitate a circle process. The circle of friends process is sometimes referred to as *personal futures planning* (Mount & Zwernik, 1988). The process, similar to the MAPs process, can be used to enlist the commitment of future involvement of peers around an individ-

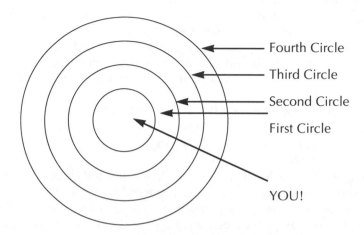

This exercise is a social scan. It will give a quick picture of who is in your life. It is very useful to gain clarity about who might be involved in certain activities or circles that need to be filled. We recommend it personally and consider it an essential preventive health check for students and teachers. The key hidden question is: "Who loves this person?"

Instructions:
1. Draw four concentric circles.
2. Put yourself right in the middle then take a few minutes to fill in the people in each of your four circles.
    First circle: The people most intimate in your life—those you cannot imagine living without
    Second circle: Good friends—those who almost made the first circle
    Third circle: People, organizations, and networks with whom you are involved (work colleagues, the church choir, the square dance club, softball team, etc.)
    Fourth circle: People you *pay* to provide services in your life (medical professionals, tax accountants, mechanics, teachers, etc.)

Note: People can be in more than one circle (e.g., your doctor or teacher could also be a very close friend; a deceased parent/friend may be an intimate personal suppport).

Figure 1.   Steps involved in conducting a circle of friends process. (From Falvey, M.A., Forest, M., Pearpoint, J., & Rosenberg, R.L. [1994]. Building connections. In J.S. Thousand, R.A. Villa, & A.I. Nevin [Eds.], *Creativity and collaborative learning: A practical guide to empowering students and teachers* [p. 350]. Baltimore: Paul H. Brookes Publishing Co. Reprinted by permission.)

ual student. For a student who does not have an extensive network of friends, a circle of friends process can be very useful.

Cooperative Groupings   As discussed in several other sections of this book (Chapters 5, 6, 12, and 13), cooperative groupings are an essential ingredient in a classroom where intentional efforts to facilitate student relationships and friendships are considered paramount. Cooperative groupings are a way to promote interdependence. Specifically, when teachers use a cooperative grouping instructional arrangement, they assign students to work on assignments or projects within small heterogeneous groups of three to six students that vary in abilities, interests, and strengths. The students working in cooperative groupings are instructed to work together and discouraged from working independently. One example of cooperative grouping is the formation of *tribes*. The major purpose of the tribes is for "positive peer support for social development and learning" (Gibbs, 1987, p. 20). A tribe is a group of students who form a social network that works together throughout a school year (and beyond, it is hoped). The students are assigned to heterogeneous groups of five to six students. The tribes share personal concerns and feelings as well as plan and problem solve to maintain a positive working atmosphere, and they work within the curriculum in a cooperative manner. All areas of the curriculum can and have been successfully addressed within the context of tribes. Chapters 5 and 12 provide additional discussions about and examples of tribes.

Community Strategies

While efforts to facilitate social relationships must include both the curriculum and instructional approaches for schools, attention must also be given to the social networking within the student's community. There are several strategies that can be used to facilitate friendships and social networks within communities. In addition to MAPs and circles, two such strategies are described below.

Citizen Advocacy Citizen advocates are volunteers who assist people who have been excluded from their communities to become better connected (O'Brien & O'Brien, 1992). These advocates are community members who provide introductions and ongoing support in order to develop sustained personal relationships for persons who have been socially excluded. For example, when Juan, a 20-year-old man with multiple disabilities, was kicked out of his group home, a citizen advocate contacted a local university housing unit and was able to identify two students who were looking for a roommate and anxious to meet Juan. Juan liked the two students and they liked him, and they all eventually agreed to share an apartment. The three young men have become compatible roommates and good friends. The citizen advocate continues to meet with Juan to assist him in identifying needs and securing the resources to meet those needs.

Connecting People to Community Associations To discover opportunities for people to become more connected to community associations such as churches, sporting activities, clubs, and other such affiliations, educators and/or service providers can enlist the participation and support of leaders of these groups (O'Brien & O'Brien, 1992). One community connection can lead to multiple connections. People with significant disabilities can contribute new energy, new abilities, and new meaning to the associations that enliven the communities in which they live.

CONCLUSIONS

Not all of the preceding strategies will work with all students, although within the numerous strategies presented there will undoubtedly be a set of effective strategies for each individual student. Educators should systematically assess the situation carefully to determine the appropriate type and amount of strategies and supports that are necessary, using the information presented in Chapter 4 of this book. In addition, educators should fade their assistance as soon as naturally occurring supports are available.

The challenge to educators is to create the optimal environment for encouraging students with disabilities to develop friendships and support networks. Numerous existing strategies can be used to assist children, adolescents, and adults to form connections with others and to nurture such connections so that they become essential friendships. Services and support should foster relationships, and "systems" support should be faded as quickly as possible in favor of natural supports (e.g., family, friends, co-workers). If schools and communities create a culture of cooperation, caring, equity, and celebration of diversity, changes in service delivery models, curriculum, instruction, and community connections will follow naturally.

REFERENCES

Amado, A.N. (Ed.). (1993). *Friendships and community connections between people with and without disabilities.* Baltimore: Paul H. Brookes Publishing Co.

Amado, R.S. (1993). Loneliness: Effects and implications. In A.N. Amado (Ed.), *Friendships and community connections between people with and without disabilities* (pp. 67–84). Baltimore: Paul H. Brookes Publishing Co.

Asher, S.R., Oden, S.L., & Gottman, J.M. (1977). Children's friendships in school settings. In L.G. Katz (Ed.), *Current topics in early childhood education* (Vol. 1) (pp. 33–61). Norwood, N.J.: Ablex.

Berndt, T.J. (1982). The features and effects of friendships in early adolescence. *Child Development, 53,* 1447–1460.

Berndt, T.J., & Perry, T.B. (1986). Children's perceptions of friendships as supportive relationships. *Developmental Psychology, 22*(5), 640–648.

Bishop, K. (1991). *The integration and employment status of adults with disabilities in supported employment.* Unpublished doctoral dissertation, University of California Los Angeles/California State University, Los Angeles.

Brown, L., Branston, M.B., Hamre-Nietupski, S., Johnson, F., Wilcox, B., & Gruenewald, L. (1979). A rationale for comprehensive longitudinal interactions between severely handicapped students and other citizens. *AAESPH Review, 4*(1), 3–14.

Buhrmester, D., & Furman, W. (1986). The changing functions of friends in childhood: A neo-Sullivan perspective. In V.J. Derlaga & B.A. Winstead (Eds.), *Friendship and social interaction* (pp. 41–61). New York: Springer-Verlag.

Cowen, E.L., Pederson, A., Babigian, M., Izzo, L.D., & Trost, M.R. (1973). Long-term follow-up of early detected vulnerable children. *Journal of Consulting and Clinical Psychology, 41,* 438–446.

Derman-Sparks, L., & the ABC Task Force (1989). *Anti-bias curriculum: Tools for empowering young children.* Washington DC.: National Association for the Education of Young Children.

Edwards, J. (1988). Sexuality, marriage, and parenting for persons with Down syndrome. In S.M. Pueschel (Ed.), *The young person with Down syndrome* (pp. 187–204) Baltimore: Paul H. Brookes Publishing Co.

Evans, I.M., Salisbury, C.L., Palombaro, M.M., Berryman, J. & Hollywood, T.M. (1992). Peer interactions and social acceptance of elementary-age children with severe disabilities in an inclusive school. *Journal of The Association for Persons with Severe Handicaps, 17*(4), 205–212.

Falvey, M.A. (1989). *Community-based curriculum: Instructional strategies for students with severe disabilities.* Baltimore: Paul H. Brookes Publishing Co.

Falvey, M., Forest, M., Pearpoint, J., & Rosenberg, R. (1994). Building connections: Circles, MAPs, and Paths. In J. Thousand, R. Villa, & A. Nevin (Eds.), *Creativity and collaborative learning: A practical guide for empowering students and teacher.* (pp. 347–368). Baltimore: Paul H. Brookes Publishing Co.

Field, T. (1984). Play behavior of handicapped children who have friends. In T. Field, J.L. Roopnarine, & M. Segal (Eds.), *Friendships in normal and handicapped children* (pp. 153–162). Norwood, NJ: Ablex.

Forest, M., & Lusthaus, E. (1990). Everyone belongs with the MAPs action planning system. *Teaching Exceptional Children, 22*(2), 32–35.

Gibbs, J. (1987). *Tribes: A process for social development and cooperative learning.* Pleasant Hill, CA: Center for Human Development.

Gottlieb, J., & Leyser, Y. (1981). Friendship between mentally retarded and nonretarded children. In S.R. Asher & J.M. Gottman (Eds.), *The development of children's friendships* (pp. 150–181). Cambridge, England: Cambridge University Press.

Guralnick, M.J. (1980). Social interactions among preschool children. *Exceptional Children, 46*(4), 248–253.

Haring, T.G., Breen, C., Pitts Conway, V., Lee, M., & Gaylord-Ross, R. (1987). Adolescent peer tutoring and special friend experiences. *Journal of The Association for Persons with Severe Handicaps, 12*(4), 280–286.

Haring, K., Farron-Davis, R., Goetz, L., Karasoff, P., Sailor, W., & Zeph, L. (1992). LRE and the placement of students with severe disabilities. *Journal of The Association for Persons with Severe Handicaps, 17*(3), 145–153.

Hartup, W.W. (1970). Peer interaction and social organization. In P.H. Mussen (Ed.), *Carmichael's manual of children psychology* (3rd ed.) (pp. 361–456). New York: John Wiley & Sons.

Hartup, W.W. (1975). The origins of friendship. In M. Lewis & L.A. Rosenblum (Eds.), *Friendships and peer relations* (pp. 11–26). New York: John Wiley & Sons.

Hartup, W.W. (1983). Peer relations. In E.M. Hetherington (Ed.), *Socialization, personality, and social development* (pp. 104–196). New York: John Wiley & Sons.

Hayes, D.A. (1978). Cognitive bases for liking and disliking among preschool children. *Child Development, 49,* 906–909.

Hojat, M., & Crandall, R. (Eds.). (1989). *Loneliness: Theory, research and applications.* Newbury Park, CA: Sage Press.

Howes, C. (1983). Patterns of friendship. *Child Development, 54,* 1041–1053.

Howes, C. (1987). Social competence with peers in young children: Developmental sequences. *Developmental Review, 7*(3), 252–272.

Howes, C., & Mueller, D. (1980). Early peer friendships: Their significance for development. In W. Spiel (Ed.), *The psychology of the twentieth century.* Zurich, Switzerland: Kindler.

Hunt, P., Haring, K., Farron-Davis, F., Staub, D., Rogers, J., Beckstead, S.P., Karasoff, P., Goetz, L., & Sailor, W. (1993). Factors associated with the integrated educational placement of students with severe disabilities. *Journal of The Association for Persons with Severe Handicaps, 18*(1), 6–15.

Hymel, S., & Asher, S.R. (1977). *Assessment and training of isolated children's social skills.* (ERIC Document Reproduction Service No. ED 136 930)

Lewis, M., & Rosenblaum, L.A. (1975). *Friendships and peer relations.* New York: John Wiley & Sons.

Lutfiyya, Z.M. (1988, September). Other than clients: Reflections on relationships between people with disabilities and typical people. *Newsletter of The Association for Persons with Severe Handicaps, 14*(9), 3–5.

Masters, J.C., & Furman, W. (1981). Popularity, individual friendship selection and specific peer interaction among children. *Developmental Psychology, 17*(3), 344–350.

Monat-Haller, R.K. (1992). *Understanding and expressing sexuality: Responsible choices for individuals with developmental disabilities.* Baltimore: Paul H. Brookes Publishing Co.

Mount, B., & Zwernik, K. (1988). *It's never too early, it's never too late: A booklet about personal futures planning.* St. Paul: Metropolitan Council.

Nisbet, J. (Ed.).(1992). *Natural supports in school, at work, and in the community for people with severe disabilities.* Baltimore: Paul H. Brookes Publishing Co.

Noddings, N. (1992). *The challenge to care in schools: An alternative approach to education.* New York: Teachers College Press.

O'Brien, J., & O'Brien, C.L. (1992). Members of each other: Perspectives on social support for people with severe disabilities. In J. Nisbit (Ed.), *Natural supports in school, at work, and in the community for people with severe disabilities* (pp. 17–64). Baltimore: Paul H. Brookes Publishing Co.

Oden, S., & Asher, S.R. (1977). Coaching children in social skills for friendship making. *Child Development, 48,* 495–506.

Perske, R. (1987, October). *Why friendship?* Presentation at the meeting of The Association for Persons with Severe Handicaps conference, Chicago.

Perske, R. (1989). *Circle of friends.* Nashville: Abingdon Press.

Robins, L.N. (1966). *Deviant children grown up.* Baltimore: Williams & Wilkins.

Roff, M., Sells, S.B., & Golden, M.M. (1972). *Social adjustment and personality development in children.* Minnesota: University of Minnesota Press.

Rubin, Z. (1982). *Children's friendships.* Cambridge, MA: Harvard University Press.

Rynders, J.E., Johnson, R.T., Johnson, D.W., & Schmidt, B. (1980). Producing positive interactions among Down Syndrome and nonhandicapped students through cooperative goal structuring. *American Journal of Mental Deficiency, 85,* 268–273.

Schaffner, C.B., & Buswell, B.E. (1992). *Connecting students: A guide to thoughtful friendship facilitation for educators and families.* Colorado Springs, CO: PEAK Parent Center.

Schnorr, R.F. (1990). "Peter? He comes and goes . . .": First graders' perspectives on a part-time mainstreamed student. *Journal of The Association for Persons with Severe Handicaps, 15*(4), 936–941.

Shapiro, J. (1993, December 13). Separate and unequal. *U.S. News and World Report, 115*(3), 46–56.

Sherwood, S.K. (1990). A circle of friends in a 1st grade classroom. *Educational Leadership, 48*(3), 41.

Stainback, S., & Stainback, W. (1985). *Integration of students with severe handicaps into regular schools.* Reston, VA: Council for Exceptional Children.

Stainback, W., & Stainback, S. (1987, March). Facilitating friendships. *Education and Training in Mental Retardation,* 18–25.

Stainback, S., Stainback, W., & Forest, M. (Eds.). (1989). *Educating all students in the mainstream of regular education*. Baltimore: Paul H. Brookes Publishing Co.

Storey, K., & Gaylord-Ross, R. (1987). Increasing positive social interactions by handicapped individuals during a recreational activity using a multicomponent treatment package. *Research in Developmental Disabilities, 8,* 627–649.

Strain, P.S. (1983). Generalization of autistic children's social behavior change: Effects of developmentally integrated and segregated settings. *Analysis and Intervention in Developmental Disabilities, 3,* 23–34.

Strain, P.S. (1984). Social interactions of handicapped preschoolers. In T. Field, J.L. Roopnarine, & M. Segal, (Eds.), *Friendships in normal and handicapped children* (pp. 187–207). Norwood, NJ: Ablex.

Strully, J.L., & Bartholomew-Lorimer, K. (1988). Social integration and friendship. In S.M. Pueschel (Ed.), *The young person with Down syndrome: Transition from adolescence to adulthood* (pp. 65–76). Baltimore: Paul H. Brookes Publishing Co.

Strully, J., & Strully, C. (1985). Friendship and our children. *Journal of The Association for Persons with Severe Handicaps, 10*(4), 224–227.

Sullivan, H.S. (1952). The interpersonal theory of psychiatry. New York: Norton.

Taylor, S.J., Biklen, D., & Knoll, J. (Eds.). (1987). *Community integration for people with severe disabilities*. New York: Teacher's College Press.

Vandercook, T., York, J., & Forest, M. (1989). The McGill Action Planning System (MAPs). A strategy for building the vision. *Journal of The Association for Persons with Severe Handicaps, 14,* 205–215.

Weiss, R.S. (1982). Loneliness: What we know about it and what we might do about it. In L.A. Replau & S.E. Goldstein (Eds.), *Preventing the harmful consequences of severe and persistent loneliness*. Rockville, MD: National Institute on Mental Health.

Weiss, R.S. (1974). The provisions of social relationships. In Z. Rubin (Ed.), *Doing unto others* (pp. 17–26). Englewood Cliffs, NJ: Prentice-Hall.

Wieck, C. (1993). Foreword. In A.N. Amado (Ed.), *Friendships and community connections between people with and without developmental disabilities.* (pp. ix–x). Baltimore: Paul H. Brookes Publishing Co.

York, J., Vandercook, T., MacDonald, C., Heise-Neff, C., & Caughey, E. (1992). Feedback about integrating middle school students with severe disabilities in general education classes. *Exceptional Children, 58*(3), 244–257.

PRESCHOOL CURRICULUM AND INSTRUCTION

11

Lisbeth J. Vincent

Through Public Law (PL) 101-476, the Individuals with Disabilities Education Act of 1990 (IDEA) and PL 102-119, the Individuals with Disabilities Education Act Amendments of 1991, children between 3 and 5 years of age are eligible for public school services if the school district's multidisciplinary assessment team finds that they are displaying a disabling condition. Specific definitions and criteria for determining whether a child qualifies vary from state to state. However, once a child is eligible, the services and program that the child is offered must meet all of the requirements of IDEA. An individualized education program (IEP) must be developed in conjunction with the child's parents, and services must be offered in the least restrictive environment (LRE). The definition of LRE implies that a child can be placed in a special education environment only if the general education environment with supplementary aids and services is not sufficient for the child to reach the goals selected. For many preschool-age children, services are now available in the general education preschool environment. Children and families are receiving their preschool services in settings that include typical children.

In communities all across the United States, children with disabilities are going to neighborhood preschool and child care centers. In some cases, these settings have specific provisions for children with disabilities (e.g., Head Start), while in others an individual child with a disability is being included at the request of the family or school district with needed support. Services and supports are following children with disabilities into "natural environments," that is, the settings where they would be if they did not have a disability. Children with disabilities attend preschool with their sisters, brothers, cousins, and neighbors. They represent one form of diversity within settings for preschool-age children, a form of diversity that is no greater, more difficult, or more important than

285

diversity in class, culture, ethnicity, language, race, religious beliefs, or other family values and experiences. They and their families are part of the overall fabric of their communities. They are beginning school fully included with the intent to remain in inclusive schools until graduation.

In programs across the country, scenarios like the following are unfolding every day. The Southside Child Care Center is operated by the public schools and is designed for children who are 2–9 years of age. Melissa and her mom drive up to the center just as Melissa's friend, Jamie, is arriving with his dad. The parents and children get out of their cars. Jamie's dad reminds him not to forget his backpack as he runs over to greet Melissa and "walk" into school with her. Melissa pushes her wheelchair and excitedly jabbers with Jamie. She stops pushing her wheelchair and holds up her backpack, shaking it. Jamie unzips it and sees several toy dinosaurs inside. "Cool," he says. "Let's go give them to Ms. Alice." Melissa grins and heads her wheelchair toward the front door to the center. Melissa's mom and Jamie's dad are left standing on the sidewalk, smiling and calling out to their children to wait for them inside the door so they can sign in and say hello to their teacher.

Building inclusive preschool settings, perhaps like Southside's, is the focus of this chapter. The foundations of effective inclusive preschool programs are described first. The development of social competence during the preschool years is then examined, and the elements of a high-quality preschool environment for all children are considered. Curricular and instructional approaches that rely on natural activities for preschool-age children are stressed. Adapting curriculum and instruction to meet individual needs of children is discussed. Special sections then highlight child assessment, goal setting (i.e., individualized education programming), family participation, and general curriculum and intervention strategies. The chapter closes with a description of a typical day for a child with significant disabilities who is included in a neighborhood preschool.

EFFECTIVE INCLUSIVE PRESCHOOL PROGRAMS

Through research and model demonstration projects in the 1970s and 1980s, educators have increased their knowledge of what constitutes an effective inclusive preschool for children with and without disabilities. The term *typical preschool* is used throughout this chapter to describe those preschools that were initially established to provide services to preschool-age children without disabilities. The term *special education preschool* is used to refer to those settings initially established to serve only children with disabilities. The term *inclusive preschool* is used to describe settings which serve preschool-age children with and without disabilities in the same programs and classrooms. Research by Guralnick and his colleagues (Guralnick, 1984, 1986, 1990; Guralnick & Groom, 1988) and by Strain and his colleagues (Sainato, Goldstein, & Strain, 1992; Strain, 1983, 1984; Strain, Hoyson, & Jamieson, 1985), among others, has clearly demonstrated that young children with and without disabilities can be successfully educated in inclusive settings.

Research in the early 1990s by Cole, Dale, and Mills (1991) and Yoder, Kaiser, and Alpert (1991) has lent support to the idea that children with more severe disabilities may be most appropriately served in inclusive settings. They found that young children show more developmental progress with child-directed as opposed to adult-directed approaches. While child-directed instructional approaches characterize most typical preschool settings, special education preschool settings have traditionally been characterized by adult-directed approaches (Odom & McEvoy, 1990; Odom & Ostrosky, 1990; Vincent, Salisbury, et al., 1980). However, in addition to child-directed activities, individualized planning and intervention is necessary for young children with disabilities to fully benefit from the inclusive setting (Johnson & Johnson, 1995; Strain, et al., 1992; Wolery & Bredekamp, 1995).

Bailey and Wolery (1992) specified seven outcomes achieved by successful services and programs for young children with disabilities. These outcomes can also be used to describe the foundation of effective inclusive preschool programs for young children with disabilities and their families. First, preschool services must not focus just on the child with a disability, but must provide support and assistance to the family as a whole. Through high-quality programs, families can identify their needs and develop strategies and resources to meet these needs. Needs may be as diverse as financial assistance for in-home medical care to information on babysitting or respite care services to emotional support for parents as they learn the extent of their child's disabilities. The family of a child with a disability who receives educational services in an inclusive preschool setting must have coordinated access to these additional services.

Second, the preschool environment itself must promote active engagement of the child with a disability with materials, peers, and adults. The child must be a participant learner and not just an observer. Independence should be encouraged through acquisition of specific skills and adaptation of the materials and setting where necessary. The child with a disability should be a contributing member of the group. The inclusive setting must truly include all children.

Third, through school and home support and facilitation, the child with a disability must be developing increased abilities in areas targeted on his or her IEP. The child should display more developmentally advanced behavior over time where appropriate. The activities in the inclusive preschool must match the child's IEP. Where physical and/or health management concerns exist, the child must be receiving appropriate supports and services in the regular classroom setting when appropriate and in alternative settings at other times.

Fourth, the inclusive preschool environment should foster social competence and self-esteem. Children need to receive guidance and support in forming friendships and learning peer-to-peer behavior. The child with a disability must receive support to become a problem solver with his or her peers. High-quality programs help children learn to express their needs, wants, and feelings in socially acceptable ways. Communication between home and school can be used to help identify new areas of social competence and promote their practice across settings.

Fifth, children with disabilities often show difficulties in generalizing skills and behavior across people, materials, and settings. An effective preschool program coordinates efforts between home and school and within school so as to foster generalization. Communication is essential between adults in the classroom and with adults who come into the classroom to provide support and assistance. Planned carryover of objectives across materials and activities is essential for most children with disabilities. The involvement of family members in promoting generalization to nonschool settings must also be planned.

Sixth, the inclusive preschool setting is one part of a normalized life experience for a child with a disability and his or her family. Planning to continue this normalization outside of the school day is essential. For example, assisting a family to plan a birthday party in which their child with a disability is an active participant in the games and activities helps normalize the child and family experience. Planning to continue inclusion beyond the preschool years into kindergarten must start early.

Seventh, an effective preschool program serves as a base of ongoing assessment for all children who are enrolled. When a child has a disability, there is a great need for ongoing monitoring of their development. Delays in one area of development can spill over into other areas. For example, a child who shows a significant delay in expressive language at 3 years of age may begin to show some difficulties in interacting with peers and resolving conflicts over toys and materials. With ongoing attention to development in all areas, these difficulties can be anticipated or discovered early and the child can be helped to learn alternative ways of responding.

Overall, an effective inclusive preschool program is built on ongoing communication between the school personnel and families, among various school personnel (both general and special), and among the school, family, and other community agencies involved. When a child has a disability, the preschool experience is more than just a classroom. It often involves coordination of a variety of resources and services provided by a variety of disciplines and agencies. However, the child's successful inclusion in the preschool classroom environment is an important piece of the program. Parents view the child's acceptance in the classroom by peers and adults as a major developmental success. Such success rests on a combination of the child's emerging social competence and adaptations to the preschool setting.

DEVELOPING SOCIAL COMPETENCE DURING THE PRESCHOOL YEARS

Educators and parents share a common concern about the development of social competence during the preschool years (Vincent, 1992). One of the major developmental tasks for *all* children during these years is the acquisition of the social skills necessary to form relationships and friendships with peers. As these skills begin to emerge by age 3, when children usually show increased interest in peers (Howes, 1988), both parents and teachers look to preschool settings to provide support for children in this developmental area. Frequently, typical preschools assign equal value to social–emotional development and to cognitive development and problem solving.

This approach has been underscored by the National Association for the Education of Young Children (NAEYC). In its position paper on developmentally appropriate practices, NAEYC stressed the development of meaningful, successful relationships among children as a major goal of a high-quality early childhood program (Bredekamp, 1987). Research has shown that the development of successful relationships among peers has a positive impact on the development of cognitive, prosocial, and communication skills (Bates, 1975; Garvey, 1986; Howes, 1988; Rubin & Lollis, 1988).

Parents of children with disabilities often state that a major long-term goal for their children is that they will have friends in the community (Vincent, 1985). They see inclusive programs as potentially encouraging acceptance and social skills development (Bailey & Winton, 1987; Blacher & Turnbull, 1982; Guralnick, 1994; Reichart et al., 1989). Parents also worry that their children will be rejected or isolated in the inclusive setting (Bailey & Winton, 1987; Guralnick, 1994; Turnbull, Winton, Blacher, & Salkind, 1982). Actually, inclusive settings offer many opportunities for children with disabilities to increase their social competence. Peer-related social interactions occur at a higher frequency in inclusive preschool programs than in special education preschool programs (Buysse & Bailey, 1993; Guralnick & Groom, 1988). In addition to these increased opportunities, quality of interaction is highly appropriate. For example, peers without disabilities are able to match their communicative and social overtures to the developmental abilities of children with disabilities and to involve these children in a variety of play and observational learning activities (Guralnick & Groom, 1988; Guralnick & Paul-Brown, 1980, 1984). Chapter 10 in this volume offers a more extensive discussion of strategies for facilitating friendships.

A note of caution is in order, however. The general approach used in typical preschool programs to foster social-emotional development does not appear *sufficient* for all children with disabilities. Children with disabilities often show social skills deficits that are greater than might be expected from their developmental abilities in communication and cognitive domains (Guralnick, 1990). Even with the increased opportunities available in the inclusive setting, children with disabilities may engage in less social interaction than might be expected based on the setting and their developmental status. A stronger focus on the development of social competence must be provided for these children in inclusive settings. This increased emphasis in the classroom on social competence is also likely to enhance the skills of children without disabilities. Communication between preschool and home should focus on ways to enhance and generalize this social competence in other community settings. The development of peer-to-peer social competence and of self-management skills are of particular importance for future inclusion experiences and for the development of relationships with adults and children in later school and community settings.

Peer-to-Peer Social Competence

During the preschool-age years, peer-to-peer social competence is built on under-standing the rules of play situations and sharing common play themes (e.g., building a road with interconnecting blocks or preparing, serving, and eating a meal). Children need to learn how to enter the play arena, maintain play themes, share materials, and resolve conflicts (Guralnick, 1990, 1992; Miller, Strain, Boyd, Jarzynka, & McFetridge, 1993). Children learn to join ongoing play activ-ities in a nonthreatening manner. They join in by adding materials that are rele-vant to the play theme, commenting on what is happening, imitating what is hap-pening, asking to share existing materials, or simply staying near the activity as an interested observer.

During the preschool years, children without disabilities are successful in joining ongoing play themes or activities about half of the time. The other half of the time their attempts are ignored or rejected (Corsaro, 1981). Particularly likely to be rejected are attempts to redirect the play, disrupt the activity, or interact without relating to the play theme. Children with disabilities are at risk to engage in behavior that leads to rejection. Their communication skills are often more limited than their peers, and their ability to join a play theme by adding relevant materials or expand a play theme by adding new dimensions may be affected by delays in the cognitive domain. Thus, proximity to the play arena may not be suf-ficient to allow a child with a disability to learn how to join in peer-to-peer play situations so vital for learning social competence.

In addition to learning how to join in social interactions, children learn to manage conflict that arises during the play situation itself. To be successful in peer-to-peer relations, a child needs to develop conflict resolution skills. The ability to recognize the desires and rights of one's peers is essential to conflict resolution. Maintaining connectedness with the activity in the face of conflict, of-fering an alternative or solution, providing reasons for one's actions, and asking and answering questions with peers are all strategies that preschool-age children have demonstrated (Eisenberg & Garvey, 1981). Maintaining play requires that children match their behavior to ongoing play themes and stay connected to the play situation during conflict (Howes, 1988).

In essence, children learn to vary the intensity of their interactions and to regulate their emotional reactions in the play context. These skills all require the ability to express one's needs, wants, and feelings to one's peers. Children with disabilities often have significant delays in communication skills. When faced with situations where they are not able to verbally express what they want, they may do so physically. They may simply reach out and take an object being used in a play theme, rather than join in by asking for a turn. Conversely, they may allow another child to take a play object from them without protesting. Thus, once engaged in a play situation, the child with a disability may not fully benefit from the learning opportunity that peer-to-peer interaction provides.

Facilitation and support from adults and peers in the play situation are needed for children with disabilities to learn to join in and stay connected to play themes. Successful strategies include 1) systematically gathering information on what parts of the play situation are causing difficulty for the child, 2) assisting the child to introduce appropriate materials to the activity, 3) modeling verbal expressions which can be used to ask to join in the activity and to resolve conflict, 4) ensuring that play materials which match the interests of the child are included in the classroom, 5) teaching the children without disabilities to initiate interaction with and include the child with disabilities, and 6) designing small group or learning center activities that assist the child to learn important play themes.

Self-Management Skills

Children's difficulties in the area of peer-to-peer relations do not usually occur in isolation. Often these children also have difficulties in meeting classroom expectations in following rules and routines and participating in classroom activities (Strain, Kerr, & Stagg, 1982; Strain & Sainato, 1987). The underlying difficulty is likely to be self-management. Early educators have acknowledged that the ability to participate in the classroom milieu without constant adult attention and supervision is essential for classroom success (Strain, 1981; Vincent, Salisbury, et al., 1980; Walter & Vincent, 1982). Expectations for self-management increase as a child grows older. Self-management is an essential skill for success not only in classrooms, but also in home and community settings.

During the preschool years, children are expected to begin the process of going from being inner-directed and following their own interests and wants to becoming outer- and other-directed. Familiar routines such as bedtime and story time are expected to guide their behavior and reactions. Activities such as music, art, and blocks produce interest and involvement. Gradually children are expected to comply with the rules of the classroom and home setting. These rules are usually still flexible at this age, but minimal expectations often exist. For example, in many preschool classrooms, children may not be required to join the opening circle, but if they do not they must engage in a quiet activity. Similarly, at home, the child may not need to go to sleep at nap time and may be allowed to have a book in bed, but he or she must rest quietly. Children with and without disabilities can experience difficulties meeting these changing and always increasing expectations.

A child's developmental status, temperament, and experience all have an impact on success in mastering self-management skills. A child's cognitive and communication abilities have an impact on how easily he or she learns new rules, routines, and activities. Often child "misbehavior" is not willful disobedience, but an indication that the child does not know or has forgotten what is expected. Children vary temperamentally in how readily they adapt to routines and changes and how able they are to calm and control their reactions to change and stress. These developmental and temperamental differences are more likely to be apparent when a child has a disability.

Children's experiences also have an effect on their learning and use of self-management skills. Part of this experience is what educators and others provide children in the preschool classroom. In special education preschool classrooms, where adult–child ratios are usually low, children often can rely on adults to do the "managing." In inclusive preschool classrooms, children must learn to rely on themselves and their peers. Fortunately, strategies to teach self-management to preschool-age children with disabilities have been identified and implemented successfully in pilot projects (Baer, 1990; Barnett & Casey, 1992; Strain & Sainato, 1987). The basic approach involves teaching children to identify what behavior is appropriate for a given situation, evaluate their behavior against this standard, determine whether they have met the standard, confirm their evaluation with an adult or peer, and determine whether reinforcement is appropriate. For example, Jason received support from teachers and peers to learn that during art time, the glue, scissors, crayons, and paper were used only at the art table. The children stayed in their own seats and let someone know if they needed to share any of the materials. Jason learned through review with the teacher, by having his peers state the rules out loud before art time started, and by being asked to join the discussion with words. During art time, the teacher asked the group, including Jason, to review the rules and asked whether they were meeting the rules. Jason signaled "yes" with words and by pointing to a picture of a smiling face. (Had he not been meeting the rules, he would have pointed to a neutral face drawing.) Jason asked his buddy if he was meeting the rules. His buddy said, "Yes, you stayed in your seat and asked me for the scissors." Jason identified that indeed he should get a reinforcer by putting up his hand for a "way to go" high-five from his buddy.

Preschool-age children who were having difficulty with classroom management have learned to use this strategy on an individual basis and when it was implemented for the whole class. Children have been observed to continue using the strategy on their own and with each other when external reinforcement was removed. Children with and without disabilities have learned the strategy and improved their overall classroom behavior. This strategy relies on teaching children to be in control of their behavior, rather than having adults control children through time-out or punishment. It is likely to contribute to positive self-esteem, as children are able to fully participate in more complex and diverse settings when they have learned self-management skills.

Overall, educators and researchers have demonstrated that children with disabilities face some challenges in the inclusive preschool setting, but that these challenges can be overcome and the setting can be highly beneficial if the opportunities offered by the inclusive setting are blended with necessary supports and adaptations for the individual child. The inclusive preschool setting offers unique opportunities for the child with a disability to capitalize on the ability to learn from natural activities and adult and peer interactions. The characteristics of a high-quality preschool setting which is likely to offer these opportunities are reviewed next.

RECOMMENDED PRACTICES FROM EARLY CHILDHOOD GENERAL EDUCATION

In 1987, the National Association for the Education of Young Children (NAEYC) and the National Association of Early Childhood Specialists in State Departments of Education (NAECS/SDE) published an extensive position statement that outlined developmentally appropriate practice (DAP) for a high-quality early childhood program for children from birth through 8 years of age. These practices have received widespread attention and refinement from both general and special educators (Bredekamp, 1992, 1993; Bredekamp & Rosegrant, 1992; Carta, 1995; Carta, Schwartz, Atwater, & McConnell, 1991; Johnson & Johnson, 1992, 1995; NAEYC & NAECS/SDE, 1991; Odom, 1995; Wolery & Bredekamp, 1995).

NAEYC advocated that early childhood programs plan a learning environment that 1) matches what is known about children at various ages of development, referred to as age appropriateness, and 2) is responsive to the individual experiences and differences of children, referred to as individual appropriateness (Bredekamp, 1987). They emphasized the role of children's play in fostering the development of conceptual, communication, social, emotional, and adaptive behavior. NAEYC provided guidelines for developmentally appropriate practice in four areas: curriculum, adult–child interaction, relations between home and school or program, and developmental evaluation of children. These guidelines have become widely accepted as reflecting recommended practice in early childhood education and have received attention and support from early childhood special educators as well. They serve as the base for an effective preschool setting into which supports and adaptations for a child with a disability can be built. The recommendations cover goals and methods of instruction in addition to providing a conceptual basis for how young children learn and develop.

Curriculum Guidelines

According to the NAEYC guidelines (Bredekamp, 1987; Bredekamp & Rosegrant, 1992; Wolery & Bredekamp, 1993), the basic premise behind the curriculum in a high-quality early childhood program is that a child's conceptual, communication, social, emotional, and adaptive development is interrelated. Thus, the curriculum must provide experiences in which these developmental areas are interrelated. The classroom is a place for the "whole" child to actively engage in learning opportunities that emphasize self-direction and child interests. The child is not broken down into subparts (e.g., speech and language or fine motor skills) for instruction. Children are given opportunities and support to select and guide their own activities. Individual child interests are supported by adults. The materials used in learning activities are selected for their relevance to the lives of young children and because they can be touched, explored, and manipulated. Curriculum planning involves knowledge of children's backgrounds and experiences to plan high-interest, nonsexist, multicultural experiences.

The child is viewed as an active leader and not just a participant in the learning process. Children's likes, dislikes, strengths, and unique needs are respected and supported in the early childhood program. The role of the teacher is to facilitate and support a child's exploration, discovery, and learning. Instruction is not directive and controlled. The adult provides opportunities for children to learn by choosing an appropriate blend of interesting and challenging active and quiet activities, both indoors and outdoors.

Early childhood special educators point out that children with disabilities often require extra planning and attention in terms of curriculum. The physical environment, materials, activities, and the daily schedule may need to be adapted in order to meet the unique social–emotional, communication, cognitive, motor, and adaptive abilities and needs of these children. Special supports may be needed in the classroom setting. Simply participating in the general early childhood curriculum may not lead to the developmental gains desired by a child's family and educational and therapeutic team. Suggested guidelines for curriculum adaptations are discussed in a later section of this chapter.

Adult–Child Interaction Guidelines

According to the NAEYC guidelines (Bredekamp, 1987; Bredekamp & Rosegrant, 1992; Wolery & Bredekamp, 1995), the basic premise that guides adult–child interaction in a high-quality early childhood program is that while each child in a program is the responsibility of an adult at all times, adults foster independence in children while keeping them safe. Adults respond to the differing needs of children in an age-appropriate fashion. They allow children to express their wants and needs. Both verbal and nonverbal communication are encouraged and responded to consistently. Signs of stress are responded to on an individual child basis. Children's self-esteem is enhanced by adults expressing support and respect, not criticism, judgment, or anger. Discipline is viewed as a way to help children learn self-control by setting realistic limits and helping children remember the limits. Children are allowed to explore and make mistakes. Learning through trial and error is encouraged and supported.

The adult acts as a facilitator; the child acts as an active, engaged learner. The adult is responsible for building an environment in which children are safe, yet able to explore, make mistakes, and learn from trial and error. Adults are responsible for supporting children during this process in ways that enhance self-esteem, assist children in relating to each other, and help children learn self-control. These skills are in the broad areas of social competence and self-management. As discussed earlier in this chapter, children with disabilities often need extra support and program adaptations to be successful in these areas.

Home–School Partnership Guidelines

According to the NAEYC guidelines (Bredekamp, 1987; Bredekamp & Rosegrant, 1992; Wolery & Bredekamp, 1995), joint planning between teachers and families is an essential element in a high-quality early education program. Parents are viewed as decision makers in their children's lives and need to be involved in deciding how to best meet the children's needs. Parents play a critical role in planning for their child's transition from preschool to kindergarten services.

Early childhood special educators recognize that for children with disabilities, a strong collaboration between home and school is essential. Families are usually the most consistent source of support and encouragement for the children. Families see the child across many settings and experiences. They are accurate observers and reporters of what their child can do and is learning to do. They play an essential role in assessment and IEP planning and implementation. They can often serve as an effective translator of the child's unique strengths and needs to the typical early childhood education setting.

Developmental Evaluation of Children Guidelines

According to the NAEYC guidelines (Bredekamp, 1987; Bredekamp & Rosegrant, 1992; Wolery & Bredekamp, 1995), the basis of developmental evaluation in a high-quality childhood program is the recognition that parents and teachers have valuable information to share about children's development. Because of the wealth of their direct observation on a day-to-day basis with a child, parents and teachers are in a unique position to choose curriculum goals. Standardized testing alone should not be used for this purpose or to exclude or include children in particular programs. If standardized instruments are used with young children, they must be interpreted with caution and must be supplemented with other sources of information about a child's development.

Early childhood special educators also value the role of direct observation in determining a child's educational goals and objectives. As is discussed in the next section, ongoing assessment of children with disabilities forms the cornerstone of a high-quality early childhood program designed to meet their special needs.

RECOMMENDED PRACTICES FROM
EARLY CHILDHOOD SPECIAL EDUCATION

The NAEYC guidelines for developmentally appropriate practice just reviewed are necessary but not sufficient for successful early childhood programs for children with disabilities. As discussed in the first section of this chapter, both research and model demonstration projects have contributed to the knowledge base of specialized strategies and resources to be used in inclusive settings that enhance the learning and development of children with disabilities. In addition, children with disabilities and their families are entitled to services from public schools beginning at 3 years of age in all states. In many states, these children and families are eligible for services through a publicly funded program beginning at birth.

Part H of IDEA, the Infant and Toddler Program, allows states to extend services for children with disabilities and their families to birth or diagnosis of a child's disability (Garwood & Sheehan, 1989). If a state chooses, they may also define conditions and provide services to children who are considered to be at risk for disabling conditions. Each child and family who is served is entitled to an individualized family service plan (IFSP). Services are to be delivered in a family-centered, as opposed to a more traditional child-centered, manner. A service coordinator is selected by the IFSP team to help the family obtain the services they and their child need to maximize the child's development. Thus, many families and children who are entering inclusive preschool settings have been receiving services for a number of years and come to the setting with goals and objectives and with needed resources, supports, and adaptations well specified.

At 3 years of age, children with disabilities and their families are entitled to the full complement of services provided to school-age children. Parental and child rights and protections are guaranteed through IDEA. Each child is entitled to a full multidisciplinary assessment, the development of an IEP that responds to his or her unique needs and abilities, and supports and services from trained professionals in areas that meet the child's needs.

The Division for Early Childhood (DEC) of the Council for Exceptional Children is the professional organization that represents the largest number of specially trained teachers, therapists, and nurses working with preschool-age children with disabilities and their families. DEC undertook a project to identify recommended practices for high-quality services for young children with special needs and their families (hereafter referred to as the DEC task force). The practices were identified by expert working groups composed of professionals and parents and then submitted to organization members for validation. Identified practices in the area of assessment, the IEP, curriculum and intervention strategies, and family participation are reviewed later in this chapter for their relevance to formulating preschool curriculum and instruction for the inclusive setting. The complete set of *DEC Recommended Practices: Indicators of Quality in Programs for Infants and*

Young Children with Special Needs and Their Families (1993) also includes sections on service delivery models; interventions to promote communication, social-emotional, adaptive, and motor skills; transition; personnel competence; program evaluation; and early intervention with children who are gifted. Incorporating these recommended practices with the developmentally appropriate practices presented earlier ensures that the individual needs of children with disabilities are fully addressed in the inclusive setting.

Recommended Practices for Assessment in Early Childhood

Assessment practices are delineated in Chapter 4; however, practices and strategies specific to preschoolers are presented here. A clear indicator of a high-quality program from the perspective of early childhood special educators is that child learning and development are monitored consistently over time. Assessment must be seen as an ongoing process. In fact, this is a requirement of IDEA. Combined with a focus on the family as decision makers and on instructional objectives that are functional and naturalistic, this requirement means that educators need to design ways of monitoring progress that measure real world skills in authentic situations. With the need to focus on social competence and self-management, measurement must look at the child as an actor and interactor in his or her environment, rather than just a performer of isolated skills. For example, in the story of Melissa and Jamie earlier in this chapter, Melissa demonstrated initiated communication, peer-to-peer interaction, motoric self-direction, and separation from her family.

Ongoing assessment and measurement can be built into the average day of the child and teacher (Bricker & Cripe, 1992). Activities can be broken down into the skills or subcomponents involved so that child progress can be monitored. A sample of an ongoing assessment tool for circle time is presented in Figure 1. Notice that not only does the teacher record whether the child can do the component, she also records what support allows the child to participate successfully. The purpose of ongoing assessment is to help determine what supports and adaptations might help a child with a disability participate more successfully in the inclusive preschool setting, not just to record what a child can and can not do. The components selected for analysis are maximally helpful when they occur across activities and classroom settings. In the example of Melissa and Jamie, responding to questions, making choices, and imitating are all skills needed for children to successfully engage and remain connected to play themes with their peers during other times of the day.

The assessment practices that were validated through the DEC task force are presented below. High-quality inclusive preschool programs must ensure that these practices are implemented consistently and effectively for children with disabilities. Assessments must identify skills that are functional, important, and worthwhile for children to learn (Neisworth, 1993). As such, assessments must be based in real-world observations of children at home and school and must in-

Circle Time	Can Do	Needs Support (describe briefly)
1. Sits appropriately		
2. Looks at adults or peers when they talk		
3. Responds to name when called		
4. Responds to questions		
5. Asks questions or makes choices		
6. Responds to request to participate		
7. Imitates actions when requested		
8. Participates with fingerplays and songs		

Figure 1.   Activity-based assessment of circle time skills.

clude the opinions of parents, teachers, therapists, and others. Because of the unpredictability of the behavior of young children, assessment must occur on multiple occasions. The assessment information gathered must be used to select appropriate goals and adapt instruction. Specific recommended practices were validated by the DEC task force in the areas of 1) preassessment activities and planning; 2) procedures for determining eligibility for services, program placement, program planning, and monitoring; and 3) reporting of assessment results. Table 1 presents a synopsis of the recommendations in each area. The story of the Menendez family at the end of this chapter illustrates these recommended practices in the area of conducting and reporting assessments.

Recommended Practices for IEP Planning

In addition to using developmentally appropriate practices to guide programs for young children with disabilities, educators and others need to develop more specific instructional objectives for the children. Both IDEA and research in early childhood special education support tying these specific objectives to assessment systems that carefully monitor progress (Bricker & Cripe, 1992; Carta et al., 1991). For example, in choosing specific instructional objectives for the IEP, the focus should be on skills that are helpful to the child now, at home as well as at school, and that will continue to be helpful in the future (McDonnell & Hardman, 1988). The concept of facilitating skills that will be helpful in the next educational

Table 1. Recommended practices for assessment

Preassessment planning activities
- Families are contacted before assessment is started by professionals who will be conducting the assessment; information about the assessment process is shared and questions are answered.
- Information from other agencies is reviewed so that duplication does not take place.
- The procedures for assessment and materials to be used are jointly selected by the family and professionals.
- The family and professionals jointly determine who will be involved in conducting the assessment.
- The unique needs of the child and preferences of the family determine what type of teaming is done for assessment.

Procedures for determining eligibility for services, program placement, program planning, and monitoring
- Information to be used in the assessment is gathered from a variety of sources (e.g., family members, current service providers) using a variety of means (e.g., checklists, interviews).
- Assessment information is gathered at a variety of times.
- Procedures and instruments used for assessment have been developed on children similar to the child of interest.
- Child and family language, culture, and experiences are respected in the assessment process.
- Instruments and procedures selected are matched to unique child strengths, likes, and dislikes.

environment is referred to as *criteria of the next environment* (Vincent, Salisbury, et al., 1980). Researchers have identified many of the skills that are necessary for success in preschool and kindergarten settings (McCormick & Kawate, 1982; McCormick & Noonan, 1984; Murphy & Vincent, 1989; Noonan, 1989; Noonan et al., 1992; Rosenkoetter, Hains, & Fowler, 1994; Vincent, Salisbury, et al., 1980; Walter & Vincent, 1982). Most of the identified skills facilitate being a member of the group, as Melissa demonstrated with Jamie in the example provided, rather than facilitate preacademic skills such as colors and numbers. These skills enable a child to adapt to new situations and children readily and thus learn in the new environment without losing significant gains due to the change. Peer-to-peer social competence and self-management skills enable a child to move readily between environments and to form new friendships and social relationships. The initial development of these relationships occurs during the preschool years and can be readily supported in the inclusive preschool settings with appropriate adaptations to the curriculum. The family's goals and short-term instructional objectives in these areas should be included on a child's IEP.

Families play a critical role in the development of the IEP. While traditionally the IEP has been seen as a document that guides professional interactions with children in school situations, increasing the role of families as assessors and teachers across settings with their children is being recognized. Particularly with children below school age, the family is seen as a central partner and decision maker in the IEP process. The DEC task force identified recommended practices to support families in this role (Turbiville, Turnbull, Garland, & Lee, 1993). These recommendations are presented in Table 2.

The intervention goals selected for children should be those that families can implement naturally in their daily routines and that teachers can also implement in classrooms (McDonnell & Hardman, 1988). The use of naturally occurring activities to facilitate the development of social, cognitive, communication, and adaptive skills has been proposed as an essential ingredient to building parent–professional partnerships (Edelman, 1991; Noonan & McCormick, 1993; Vincent, Laten, Salisbury, Brown, & Baumgart, 1980).

The inclusion of parents as equals in decision making (Vincent, 1985) is the cornerstone of a family-centered model. Accepted recommended practice is that agencies, programs, and professionals shift their focus from the child to the family as a whole. Families are viewed as capable and competent decision makers on behalf of their young children with special needs (Dunst & Trivette, 1989; McGonigel, Kaufmann, & Johnson, 1991; Vincent, 1985, 1993). Family concerns, priorities, and preferred resources are to be the major determiners of a child's IEP. Family preferences regarding variables such as setting and type of service delivery are to be respected. Families are increasingly requesting inclusive preschool placements, as did Melissa's mom in the earlier example. Recommended practices in the area of family participation were generated by the DEC task force for program advising/policy making; staff training, hiring, and evaluation; family-to-family support; intervention; interagency collaboration; legislative issues; advocacy; procedural safeguard development; and leadership training. For the purposes of this section, only those practices in the area of intervention are discussed and presented in Table 2.

The DEC recommended practices support families as competent decision makers (Vincent & Beckett, 1993). Families are seen as being capable of involvement in determining goals, setting short-term objectives, and deciding the place and pace of service delivery. Family-chosen options are to be supported and developed as needed. No longer is it the role of professionals to decide without the family how and where a child with a disability will be educated.

Recommended Practices for Curriculum and Intervention Strategies

A focus on activities as the basis for adapting instruction is also an indicator of high-quality practice. In fact, activity-based intervention (ABI) is receiving increased attention as a successful intervention planning and implementation strategy:

> Activity-based intervention is a child-directed, transactional approach that embeds intervention on children's goals and objectives in routine, planned, or child-initiated activities, and uses logically occurring antecedents and consequences to develop functional and generative skills. (Bricker & Cripe, 1992, p. 40)

Table 2.   Recommended practices for IEP planning and family participation

- Families receive information about the IEP process, its purposes, and their rights in a supportive manner.
- Families can select a service coordinator to help them with the development of the IEP; this person can be another parent of a child with a disability, if the family chooses.
- The service coordinator assists the family to identify their concerns and priorities and to share these with the IEP team.
- Families are equal members of the IEP team and can include others who they believe should have a role in program planning or who would be supportive of them.
- Families can select the type and level of their decision making in the process.
- Families receive assistance as necessary in understanding the information brought to the IEP team by professionals.
- Goals and objectives are developed jointly with families; family concerns and priorities guide the selection of objectives.
- Families can choose the settings where services are delivered.
- Families' preferences regarding instructional strategies are honored.
- Instruments, methods, and procedures of assessment take into account any sensory or physical limitations of the child.
- Child strengths and capabilities are as much a focus of the assessment as child deficits or problems.
- Assessment results lead to choosing intervention goals, not just documenting child deficits and disabilities.
- Measures are selected that can be used on an ongoing basis to document success in reaching objectives and generalizing skills to new situations and settings.
- Measures are selected that can be used across disciplines and foster cross-disciplinary planning of functional goals and objectives.

Reporting the Results of Assessment
- Reports are organized by functional areas rather than by instruments used.
- Rather than documenting deficits, reports focus on results that are useful for program planning and selecting goals and objectives.
- Families are able to understand assessment results.
- Assessment reports contain information on capabilities as well as disabilities.
- Any factors that may have adversely affected a child's performance are fully reported and addressed (e.g., lack of rapport with the assessor).
- Reports focus on how the child has compensated for any limitations and how development in general is being affected by the disability.

Family Participation in Intervention
- Families receive assistance in obtaining early intervention services and supports in natural community settings.
- Family preferences have priority in determining the intervention setting.
- Families receive assistance in applying intervention strategies across settings.
- The intensity of child and family participation in early intervention services is determined by the family.
- Hopes and dreams that families have for their children are supported by staff.

Adapted from *DEC Recommended Practices* (1993).

ABI allows the principles of developmentally appropriate practice from NAEYC to be applied to children with disabilities, while ensuring truly individualized planning, intervention, and monitoring of progress from the DEC recommended practices. ABI has the potential to achieve optimal levels of child engagement because the child is the initiator of activities or at least of the direction that activities take (Warren, 1992). Such engagement allows superior learning and assists in generalization. ABI is highly consistent with the tenets of developmentally appropriate practice, particularly in that the child is the initiator and director of play activities. Because of its focus on the use of routine and planned activities, ABI also allows planning for individualized instructional objectives and monitoring of progress as specified in the DEC recommended practices. ABI also meets the tenets of functional behavior for today and in the future because it relies on naturally occurring interactions during routine activities between children and adults. For example, learning to turn on the water faucet after washing one's hands (rather than working on wrist rotation in an isolated therapy session) or learning dressing skills in the context of a play activity with other children and in preparation for departure (rather than at a button board or during time scheduled in isolation from a functional need to dress) are both functional activities. Additional strategies for teaching skills within functional activities are outlined in Chapter 8 of this volume.

Naturalistic teaching approaches and the use of small-group rather than one-to-one instruction are essential curriculum adaptations. In inclusive preschool settings, children usually receive support and facilitation during group activities on an ongoing basis from either adults or peers in the classroom. Adapting activities, materials, daily scheduling, and expectations of child behavior are all ways of optimizing the inclusion of children with disabilities (Cook, Tessier, & Klein, 1992; Noonan & McCormick, 1993).

The recommended practices from the DEC task force in the area of curriculum and instruction include outcomes that should be achieved with high-quality practices, factors that should influence the selection and modification of curriculum and instructional strategies, and specific strategies that have been demonstrated to be effective (Wolery & Sainato, 1993). These aspects are presented in Table 3.

These validated curriculum strategies can be used and modified to accomplish the outcomes of active engagement, increased independence, and generalization of learned skills. The outcomes are similar to the description of desired child behavior and assumptions about child learning that guide developmentally appropriate practices for typical children. The strategies specified allow the educator to supplement such practices with more systematic intervention techniques if child learning lags. By incorporating the recommended practices for assessment, family participation, and IEP development, consistency between home and school is ensured.

THE MENENDEZ FAMILY: A CASE STUDY

Alex was just turning 3 years of age and would begin his public school experiences for children with disabilities within a month. Because the family lives in a state that participated in the Part H program, they were already receiving services from an early intervention program. Personnel from this program and the public school early childhood program for children with disabilities worked together with the

Table 3. Recommended practices for effective curriculum and instruction

Desired outcomes
- Children will be actively engaged with their environment.
- Children will demonstrate increasing independence and initiative in prosocial behavior.
- Children will demonstrate generalization of learned skills across a wide variety of age-appropriate and culturally appropriate contexts.
- Children will be supported to participate to the extent of their abilities in all classroom routines and activities.

Strategy selection and modification
- Value the diversity of families, their experiences, and their preferences for teaching methods.
- Recognize the individuality of children.
- Bring together information from diverse disciplines and perspectives.
- Provide a balance of adult-initiated and child-directed activities.
- Use ongoing classroom routines and activities for teaching.
- Focus on generalization and not just initial acquisition of skills.
- Utilize the most normalized teaching methods possible.

Characteristics of effective strategies
- Use of age-appropriate, functional materials.
- Naturalistic, activity-based strategies.
- Participation of peers.
- Imitation of child behavior.
- Expansion and elaboration of child behavior.
- Prompting strategies and fading of prompts.
- Use of natural reinforcers and ignoring of undesirable behavior.
- Teaching self-management strategies.
- Reinforcing successive approximations of the desired behavior.

Adapted from *DEC Recommended Practices* (1993).

family to develop his new IEP and program. The Menendez family met with their service coordinator from the early intervention program for infants and toddlers and the coordinator of preschool special education services from their school district to plan for the inclusion of their son, Alex, in a neighborhood preschool. They completed a transition plan to guide Alex's move to preschool services.

Because the program followed a family-centered model, the parents were equal partners in determining how Alex's transition or program exit assessment would be conducted and what goals and objectives would be set for the next year in his new program. In completing this assessment, the family and service coordinator followed the guidelines of developmentally appropriate practice from NAEYC and recommended practices from DEC. A copy of the plan that would guide Alex and his family's transition from infant/toddler services to preschool-age services is reproduced in Appendix A at the end of this chapter. This plan includes information about the family's concerns, priorities, and preferred resources; Alex's strengths and needs; and the team's desired outcomes and strategies for obtaining them. After Alex spent 1 month in the preschool, the team met again to write a specific section of the IEP related to Alex's program in the preschool classroom.

Inspection of the IEP reveals that the move to a full-inclusion preschool was only one of several priorities for the family. They also wanted assistance with helping Alex communicate more effectively in all environments. They recognized that his success in the community would be greatly enhanced if others could understand him and he could make his needs and wants known. His parents were also interested in capitalizing on Alex's strengths in the area of learning through videos. They wanted to explore using this medium to work on preacademic skills and to build relationships with other children. Finally, his mother anticipated returning to work full-time once Alex was settled in his new program. This would mean finding extended child care and helping this person or staff work successfully with Alex.

Alex's transition to preschool went smoothly. Alex gradually began spending time in the preschool setting 1 month before his third birthday. This enabled staff, children, parents, and Alex to adapt slowly to the changes between this classroom setting and his previous program. As suggested by developmentally appropriate and recommended practices, it also allowed goals and objectives to be selected after people got to know Alex and his reactions in the new setting. He was attending full-time (i.e., five mornings a week), following his third birthday. Alex, his parents, the infant program staff, the preschool program staff, and his new classmates had all learned adaptations that resulted in successful inclusion. A description of a typical morning for Alex can be found in Appendix B at the end of this chapter.

SUMMARY

The inclusion of children with disabilities in typical preschool settings can enhance their development. Developmentally appropriate practices that guide these environments are applicable to the education of children with disabilities. Careful attention must be paid to supporting children's learning of peer-to-peer social competence and self-management, as well as appropriate skills in communication and cognition and in motor, social-emotional, and adaptive areas. Adapting classroom expectations and instructional strategies, within the context of naturally occurring rules and routines, represents recommended practice from the perspective of early childhood special education. Families and children must be placed in a leadership role and seen as capable and competent actors on and interactors in their environment. Successful inclusive preschool settings incorporate both developmentally appropriate and recommended practices for young children with special needs.

REFERENCES

Baer, R. (1990). Correspondence training: Review and current issues. *Research in Developmental Disabilities, 11*, 379–393.

Bailey, D.B., Jr., & Winton, P.J. (1987). Stability and change in parent's expectations about mainstreaming. *Topics in Early Childhood Special Education, 7*, 73–88.

Bailey, D.B., and Wolery, M. (1992). *Teaching infants and preschoolers with disabilities* (2nd ed.). New York: MacMillan.

Barnett, D.W., & Casey, K.T. (1992). *Designing interventions for preschool learning and behavior problems*. San Francisco: Jossey-Bass.

Bates, E. (1975). Peer relations and the acquisition of language. In M. Lewis & L.A. Rosenblum (Eds.), *The origins of behavior: Vol. 4, Friendship and peer relations* (pp. 259–292). San Francisco: Jossey-Bass.

Blacher, J., & Turnbull, A.P. (1982). Teacher and parent perspectives on selected social aspects of preschool mainstreaming. *Exceptional Child, 29,* 191–199.

Bredekamp, S. (Ed.). (1987). *Developmentally appropriate practice in early childhood programs serving children from birth through age 8.* Washington, DC: National Association for the Education of Young Children.

Bredekamp, S. (1992, December). *Developmentally appropriate practices for children with special needs: Myths and realities.* Paper presented at the International Early Childhood Conference on Children with Special Needs, Washington, DC.

Bredekamp, S. (1993). The relationship between early education and early childhood special education: Healthy marriage or family feud? *Topics in Early Childhood Special Education, 13,* 258–273.

Bredekamp, S., & Rosegrant, T. (1992). *Reaching potentials: Appropriate curriculum and assessment for young children* (Vol. 1). Washington, DC: National Association for the Education of Young Children.

Bricker, D., & Cripe, J. (1992). *An activity-based approach to early intervention.* Baltimore: Paul H. Brookes Publishing Co.

Buysse, V., & Bailey, D.B., Jr. (1993). Behavioral and developmental outcomes in young children with disabilities in integrated and segregated settings: A review of comparative studies. *Journal of Special Education, 26,* 434–461.

Carta, J.J., Schwartz, I.S., Atwater, J.B., & McConnell, S.R. (1991). Developmentally appropriate practice: Appraising its usefulness for young children with disabilities. *Topics in Early Childhood Special Education, 11*(1), 1–20.

Cole, K., Dale, P., & Mills, P. (1991). Individual differences in language delayed children's responses to direct and interactive preschool instruction. *Topics in Early Childhood Special Education, 11*(1), 99–124.

Cook, R.E., Tessier, A., & Klein, M.D. (1992). *Adapting early childhood curricula for children with special needs.* New York: Merrill.

Corsaro, W.A. (1981). Friendship in the nursery school: Social organization in a peer environment. In S.R. Asher & J.M. Gotman (Eds.), *The development of children's friendships* (pp. 207–241). New York: Cambridge University Press.

DEC recommended practices: Indicators of quality in programs for infants and young children with special needs and their families. (1993). Reston, VA: Division for Early Childhood of the Council for Exceptional Children.

Dunst, C.J., & Trivette, C.M. (1989). An enablement and empowerment perspective of case management. *Topics in Early Childhood Special Education, 8*(4), 87–102.

Edelman, L. (1991). *Family centered home visits* [Videotape]. Baltimore: Kennedy Krieger Institute.

Eisenberg, A.R., & Garvey, C. (1981). Children's use of verbal strategies in resolving conflicts. *Discourse Processes, 4,* 149–170.

Garvey, C. (1986). Peer relations and the growth of communication. In E.C. Mueller & C.R. Cooper (Eds.), *Process and outcome in peer relationships* (pp. 329–345). Orlando, FL: Academic Press.

Garwood, G., & Sheehan, R. (1989). *Early intervention system: The challenge of Public Law 99-457.* Austin, TX: PRO-ED.

Guralnick, M.J. (1984). The peer interactions of young developmentally delayed children in specialized and integrated settings. In T. Field, J. Roopnarine, & M. Segal (Eds.), *Friendships in normal and handicapped children* (pp. 139–152). Norwood, NJ: Ablex.

Guralnick, M.J. (1986). The peer relations of young handicapped and nonhandicapped children. In P.S. Strain, M.J. Guralnick, & H. Walker (Eds.), *Children's social behavior: Development, assessment and modification* (pp. 93–140). New York: Academic Press.

Guralnick, M.J. (1990). Peer interactions and the development of handicapped children's social and communicative competence. In H. Foot, M. Morgan, & R. Shute (Eds.), *Children helping children* (pp. 275–305). New York: John Wiley & Sons.

Guralnick, M.J. (1992). *Assessment of peer relations*. Seattle: University of Washington Child Development and Mental Retardation Center.

Guralnick, M.J. (1994). Mother's perceptions of the benefits and drawbacks of early childhood mainstreaming. *Journal of Early Intervention, 18*(2), 168–184.

Guralnick, M.J., & Groom, J.M. (1988). Peer interactions in mainstreamed and specialized classrooms: A comparative analysis. *Exceptional Children, 54*, 415–425.

Guralnick, M.J., & Paul-Brown, D. (1980). Functional and discourse analysis of nonhandicapped preschool children's speech to handicapped children. *American Journal of Mental Deficiency, 84*, 444–454.

Guralnick, M.J., & Paul-Brown, D. (1984). Communicative adjustments during behavior-request episodes among children at different developmental levels. *Child Development, 55*, 911–919.

Howes, C. (1988). Peer interaction of young children. *Monographs of the Society for Research in Child Development, 53*(1, serial no. 217).

Individuals with Disabilities Education Act Amendments of 1991, PL 102-119. (October 7, 1991). Title 20, U.S.C. 1400 et seq: *U.S. Statutes at Large, 105*, 587–608.

Individuals with Disabilities Education Act of 1990 (IDEA), PL 101-476. (October 30, 1990). Title 20, U.S.C. 1400 et seq: *U.S. Statutes at Large, 104*, 1103–1151.

Johnson, J.E., & Johnson, K.M. (1992). Clarifying the developmental perspective in response to Carta, Schwartz, Atwater, and McConnell. *Topics in Early Childhood Special Education, 12*, 439–457.

Johnson, J.E., & Johnson, K.M. (1995). The applicability of developmentally appropriate practice for children with diverse abilities. *Journal of Early Intervention, 18*(4), 343–346.

McCormick, L., & Kawate, J. (1982). Kindergarten survival skills: New directions for preschool special education. *Education and Training of the Mentally Retarded, 17*, 247–252.

McCormick, L., & Noonan, M.J. (1984). A responsive curriculum for severely handicapped preschoolers. *Topics in Early Childhood Special Education, 4*(3), 79–96.

McDonnell, A., & Hardman, M. (1988). A synthesis of "best practice" guidelines for early childhood services. *Journal of the Division for Early Childhood, 12*, 328–341.

McGonigel, M.J., Kaufmann, R.K., & Johnson, B.H. (Eds.). (1991). *Guidelines and recommended practices for the Individualized Family Service Plan*. Bethesda, MD: Association for the Care of Children's Health.

Miller, L.J., Strain, P.S., Boyd, K., Jarzynka, J., & McFetridge, M. (1993). The efforts of classwide self-assessment on preschool children's engagement in transition, free play, and small group instruction. *Early Education and Development, 4*, 162–181.

Murphy, M., & Vincent, L.J. (1989). Identification of critical skills for success in day care. *Journal of Early Intervention, 13*, 221–229.

National Association for the Education of Young Children and the National Association of Early Childhood Specialists in State Departments of Education. (1991). Guidelines for appropriate curriculum content in programs serving children 3 through 8: A position statement. *Young Children, 46*, 21–38.

Neisworth, J.T. (1993). Assessment. In *DEC recommended practices: Indicators of quality in programs for infants and young children with special needs and their families* (pp. 11–17). Reston, VA: Division for Early Childhood of the Council for Exceptional Children.

Noonan, M.J. (1989). *An eco-behavioral approach to curriculum development for infants with special needs*. Paper presented at the Division for Early Childhood Annual Conference, Minneapolis.

Noonan, M.J., & McCormick, L. (1993). *Early intervention in natural environments.* Pacific Grove, CA: Brooks/Cole.

Noonan, M.J., Ratokalau, N.B., Lauth-Torres, L., McCormick, L., Esaki, C.A., & Claybaugh, K.W. (1992). Validating critical skills for preschool success. *Infant-Toddler Intervention, 2*(3), 187–202.

Odom, S.L. (1995). Developmentally appropriate practices, policies, and use for young children with disabilities and their families. *Journal of Early Intervention, 18*(4), 346–348.

Odom, S.L., & McEvoy, M.A. (1990). Preschool mainstreaming: Potential barriers and tasks for the field. *Topics in Early Childhood Special Education, 10*(2), 48–61.

Odom, S.L., & Ostrosky, M. (1990). Ecobehavioral analysis of early education/specialized classroom settings and peer social interaction. *Education and Treatment of Children, 13*(4), 316–330.

Reichart, D.C., Lynch, E.C., Anderson, B.C., Svobodny, L.A., DiCola, J.M., & Mercury, M.G. (1989). Parental perspectives on integrated preschool opportunities for children with handicaps and children without handicaps. *Journal of Early Intervention, 13,* 6–13.

Rosenkoetter, S.E., Hains, A.H., & Fowler, S.A. (1994). *Bridging early services for children with special needs and their families: A practical guide for transition planning.* Baltimore: Paul H. Brookes Publishing Co.

Rubin, K.H., & Lollis, S.P. (1988). Origins and consequences of social withdrawals. In J. Belsky & T. Nezworski (Eds.), *Clinical implications of attachment* (pp. 219–252). Hillsdale, NJ: Lawrence Erlbaum Associates.

Sainato, D.M., Goldstein, H., & Strain, P.S. (1992). Effects of self-evaluation on preschool children's use of social integration strategies with their classmates with autism. *Journal of Applied Behavior Analysis, 25,* 127–142.

Strain, P.S. (Ed.). (1981). *The utilization of classroom peers as behavior change agents.* New York: Plenum.

Strain, P.S. (1983). Generalization of autistic children's social behavior change: Effects of developmentally integrated and segregated settings. *Analysis and Intervention in Developmental Disabilities, 3,* 23–24.

Strain, P.S. (1984). Social behavior patterns of nonhandicapped and developmentally disabled friend pairs in mainstream schools. *Analysis and Intervention in Developmental Disabilities, 4,* 15–28.

Strain, P.S., Hoyson, M., & Jamieson, B. (1985). Class deportment and social outcomes for normally developing and autistic-like children in an integrated preschool. *Journal of the Division for Early Childhood, 10,* 105–115.

Strain, P.S., Kerr, M.M., & Stagg, V. (1982, May). The makings of success in the early elementary grades. Paper presented at the conference of the Analysis of Behavior Association, Milwaukee.

Strain, P.S., McConnell, S.R., Carta, J.J., Fowler, S.A., Neisworth, J.T., & Wolery, M. (1992). Behaviorism in early childhood. *Topics in Early Childhood Special Education, 12,* 121–141.

Strain, P.S., & Sainato, D.M. (1987). Preventive discipline in the preschool class. *Teaching Exceptional Children, 19,* 26–30.

Turbiville, V., Turnbull, A., Garland, C., & Lee, I. (1993). IFSPs and IEPS. In *DEC recommended practices: Indicators of quality in programs for infants and young children with special needs and their families* (pp. 29–38). Reston, VA: Division for Early Childhood of the Council for Exceptional Children.

Turnbull, A.P., Winton, P.J., Blacher, J., & Salkind, M. (1982). Mainstreaming in the kindergarten classroom: Perspectives of parents of handicapped and nonhandicapped children. *Journal of the Division for Early Childhood, 6,* 14–20.

Vincent, L. (1985). Family relationships. In *Equals in the partnership* (pp. 23–31). Washington, DC: National Center for Clinical Infant Programs.

Vincent, L. (1992). Families and early intervention: Diversity and competence. *Journal of Early Intervention, 16*(2), 6–12.

Vincent, L. (Ed.). (1993). *Implementing the Individualized Family Service Plan: A process manual.* Los Angeles: Los Angeles Early Intervention Project.

Vincent, L., & Beckett, J. (1993). Related to family participation. In *DEC recommended practices: Indicators of quality in programs for infants and young children with special needs and their families* (pp. 18–29). Reston, VA: Division for Early Childhood of the Council for Exceptional Children.

Vincent, L.J., Laten, S., Salisbury, C., Brown, P., & Baumgart, D. (1980). Family involvement in the educational processes of severely handicapped students: State of the art and directions for the future. In B. Wilcox & R. York (Eds.), *Quality education for the severely handicapped: The federal investment.* Washington, DC: U.S. Department of Education.

Vincent, L.J., Salisbury, C., Walter, G., Brown, P., Grunewald, L.G., & Powers, M. (1980). Program evaluation in early childhood/special education: Criteria of the next environment (pp. 303–328). In W. Sailor, B. Wilcox, & L. Brown (Eds.), *Methods of instruction for severely handicapped students.* Baltimore: Paul H. Brookes Publishing Co.

Walter, G., & Vincent, L.J. (1982). The handicapped child in the regular kindergarten classroom. *Journal of the Division for Early Childhood, 6,* 84–95.

Warren, S. (1992). Foreword. In D. Bricker & J. Cripe, *An activity-based approach to early intervention.* Baltimore: Paul H. Brookes Publishing Co.

Wolery, M., & Bredekamp, S. (1995). Developmentally appropriate practices and young children with disabilities: Contextual issues in the discussion. *Journal of Early Intervention, 18*(4), 331–341.

Wolery, M., & Sainato, D. (1993). General curriculum and intervention strategies. In *DEC recommended practices: Indicators of quality in programs for infants and young children with special needs and their families.* Reston, VA: Division for Early Childhood of the Council for Exceptional Children.

Yoder, P., Kaiser, A., & Alpert, C. (1991). An exploratory study of the interaction between language teaching methods and child characteristics. *Journal of Speech and Hearing Research, 34,* 155–167.

Appendix A
IEP for the Menendez Family

Family concerns, priorities, and preferred resources: Identify with the family major areas of concern for the child with special needs and the family as a whole. Also identify how the family solves problems and what types of resources they find helpful.

Alex lives with his mother, father, grandfather, and younger brother. The family is involved with extended family members and friends from church and their community center. They prefer to use the resources of their local community. They recognize that, due to Alex's unique developmental needs, this will not always be possible. They have already become involved in a parent support group for children with autism through a Children's Hospital 1 hour from their home. They believe that Alex is best served when he is a full, participating member in his local community. They would like to see the specialized services he receives delivered in these environmentally congruent settings. They want him to attend a neighborhood preschool when he turns 3 years of age. They want support staff to work with them, their extended family, friends, and community to make this effort successful for Alex.

   The family held several discussions to decide what their highest priorities for Alex are right now. They tried to think about what would help them continue to fully integrate him into the family and community. They also tried to keep in mind what Alex would choose if he were selecting his goals. They all agreed that Alex seems to understand more than he can express. They would like to see a focus on a communication system for him and them. They want this system to help him relate to other children as well as adults. He is interested in what other children are doing and needs a way to engage with them. Mom and Dad are concerned that he is progressing with feeding himself very slowly. They worry that this will decrease his ability to fully participate in the preschool setting. They have had excellent success this past 6 months on toilet training Alex and teaching him to follow simple household rules, and they feel confident that they can carry out a program that is designed around their family's schedule and teaching style. They believe that young children need support and guidance, not punishment.

   They recognize that Alex's favorite activities are to read magazines, such as *TV Guide,* and watch videos of *Sesame Street* and *Mr. Rogers.* They get tired of the same ones over and over, but he does not. They would like to figure out ways to incorporate the videos and magazines into family activities. The family also discussed increasing their financial resources as an area of priority. Alex's medical bills from evaluations and specialized ongoing care by a neurologist are not fully covered by their medical insurance. Also while Alex's grandfather and other family members and friends are very willing to babysit on a periodic basis, Mom and Dad are finding that they need more consistent child care than this. Mom is hoping to return to work part time after Alex settles into the preschool setting, and both Mom and Dad are becoming increasingly involved in advocacy efforts on behalf of young children with special needs. They will begin to plan in this area after the upcoming transition to preschool, probably in 6–9 months.

Outcomes: Identify with the family what goals they would like to work on in the next 6–12 months.

Five outcomes were selected by the family in consultation with the early intervention team:

1.   Development of a communication system using pictures, signs, gestures, and words that allows Alex to initiate and respond communicatively.
2.   Reassessment by an occupational therapist for guidance on a self-feeding program.
3.   Development of a transition plan for Alex to enter a community preschool with appropriate support services and planned adaptations in the curriculum and instructional strategies.
4.   Brainstorming with other parents of children with autism and with early intervention staff on how to use Alex's interest in books and videos in a family context.
5.   Planning for Mom's return to work and the need for consistent child care in addition to a preschool program.

Child's strengths and needs: Identify with the family what the child can do and is learning to do, and identify concerns about his development; include information on cognition, fine motor, gross motor, hearing, language, self-help, social–emotional development, and vision.

Alex sleeps in his own room, gets out of bed on his own, and comes down a flight of six steps unassisted to the kitchen in the morning. He goes down holding onto the banister, one tread at a time. He indicates that he is hungry by trying to open the refrigerator or by climbing on a step stool to get food off the kitchen counter. He sometimes gets up like this and wanders downstairs into the kitchen in the middle of the night. Once he is up, he does not go back to sleep and someone must stay up with him to supervise. He is starting at these times to settle down onto the couch and watch one of his videos rather than running around. He will mimic the motions from the songs and jabber when Big Bird or Mr. Rogers talks to the kids. He usually watches the video with a sideways glance rather than face forward. He seems to know the songs and characters by the animation on his face and his body language. At his infant program when some of the same songs are sung, he is also beginning to show the sideways glances of attention, although he has not mimicked the teachers or other children yet.

Alex is beginning to play with small manipulative toys in the classroom and at home. He likes to put beads in a bottle, shake them, watch them spin, dump them out, gather them up, and put them in again. He can operate all of the switches on his pop-up toys. He likes the *Sesame Street* one the best. He can pick up the receiver of the phone and push the buttons and both listens and jabbers. He only does this with a real telephone. He is beginning to operate the switches on the VCR at home; he has a child's tape recorder he can operate. He will stab a spoon into food, such as pudding, and bring it to his mouth. About half of the time it is right side up. He is very interested in sawing butter and bread with a knife. He drinks unassisted from a cup. He does not spill the liquid or tip the cup over, even when it is quite full. He drinks soda through a straw, reacts by shaking his head to the carbonation, and then reaches out for more. He will engage in pretend eating activities in the kitchen play area of the classroom. Alex indicates that he needs to go to the bathroom by coming to an adult and holding his pants in the crotch. He is able to pull his pants up and down by himself. He tries to zip and snap. He prefers to stand to urinate, rather than sitting on a potty chair.

Alex has a vocabulary that is hard to predict because he seems to acquire and then lose words and phrases. For example, he mastered "open them, shut them" and did it to the song for 6 weeks and has now stopped. He said "bye-bye" at 14 months, stopped at 18 months, and has recently started again. He says "up" when wanting to be carried or allowed to get to something that has been put away. He has learned 10 signs in the last 6 months and is using them with reminders to communicate his desires for drinks, food, going outside, and so forth. If you focus Alex's attention and then ask him a question about his day at school or somewhere he went with his family, he will look at you sideways and jabber intently, use hand motions and seeming to attempt to answer your question. He initiates interactions with peers in the classroom and in family and neighborhood situations. If you attempt to prevent Alex from engaging with the other children he will scream, throw toys, and hit out at adults. He communicates by watching, touching, and rubbing against them. He will join in a play theme in the kitchen area if reminded by an adult.

Summary of developmental levels: This summary of developmental levels is only useful in the context of the preceding discussion of the child's strengths and needs. The numbers should not be used in isolation to characterize a child's development or determine services.

Child's age when developmental levels were determined: 34 months

Cognitive	25 months	Fine motor	32 months
Gross motor	34 months	Language	16 months
Self-help	22 months	Social-emotional	17 months
Hearing	within normal limits	Vision	within normal limits

Outcome #1:   What does the family wish to accomplish? Briefly explain.

The family and early intervention team would like to develop a consistent strategy for how they will approach communication with Alex. Everyone is finding different methods effective, but all are concerned about confusing Alex and themselves. Mom and Dad's priority is that he use verbal expression as much as possible. However, they have seen some new work with children with autism that has shown how helpful letter boards and computers are, and they do not want to rule this out. They are concerned that he is easily frustrated when he wants something and they cannot figure out what exactly it is. They would like a way for him to indicate his choices and then maybe work on saying the words when he has gotten what he wants. The early intervention team is pleased with how quickly he has picked up on signs and how willing he is to use them in the classroom. They too have seen his frustration when he is not understood and would like to support his making choices.

The outcome of this objective is that Alex will increase his use of words, signs and pictures to indicate what he wants; he will decrease screaming and grabbing.

(Identified by: Family and early intervention team)

Strategies/activities: Who will do what, and when will they do it in order to accomplish the outcome?

1. The speech-language therapist from the early intervention team will explore having a communication assessment conducted with Alex. He will report back to parents on the details of proceeding within 1 month.

2. The family will make up a picture book of Alex's favorite drinks, snacks, videos, magazines, and toys; they will try using this to assist him in communicating what he wants. The teacher or speech therapist will make a home visit if Mom and Dad wish to observe and brainstorm. Successful strategies will be conveyed to staff at the preschool.

3. Alex's favorite assistant teacher will make a picture book for him to use at school during playtime. It will include pictures of children, activities, and toys. He will practice with this book twice during each infant session he attends. He will attend three sessions per week. He will begin to attend the preschool classroom once per week in the next month. His picture book will go with him.

4. The speech therapist will develop a list of 25 new signs in conjunction with family, infant program staff, and new preschool staff. School staff will develop activities and materials to work on the new signs and practice old signs at each infant and preschool session he attends. New signs will be introduced gradually, approximately three to five each week.

5. All will remember to repeat what they hear Alex say, expand it to a two- to three-word phrase he is capable of saying, and give him many opportunities to use his words, signs, and pictures.

6. Interactions with other children that involve the songs and games he sees on his *Sesame Street* and *Mr. Rogers* videos will be facilitated by school staff at both infant and preschool programs. At least one such activity will be included during each session.

Criteria/timelines: How will we know if we're making progress?

The family will be asked monthly to complete a status report on the choices Alex is making and how; they will rate whether the screaming and grabbing continues to be a problem. The school staff will keep a weekly log of new words, phrases, signs, and picture choices he has made. They will note whether his screaming and grabbing continues to be a problem. His interactions with peers will be observed twice monthly at play time at the infant and preschool programs.

Outcome #2: What does the family wish to accomplish? Briefly explain.

Alex learned to drink from a cup at 18 months of age. An occupational therapist helped the family with teaching him this skill. The therapist also helped them get him started on feeding himself with a spoon. During the past year, Alex has made little progress in this area. He prefers to use his fingers, be fed by others, or not eat. Pushing him to use the spoon results in crying, screaming, spitting, and so forth. Family and infant teachers are not sure what is happening.

The outcome is that a reevaluation will be conducted by an occupational therapist who has experience in working with children with autism.

(Identified by: Family and infant teachers)

Strategies/activities: Who will do what, and when will they do it in order to accomplish the outcome?

1. The infant teacher, who is Alex's service coordinator, will contact the county early intervention evaluation team. Information will be required on obtaining occupational therapy evaluation services. Information will be discussed with the family within 2 weeks.
2. The family will talk to other parents of children with autism in their support group and find out what strategies and personnel they used for teaching self-feeding skills. Results will be shared with the service coordinator and infant teacher within 1 month.
3. Reevaluation will be completed within 2 months and a new program developed and initiated within 3 months.

Criteria/timelines: How will we know if we're making progress?

The service coordinator will monitor the attainment of the reevaluation. Family will give input on whether they are getting the information they need to move forward on self-feeding.

Outcome #3:   What does the family wish to accomplish? Briefly explain.

The family wishes Alex to move to a preschool program in their local community that is fully inclusive at age 3. The early intervention team agrees that such a placement would be ideal for Alex. Both are concerned that the necessary support services be identified and provided for this experience to be successful for all (i.e., family, Alex, preschool program, other children).

The outcome of this objective is that Alex will begin the transition to a preschool program in his local community and receive the support he needs to be successful. He will start attending 1 day per week, move to 2 days per week in 1 month, 3 days in 2 months, and full time in 3 months.

(Identified by: Family)

Strategies/activities: Who will do what, and when will they do it in order to accomplish the outcome?

1.   The family has already visited three preschools and feels that two are possible placements. The infant teacher and assistant teacher have visited these two programs. One program has expressed a desire to include Alex and has included children in the past.
2.   The school district has been forwarded appropriate paperwork to begin transition planning. This was handled by Mom and assistant teachers.
3.   The initial meeting with the school district is scheduled this month. The family would like to have reports complete by that time and a statement from the infant program supporting full inclusion.
4.   The speech-language therapist knows three other families whose children are fully included. Mom and Dad indicated they would like to talk with these families to see what support services have been helpful. The therapist will contact other families and get permission for Alex's parents to contact them. He will do this within the week.
5.   The family would like the assistant teacher and teacher to accompany them to the first meeting with school personnel. Staff will try to arrange their schedules to meet this request. School district schedules do not always match infant program schedules. The family will request of the school district that the meeting be held in the early afternoon.

Criteria/timelines: How will we know if we're making progress?

The service coordinator and family will schedule a weekly contact to keep up with the transition process. Alex's placement in a fully inclusive preschool setting with appropriate support services will be seen as success. The family will evaluate whether the placement meets these criteria.

Outcome #4: What does the family wish to accomplish? Briefly explain.

The family has heard from other parents of children with autism that Alex's interest in magazines and videos is something some of their children show as well. They hope that they can use this interest to foster preacademic and academic skills and to build interactions with other children. Right now it is something Alex does alone, and in fact he will usually drop the magazine or walk away from the TV screen if someone tries to interact with him.

The outcome is that Alex's magazines and videos will be incorporated into family activities at home and activities with other children at school.

(Identified by: Family)

Strategies/activities: Who will do what, and when will they do it in order to accomplish the outcome?

1. Mom and Dad will talk to other parents at their support group meeting about this issue. They will keep staff posted on what they hear.
2. Family and early intervention staff will explore ways to use magazines and videos at school with Alex and one or two other children. Preschool staff will be asked to incorporate use of these materials into free play or choice time in their setting.

Criteria/timelines: How will we know if we're making progress?

When Alex's interest in magazines and videos is incorporated into his interactions with family members and children at school, progress will have been made. Staff and parents will discuss this monthly.

Outcome #5: What does the family wish to accomplish? Briefly explain.

Mom is planning to return to work after Alex is settled in his new placement. He will probably need child care in addition to the preschool program. She would like for this to also include Alex's younger brother, who is 14 months old. Mom and Dad see planning for this objective as taking place after the preschool program transition.

(Identified by: Family)

APPENDIX B
SAMPLE OF ALEX'S MORNING IN HIS NEIGHBORHOOD PRESCHOOL

8:30–8:45 A.M. Families and children arrive. Alex has been assigned a cubby next to Irena, who lives on his block and likes to play with him outside on the playground. Alex takes his backpack and puts it in his cubby and then removes his jacket and drops it onto the floor. Irena tells him to put it on the hook. He turns aways and swings his hands in front of his face. His mom comes over and turns him around and helps him pick it up and put it on the hook. Irena takes his hand and asks him to come with her to the free play rug. He follows and watches as she, David, LaTisha, and Monte build with bristle blocks. He picks up one lying near him on the floor. Monte tells him to come stick it on and make the stack higher. As he does so the whole pile falls over and all the kids laugh. They begin to build again. Alex sits and stares out a classroom window until Irena hands him the block, and then he joins in to build again. David starts to take the stack apart rather than build it up. LaTisha tells him that is not fair. He has to wait. Alex stops and watches as the children negotiate to determine whether they are building or taking it down.

8:45–9:15 A.M. Circle time. Ms. Sanborn calls for her helper to come ring the bell and signal to the children that it is time to come to the circle. Monte is the helper and goes over. Alex follows him. The 15 children in the preschool classroom gather around Ms. Sanborn on the rug to share songs and stories. Ms. Sanborn starts with the "Hello" song, calling each child's name and having the child indicate he or she is present. Alex smiles when his name is called and rolls his head back and forth repetitively. Other children wave, hide their faces, stand and so forth. Ms. Sanborn asks if anyone has a song he or she would like to sing. Brianna asked for the "Itsy, Bitsy Spider." Alex puts his fingers together to start the spider climbing. He watches as the teacher and children do the other motions. Irena reaches over and tries to help him do the motion for "down came the rain." He laughs. Sam asks for "The Wheels on the Bus." Children chime in to show which hand and body motions to do. Alex excitedly swings his arms back and forth in front of him. Ms. Sanborn asks him if he wants to do the windshield wipers. He does not respond, but she has all the other children imitate him. He stops and watches them and then laughs. Ms. Sanborn tells the children she has a new story to read. It's from *Sesame Street,* and she asks the children to guess who is in it. Children start calling out Oscar, Big Bird, and other names. She laughs and says, "You're right. They are all in it." Alex crawls over to where she has the book, to pick it up and look at it. She says to him, "Would you like to be the page turner? You can sit next to me and help." She reads the story and hands Alex the book when she is finished.

9:15–10:15 A.M.   Ms. Sanborn tells the group now its time for Choices. She asks, "Can anyone remember what they are?" The children remember art, blocks, house, dress-up, books, sand table, and puzzles. "Think about what you'd like to do first," she says. "Remember, you can change, but first clean up where you are." She turns to Alex and says, "What do you choose, Alex? Let's look around and see where you want to go." She helps Alex scan the room. He chooses the house corner and goes and joins Matthew, David, Brianna, and Toni. The teacher assistant, Ms. Malana, goes to this area once she sees Alex make his choice. She joins the children's play, following their lead, using this opportunity to repeat and/or expand on what Alex is saying. Toni follows her lead and begins to do this also. Ms. Malana gradually fades out and the children continue to play. He spends time playing with the toys, materials, and other children, but part of the time he stands and stares across the classroom out a window. Alex remains in the house corner for 20 minutes. He then gets up and goes over to the art area, where Ms. Sanborn is helping the children make paper bag puppets. He watches the activity for several minutes and then sits down. Ms. Sanborn waits for him to ask for materials. When he doesn't, she says, "What do we need to make a puppet?" Alex remains silent. Dusty looks up and says, "Alex, you need a bag." Alex points to the bags and then to crayons and stickers. Dusty says, "I'll help you with the stickers; I can pull off, you can stick on." Alex takes stickers from Dusty and smiles as he pastes them on his bag. "You can color, too!" Dusty says, and goes back to his own puppet. Ms. Sanborn helps the children cut out faces and run a piece of yarn through holes in the top of the bag, so they can tie the puppets on their hands. Alex does not want his tied on, nor does Irena. He leaves his puppet and goes over to the record player and starts to turn it on. Ms. Malana comes over and asks him, "Where can you be now?" Alex stops trying to turn the record player on. "This is not one of the choices. Where would you like to go next?" Ms. Malana asks. He looks around and walks over to the books. He settles in a bean bag and "reads" several *Sesame Street* stories.

10:15–10:30 A.M.   Ms. Sanborn gets her helper Monte. He rings the bell and she announces, "It's time to clean up. Put away your toys and come to the door to go to the bathroom." Alex continues "reading" until Brianna says, "Clean-up time Alex," and points to the shelf where the books go. He puts his book there and follows her to the door.

10:30–10:45 A.M.   Bathroom and handwashing. Ms. Sanborn and Ms. Malana have the children divide into boys and girls and go into the bathrooms. Ms. Malana encourages Alex to stand at the commode and pull his pants down so he can urinate. He uses the toilet and pulls his pants up. She helps him tuck his shirt in, and then he washes his hands and goes back to the classroom to the snack table. Dusty's mom, Ms. Rivera, is volunteering and gets the children seated as they return. Alex drinks his juice immediately and holds the cup up for more. Ms. Rivera tells him to eat some of his apple slices first. He picks one up, chews on it, and spits out the skin on the table. She reminds him that if he does not like it, he should put it on his napkin. He holds up his glass again for juice. "So, you still want some more juice, Alex. Can you tell me with your words? Juice, please." He says, "Ju . . . ju." She pours his juice. As the children finish, they take their cups and napkins and throw them in the trash. Alex does so with no reminders. He wanders over to the record player. Ms. Sanborn sees him and redirects him to get ready to go outside. She asks him, "Where do you need to go wait?" He sits down on the floor where he is and begins to wave his arms. She says, "Alex, you need to go sit in the circle on the rug. Would you like to walk with me over there?" Alex stays seated. She extends her hand and says, "Let's go now so we can find out what games we'll be playing outside. Maybe you can play on the slide." Alex smiles, gets up, and walks over to where the other children are gathering to hear about the activities.

10:45–11:30 A.M.   Outdoor activities are announced. Children have choices including sandbox, wheel toys, balls, big building blocks, climbing equipment, water table, trucks and cars, and dolls and strollers. Alex immediately goes to the climbing area and goes up and down the slide, taking turns with LaTisha and David. He follows LaTisha to the water table and starts to pour water onto the pavement and stamp his foot in it. She tells him, "Water stays in the table, Alex." He screams and throws his cup back into the table. He leaves and goes to the sandbox. He takes a shovel and bucket from Brianna, who promptly takes it back. He begins to pick up and shift sand through his fingers and then begins to throw it in the air. Ms. Sanborn comes over and says, "Alex, you need to make a plan for what to play with. Where would you like to go next? Have you ridden on the bikes?" Alex smiles. She says, "Let's go get in line for your turn. How many other children are waiting today?" She walks him over and has Monte help count how many are in line. After Alex's turn on the bike, she watches to see if he needs some support to choose again. This time he heads over to where three of the children are throwing and chasing balls. He remains there for the rest of the outdoor time, running, throwing, laughing, and rolling over on the biggest ball. Ms. Malana joins the activity for a few minutes and models action verbs that correspond with what the children are doing.

11:30–11:45 A.M.   Closing circle and departure. The children come inside and sit on the rug for a review of the day's activities and the closing song. Each child shares something she or he did that day. Alex is helped to share that he played with the balls. His mom has come into the classroom at this point and gets to hear him contribute. She then follows up and asks him what he did when he comes over to her. He looks up and says, "ball." Ms. Sanborn calls out to him that she has something of his. He takes his mom over to the puppets and gets his to put in his backpack. He and his mom get his backback and coat. He waves good-bye to Irena and David when they say "bye" to him.

12 ELEMENTARY CURRICULUM AND INSTRUCTION

MARQUITA GRENOT-SCHEYER, PEGGY ANN ABERNATHY,
DEBBIE WILLIAMSON, KIMBERLEE A. JUBALA, AND JENNIFER J. COOTS

In some parts of the United States of America, elementary schools embrace diversity and are designed to serve all children. Such schools provide students with curriculum rich in meaning; instruction that emphasizes function, purpose, and real-life application; frequent opportunities to engage in collaborative learning experiences with peers; and a community spirit of caring and belonging

Yolanda, a fifth-grade student with significant disabilities, attends such a school. Her school is a small elementary school in an urban district. The sense of community is apparent when one walks onto campus. Early in the morning, there are parents with their infants waiting for an English as a Second Language (ESL) class to begin. Several elderly individuals are escorted by children to classrooms to begin their volunteer activity in a recently developed "Grandparents" program. Two high school students, one of whom has Down syndrome, assist the teachers in the Head Start classrooms as part of a work-experience/transition program. A group of students, including Yolanda, gather outside their classroom to work on their math assignment. Their task is to interview students regarding their favorite colors, flavors of ice cream, and television shows and to graph their results. Yolanda is actively involved in interviewing students, with the use of her electronic Canon communicator, and in displaying the results on a bulletin board. With the help of her peers, Yolanda is able to color in a bar graph to show that

Preparation of this chapter was supported in part by Cooperative Agreement No. HO86A20003 to Syracuse University, with a subcontract to California State University, Long Beach, from the Office of Special Education Programs, U.S. Department of Education. This material does not necessarily reflect the position or policies of the U.S. Department of Education, and no official endorsement should be inferred.

Family Matters and *The Simpsons* are the favorite television shows of the majority of her fifth- and sixth-grade peers.

This chapter provides strategies to support the inclusion of elementary students with significant disabilities, such as Yolanda, in general education classrooms and schools. More specifically, the chapter focuses on how schools can become caring communities where students are taught to rely upon each other in the process of acquiring academic and social skills. It also discusses how peer support networks facilitate prosocial behaviors and the inclusion of all students. The first section describes the nature and function of elementary schools as places of caring and active learning. The last section presents a typical day for an elementary student with severe disabilities who is an integral member of her fifth grade learning community.

NATURE AND FUNCTION OF ELEMENTARY SCHOOLS

Educators can use a variety of strategies such as peer support networks, cooperative learning, circle of friends, and tribes to assist students to be members of their school community.

Schools as Caring Communities

Elementary schools can set the stage for feelings of self-worth, social responsibility, and belonging, all of which are necessary for developing compassionate citizens within a caring school community. In schools that foster caring and a sense of community, students are encouraged to ask "What kind of school do we want to have?" and are invited to be active participants in this decision-making process. By assisting students with and without significant disabilities to feel that they are valued members of the school community, educators can be more effective in fostering development in all critical curricular areas. Such active student involvement in decision making can help to teach the skills and values, including social responsibility, that are critical for developing caring communities. Schaps and Solomon (1990) describe social responsibility as

> more than a set of learned skills or acquired habits . . . it is anchored in the development of deeply personal commitments to such core social values as justice, tolerance, and concern for others. We cannot expect our children to develop commitments of this kind in a vacuum. They must be able to see and experience these values in action in their daily lives, including their lives in schools. This is why schools must strive to become "caring communities. . . ." (p. 38)

Central to the development of a caring school is the promotion of pro-social development (Schaps & Solomon, 1990). Schools and classrooms can be structured to facilitate kindness, consideration, empathy, concern, and care for others. Educators can structure learning experiences so that students who have the capacity to support others will have frequent opportunities to do so and will see the benefits of learning in a place that is defined by care.

This notion of caring is critical in contemporary elementary schools because students are required to develop skills necessary to learn, play, live, and work with people who are different in a variety of dimensions, including ethnicity, culture, ability, and socioeconomic status (Nevin, 1993). As educators attempt to meet the ever-broadening needs of a heterogeneous student population, it is clear that the school response to diversity will have a strong effect on student outcomes. If diversity is valued, then students can have numerous opportunities to learn to accept diversity and see difference as typical.

Peer Support Networks

Peer support networks are one type of natural support that can assist teachers to facilitate children coming closer together as friends and learning partners. Natural supports may include peers, curricula, materials, and technology that assist all students to be full members of regular classrooms, schools, and communities (Jorgensen, 1992).

Such supports are particularly important for elementary-age children. Among many families who have sons or daughters with significant disabilities who are included in general education classrooms stories of the positive impact of such supports are frequent. For example, Blair, a second grader with significant disabilities, has been included in a general education classroom. According to her mother, Blair's classmates, although aware that Blair needs various levels of support throughout her school day, comment that "everyone needs support," "it's okay to need support," and "it's no big deal."

Besides such personal narratives from families, as well as from peers and others, there is a rich and informative literature regarding the importance of social relationships, including friendships, for elementary-age children (also see Chapter 10). Friendships are especially important for various developmental (Guralnick, 1980; Hartup, 1983; Howes, 1983, 1987; Rubin, 1982), psychological (Berndt & Perry, 1986; Weiss, 1974), and sociological reasons (Forest & Lusthaus, 1989; Grenot-Scheyer, Coots, & Falvey, 1989; Snow, 1989; Taylor, Biklen, & Knoll, 1987).

Chapter 11 has already addressed useful strategies for fostering friendships among preschool children. Numerous additional strategies, from both general and special education, can facilitate the development of natural supports among elementary school children with and without significant disabilities in general education settings. These are described below.

Cooperative Learning   Cooperative learning is a powerful instructional method for both the acquisition of knowledge and the promotion of pro-social behavior in children. (See Chapter 5 for more detail on this strategy.) The essence of cooperative learning is that all students are concerned about the performance and behavior of all group members (Putnam, 1993). Because cooperative learning places the onus of responsibility on the group for involving all students, opportunities to practice critical social interaction skills are created and supports for students develop naturally. While the advantages of cooperative learning arrangements for knowledge building have been stressed in Chapter 5, it is important to emphasize here the role of cooperative learning in the development of social skills for elementary-age children. Through peer interaction, students can develop an increased awareness and sensitivity to others and engage in essential interpersonal communication skills (Putnam, 1993). Cooperative learning "guarantees . . . interaction on a regular basis and on a more intimate and mutually interdependent level" (Putnam, 1993, p. 27), which is critical to the well-being of all students and to the development of friendships.

Circle of Friends   Circle of friends (Forest & Lusthaus, 1989) is a strategy that can be used to provide opportunities for all students to become more fully participating members of a class, to be active within their own school, and to build lasting friendships within the community. Using this strategy (see Chapter 10 for more detail on implementation), teachers can arrange opportunities that allow students with and without significant disabilities to interact with one another and to become more involved in each other's social network. This process facilitates innovation and creativity, caring, and genuine involvement among children. For example, Stephanie is a second grader with multiple physical disabilities and health impairments who uses a wheelchair yet had a great desire to jump rope with her friends at recess. Since she has no intentional or reliable motor movement except in her right leg, it was difficult for her classroom teacher to assist Stephanie in moving from passive partial participation to more engaged interaction. Stephanie and her circle of friends thought about the challenge and came up with an innovative solution. With the help of her health aide, the children taped the rope to Stephanie's right ankle using masking tape. With another child holding and turning the other end of the rope, Stephanie was able to "turn" the rope and watch her friends jump. In addition, she was able to sing along with the jump-rope chants. Both Stephanie and her peers benefited from this innovative solution.

The circle of friends strategy can also give children without disabilities more insight into their own thinking, attitudes, and behaviors. It is easy to focus upon the student with a disability and decide that there are things that could be done to "help" that student. But what is not always acknowledged is the fact that often students without disabilities can be "helped," too. For example, Aaron, a fourth grader with severe disabilities, had difficulty standing in the long lunch line. The boys in his class were loud and boisterous and teased each other. Aaron imitated his peers and at times ended up pushing others in line too hard or being too silly and noisy, which often resulted in adult intervention. Frequently, Aaron and some of his peers were directed to go to the back of the line. When this situation was brought up for discussion within the circle of friends during recess, the boys realized that their inappropriate behavior had a negative effect upon Aaron. They genuinely cared for him and felt bad when he was reprimanded. As a result of the discussion, they changed their own behaviors, helping Aaron to stand in line and demonstrating how to act "cool" when adults were present (i.e., showed him how not to get "caught"). As a result of this process, the fourth-grade boys began to stand in line much better, to the delight of the noon duty aides. By giving some insight, power, and control to the students, and by allowing shared responsibility for social decisions (Paley, 1992), Aaron's peers were able to effect change in a positive manner. The circle benefited all the children.

Tribes Tribes (Gibbs, 1987) is a systematic process to increase self-esteem, social responsibility, and academic achievement in children. Underlying this process is the belief that children who maintain long-term membership in supportive classroom peer groups will improve in self-image and demonstrate more responsible behavior and motivation toward academic achievement. Tribes are composed of groups of five to six students who meet regularly throughout the school year to promote a sense of belonging and caring. A sequence of group activities facilitated by the classroom teacher develops trust and respect for others. As tribes become supportive working groups, they are used for the management of behavior, problem solving, decision making, and teaching of subject matter through peer interaction. An example of the reciprocity inherent in the beginning stages of this process follows. In Carla's second-grade class, all of the students were asked to write down the names of several classmates with whom they would like to sit and work. The teachers described the idea of creating tribes and the importance of the list. He stressed that this was a private matter and that no one but he would see the lists. Carla spelled out s-A-N-D-E on her letterboard with her teacher as the facilitator, and the teacher asked, "Oh, would you like to sit by Sandy?" Carla excitedly said "yes." At the end of the day, the teacher discovered that Sandy had also included Carla on her list of people she wanted included in her tribe. The strategy of using tribes is then another example of how teachers can systematically facilitate the development of peer support networks and help schools to become caring communities.

Cooperative learning, circle of friends, and tribes are specific strategies that teachers can use to help elementary-age students reach important goals. As noted earlier, a primary function of elementary schools is to teach social-moral responsibility and prosocial behaviors, as well as to encourage the acceptance of widely diverse student populations. For students to be successful in junior high, high school, and postschool settings, elementary school personnel must lay the groundwork for a sense of belonging and for the acquisition of those skills necessary for students to cooperate and collaborate, both in and out of the classroom, to achieve social, academic, and personal success. The next section focuses on strategies for developing schools as active places of learning.

Schools: "Learning by Doing"

In addition to creating caring communities, elementary schools can provide students with active learning opportunities that emphasize functionality and meaning. Many exemplary elementary schools reflect the principles of John Dewey

(1956). Dewey saw schools as agencies of society designed to improve our democratic way of life (Wiles & Bondi, 1989). Furthermore, he believed that schools should reflect community life, with students studying about home, neighborhood, and community, a perspective congruent with many current practices in both special and general education. "Learning by doing" was a principle central to Dewey's ideas about schools. Quite simply, it was proposed that active children learn more. Dewey maintained that the curricula of the elementary school should reflect the informal style of active learning that is characteristic of learning opportunities outside of school. Thus, elementary schools should not be characterized by rote or mechanistic learning, but rather should reflect a variety of creative activities where students are active participants in the learning process (Wiles & Bondi, 1989).

Elementary schools that reflect active learning, encourage peer support networks, and emphasize the importance of a caring community can be optimal learning environments for *all* children. The rationale for this proposal for schools has been reviewed in the initial sections of this chapter, along with strategies to help create such learning environments. Additional characteristics of optimal learning environments are delineated in Table 1.

In the next section, considerations and suggestions for assessment and goal development and curriculum and instruction for elementary-age students are presented. These suggestions build upon the frameworks presented in previous chapters.

Table 1.   Quality characteristics of inclusive, caring school communities

1. Students are grouped heterogeneously within age-appropriate classrooms and with full membership status.
2. All students follow age-appropriate daily schedules and routines, including academic class enrollment, and nonacademic activities and routines.
3. Individually appropriate educational supports and services identified on the student's IEP are provided to the student in the general education setting, through the use of supplementary aids and services.
4. Curricular, instructional, and materials adaptations and modifications are evident at all ages, reflecting multi level and multi modal student needs and learning styles as an integral aspect of general education practices with special education and other mandated support services.
5. Varied student needs are addressed using age-appropriate activities and curricular adaptations.
6. Instructional practices are congruent with community values.
7. Instructional grouping arrangements incorporate social and behavioral considerations to ensure that students have daily opportunities to practice problem solving, to develop positive attitudes and social behaviors in interactions with students from diverse backgrounds, and to facilitate community building.
8. School support resources and activities are available and provided to enhance positive social relationships among children.

Adapted from Meyer (1993).

ASSESSMENT AND GOAL DEVELOPMENT

Working with children with disabilities requires an IEP, but the IEP is really a model for educational planning and instruction for all teachers: "Collecting diagnostic data, setting goals and objectives, selecting instructional materials, and evaluating student performance are all steps in the instructional process" (Wiles & Bondi, 1989, p. 266). As part of school restructuring, many general educators are implementing a similar process for their students.

For example, the California Learning Record (CLR) (1993) is an annual portfolio of information about a student's progress, development, and achievement. One parent of a child with significant disabilities who is fully included in a second grade classroom noted that the CLR "is just like the IEP process . . . but for all children" (S. Brown, personal communication, July, 1993). The three major sections of the CLR are shown in Table 2.

The CLR represents a new way of thinking about how students learn and about how they are evaluated and represents the merging of general and special education practices. In collaboration with one another, general and special education teachers can develop comprehensive assessment plans for all students. As described in detail in Chapter 4, elementary teachers can use observation, family and significant other interviews, teacher-made assessments, portfolios, ecological

Table 2.   Summary of the California Learning Record

Part A: Documenting Prior Experiences:
The first part involves a parent conference to develop an individualized learning plan. During this conference, general information about the child is obtained from the parents or guardians.
The purpose of the parent conference is to draw on the knowledge you have about your children which is related to learning at school. You contribute your observations about how your child learns best, what you know about your child's interests, and what your hopes and concerns are for the school year. (CLR, 1993, p. 2)
The student is also included in this conference and is encouraged to talk about his or her interests, strengths, experiences, and personal goals. The information gathered from this conference helps the teacher to develop curriculum and instructional plans that build upon the child's prior experiences.

Part B: Documenting Student Learning:
During this phase, teachers gather evidence of student learning through observations, projects, and other assessment data typically found in student portfolios. During the early elementary years, the teacher takes full responsibility for gathering the data needed for the CLR. As students develop, they contribute more of the evidence necessary to develop a comprehensive view of their abilities. By high school, the responsibility for documentation of progress may shift almost solely to the student, with support as necessary.

Part C: Reflecting on the Year's Work:
Toward the end of the school year, parents are once again asked to contribute to the portfolio of student observations. The student is also asked to reflect on his or her personal experiences as a learner during the year. The child's comments along with those of the teacher and the parents provide a complete and meaningful portrait of the child's achievement and progress.

and student repertoire inventories, and other authentic assessment strategies to comprehensively assess and plan for all students.

CURRICULA AND INSTRUCTION

Curricula and instruction must be broadly based to accommodate a wide variety of learners (Wiles & Bondi, 1989). Unfortunately, however, some contemporary schools are characterized by "predefined" curricula, which means that educators start with the curriculum rather than the child, often resulting in students who are bored, unmotivated, or simply do not show up at school (Stainback, Stainback, & Moravec, 1992). Such curricula typically include discrete categories of information that are delivered in unimaginative and artificial ways. These narrowly defined curricula eliminate many students from the educational experiences they need to become contributing members of a democratic society. School restructuring efforts in both general and special education focus on addressing this problem and on assisting the growing number of students for whom school has limited relevance.

Most educators would agree that curriculum reform is a central issue in restructuring. Despite the many efforts to provide updated technology and interesting supplemental materials to enhance learning, educators cannot anticipate long-term student success if the nature and delivery of the curriculum are not fundamentally changed across all subject areas. Students learn best when the content of their learning is meaningful and useful for daily living and builds upon their own personal experiences (Kovalik, 1993). This notion echoes the early contributions of Dewey (1956), which suggest that students learn best when they are actively involved in real-life activities with real-life outcomes.

Recent research on learning suggests that although we only retain up to 40% of what we see, hear, and discuss, we retain 80% of what we "experience directly or practice by doing," and up to 90% of what we "attempt to teach others" (Roy, cited in Kovalik, 1993, p. xii). With this in mind, it is easy to see that traditional curricula, with an emphasis on abstract and symbolic learning (e.g., worksheets, memorization of formulas), limits students to retaining less than half of what they are taught. It is no wonder that many students without disabilities, let alone those with special needs, are unable to acquire academic skills despite many years of education. The problem must be recognized as lying not with the students, but rather with external factors such as the curriculum and instruction.

Integrated Thematic Instruction

Integrated thematic instruction (ITI) is perhaps the most comprehensive and inspired of recent curriculum reform efforts (Kovalik, 1993). The primary focus of ITI is the "here and now." Students are given the opportunity to attach personal meaning to the curriculum. For example, thematic units often begin by using inquiry charts where students are asked what they know about a particular subject and what they would like to know about it. Teachers then build upon *student-*

generated areas of interest to expand the knowledge base of a subject. This curricular approach attempts to teach students about those aspects of the world with which they already interact, and ultimately helps them develop the skills necessary to do so successfully, thus providing preparation for living in the community now and in the future (Kovalik, 1993). Solidly based upon the brain research of Gardner (1983), Hart (1983), and others, ITI is a model for developing and managing curricula that is meaningful and useful to the learner and takes into account multiple learning styles and abilities.

In an ITI model, science and social studies drive the content of thematic curriculum as well as serve as vehicles for instruction in all other content areas. Essentially, daily schedules that segregate math, science, social studies, music, art, and language arts into neat 45-minute or 1-hour units are replaced by day-long social studies and science thematic units, where basic skills such as math, reading, and writing are infused into these larger content areas. A daily schedule might include 2–4 hours on a social studies or science theme and varying degrees of instruction in basic skill areas related to the theme. Although there are times when basic skills are taught apart from the overall thematic unit, teachers in ITI classrooms maintain flexibility and are continually alert to optimal opportunities for such instruction.

There are several reasons for this curricular focus on science and social studies. First, research on learning indicates that the brain's natural tendency is to assess stimuli (research) and construct meaning (evaluate) (Hart, 1983). Both research and evaluation are common methods used in the social studies and science content areas. Second, a portion of our brain is "programmed to learn from the natural world" (Kovalik, 1993, p. 41). Again, science and social studies readily provide concrete and "natural-world" kinds of learning experiences for students. Furthermore, these learning experiences can often be found in surrounding neighborhoods and communities. ITI recommends that, before planning a thematic unit, teachers should "scout" or inventory the school and community for resources upon which to develop the unit. Indeed, teachers are discouraged from developing thematic units based upon material other than those that are realistic and readily available. Third, these content areas provide multiple opportunities to use basic skills in a variety of ways that are meaningful to the learner because they are embedded in real-life experiences. Fourth, and most important, it is in these content areas that skill differences between students are least. Curricular modifications and alternative instructional strategies are more easily developed in social studies and science for all students, including those with significant disabilities.

The seven characteristics of ITI according to Kovalik (1993) are as follows:

1. ITI is based upon the fundamental value that the purpose of public education is to create an enlightened and caring citizenry capable of participating in and maintaining a democracy.

2. Students learn best when they are actively engaged in real-life situations and activities.
3. Students learn in different ways and at different paces.
4. Curricula should center around the acquisition of concepts. Basic skills, such as reading, writing, and mathematics, should be infused into and support a curriculum that focuses primarily on shared values and attitudes.
5. Students should continually be provided with choices to allow for variability in learning style and positive reinforcement.
6. Lecture should be limited, and opportunities for exploration, discovery, and application of concepts to the real world extended.
7. Meaningful, "reality-based" assessment practices should be used.

Curriculum can be delivered through six input levels (Kovalik, 1993). From most to least effective, the levels are the following:

1. First-hand or "being there" learning experiences
2. Immersion into a content area
3. Physical manipulation or hands-on participation with real-life objects
4. Hands-on participation with representational objects
5. Second-hand information obtained through videos, television, and films
6. Symbolic learning experiences (e.g., mathematical formulas, rules of grammar)

In an ITI classroom, much of the curriculum is developed and presented at the first, second, and third levels of input to ensure that students are participating and adequately motivated. For example, an ITI unit on oceans and sea life might include a great deal of real objects, such as shells, different types of shell fish, starfish, and jars containing other kinds of fish for students to manipulate and examine. Field trips to local fishing areas, beaches, or perhaps amusement parks focusing on marine life might also be included.

Other disciplines, such as biology, art, chemistry, and math are integrated into the selected theme. In the case of oceans and sea life, students might be required to dissect various fish; to perform experiments involving the density of salt and sea water; and to categorize sea life according to its various characteristics such as habitats, colors, and sizes. Ways to integrate art might include fish prints and/or watercolor and other media presentations to be displayed around the classroom.

The tenor of an ITI classroom is one of cooperation and collaboration. For students to learn, they must feel safe and there must be a complete "absence of threat" in the classroom (Kovalik, 1993). In addition, classrooms that are implementing this curricular approach are characterized by "trustworthiness, truthfulness, active listening, no put downs and personal best" (Kovalik, 1993, p. 29). The primary instructional strategy in ITI classrooms is cooperative learning. Lecture ("chalk and talk") is dispersed throughout the day and limited to short periods. Students spend the majority of their day in interaction with one another and the teacher. In ITI classrooms, students rely heavily on each other for the information and skills necessary to demonstrate knowledge of the curriculum. The ultimate outcomes of thematic instruction are complete mastery of smaller components of the curriculum and enhanced skills in problem solving, collaboration, and cooperation.

Because students help generate curriculum in thematic classrooms, they can bring their unique cultural heritage and background into the learning process. Cross-cultural sensitivity and understanding is not achieved by simply placing students from diverse cultures in close physical proximity. Such understanding occurs when all students are empowered to interact and make choices from their various frames of reference about what and how they will learn.

Community-Based Instruction

Past practices in special education provide examples of other strategies for making the curriculum meaningful for all students and are consistent with methods in general education. For example, community-based, or community-referenced, instruction is a service delivery model that personnel trained in special education can share with their colleagues in general education. Community-based instruction involves the teaching of meaningful skills in natural environments. Such community experiences can be beneficial for all students. Along with a thematic approach to curriculum, community-based instruction facilitates the acquisition of real-life experiences for students without disabilities alongside peers with disabilities. For example, José, a fourth-grade student with significant disabilities, is accompanied by two peers without disabilities once a week for community-based instruction. José's goals include initiating a request using his communication board, extending his arms and hands to reach grocery items on shelves above the level of his wheelchair, and engaging in an appropriate social exchange. The goals for Steven and Raoul, two peers without disabilities, include estimation (how much do the desired snack items cost?), rounding to the nearest 10s and 20s (to determine if they have enough money), and determining the tax on all the items purchased for the group (multiplication and addition). This example illustrates how the combined expertise and knowledge of both general and special educators can work to benefit all children.

There has been some discussion in the professional literature regarding how much time students with significant disabilities should spend in the general education classroom relative to time spent in community-based activities (see Brown et al., 1991). The location of learning for students with severe disabilities should parallel that of students without disabilities. Suggested percentages of time to be spent in various settings (Sailor et al., 1986) may be useful as a rule of thumb, but these guidelines can also become problematic if they overshadow individualization based upon unique student needs. In addition, there are virtually no empirical data to support the use of such percentages (Giangreco & Putnam, 1991). As suggested by Stainback, Stainback, and Moravec (1992),

> It is a major mistake to take students who are classified as having disabilities into the community during school hours to learn "functional, community-referenced, or vocational skills" unless other students in the general education classes are also doing this. (p. 79)

While thematic approaches and real-life experiences are necessary to make the curriculum meaningful for all students, there are some students, including those with significant disabilities, for whom specific adaptations and modifications may be necessary to further enhance their access to the curriculum. Specific curricular modification strategies and instructional considerations are presented in the following section.

Strategies to Modify Curricula and Instruction

Educators have a variety of curricular modification and instructional strategies from which to choose when deciding how best to match the needs of the students with instruction in the general education classroom. Effective teachers employ a variety of strategies including demonstrations, small-group activities, cooperative learning, peer tutoring, and individual work.

The variables that may be manipulated to individualize curriculum and instruction include the following components:

1. *Materials for study*   Along with selecting materials varied in level of difficulty, teachers can choose from a wide array of materials, including those that provide "being there" experiences as well as literature, art, music, newspapers, journals, and magazines, rather than standard textbook materials.
2. *Method of study*   This refers to types of instructional strategies, such as thematic instruction and cooperative learning, which are among those strategies best suited to meeting the learning needs of diverse learners.
3. *Pace of study*   To accommodate the wide range of ability levels of today's students, it may be necessary to change the pace of study for some students so that they will feel successful in mastering portions of the curriculum.
4. *Sequence of study*   Students should be able to select and master salient portions of the curriculum, rather than be made to feel overwhelmed at the prospect of mastering an entire unit.
5. *Learning focus*   Learning should identifiy and focus on shared values, attitudes, and the problem-solving process that are most relevant and interesting to all students.
6. *Place of learning*   Teachers should not limit themselves to classroom instruction but should provide as many opportunities as possible for students to acquire skills in the community and other nonschool environments.
7. *Evaluation of learning*   To make learning more relevant for students, they should be provided with structured self-evaluation opportunities. Teachers

can provide such learning experiences by using authentic assessment strategies.

As previously mentioned, the primary function of elementary schools is to teach students prosocial behaviors, problem-solving skills, and skills that enable them to cooperate and collaborate in the learning process. When curriculum focuses on real-life issues and concerns, students can relate to learning in a personal way, and active participation and success are more readily achieved. The essence of effective regular class placement is that specially designed curricula and instruction are provided within general education environments (Giangreco & Putnam, 1991) and that curricular modifications are only "as special as necessary" (Schuh, 1993, p. 1). Presented below are two examples of curricular modifications that were developed for Hannah, a third-grade student with significant disabilities.

During language arts, the class is asked to sit on the rug to listen to a story read by the teacher. Hannah, who has visual impairments, is given a copy of the same book that the teacher is reading from, which she holds close to her face so that she can more clearly see the illustrations and thus follow along more easily. This strategy also helps to "center" her, because she has an object at close range upon which she can focus. This example of material adaptation helps Hannah to sit for longer periods of time and thereby derive more meaning from the activity.

While her peers without disabilities are completing addition and subtraction of double-digit number worksheets as a follow-up to a lesson on budgeting their allowance, Hannah works with a peer without disabilities and an adult assistant to complete single-digit addition. Through facilitation and a number board, Hannah is able to correctly answer several simple math problems. The peer, who has completed her own assignment, writes down the answer for Hannah on a worksheet.

This example illustrates how a multilevel curricular adaptation allows Hannah to work in the same curricular area as her peers without disabilities, as well as work on individualized goals. As shown, teachers can use a variety of methods to adapt curriculum and instruction to better meet the needs of all their learners. In the following section, strategies for encouraging collaboration among general and special educators are presented.

COLLABORATION AMONG ELEMENTARY SCHOOL PERSONNEL TO FACILITATE INCLUSION

General and special education teachers may find themselves asking a series of questions as they plan to include students with severe disabilities in general education programs. Based upon informal interviews with elementary teachers in one urban school district, the following questions were raised:

How can I plan and structure the curriculum to benefit all of my students?

What kinds of instructional strategies are most conducive to facilitate learning for my students?

How can I work with other adults to ensure an appropriate educational program?

What is the role of the inclusion facilitator/case manager/support teacher?

In collaboration with one another, general education teachers and special education personnel developed the list of strategies in Table 3 to assist teachers to more fully include students with significant disabilities as well as to make curriculum and instruction meaningful for all students.

The information and strategies presented in Table 3 can be used to form a comprehensive and supported educational program for elementary-age students, including those with severe disabilities. To illustrate these concepts and strategies, a composite portrait of a student is presented in the following section.

PORTRAIT OF MEGHAN

Meghan is a child with strawberry blonde hair and as many labels as she has freckles. While Meghan is the only child with severe disabilities in the room, this fifth-grade general education class also includes 34 of Meghan's peers, who speak several different languages among them and have a variety of labels such as "high achiever," "learning disabled," "average student," "emotionally disturbed," "gifted," and "limited English proficient." While these students have many different challenges and talents, they all share in the responsibility for Meghan's learning.

Recently three of Meghan's friends helped to write her IEP. "An IEP is like a report card, only it has more pages," explained one 10-year-old. Together, these students wrote assessment reports that included comments like these: "Meghan can count to 10, but sometimes she skips 6 and 7," and "Meghan is working better at her desk. Sometimes she writes on the table, but that hardly happens anymore—and if you ask her, she'll stop."

Table 3.   Strategies to facilitate inclusion

1. Assess (and teach) age-appropriate behaviors and norms (e.g., teach student how to "hang" during recess).
2. Assess (and facilitate) social networks among peers.
3. Use and modify general education assessment procedures (e.g., help develop portfolios for students with significant disabilities).
4. In collaboration with classroom teacher, modify core curriculum and infuse student needs into lessons.
5. Provide direct instruction to students both with and without severe disabilities.
6. Function as "case carrier" (e.g., convene and facilitate IEP meeting).
7. Be a liaison for support personnel and parents, classroom teacher and administrators.
8. Provide suggestions to assist students to manage their behavior (i.e., consult with behavior specialist).
9. Be the initial liaison with family on behalf of the school.
10. Facilitate (i.e., coordinate and moderate) school-site team meetings.

These students then helped to write Meghan's goals for the current year. "We know what fifth graders need to learn to do," begins one student. "Meghan needs to learn to play more games at recess. And she needs to get better at using her calculator or she doesn't get her math problems right. And she needs to learn how to read more words because right now she can only read a few."

Meghan's friends recognize that she has many things to learn and that things in the classroom don't always run smoothly. Meghan demonstrates some behavior problems, and, at times her skills seem limited. Her peers have a positive attitude, however. They have watched Meghan change from the beginning of the year, and they know that they have played an important role in her success. Meghan continues to grow and learn. These students' ideas and strategies are often incorporated into the life of the classroom.

Meghan's parents are excited about the changes they have seen in Meghan. They have watched Meghan develop friendships. They have seen her IEP goals change to include academic and other classroom skills. And they have provided insight and encouragement in helping to reduce problem behaviors that had been present at the beginning of the year. Meghan's parents have provided input to Meghan's educational program from the start, and they have remained an active part of the IEP team.

Meghan's parents, the general education teacher, the special education teacher designated as the inclusion case manager, the principal, the adapted physical education teacher, the general physical education teacher, the communication specialist, and Meghan's peers worked together to help plan Meghan's goals for this school year. These goals include these:

1. Type three sentences on the computer to share about her day.
2. Use a calculator to compute sums, differences, and products in order to participate in math games and activities.
3. Increase sight reading vocabulary to read a teacher-made or peer-made book.
4. Demonstrate appropriate greeting behavior (say "Hi" and/or "I like you" instead of hugging and kissing) with classroom and playground peers.
5. Participate in cooperative learning activities in social studies and/or science.
6. Secure and put away art materials and use them appropriately.
7. Pack and unpack her backpack, putting homework in the right place and keeping track of her glasses.
8. Produce initial and medial "th" and "f" sounds in words when interacting with peers and adults.
9. Move right or left to catch or return a ball during recess and physical education activities.
10. Run continuously for 3 minutes during physical education warm-up activities.

These goals are addressed throughout the school day and are infused into the schedule and curriculum of the fifth-grade classroom. For example, Meghan works on sight reading vocabulary during journal, language arts, community circle, math, social studies, and science activities. Meghan receives support in the general education classroom from her peers, the fifth-grade teacher, an aide from the special education program for 3 hours a day, the communication specialist for 30 minutes a week, the adaptive physical education teacher for 30 minutes a week, and the special education teacher during weekly consultation. Figure 1 shows a support plan that was developed for Meghan.

Meghan's schedule is carefully planned to coordinate this support during the times of the day when Meghan needs the most assistance. Roles, responsibilities, and support schedules continue to change as both Meghan's needs and the needs of her classroom teacher change over time. The following scenarios are excerpts from a day in fifth grade, including interactions between Meghan and her peers.

Opening

As the day begins, children enter their classrrom and find their seats. The students are grouped into tribes (also see Chapter 3), and there is laughter and quiet conversation as they "check in" with their tribe members.

Each student has a morning job, including tasks such as collecting homework, tutoring in the kindergarten classroom, being an office monitor, or watering the plants. Meghan's job is to feed the fish. Meghan checks the schedule taped to her desk and walks to the aquarium. She begins to drop the contents of the entire canister into the aquarium. Then she stops. "Only a little," Meghan reminds herself, as she carefully sprinkles a small amount of food into the tank. "Feed fish," Meghan announces as she crosses her name off the job list.

Journals

Meghan returns to her desk and checks her schedule. "Journals," she says, pointing to the picture symbol. Meghan elbows her table partner. "Karen, journals!" Karen hands Meghan a collection of photographs taken at Meghan's home and at school. Meghan selects one and points to the figures in the picture. "I Girl Scouts!" "You went to a Girl Scout meeting?" asks Karen. "Yes," agrees Meghan. "Ate cookies!" "Okay Meghan," says Karen, carefully printing the sentences. "Let me see if I got this right. 'I went to Girl Scouts. I ate cookies.' Anything else?" Meghan studies the picture. "No," she says at last.

Karen helps Meghan read the sentences several times. "Okay, you're ready to copy," she says, as she paper clips the photographs into Meghan's journal. Around them other children work in their journals, some writing, some drawing, some engaging in a written conversation. Karen begins working on her own journal and slowly, with concentration, Meghan begins to copy the letters.

Language Arts

"I think that Leigh's dad will find his dog, Bandit," predicts Carey. The children are working in literature study groups discussing the next chapter in the novel

Full Inclusion Support Plan

Date: _August 1994_

Student: _Meghan S._

School: _42nd Street_

Age/birthdate: _11 / 2-11-83_

Teacher/grade: _C. Campbell / 5th grade_

Case manager: _D. Williamson_

Related services/support staff:

Communication specialist: _C. Pennington_

Adaptive physical education teacher: _J. Porter_

Instructional aide: _M. Ramirez_

Class schedule:

Student goals:	Opening	Journals	Language Arts	Recess	Social Studies	Science	Lunch & play	P.E.	Math	Closing
Type 3 sentences			D /5,8							
Use Calculator									D,C/8	
Increase sight vocabulary		A,D /5,8	C,D /8,5		D,C /,8	D,C /8			D,C /8	
Demonstrate appropriate greeting	A /8			A /5,8			A /8			A /8
Participate in cooperative groups	A /8				D /8	D /8			D /8	
Secure and put away art materials	A /9	A /8			A /8					
Pack/unpack backpack	A /9									A /8
Produce initial & medial "th" and "f"	A,E/	A,E /5,8	A,E /9		A,E /9	A,E /9			A,E/9	A,E/9
Move right/left to catch a ball				A /2,8			A /8	A /2,8		
Run continuously for three minutes								A /2,8		

KEY: **Curriculum adaptations:**

A = As is; B = Physical assistance; C = Adapt materials; D = Multilevel;
E = Different goals; F = Substitute curriculum

Levels of assistance:

1 = No additional; 2 = DIS/Related service; 3 = Case manager; 4 = RSP;
5 = Aide; 6 = Staff; 7 = Cross-age tutor; 8 = Peers; 9 = General education teacher

Figure 1.   A sample full inclusion support plan for Meghan. (From Grenot-Scheyer, M., Koert, M., & Sims, S. [1992]. *Full inclusion support planning grid.* Unpublished manuscript, California State University, Long Beach.)

Dear Mr. Henshaw. "I think that Bandit is going to run away and find Leigh's house," suggests Paloma. "No way!" counters José. "The dog got out of the truck somewhere in the mountains! How could he find his way back to Pacific Grove?" "What character do you like, Meghan?" asks Stephanie. She thinks for a minute and says, "I mean, who do you like?"

Meghan searches the pages for the right pictures. Each day, one of her peers summarizes the chapter in a sentence or two. The sentence is then printed in large type on the computer, and another student illustrates the page and adds it to Meghan's version of the classroom novel. For this novel, the teaching assistant from the special education program has also added picture symbols to the children's sentences.

"I like the dog!" Meghan decides. She points to the picture and says, "Funny dog! Molly my dog." "That's right, Meghan. That does look like your dog, Molly," agrees Paloma. "Do you think Leigh's mom would let him keep the dog if it came home?" George asks the group. The discussion continues as children thumb through their books and talk about the issues.

Writer's Workshop finds the children working at different stages on different pieces from their writing folder. "I need a peer editor," John calls out from the editing table. "I'm ready for peer editing too," says Hoai, exchanging papers with John. "I'm ready to publish," announces Shannon as she walks over to the computer. A high school tutor is helping Meghan type her name and some of the sentences from her journal.

"Her typing is getting a little bit better," comments Shannon. "Yesterday she typed a whole sentence from her journal before recess time." "R-E-C-E-S-S," recites Meghan as she follows the letters in her journal.

Recess

The bell rings and the students hurry to put things away, gather snacks, and select playground equipment. "I like you," Meghan says to Nicole as they walk out the door together. "I like you too, Meghan!" says Nicole, smiling. "When I came to this school last week, Meghan was the first person who said hello to me!" Nicole tells Mrs. Gobat, an aide who helps supervise the students on the playground. "Meghan was my first friend here."

"Come on Meghan, let's go play four square," shouts Alex. Alex, Jeff, and Damian reach the square first. Vanezza and Meghan take the fourth square together. In tandem, they hit the ball back to Alex. A child from another classroom is in line waiting for his turn. He watches the girls playing together. "No fair!" he protests. Alex catches the ball and stops playing. "Everyone on the playground has an equal opportunity to play. Without help, Meghan can't play . . . yet. She's learning. We're helping her. You can play here if you want to, or you can play at a different square." Alex blushes at his new-found advocacy skills.

The boy agrees to play and Alex serves again. With Vanezza's help, Meghan smacks the ball, which lands squarely on Alex's foot and bounces away. Alex laughs and takes his place in line to play again. "Next time," he teases. "Oh, Meghan," giggles Vanezza, "We got a *boy* out . . . !" The bell rings, and the students return to their room for social studies.

Social Studies

"Each group needs to find a comfortable work area," begins the teacher. "If you are working on Native American masks, you will find your materials on the table in the tiled area. Please try to be careful with the paint and glue."

"What are you making today, Meghan?" Karl asks. Meghan looks through the pictures that display her choices for art projects. "You can make a mask or moccasins, or paint symbols on the tepee. Or you can make a basket or a necklace or a weaving," explains Karl.

Meghan chooses to make a mask and joins a group of students hard at work on the projects. Andrea cautions, "Be careful with the paints, Meghan. Do you want me to help you?" "No," says Meghan, as she dips the brush in the paint. "Be careful!" she tells Matthew who is sitting next to her. Together they work on their masks, pausing only to wipe up the errant paint drips.

"Fedders," says Meghan reaching for feathers to add to her mask. "Feathers," corrects Laura. "Meghan, remember 'Feathers' has a 'th' in the middle." Laura and Meghan had been partners the previous day when the communication specialist came to help in the classroom. Together, Laura, Meghan, and the communication specialist had read some books pointing out items containing the "th" sound. "Fedders," says Meghan with great concentration, putting her finger on her teeth as the communication specialist had demonstrated. "Good try, Meghan," praises Laura, "You have a lot of feathers."

Science

Today's science activity finds Meghan carefully counting Cheerios and stringing them onto yarn. "Myself," says Meghan as she carefully adds another piece of cereal to the yarn. "We're making a model of the nervous system," explains Maggie, her table partner. "The cereal is the vertebrae—that's what protects the spinal cord." "Foot," says Meghan as she points to the foot on the model. "Right, Meghan. The nerves take messages from the brain all the way to your foot," continues Maggie. "More cereal, please," interrupts Meghan. "You need 33 pieces, Meghan. Count how many you have. Here, I'll help you," says Maggie as she points to the cereal. "1, 2, 3 . . . " Meghan begins.

Physical Education

After lunch, Meghan joins her friends for physical education. The adapted physical education teacher has helped the general education teacher devise some new strategies so that Meghan can participate in today's mile run. A series of fluorescent cones have been set up for Meghan to follow. She runs to each cone, where she then stops to rest. Then she starts out again, running toward the next cone. "Run with me Meghan," urges Nina as they run together toward the first cone.

Math

When the children return from physical education, they find newspapers piled on their desks. "Newspaper math" is a favorite in the classroom, and the students quickly get to work cutting items from the advertisements. With a roll of the die, students determine how many of each item they will buy.

"I'm buying four cans of chicken soup," says Nate. "Four times 89 cents is . . . " he calculates. "$3.56!" He removes a twenty dollar play bill from his wallet, counts back the change, and begins considering his next purchase. Meghan has glued her pictures onto her paper shopping list. With help from the teacher, she copies the amount alongside each picture. She is just learning how to use her calculator and needs some help with the buttons. "I'm finished, so I can help her," offers Melina. Meghan names each item on her list, and then reads the individual numbers in the price. Once Meghan has arrived at the total, Melina helps her count out the correct amount of money using the dollar-more strategy, which is a method to teach estimation and addition.

Closing

The day winds to an end with all of the children gathering for community circle. The teacher begins. "Please think of one positive experience that you would like to share about your day. But first, is there any further discussion about the changes in the playground rules?" Dustin and Kirsten volunteer, discussing their new roles as game leaders for the first graders. "I think we should be able to play chess outside," adds Vera. "I will write a letter to the vice principal suggesting that." "I'll help you," offers Dane. "I have a concern," begins Mike. "If the fifth graders can only play on the high bars, Meghan won't be able to play on the bars any more. That's like taking her favorite thing in the world and making it too hard for her to do. That wouldn't be fair."

The discussion continues and the teacher suggests that a group of students work together to find some solutions. Each child shares a positive moment about his or her day.

"I finished my story about the girl who is lost in the river," begins Terese. "I helped my kindergarten buddy read his name," adds Clara. "I made it to second base in kick ball," Chris shares. When Meghan's turn arrives, she proudly holds up her mask. "My mask has fedders!" she says, grinning.

The bell rings and there is a flurry of energy as books are collected, backpacks are secured, and good-byes are exchanged. Meghan sees her mom standing outside. "Mom! Mom!" she shouts, running out the door. "My mask has fea . . . fea . . . fea*th*ers!"

SUMMARY

This chapter has described the nature and function of elementary schools as caring communities and places of active learning for all students, including those with significant disabilities. Such caring and active communities can effectively meet the needs of *all* students through the use of individualized assessments and curricular and instructional adaptations. Meghan's portrait is one example of how such optimal learning environments can effectively meet the needs of a diverse group of students.

REFERENCES

Berndt, T.J., & Perry, T.B. (1986). Children's perceptions of friendships as supportive relationships. *Developmental Psychology, 22*(5), 640–648.

Brown, L., Schwarz, P., Udvari-Solner, A., Frattura Kampschroer, E., Johnson, F., Jorgensen, J., & Grunewald, L. (1991). How much time should students with severe intellectual disabilities spend in regular education classrooms and elsewhere? *Journal of The Association for Persons with Severe Handicaps, 16*(1), 39–47.

California Learning Record: Handbook for teachers, K–6. (1993). California Learning Record Project, University of California, San Diego.

Dewey, J. (1956). *The child and the curriculum: The school and society.* Chicago: University of Chicago Press.

Forest, M., & Lusthaus, E. (1989). Promoting educational equality for all students: Circles and maps. In S. Stainback, W. Stainback, & M. Forest (Eds.), *Educating all students in the mainstream of regular education* (pp. 43 57). Baltimore: Paul H. Brookes Publishing Co.

Gardner, H. (1983). *Frames of mind: Theory of multiple intelligences.* New York: Basic Books.

Giangreco, M.F., & Putnam, J.W. (1991). Supporting the education of students with severe disabilities in regular education environments. In L.H. Meyer, C.A. Peck, & L. Brown (Eds.), *Critical issues in the lives of people with severe disabilities* (pp. 245–269). Baltimore: Paul H. Brookes Publishing Co.

Gibbs, J. (1987). *Tribes: A process for social development and cooperative learning.* Pleasant Hill, CA: Center for Human Development.

Grenot-Scheyer, M., Coots, J., & Falvey, M.A. (1989). Developing and fostering friendships. In M. Falvey, *Community-based curriculum: Instructional strategies for students with severe handicaps* (2nd ed.) (pp. 345–355). Baltimore: Paul H. Brookes Publishing Co.

Grenot-Scheyer, M., Koert, M., & Sims, S. (1992). *Full inclusion support planning grid.* Unpublished manuscript. California State University, Long Beach.

Guralnick, M.J. (1980). Social interactions among preschool children. *Exceptional Children, 46*(4), 248–253.

Hart, L.A. (1983). *Human brain and human learning.* Oak Creek, AZ: Books for Educators.

Hartup, W.W. (1983). Peer relations. In P.H. Mussen (Ed.), *Handbook of child psychology: Socialization, personality and social development* (4th ed.) (pp. 103–196). New York: John Wiley & Sons.

Howes, C. (1983). Patterns of friendship. *Child Development, 54*(4), 1041–1053.

Howes, C. (1987). Social competence with peers in young children: Developmental sequences. *Developmental Review, 7*(3), 252–272.

Jorgensen, C.M. (1992). Natural supports in inclusive schools: Curricular and teaching strategies. In J. Nisbet (Ed.), *Natural supports in school, at work, and in the community for people with severe disabilities* (pp. 179–215). Baltimore: Paul H. Brookes Publishing Co.

Kovalik, S. (1993). *Integrated thematic instruction: The model* (2nd ed.). Oak Creek, AZ: Books for Educators.

Nevin, A. (1993). Curricular and instructional adaptations for including students with disabilities in cooperative groups. In J.W. Putnam (Ed.), *Cooperative learning and strategies for inclusion* (pp. 41–56). Baltimore: Paul H. Brookes Publishing Co.

Paley, V.G. (1992). *You can't say you can't play*. Cambridge, MA: Harvard University Press.

Putnam, J.W. (Ed.). (1993). *Cooperative learning and strategies for inclusion*. Baltimore: Paul H. Brookes Publishing Co.

Rubin, Z. (1982). *Children's friendships*. Cambridge, MA: Harvard University Press.

Sailor, W., Halvorsen, A., Anderson, J., Goetz, L., Gee, K., Doering, K., & Hunt, P. (1986). Community intensive instruction. In R.H. Horner, L.H. Meyer, & H.D.B. Fredericks (Eds.), *Education of learners with severe handicaps: Exemplary service strategies* (pp. 251–288). Baltimore: Paul H. Brookes Publishing Co.

Schaps, E., & Solomon, D. (1990). Schools and classrooms as caring communities. *Educational Leadership, 48*(3), 38–42.

Schuh, M. (1993, October). *Adapting regular education for all students*. Paper presented at the Autism Society of Los Angeles, Toward Full Inclusion Conference, Los Angeles.

Snow, J.A. (1989). Systems of support: A new vision. In S. Stainback, W. Stainback, & M. Forest (Eds.), *Educating all students in the mainstream of regular education* (pp. 221–231). Baltimore: Paul H. Brookes Publishing Co.

Stainback, W., Stainback, S., & Moravec, J. (1992). Using curriculum to build inclusive classrooms. In S. Stainback & W. Stainback (Eds.), *Curriculum considerations in inclusive classrooms: Facilitating learning for all students* (pp. 65–84). Baltimore: Paul H. Brookes Publishing Co.

Taylor, S.J., Biklen, D., & Knoll J. (Eds.). (1987). *Community integration for people with severe disabilities*. New York: Teachers College Press.

Weiss, R.S. (1974). The provisions of social relationships. In Z. Rubin (Ed.), *Doing unto others* (pp. 17–20). Englewood Cliffs, NJ: Prentice Hall.

Wiles, J., & Bondi, J. (1989). *Curriculum development: A guide to practice*. New York: Merrill.

13 SECONDARY CURRICULUM AND INSTRUCTION

Mary A. Falvey, Susann Terry Gage, and Lori Eshilian

Since the mid-1980s, secondary schools across the United States, Canada, and many other countries have been restructuring their educational programs to better prepare their students for adult life. Secondary schools are successful when all students learn and develop to their full potential as responsible, caring, and contributing members of a community. A successful secondary school provides each student with personal attention; ongoing advisement; effective instruction; an interrelationship between subjects taught; critical thinking and problem-solving skills expected in jobs, homes, and community settings; parent and community involvement; and appropriate supports.

In an attempt to restructure high schools to reflect these characteristics, the staff and students in partnership with parents and community members have come together in many communities. They share the vision that students should learn to use their minds, bodies, and hearts, and to live productive, socially useful, and personally satisfying lives.

In some schools, these restructuring efforts have resulted in the assignment of all students to age-appropriate "houses" instead of ability groupings. A house is like a "school within a school," formed by a group of approximately 120–180 students and a team of 5–7 teachers. Typically students, particularly freshmen and sophomores, have no more than three different teachers in one day, since the subjects that are taught are integrated and often team taught. These houses contain a common core of learning in English, social studies, math, and science or electives. Student placement in houses is done randomly. Each house has its own uniqueness based upon the interests and needs of its students and teachers. Juniors and seniors determine their career paths, completing both community service requirements and internships with employers. Not all students have the same program; however, all students, those with and without disabilities, receive a rigorous core of learning based on the same desired student outcomes.

This example illustrates some of the strengths of this approach. It is Tuesday morning, the day after the holiday for Martin Luther King, Jr.'s, birthday. The students are arriving to school on foot, bicycle, school buses, public buses, cars driven by family members or friends and their families, and a few in their own cars. Joaquin, Carlos, Nathan, and Meagan are talking together on the grass in front of the school when Anthony, being pushed in his wheelchair by his brother, goes by. Immediately, all four students stop what they are doing in order to ask Anthony if he had been invited to or heard the rumor about the party at Maria's house the following weekend. Anthony responds with a big smile and nod, which for those who know him translates to, "Yes, I was invited." They all had been invited—this was going to be an enormous party.

The students discussed the homework assignment they had: to pretend that Martin Luther King, Jr., was alive at the time of the Rodney King beating in Los Angeles and present what they thought he would have said and/or done. Joaquin painted a series of pictures depicting what he thought Dr. King would have been doing, while Carlos and Anthony had typed their description into a computer. Nathan had written and recorded a song, and Meagan had cut pictures out of magazines to create a collage of her thoughts. The bell rings, indicating that it is time to head to class. Since these students, except Anthony's brother, are all assigned to the same house, Anthony's brother motions to the group to grab Anthony's wheelchair handles, which Carlos does, and proceeds to go to his own class.

Ms. Peel, their first-period "advisory" (formerly known as "homeroom") teacher, says hello and tells the students how nice it was to see so many of them at the rally held the day before in honor of Dr. King. The students discuss the rally and other business during their advisory period. Anthony and his friends proceed through their day asking questions, thinking, communicating information, and participating in a variety of teaching experiences. Anthony's schedule for the first semester of his freshman year is included in Figure 1. This example summarizes the key advantages of a secondary school that has been restructured for greater effectiveness.

Secondary schools include middle, junior, and senior high schools, and although differences among these three types of schools do exist, particularly with regard to the age of the students that attend, these differences go beyond the scope and purpose of this chapter and therefore are not discussed. Rather, the term *secondary* is used to refer to all three types of schools unless otherwise indicated.

The secondary school, as seen in contemporary times, was established in the latter half of the nineteenth century. In 1892, the Committee of Ten, a committee established by the National Education Association (NEA), identified the early introduction of the fundamentals of subjects into the upper elementary grades and the

Time	Period	Class
7:35–7:53	Advisory	Greeting, summary of day, current events
8:00–8:53	1	Foods 1
9:00–9:53	2	Course 1 math (algebra)
10:00–10:15	Nutrition	
10:15–12:15	3 & 4	Humanities (integration of English and social studies)
12:15–1:00	Lunch	
1:00–1:53	5	Fitness for life (physical education)
2:00–2:53	6	Academic enrichment (counseling, homework help)

Figure 1. Anthony's freshman class schedule.

standardization of subject matter for all high school students (Report of the Committee on Secondary School Studies, 1893). This committee recommended a list of courses that has shaped the basic outlines of today's high school curriculum:

- English language and literature
- Foreign language, such as Greek, Latin, German, French, and Spanish
- Mathematics, such as algebra, geometry, and trigonometry
- Natural sciencies, such as astronomy, meteorology, botany, zoology, physiology, geology, and physical geography
- Physical sciences, such as physics and chemistry (Gutek, 1992, p. 301)

In 1918, the NEA established the Committee on the Reorganization of Secondary Education to review the purpose of the high school. This report em phasized the importance of health, a command of basic skills including those necessary to function within the home, vocational preparation, citizenship skills, skills needed to engage in leisure activities, and skills needed to develop an ethical character within secondary schools. This commission viewed the secondary school as both an academic institution and an agency of social integration (Gutek, 1992).

In 1959, James Conat made a number of recommendations to create and restore a comprehensive high school. He insisted that the comprehensive high school be socially comprehensive (so that it enrolls a heterogeneous population of students) and that the high school be large enough to provide broad curricular possibilities to meet the vocational and academic needs of students who were college bound as well as those who were not.

Secondary schools have experienced extensive reviews and criticism over the past years (Boyer, 1983; Sizer, 1984). Contemporary efforts to reform the secondary schools have addressed both declining academic standards and deteriorating moral and social values (Gutek, 1992). In the 1980s, several reports examined the conditions specific to secondary schools in the United States. The

High School: A Report on Secondary Education in America (Boyer, 1983) was sponsored by the Carnegie Foundation for the Advancement of Teaching, and *Horace's Compromise: The Dilemma of the American High School* (Sizer, 1984) was cosponsored by the National Association of Secondary School Principals and the Commission on Educational Issues of the National Association of Independent Schools. These reports found that high schools lacked a clear and vital vision of their mission and that teachers and administrators had been unable to establish educational priorities. Specifically, Boyer (1983) proposed a core curriculum that was presented in such a way as to expose students to a commonly shared, interdisciplinary body of knowledge. He proposed that students be required to complete an independent project during their senior year that examined a significant contemporary issue.

In his secondary school reform efforts, Sizer (1984) recommended an increase in students' expectations of themselves and their achievements by creating more flexible and "friendly" schools. He particularly emphasized the need to create schools that teach in an interdisciplinary manner and use meaningful evaluation procedures to determine learning outcomes. Sizer's work led to the creation of the Coalition of Essential Schools at Brown University. This coalition has identified nine common principles that have driven much of the restructuring effort in secondary schools in the United States. These principles are delineated in Table 1.

Secondary schools are particularly influenced by societal attitudes and climates; therefore, schools often reflect the communities' successes and struggles. On the one hand, in a community where there is harmony among its participants, the secondary schools are likely to reflect such harmony. On the other hand, secondary schools located in communities where there is tension among its members are more likely to reflect the same tension in the schools. The communities and schools that experience such tension are often located in deteriorating neighborhoods where people live in poverty and where drugs, gangs, and violence are a way of life. In order for schools to successfully restructure, they must address the needs of the community. Without a concerted effort to build a sense of a just community, restructuring secondary schools is more difficult. The purpose of this chapter is to identify strategies for creating secondary schools that effectively teach *all* students about surviving and thriving in diverse communities.

PREPARATION FOR ADULT LIFESTYLES

General Education Preparation: Postsecondary Education or Employment

Today, the majority of secondary schools are designed to prepare students for traditional postsecondary education (Goodlad, 1984; Sizer, 1989). Schools with such an orientation have become less effective for most students. Many high schools lack the technological equipment and knowledge to prepare students for

Table 1.   The common principles of the coalition of essential schools

1. The school should focus on helping adolescents learn to use their minds well. Schools should not attempt to be "comprehensive" if such a claim is made at the expense of the school's central intellectual purpose.
2. The school's goals should be simple: that each student master a limited number of essential skills and areas of knowledge. While these skills and areas will, to varying degrees, reflect the traditional academic disciplines, the program's design should be shaped by the intellectual and imaginative powers and competencies that students need, rather than necessarily by "subjects" as conventionally defined. The aphorism "less is more" should be guided by the aim of thorough student mastery and achievement rather than by an effort merely to cover content.
3. The school's goals should apply to students, but the means to these goals will vary as these students themselves vary. School practices should be tailor-made to meet the needs of every group of adolescents.
4. Teaching and learning should be personalized to the maximum feasible extent. No teacher should have direct responsibility for more than 80 students; decisions about the course of study, the use of students' and teachers' time and the choice of teaching materials and specific pedagogies must be unreservedly placed in the hands of the principal and staff.
5. The governing practical metaphor of the school should be student as worker, rather than the more familiar metaphor of teacher as deliverer of instructional services. Accordingly, a prominent pedagogy will be coaching, to provoke students to learn how to learn and thus to teach themselves.
6. Students embarking on secondary school studies are those who show competence in language and elementary mathematics. Students of traditional high school age who do not yet have appropriate levels of competence to start secondary school studies will be provided with intensive remedial work so that they can quickly meet those standards. The diploma should be awarded on a successful final demonstration of mastery for graduation—an Exhibition. This Exhibition by the student of his or her grasp of the central skills and knowledge of the school's program may be jointly administered by the faculty and high authorities. Because the diploma is awarded when earned, the school's program proceeds with no strict age grading and with no system of credits earned by time spent in class. The emphasis is on the students' demonstration that they can do important things.
7. The tone of the school should explicitly and self-consciously stress the values of unanxious expectation ("I won't threaten you, but I expect much of you"), of trust (unless it is abused), and of decency (the values of fairness, generosity, and tolerance). Incentives appropriate to the school's students and teachers should be emphasized, and parents should be treated as essential collaborators.
8. The principal and teachers should perceive of themselves first as generalists (teachers and scholars in general education) and next as specialists (experts in a particular discipline). Staff should expect multiple obligations (teacher–counselor–manager) and a sense of commitment to the entire school.
9. Administrative and budget targets should include substantial time for collective planning by teachers, competitive salaries for staff, and an ultimate per-pupil cost not more than 10 percent higher than that at a traditional school. Administrative plans may have to show the phased reduction or elimination of some services now provided for students in many traditional comprehensive secondary schools.

Adapted from Sizer, 1992.

current and future job markets. In addition, far fewer than 50% of high school graduates in the United States enroll in postsecondary education institutions (Black, 1993). Pressure has been placed on restructuring secondary schools to more effectively educate students who have been referred to as the "forgotten half," that is, those students who do not go on to postsecondary education.

All students need a different and more functional approach to education. Secondary schools must adapt to the current and future world of work and community without losing their strong college preparatory programs. Secondary schools must provide systematic and structured experiences to teach the skills to be successful in work and the community as well as in postsecondary education.

The 1994 School-to-Work Opportunities Act (PL 103-239) provided federal aid to states and communities to develop school-based job training for all students. With such legislation and pressure to more adequately prepare students for work and community life, we can expect to see more high schools restructuring to better prepare students for postsecondary education as well as career options.

Special Education Preparation: Community-Based Training and School-Based Academics

In 1990, PL 101-476 amended PL 94-142 (the Education for All Handicapped Children Act) and renamed it the Individuals with Disabilities Education Act (IDEA). IDEA requires that students 16 years of age and older be provided with an individualized transition plan (ITP) in addition to the already required individualized education program (IEP). An ITP includes goals and objectives for the student to make a successful transition from school to postschool and/or job settings. Over the past decade, general education has taken place within the school campus, while the majority of secondary-age students with significant disabilities have been enrolled in job-skills and community-based training programs as the primary focus of their secondary schooling experience (Falvey, 1989; Sailor et al., 1989). Although this opportunity has provided important job and community skills training, it raises several serious concerns.

First, as a result of off-campus job-training programs, students with significant disabilities have not been given the same access to school-based academic programs as their peers without disabilities. Traditional belief that students with disabilities would not benefit from academic secondary educational programs are being challenged (Tashie & Schuh, 1993). Skills necessary to acquire and maintain jobs, as well as those necessary to use community settings, are important and essential for all students. However, students with disabilities can participate in community and job-training opportunities after school, on weekends, and/or during school breaks and vacations, as do the majority of students without disabilities (Tashie & Schuh, 1993). In addition, students with disabilities often attend school beyond the age of 18, the typical age for graduation from high school (state regulations vary; however, the majority of states enroll students with disabilities in the public schools until the age of 21). For those states that enroll students beyond the high school graduation age, continuing education and job and community-based training can be the focus of their education during the years that follow high school. For more information about and strategies for designing postsecondary education for students with significant disabilities, see Chapter 14, this volume.

More important, programs that do not focus on school inclusion limit students' opportunities to develop friends, social networks, and natural supports within their peer group. Staff providing services to adults with significant disabilities as well as graduates of special education community-based programs indicate that establishing strong networks of friends and natural supports as adults is extremely challenging when such networks have not already been established during the high school years. In contrast, adults who are able to develop such networks while attending their neighborhood high schools increase their opportunities and participation in their communities as adults.

These social networks are crucial. Research regarding the job retention rate of adults with disabilities indicates that the most frequent reason for job loss is a lack of social skills. Such social skills are most often learned and practiced in settings where those skills are expected. High school campuses and a full range of extracurricular activities offer many more opportunities to practice and learn appropriate social skills, particularly those used when interacting with peers, teachers, and/or supervisors, than those typically provided by special education community-based instructional programs.

Opportunity to Develop Individual Potential

Students must have the opportunity to develop a plan for their educational and career paths, as well as strategies for achieving those goals. Schools that pigeonhole students based on similar test scores are using the frequently criticized yet common practice of *tracking*—clustering students by certain categorical programs or high, medium, and low ability groupings. Tracking is usually accomplished through the results of students' standardized intelligence or achievement tests. Such practice has done great harm to large numbers of students, because it often denies them equal access to the curriculum and instructional practices (Oakes, 1985). A disproportionate number of non-white and/or economically disadvantaged students are assigned to lower tracks and categorical programs. Tracking can perpetuate the achievement gap between lower income and minority students and their more affluent, often white peers (Kozol, 1991).

The opposite of tracking schools are those schools that promote and encourage heterogeneous classroom arrangements. Within these programs, all students have access to the same information and opportunities. Individual abilities and needs are addressed by providing students with a wide range of options for demonstrating mastery of learning outcomes. Within these settings, modifications of curriculum and a variety of teaching strategies are employed to allow for student differences. In addition, modifications are necessary to the traditional grading system to assess each student based on individual growth and progress rather than on a comparison of students against a predetermined standard. A heterogeneous school allows for all students to have equal access to a "core" curriculum that will support all options for future career or life paths, through a use of individualized plans for each student. These plans, much like an IEP or ITP, are developed in conjunction with family members, teachers, and friends and should not be static, but rather a flexible blueprint of the student's future. The plan should plot a course for the student's academic program and career choices. The plan can be dynamic as the student progresses and as his or her goals change because each student's secondary academic opportunity begins with experiences that allow him or her to move in a variety of directions.

Preparing Critical Thinkers and Problem Solvers

In order to effectively educate students with diverse learning styles and needs, educators must view the curriculum as a dynamic set of information. A curriculum that teaches students a knowledge base, upon which they can continue to learn information and skills, must be developed. (Paul, 1990). In addition, information can become obsolete; for example, only one half of the jobs existing in the 1970s were still around in the 1980s (Wiles & Bondi, 1987). Strategies for incorporating this new information into instruction must be developed.

Classrooms and schools that offer opportunities for students to learn and practice critical thinking skills also emphasize the need for students to have more than superficial exposure or mastery of basic skills (Paul, 1990). Teaching basic skills without emphasizing critical thinking often results in learning a little about a lot of different things, as opposed to gaining a deep understanding of a few key concepts that can be applied to many different situations (Porter, 1989). Critical thinking has often been ignored or intentionally omitted from the education of students with disabilities due to the prejudices and limited expectations that others have of them. However, these skills are essential for all students' participation in postsecondary education, jobs, the community, and home settings, and must be systematically taught, encouraged, and facilitated. Teachers need to facilitate the development of all students' critical thinking abilities by offering numerous opportunities for them to demonstrate their knowledge base in a variety of ways.

Participants in a Democracy

The United States Constitution and Bill of Rights established a country founded on democratic principles. These principles create a sense of fairness and justice. The most effective way to teach students about democratic principles is to govern schools and classrooms in a manner consistent with these principles. (For a more detailed discussion on building democratic classrooms and schools, see Chapter 5.)

Some of the most critical social values associated with a democracy are justice, tolerance, concern, and respect for all citizens (Solomon, Schaps, Watson, & Battistich, 1992). Schools assume both explicit and implicit responsibility in the development of student values. These values must be deliberately incorporated into classrooms, curriculum, and instruction. Specifically, students must be given opportunities to practice self-direction. Students who learn only to follow teachers' instructions and directions will not gain the necessary skills to initiate and make decisions involving social values and morals. In addition, students trained for compliance can easily become society's victims.

All students must be given input and feedback about their competencies and areas of strength. Students who are only corrected, criticized, compared with, or segregated from others who have more skills will not develop the self-confidence necessary to build moral character. All students must be encouraged to think for themselves. They should receive constructive, positive feedback from teachers about both their behavior and their ideas, and they should learn to take responsibility for themselves and their actions. In addition, students who feel connected and have a sense of belonging are more likely to consider both the feelings of others and the consequences of their behavior on others when making decisions. Students who have experienced isolation and deprivation are not likely to learn these essential values and life skills. If students are not taught the critical social values of fairness, tolerance, concern, and respect for others, the democratic traditions of this country are in jeopardy. When students are taught such values they are more likely to be motivated to be responsible and productive citizens.

ASSESSMENT AND CURRICULUM

In restructured high schools, learning outcomes for all students must reflect application of knowledge and demonstration of problem-solving skills, as opposed to the ability to recall facts, formulas, and routine information (Sizer, 1989). For example, students might be asked to demonstrate the skills to interview 10 different people who are employed full time in a particular field and develop some hypotheses about that particular career and analyze the personal compatibility for this career. This form of evaluation would provide students and their families and teachers with a great deal of useful information in order to assess their knowledge base and abilities to problem solve.

The organization of the curriculum within the secondary schools has experienced little change over the years until recently. Historically, students in secondary schools have been required to enroll in and pass a certain number of credits in various subject areas, such as English, social studies, foreign language, math, science, arts (music, visual arts, dance, and theater), physical education, and sometimes vocational education. Students are ready to graduate once they pass all the required courses, and graduation has been considered a major rite of passage (Sizer, 1992). The curriculum should be driven by desired student outcomes, not by a list of graduation requirements based on textbooks or college entrance requirements.

Promising Alternatives

Assessment was discussed in Chapter 4, this volume. Along with curriculum, assessment plays a particularly significant role in restructuring at the secondary level. Traditional assessments used in secondary education, particularly multiple-choice, standardized tests, do not adequately assess students' performance levels beyond their ability to recall facts and information on a particular day. More authentic assessments are based on performance and provide teachers with an array of tools to assess the quality and depth of a student's learning. Students generate a response to a question or situation rather than choose an answer. These assessment procedures are frequently outcome based and may require students to perform some or all of the following critical thinking skills: interpret, explain, synthesize, analyze, or organize information. Procedures may include essay examinations, research projects, behavior counts, scientific experiments, parent inventories, exhibitions (mini-exhibitions and exit-level exhibitions), videotape productions, theatrical student performances, student repertoire inventories, debates, and/or samples of work compiled into portfolios. Exhibitions in particular are used at the secondary level as a primary vehicle for students to demonstrate their knowledge of a rich core of subject matter (Sizer, 1989). Mini-exhibitions can include work done in a particular subject area, and exit-level exhibitions refer to culminating work demonstrating that students possess the necessary skills and knowledge their school deems essential to earn a diploma (Podl & Metzger, 1992). An example of a mini-exhibition for a literature class might be a written or visual presentation of a book or series of books that address an essential question. In an exit-level exhibition they have completed that year, the student might be asked to develop a comprehensive presentation reflective of the essential questions previously addressed and the books previously read and reviewed for the mini-level exhibitions. The presentation should demonstrate the student's literary reflectiveness and the capacity to communicate ideas in the chosen form. The high school diploma should be granted contingent upon the successful final demonstrations (e.g., exhibitions) of skill mastery determined for graduation (Podl & Metzger, 1992; Cushman, 1990). Educators must be very clear on the general yet individualized qualities that students must display and what they must do to earn a diploma. Goals must be clearly stated, not only for students, but also for the school as a whole, and must reflect the larger priorities of the community.

Outcome-based education (OBE), a particularly important feature of restructured secondary schools, has a direct impact on the assessment strategies and curriculum used. OBE can be equated with the planning that occurs for the development of an IEP or ITP for a student with a disability. A collaborative team, including the student, works together to assess the student's current level of performance. The data gained from assessment are used to generate appropriate learning goals and objectives that the student will work toward during the year. The team decides what curriculum priority areas should be addressed and attempts to project student performance levels at the end of a year. The student, with the support and facilitation of the teaching staff, attempts to achieve the goals and objectives.

OBE implies establishing outcomes for all students that are likely to be achieved differentially by each of the students. With this system, other forms of assessments are used in place of standard grading methods and bell-curve quotas (Darling-Hammond, 1991; Sizer, 1991). In addition, a system defined by the calendar or clock is replaced by a system that emphasizes "whether," as opposed to "when," students learn (Glickman, 1991; Schlechty, 1990; Weiss, 1988). School goals should drive the curriculum and assessment process. Outcome goals determine the curriculum, which in turn drives the assessment process. The following is an example of school-wide outcomes for one restructured secondary school. Graduates from this high school will be able to

Compete successfully in a changing and increasingly technological job market.
Participate and work collaboratively in a democratic, multicultural society.
Exhibit the habits characteristic of strong moral and ethical values.
Take responsibility for their own learning by setting priorities, developing personal goals, and monitoring their progress.
Demonstrate critical thinking skills in a variety of situations.
Demonstrate basic literacy skills such as reading, writing, and mathematical computation.

Within each of these general outcomes, individual students can demonstrate mastery in a variety of ways. OBE allows for this variety in students' abilities, interests, strengths, and needs. This structure allows and even encourages demonstration in less academic formats and functional, real-life exhibitions for those students who are the most academically challenged.

A curriculum driven by functional assessment for each student can become a more functional curriculum, focused on critical life skills identified by the IEP and ITP teams. Such a curriculum can assist students' to select functional career and life paths during their high school years.

Most restructuring movements have addressed the need to provide a core curriculum for all students at least within their first 2 years of high school. Such a curriculum encourages all students to be lifelong learners and allows equal access to the skills necessary for the full range of postschool options (college, trade school, work, or family life). Once students have completed the core curriculum, they along with families and school personnel can plan for the future in selecting career or life paths that will help determine each student's future curriculum choices. Many school districts are developing magnet schools that help students focus on specific career plans.

Special Education Support Services in Secondary Schools

Since secondary schools often offer students instruction in a variety of subjects from specialists (secondary teaching with in-depth training in one or two related subjects), special education support personnel should be familiar with and have knowledge in all areas of the curriculum. Support personnel should be familiar with the content, schedule, textbooks and materials, and various teaching styles used (including teaching philosophies and various teaching strategies) and should possess effective communication abilities and strategies. Special education support personnel and general education teachers should discuss students' specific goals and objectives, learning styles, medical considerations, and behavioral concerns. They should discuss grading procedures and differential standards that should be applied. This information helps in the design and implementation of IEPs for students with disabilities within general education settings. Figure 2 provides a sample vehicle for facilitating communication between special and general educators.

To allow some students to be active participants, the curriculum, instructional strategies, and/or materials may need to be adapted. A variety of curricular modifications can facilitate a student's learning in various academic classes. Different levels of "people" supports can be provided to the student. These levels, from the least to the most intensive supports, include the following:

Special education support personnel might meet with the general education teacher *once or twice a month* so that a friendly and mutually supportive relationship develops. This might include the special education support personnel providing supplemental materials when and where needed.

Special education support personnel might visit the classroom a *couple of times a week* to observe students, determine any possible need for increased support, assist the general education teacher in setting up peer supports, suggest cooperative learning group combinations, and maintain open communication with and accessibility to the general education teacher.

Special education support personnel might provide *part-time but daily support* to the general education teacher, who may assign them to assist students with assignments, make and bring supplemental materials as needed, or provide tutorial support.

A *classroom companion* involves assigning a student volunteer to assist another student in attendance and participation in a class. The classroom companion might be a member of the same class or enrolled in a service club or class that provides such a service.

Special education support personnel might provide *daily full-time support to the general education teacher*, who may assign them to assist students with assignments, make and bring supplemental materials as needed, or provide tutorial support.

Special education support personnel might provide *one-to-one support directly to the student* with disabilities. In this situation, the support person usually remains in close proximity to the student and provides the support needed.

Like all supports and modifications, the least intrusive intervention should be used, and the supports should be faded as soon as possible while maintaining students' active participation in the general education classroom. Table 2 provides several examples of curriculum modifications that can be used for various subjects. Chapter 6 provides more details about curricular modifications.

Inclusion Teacher Communication Form

Student name: Sue Rubin   **Case manager:** Lori Eshilian

Classes in which enrolled this semester: Freshman studies, algebra, English, ceramics, physical education

Student's strengths: Sue can type with facilitation, has a good sense of humor, and is very motivated.

Student's needs: Sue needs a support person to assist her in classroom assignments and in maintaining appropriate social behaviors, especially in new situations. She has a strong need for a routine.

IEP objectives specific to classroom participation: Will utilize support from facilitators (staff and peers) in classroom assignments. Will use strategies to maintain appropriate behavior in class.

Differential standards (e.g., grading, amount of work required, quality of work, attendance, and punctuality): May need to have some assignments decreased in length and/or take assignments home in order to complete. May need hand-over-hand (facilitation) for activities involving fine motor skills.

Adaptations and considerations that have been successful in the past: Use of staff or peer for facilitation (uses a Franklin Spelling Ace) for taking notes and providing verbal feedback on appropriate behavior. If teacher leaves class, it is helpful to leave his or her pen or pencil with Sue, to assist her in fighting her tendency of needing "sameness."

Additional comments:
Sue should not be allowed to disrupt the class; if she does, she should be directed to leave and go to the counselor's office.
Sue often needs physical support to move through changes.
For ceramics, Sue may need hand-over-hand (facilitation) support to initially work wth clay. May need to adapt grading standards (e.g., accept written essay on art appreciation to substitute for drawing assignment, due to her difficulties in fine motor skills).

Figure 2.   Sample form for documenting information essential to Sue's inclusion.

INSTRUCTIONAL ARRANGEMENTS

Educators can use a variety of instructional arrangements to facilitate students' active learning and participation in secondary school programs. Recognizing the deterioration of the traditional family and many communities, Sizer (1992) has suggested that larger high schools be broken up into smaller units, houses, or teams to become a closer, more personalized experience for both students and educators. It is also difficult for educators to develop individualized programs for 150–180 diverse students, the average number of students that traditional high school teachers teach each day. Smaller units can reduce the student–teacher

Table 2.   Examples of curricular modifications within secondary education

Subject	Type of modification	Description of modification
Math	materials	Using a calculator
	materials	Enlarging the print of the assignment
	materials	Using manipulatives (age-appropriate)
English/Language arts	assignment	Instead of a written paper, do a collage, oral report, computer-activated report, dictated report, or visual representation
Home economics/foods	materials	Create a set of picture recipes
	materials	Use switches hooked up to electronic appliances
	materials	Use mixer or blender in place of stirring
	assignment	Work in small groups
Art	materials	Use paint squeeze bottles instead of paint brushes
	assignment	Critique a work of art instead of creating art
Physical education	rules	Modify the rules, standards, and expectations for games
Drama	materials	Student activates a switch with tape-recorded voice
	rules	Student uses sign language to participate
	assignment	Videotape scene
Social studies/history	assignment	Instead of one written paper, do a collage, oral report, computer-activated report, dictated report, or visual presentation; or act out a historical scene
General classes	assignment	Request another student to take notes on NCR paper; make a copy of another student's notes
	assignment	Highlight with a marker the critical elements of the textbook; tape record the critical elements of the textbook; tape record the lecture or class activity

ratio, which may allow schools to design more effective programs for their students.

Another suggestion by most leaders in the field regarding restructuring high schools is that instruction occur in blocks of time rather than brief periods. Within these blocks, there should be less focus on quantity than on quality of instruction. Less content should be covered to allow for more in-depth instruction, the aim being more thorough student investigation, mastery, and achievement. Within these blocks, instruction should be interrelated and strongly connected to functional career/life expectations beyond the high school setting.

Although a *thematic approach* is more often referred to in the context of elementary education (Kovalik, 1993), the notion that the curriculum offered to secondary students should be interrelated and connected to their daily lives is of equal importance. Due to the traditional structure of the secondary school, however, approaching the curriculum thematically is particularly challenging. The selection of a thematic approach must be a school, grade-level, or "house" decision to ensure that the in-depth study of the selected theme crosses all disciplines. This approach can be difficult in high school. Current practice is to teach different subjects in isolation from each other, most often based on textbooks that do not encompass interrelated themes. In addition, most teachers are trained to be experts in one field rather than generalists with interdisciplinary skills. Adopting a thematic approach, however, can be a very effective means of restructuring curriculum and making learning more relevant to students' lives.

Secondary teachers need to work together collaboratively to effectively plan themes that could incorporate multiple subject areas. For example, if math, health, history, and English teachers collaborated, they could develop a theme for teaching students to survive in a place in the world currently uninhabited by people. The math teacher could present data on the climate and geography and ask that the students use algebraic computations to predict weather patterns and geographic characteristics of the region. The history teacher could discuss the region's history, while the health teacher could discuss humans' essential needs in order to survive. The English teacher could assign books to read and discuss that are set in that general region and/or similar regions throughout the world.

Another critical element when arranging for instruction is the development of *peer support systems*. People should be trained to provide services and support to community members who need it in order to form or participate in peer support systems. Circle of friends and futures planning processes, as described in Chapter 10, can facilitate establishing and participating in peer networks and supports. With the passage of the Americans with Disabilities Act, a disability civil rights law mandating nondiscriminatory practices in all aspects of the community, schools and businesses are in need of trained personnel to establish appropriate programs and to provide support to persons with disabilities. With the advent of highly individualized teaching strategies and support systems, there is an even greater need for people to be trained in techniques that allow individuals who use those strategies to have a high quantity and quality of participation in their schools and communities.

Secondary schools as a community share this need for students to support other students. Peer support services provide opportunities for students with disabilities to gain experience and confidence as well as to attend and participate in all aspects of secondary school life. The benefits for students who participate as peer supports are tremendous. Teachers and parents of students who have been peer supports indicate that these students demonstrate an increase in the highest values of fairness, tolerance, acceptance of differences, and respect for others. The training and experience that peer supports receive is also beneficial in securing future jobs, raising a family, and supporting other relatives or friends.

Another advantage of peer support services is that positive social interactions among students with differing abilities are modeled for a larger peer group impact. This can be especially beneficial if peer relationships extend beyond the classroom setting to extracurricular school activities and community events. It is important for all students to develop social and communty skills that are appropriate outside of a school setting. Often those social contacts and skills lead to the development of reciprocal relationships, the development of social networks, friendships, and natural supports.

SUE RUBIN'S STORY

People who have known her for most of her life refer to her as Susie; however, as she approached high school a year and a half ago, she requested that people call her Sue. Life has changed so dramatically for Sue this past year and a half that she wanted to start anew.

Although not diagnosed until the age of 3 as autistic, her parents recognized her development as different from that of other children, including a brother who was 2 years older. During the years that followed, her parents desperately tried every therapy and special program that came along, hoping that they would find ways to help her learn and become an active member of her family and community. Until recently, Sue's life was similar to the lives of thousands of children with severe disabilities throughout this and other countries. She attended segregated preschool, elementary, and junior high school classrooms, especially designed to teach students functional skills. She participated in a community-based program throughout these years. She did not have access to general education academic classes, curricula, or strategies. She had little intelligible speech and had difficulty communicating with her family, peers, teachers, and others. Sue's behavior also challenged her teachers, parents, and some of her peers. For example, she did not focus on the task or the activity, and when she was upset she banged her head, scratching and biting herself and others if they were in her way. She would choose repetitive activities and was often observed collecting and holding onto long narrow objects, such as spoons and pencils.

During her last year in junior high school, Sue was introduced to facilitated communication.[1] Although her initial responses were slow, she began typing more regularly and fluently and used more complex language. Prior to using this method, she frequently indicated that she was unaware of her own abilities. The more Sue typed, the more she was treated as a "thinking person," which influenced her own attitudes about herself and her capabilities. Over time, the amount and level of facilitation has been faded. There are many days that just having the facilitator sit next to her is enough support, especially for work that involves multiple-choice responses.

By the time she was to begin high school, she was typing regularly. The high school she was to attend had restructured and would no longer be offering a segregated special education program for students with disabilities. The school had

---

[1]See Chapter 6 for a brief discussion of facilitated communication and some of the controversy surrounding its use.

built inclusive services where special education resources would be used to support students in general education settings. Sue began her freshman year enrolling in a full load of classes, freshman studies, English, algebra, physical education, ceramics, and a practical arts class where she had the opportunity to practice typing skills. She received support from special and general education teachers, instructional aides, and other students in all of her classes. However, she indicates a strong preference for students helping her rather than adults. She says, "I just feel more like a person when a student likes me enough to learn how to feel my movements," referring to facilitation strategies.

Sue's high school no longer used categorical or tracked programs and services to segregate students; rather, the school was redesigned to meet the needs of a heterogeneous population of learners. In addition, her teachers used authentic assessment procedures to measure the progress of Sue and her classmates. After receiving a variety of training formats, the faculty began to use multiple forms of instruction, with an emphasis on multiple intelligence strategies (see Chapters 4 and 6 for more detailed discussion on multiple intelligences). In addition, as the faculty worked more frequently together in teams with students, the curriculum became more integrated.

Sue describes that stress of initially going to an inclusive high school where she had to demonstrate a set of behavioral controls that she was unable to display without support, strategies, and significant amounts of practice. To encourage her to participate appropriately in activities within general education classes, a variety of supports were used. For example, a teacher or instructional assistant sat next to her, speaking to her in a very low voice, providing her with verbal reminders for developing self-control over her inappropriate behaviors. In addition, sometimes the staff used a physical reminder, an object that had been paired with certain behaviors, which gave a sense of security and confidence. These supports gave her the opportunity to, as she says, "save my dignity when I could not control myself."

As her ability to communicate using facilitated communication has increased, and as she has had more experience at actively participating in general education classes, the supports have decreased. In place of the supports she required in the beginning of her high school years, other strategies have been employed that have been successful throughout her sophomore year, as she has continued to take a full load of general education classes. For example, peers were asked to take notes with carbon paper so that Sue, who cannot write or type fast enough, even with facilitation, would have notes to study. Numerous peers volunteered throughout the year and were very diligent in providing this service. Another example was that peers volunteered to assist Sue in going from one class to another, because she had difficulty getting there on time on her own. These opportunities to connect with peers have facilitated her involvement after school and on weekends with some of the same peers and their friends.

In the beginning, Sue reacted in a very negative way when a general education teacher left the classroom for any reason. For example, one of the special education teachers team-taught the freshman studies classes with a general education teacher. When the special education teacher was responsible for teaching and the general education teacher had to leave the class, Sue would bang her head, scream, and run out of the classroom until he returned. Through a functional analysis (described in Chapter 7), the staff developed a strategy that resulted in the elimination of this reaction to the teacher leaving the classroom. Before the teacher leaves the classroom, he tells Sue he is leaving and requests that she hold his pen or keys for him until he returns. Once this strategy became effective for this teacher, it was shared with all her other teachers and used successfully in other classes.

As part of Sue's empowerment gained with the provision of facilitation and inclusion, she is an active participant in the design of her IEP. Figure 3 lists her IEP objectives from her past (sophomore year). An interesting feature of Sue's IEP is that her objectives are stated in first-person rather than the usual third-

---

Sue Rubin's IEP Objectives

1. I will self-regulate my impulsive behaviors by labeling my emotions through facilitation and a keyboard or phrase board, and generate and employ appropriate problem-solving strategies, 9 out of 10 occurrences for 5 consecutive days.

2. With the use of facilitation, I will type out messages for my parents and teachers to which they do not know the answer, 10 consecutive times.

3. I will self-regulate my reactions to changes (including my brother Gary's departure to college) by demonstrating attendance and self-control in all my classes for 10 consecutive days.

4. I will maintain eye contact with the keyboard while typing, 19 out of 20 occurrences for 5 consecutive days.

5. I will continue to type with fluency and use complex language concepts, while my facilitator fades his or her support to my forearm 5 out of 6 consecutive occurrences within 4 days.

6. I will initiate conversation with others by approaching them with my Franklin Spelling Ace, 8 times a day for 10 consecutive days.

7. I will maintain conversation taking 3 or more turns in group discussions, 4 times a day for 10 consecutive days.

8. I will be an active member of class discussions by initiating responses, 5 times a day for 10 consecutive days.

9. I will participate in a peer support group once a week by indicating my needs and generating strategies for connecting with my peers for 5 consecutive weeks.

10. I will increase my skills at taking public transportation home from school with 4 of my peers, but without their assistance, for 10 consecutive days.

Figure 3.   IEP objectives developed for Sue Rubin, with her participation, with use of first-person pronouns.

Name: Sue Rubin   Grade/age: Sophomore/15   School year: 1993–1994

IEP Objectives	World civics	Geometry	English	Physical education	Biology	Counseling	Lunch nutrition	Assemblies	Club meetings	Passing periods	Peer support groups	After school
1. Self-regulate impulsive behaviors	X	X	X	X	X	X	X	X	X	X	X	X
2. Type out a message					X					X		
3. Self-regulate to changes	X	X	X	X	X	X	X	X	X	X	X	X
4. Eye contact with keyboard	X	X	X		X	X	X	X	X	X		
5. Type while fading support	X	X	X		X							
6. Initiate conversation	X	X	X	X	X	X	X	X				
7. Maintain conversation	X	X	X	X	X	X	X	X				
8. Active member of class discussions	X	X	X	X	X							
9. Participate in a peer support group											X	
10. Public transportation skills												X

Figure 4.   Sample matrix and schedule of Sue's IEP objectives.

person pronouns. This was a collaborative decision between Sue, her parents, and her teachers to emphasize her substantial contributions to the creation of her objectives as well as her commitment to meeting those objectives. In addition, in order to ensure that all of Sue's objectives on her IEP are systematically taught throughout the school day, a matrix demonstrating the relationship between her schedule and her IEP objectives was developed. A copy of this matrix is contained in Figure 4. Sue's own communications showed tremendous gratitude for the new respect she received from others and for her own "awakening."

SUMMARY

This chapter has discussed some of the essential secondary school restructuring efforts and described how the inclusion of students with disabilities plays an integral part in such restructuring efforts. In addition, strategies for preparing students for adult lifestyles were discussed. Finally, strategies specific to assessment, curriculum, and instructional arrangements were delineated.

Secondary schools must provide a curriculum and set of instructional opportunities such that all students learn the essential skills to live productively, act in socially responsible ways, and work towards the fulfillment of their dreams. A large number of secondary schools have already embarked on the necessary restructuring activities to create such a reality. All secondary school staffs should seriously consider such restructuring efforts.

REFERENCES

Americans with Disabilities Act of 1990 (ADA), PL 101-336. (July 26, 1990). Title 42, U.S.C. 12101 et seq: *U.S. Statutes at Large*, *104*, 327 378.

Black, S. (1993, December). Real life 101. *Executive Educator,* 24–27.

Boyer, E.L. (1983). *High school: A report on secondary education in America.* New York: Harper & Row.

Conat, J.B. (1959). *The American high school today.* New York: McGraw-Hill.

Cushman, K. (1990). Practice into theory: Teachers coaching teachers. *Horace, 7*(2), 1–8.

Darling-Hammond, L. (1991, November). The implications of testing policy for quality and equality. *Phi Delta Kappan,* 220–224.

Education for All Handicapped Children Act of 1975, PL 94-142. (August 23, 1977). Title 20, U.S.C. 1400 et seq: *U.S. Statutes at Large, 89*, 773–796.

Falvey, M.A. (1989). *Community-based curriculum: Instructional strategies for students with severe handicaps* (2nd ed.). Baltimore: Paul H. Brookes Publishing Co.

Glickman, C. (1991). Pretending not to know what we know. *Educational Leadership, 48*(8), 4–10.

Goodlad, J.I. (1984). *A place called school.* New York: McGraw-Hill.

Gutek, G.L. (1992). *Education and schooling in America* (3rd ed.). Newton, MA: Allyn & Bacon.

Individuals with Disabilities Education Act of 1990 (IDEA), PL 101-476. (October 30, 1990). Title 20, U.S.C. 1400 et seq: *U.S. Statutes at Large, 104*, 1103–1151.

Kovalik, S. (1993). *Integrated thematic instruction: The model* (2nd ed.). Oak Creek, AZ: Books for Educators.

Kozol, J. (1991). *Savage inequalities.* New York: Harper Perennial.

Oakes, J. (1985). *Keeping track: How schools structure inequality.* New Haven, CT: Yale University Press.

Paul, R. (1990). *Critical thinking: What every person needs to survive in a rapidly changing world.* Rohnart Park, CA: Center for Critical Thinking and Moral Critique.

Podl, J., & Metzger, M. (1992). Anatomy of an exhibition. *In Coalition of Essential Schools.* Providence, RI: Brown University.

Porter, A. (1989, June/July). A curriculum out of balance: The case of elementary school mathematics. *Educational Researcher,* 9–15.

Report of the Committee on Secondary School Studies. (1893). Washington, DC: United States Government Printing Office.

Sailor, W., Anderson, J.L., Halverson, A.T., Doering, K., Filler, J., & Goetz, L. (1989). *The comprehensive local school: Regular education for all students with disabilities.* Baltimore: Paul H. Brookes Publishing Co.

Schlechty, P.S. (1990). *Schools for the 21st century.* San Francisco: Jossey-Bass.

School-to-Work Opportunities Act, PL 103-239. (May 4, 1994). Title 20, U.S.C. 6101 et seq: *U.S. Statutes at Large, 108,* 568–608.

Sizer, T.R. (1984). *Horace's compromise: The dilemma of the American high school* Boston: Houghton Mifflin.

Sizer, T.R. (1989). Diverse practice, shared ideas: The essential school. In *Organizing for learning: Toward the 21st century.* Reston, VA: The National Association of Secondary School Principals.

Sizer, T.R. (1991). No pain, no gain. *Educational Leadership, 48*(8), 32–34.

Sizer, T.R. (1992). *Horace's school: Redesigning the American high school.* Boston: Houghton Mifflin.

Solomon, D., Schaps, E., Watson, M., & Battistich, V. (1992). Creating caring school and classroom communities for all students. In R.A. Villa, J.S. Thousand, W. Stainback, & S. Stainback (Eds.), *Restructuring for caring and effective education: An administrative guide to creating heterogeneous schools* (pp. 41–60). Baltimore: Paul H. Brookes Publishing Co.

Tashie, C., & Schuh, M. (1993, Spring). Why not community-based instruction?: High school students belong with their peers. *Equity and Excellence,* p. 15–17.

Weiss, A. (1988, June). *Restructuring schools.* Presentation to the Annual Georgia Leadership Institute, Athens, Georgia.

Wiles, J., & Bondi, J. (1989). *Curriculum development: A guide to practice* (3rd ed.). Columbus, OH: Charles E. Merrill.

14 POSTSECONDARY CONSIDERATIONS

Kathryn D. Bishop, Sandra L. Amate, and Pamela J. Villalobos

With enactment of the Individuals with Disabilities Education Act (IDEA) (PL 101-476), the development of augmentative communication and other adaptive technology, emphasis on positive behavior supports, and increased opportunity for full inclusion, education for students with severe disabilities has improved dramatically. Similarly, with implementation of the Rehabilitation Act Amendments of 1986 (PL 99-506) and the Americans with Disabilities Act (PL 101-336), subsequent improvements in transition services, supported employment, and supported living options have increased the quality-of-life potential for adults with severe disabilities.

As students with and without disabilities are expanding their opportunities to learn and play together, adults with and without disabilities are expanding their opportunities to live and work together. The general community has begun to have an important role in the lives of adults with disabilities, who are no longer limited to segregated activities in sheltered workshops, group homes, and Special Olympics. The concepts of full and partial participation, adaptation and accommodation, self-advocacy, and choice making reinforce the rights of adults with significant disabilities to live their lives in a manner that is culturally valued and productive for both the individual and the community. This chapter identifies and discusses some of the critical components that must be addressed by educators and other service providers in an attempt to support that lifestyle. Although school personnel may not be directly responsible for providing services to students beyond a certain age, it is their responsibility to educate parents about their child's options and to advocate for and empower individuals in developing future plans.

TRANSITION SERVICES

Facilitating the transition from school-age community life to adult community life for persons with disabilities has been increasingly recognized as an important role for school and support personnel since the passage of IDEA. Assisting with the transition into adult lifestyles for persons with severe disabilities requires comprehensive planning. A range of supports that allow individuals to live and participate fully as community members must be available. The following sections look at the need for transition services, the locus of service delivery, and appropriate methodology.

The Need for Transition Services

Data gathered in one school district (Madison Metropolitan) a few years after passage of the Education for All Handicapped Children Act (PL 94-142) indicated that although the quality of school-age services was improving, the actual impact on postgraduation lifestyles was negligible (Van Deventer et al., 1981). This study reviewed the lifestyles of 53 individuals with severe disabilities who completed their special education program in the Madison schools. Of these graduates, only one worked in a nonsheltered vocational environment. Forty-nine graduates attended segregated sheltered workshops or day activity centers, and three persons had no employment or day program involvement at all. Of those 49 individuals participating in sheltered settings, almost all were underachieving socially, emotionally, and vocationally.

Such local-level evidence of the critical role transition planning could play was supported at the national level by then Assistant Secretary of Education, Office of Special Education and Rehabilitative Services, Madeleine Will, in a 1983 speech stressing that the efforts by school personnel must not be "rendered futile by the failure of the vital transition process" (Will, 1983). Another vocational follow-up study in Madison, reviewing the status of 32 students with severe disabilities who left school in 1984, supported Will's assertions. These students received transition services, and 29 of 32 were functioning in integrated work settings with support (Brown et al., 1986).

Despite recognition of the need for transition and adult services, progress in their provision has been slow. In a 1992 review of the research on "post-21" outcome studies for people with disabilities, Peraino estimated an unemployment rate of 80% for young adults with moderate, severe, and profound mental retardation. Peraino (1992) also reported that the only variables that educators can manipulate to effect change are vocational education and training, graduation status, and social and interpersonal skills. Although not established as such, independent living skills training also appears to have substantial positive impact on individual lives (Peraino, 1992).

On a more positive note, a Harris poll (American Association on Mental Retardation, 1992) indicates that the attitudes of Americans are more open than ever to involving individuals with disabilities in all aspects of community life, including employment in local businesses. Given the legal mandates mentioned above and this social atmosphere, individuals, their families, and the network of service providers should be able to facilitate inclusive and meaningful lifestyles for adults with disabilities. The challenge is to work together to obtain and maintain the opportunities and supports that make such lifestyles realities.

Quality-of-life issues for adults with severe disabilities have tended to be addressed in terms of success in vocational settings (Albin, 1992; Kerachsky & Thornton, 1987; Wehman, Kregel, Barcus, & Schalock, 1986). The vocational arena is undoubtedly essential in an adult's life, but it must not be viewed as the only critical arena in life. Being productive in a daily work setting can assist the individual in developing a quality adult lifestyle; however, productivity itself will not ensure such a lifestyle. Inclusion and active participation with peers without disabilities must exist throughout all aspects of life.

Locus of Service Delivery

Transition services are intended to serve students who are in their last years of school-age eligibility, typically throughout their teenage years and into adulthood. Many times students with severe disabilities entitled to these services are 19–22 years old. Unfortunately, these services continue to be operated from high school or segregated school campuses. The principles of normalization, full inclusion, and chronological age appropriateness reinforce the inappropriateness of these settings: there are no same-age peers without disabilities on a high school or segregated school campus, nor are the experiences and opportunities afforded on those school campuses appropriate for the inclusion of 19- to 22-year-olds. Transition services should instead be provided from an office on an adult school campus, a community college campus, a 4-year college campus, or even a store front in the local business district. These settings provide for opportunities and experiences with other young adults in the general community and help disassociate young adults with disabilities from the notions of perpetual childhood, continual readiness services, and "prerequisite-to-life" training.

Whereas preschool, elementary, and secondary school-age services provide basic skill instruction and experience for furthering growth and development, transition services focus on skill acquisition and educational and vocational experiences leading to full participation as an adult in the community. Careful planning and cooperation among school and adult services agencies, as well as attention to where these services are based, are necessary.

Interagency Collaboration and Core Teams

A vital characteristic of transition programming is an interagency approach (Powell et al., 1991; Wehman, 1992). Parents, special and general education support personnel, and agencies concerned with vocational education, colleges and universities, rehabilitation, and developmental disabilities must work together to build the transition framework. Needed support services and/or resources must be identified and procured. The interagency model is one way to ensure a wide range of input for this process. Furthermore, the development of a core team in decision making is central to good transition planning. Each team member brings valuable perspectives and can provide insight to program development. Proper planning can prevent implementation difficulties that may threaten program success. (Specific strategies for collaboration are delineated in Chapter 3 of this volume.)

Coordination and collaboration between school and adult services providers have been bolstered by the Carl D. Perkins Vocational and Applied Technology Education Act (PL 101-392), the Rehabilitation Act Amendments of 1986 (PL 99-506) and of 1992 (PL 102-569), and IDEA (PL 101-476). These legislative acts encourage defined roles and shared responsibilities among school and adult services providers. Frequent person-to-person interactions between the different service providers is also beneficial. Wehman (1992) identifies the activities of the local interagency collaborative team:

1. To establish a reason for its existence (i.e., to improve and coordinate the provision of services for youth making the transition from school to adult community living);
2. To delineate the goals of the transition planning team, which include completing a local level needs assessment and writing an interagency agreement;
3. To list and ranking by priority the activities that will enable the team to accomplish its goals;
4. To divide the list of activities and assign persons or work groups to be responsible for completion of activities; and
5. To establish deadlines for completion of all activities. (p. 123)

Entering into general interagency agreements for transition services provides a foundation for the creation of effective transition plans and activities for individual students. For example, an agreement may be reached that school district personnel will be responsible for job development and initial on-the-job support. Another agreement may be made that a specific supported employment adult agency will step in and continue support during the last 6 months of school eligibility. By planning for each particular individual, considerations like these can be taken into account and appropriate support decisions made. Without interagency agreements, individuals may have no support or inappropriate support for several months while completing the adult services agency's "intake" procedures.

Interagency collaboration teams are also valuable in determining what types of changes are needed in the community to provide the most appropriate services for people with disabilities. Teamwork brings the "strength in numbers" notion into practice. Presenting collaborative fronts and combining efforts across agencies signals consensus for change in a community. For example, in one community, an agreed-upon change in public bus routes not only accommodated people with disabilities who were entering the work force from their neighborhood homes instead of the downtown workshop but also improved service to those without disabilities. In another community, curb cuts and traffic lights with auditory signals were installed in a short period of time. Although many such services are mandated by law, collaborative advocacy efforts can speed up the process and help identify needed changes as priorities.

After general interagency agreements and roles are defined and the overall transition programming format is in place, individual students can be considered and core teams (or circles of support) developed. Team composition varies; members should be chosen by the individual him- or herself and/or should be those people most likely to advocate for the student. Typically, core team members include the individual, one or both parents (or residential support person), friends, siblings, neighbors, employers, co-workers, special and general education support personnel, representatives from selected adult services agencies, and the social services case manager.

These people will all play key roles in core team meetings, which are run similarly to the MAPS process or futures planning meeting discussed in Chapter 4. At these meetings, members identify the goals and dreams of the student, the skills and opportunities he or she will need in order to meet those goals, the perceived systemic or other barriers to meeting those goals, strategies for addressing those barriers, identification of other key players, and action plans with clearly identified responsibilities and timelines. These meetings should address immediate needs but will predominantly focus on the future needs and lifestyle of the student as an adult in the community. Bates (1989) defines these planning meetings as outcomes-oriented processes that should be highly individualized in nature.

Individualized Transition Plans

One documented result of these planning meetings may be an individualized transition plan (ITP). As mandated in IDEA, the ITP is developed along with the IEP when the student turns 16 (or, in some states, 14) and enters a transition program. IEPs should reflect all areas of the person's life (e.g., vocational, residential, recreation/leisure, social/interpersonal, mobility); be focused on inclusive community, work, and living settings; and encompass goals reflecting activities relevant to maximal participation in adult life. The ITP is used to facilitate and encourage the support and involvement of students, friends, parents, employers, co-workers, postsecondary agencies (rehabilitation counselor, social services case manager, supported employment service agency, supported living agency), and other community members (e.g., community recreation representatives). Figure 1 provides a sample ITP format.

The purposes of an ITP are to anticipate an individual's needs upon graduation and to determine who will provide the support necessary to help meet those needs. The ITP team, as described above, participates in long-range planning,

**Parent Survey of Student's
Use of Time Outside of School**

*Please answer the following questions, regarding your son's/daughter's
use of spare time, to the best of your knowledge. Please consider what
your son/daughter does independently.*

I. **Domestic skills**
1. Does his/her own/other's laundry _____ x per week
2. Cooks meals for self/others _____ x per week
3. Bathes/showers independently _____ x per week
4. Cares for other hygiene needs (e.g., shaving, makeup) _____ x per week
5. Selects own clothes from closet _____ x per week
6. Cleans own room/other rooms of house _____ x per week

Examples of domestic activities: _____
_____
_____

II. **Recreation/leisure activities**
1. Participates in activities with family away from home _____ x per week
2. Participates in activities without family away from home _____ x per week
3. Participates in activities or hobbies at home other than watching television (e.g., sewing, shooting baskets, gardening) _____ x per week
4. Participates in "handicapped only" events _____ x per week
5. Participates in events with nonhandicapped peers _____ x per week

Examples of leisure/recreation activities: _____
_____
_____

III. **Mobility skills**
1. Walks to places independently _____ x per week
2. Walks to places with family _____ x per week
3. Walks to places with friends (peers) _____ x per week
4. Rides bicycle outside of yard _____ x per week
5. Uses public transportation independently _____ x per week
6. Uses public transportation with family _____ x per week
7. Uses public transportation with friends _____ x per week
8. Is driven by family or friend _____ x per week
9. Uses private transportation (e.g., taxi, Dial-A-Ride, school bus) _____ x per week

IV. **Consumer skills**
1. Does grocery shopping _____ x per week
2. Selects and purchases own clothes _____ x per week
3. Goes to restaurants (independently or with friend/peer) _____ x per week

(continued)

Figure 1.   Sample format for an individualized transition plan (ITP).

**Parent Survey of Student's
Use of Time Outside of School**
(continued)

4. Buys own bus pass ___ x per week

5. Pays bills ___ x per week

6. Utilizes a bank ___ x per week

7. Plans and prepares for leisure activities (e.g., calls theatre for show times, registers for classes) ___ x per week

V. **Vocational skills**

1. Participates in nonpaid jobs outside of school and home ___ x per week

2. Receives pay for work done outside of school time.
Specify amount earned. $___ per week

VI. **General Community**

1. Based on your experiences with your son/daughter, how do you think he/she would respond if approached by a police officer (e.g., run away, speak out, refuse to talk) _____

_____

_____

2. Can your son/daughter tell the difference between a friend and a stranger?

_____

_____

determining when to enter into contractual agreements with specified agencies. The team members' involvement and shared responsibility during the transition program will develop a broader and more solid foundation for activities and support after graduation. The ITP can be a separate document from the IEP; however, the ITP can also be one specific outcome of the IEP, linking appropriate adult agency supports(s) to the IEP. The most essential characteristic of the ITP is that all decisions reflect the student's preferences and desires, as well as those of the family, school, and supporting agencies.

School district personnel in the role of the transition teacher can support the efficiency and effectiveness of the transition core team meetings by preparing ahead of time. Assessments related to the skills, interests, and desires of the student will help team members gain an understanding of the student's strengths, needs, and personal goals. Meeting with parents can reinforce that information and provide an accurate account of their own desires, fears, and ability to provide support in the future. Visiting the sites in the community where the individual works and spends free time, if done unobtrusively, will also provide valuable information. Again, establishing general agreements with nonschool agencies as a foundation of the transition program will make individual plans and requests much easier to accommodate.

ITP Structure and Transition Activities

The structure and activities of a transition program are developed in accordance with the needs of the individuals being served, as identified through the IEP/ITP. Some service providers attempt to develop a structure and then battle to force students with disabilities to fit into that structure. More successful service providers assess the needs of the student and then develop a program of support to address those needs. Wehman, Kregel, and Barcus (1985) state that there are three fundamental characteristics of services that are critical for successful transition. These characteristics are integrated schools, community-based services and instruction, and functional curricula addressing individual needs. The least successful services consist of segregated service delivery with classroom-only instruction and a developmental curriculum.

Because most school-funded transition services must operate within the parameters of school services (e.g., number of hours per day, staff–student ratio), each student's activities must be carefully planned to ensure comprehensive services. Comprehensive services also include systematic instruction and active participation leading to skill acquisition in all lifestyle domains. Independence, or at least increased participation and support gained in any or all of these areas, leads to less responsibility and supervision on the part of parents, siblings, and other members of the community. In addition, the student will have increased opportunities and a more meaningful adult life whether he or she becomes independent or remains interdependent in the community.

There are certain standards that must be reflected in instruction across the curriculum of comprehensive transition services. Following is a list of those standards essential to the implementation of successful transition services:

1. *Chronological age appropriate*   Skills, activities, and environments must reflect those typical for peers without disabilities of the same chronological age.
2. *Functional/critical skills*   These include skills or activities that are required or expected of peers without disabilities. They are essential to the student's performance and participation in a variety of community environments.
3. *Cultural/linguistic sensitivity*   Activities must reflect on awareness and appreciation of the skills, values, customs, and heritage that are important in the individual's cultural/linguistic/religious background.
4. *Natural environments*   Teaching and participation in activities should take place in environments where they would naturally occur (as opposed to pretend grocery stores, for example).
5. *Zero inferences*   Once a student has acquired a skill, inferences would not be made concerning the student's performance of similar skills at a different time or in a different environment. Instruction must occur across a variety of natural environments, persons, cues, and materials, instead of inferring generalization.

6. *Physical and social integration*   Instruction and participation should include
   a. Presence of same-age peers without disabilities
   b. Ongoing interactions with peers without disabilities in natural environments
   c. A ratio of people with and without disabilities that reflects natural proportions
   d. Equal access to community facilities
   e. Qualified, appropriate personnel to provide the necessary training and support
7. *Student preferences*   Activities and curricula must emphasize student preferences and ongoing choice-making opportunities. Although all students may not be able to communicate preferences verbally, teachers and parents must work together to ascertain such preferences (e.g., examining behavior patterns, affect, eye contact, attention span, and attendance).

The activities that transition services provide for students differ based on the individual student, in terms of both type of activity and frequency of opportunity for instruction and engagement in that activity. Activities that reflect student needs and interests should be addressed in natural, inclusive environments. Typical transition services focus primarily on the student's employment opportunities. Although nonpaid work experiences may be of some value to younger students, students in transition are entitled to benefit from paid employment opportunities. Providing supported employment services has become an integral part of transition services for students with significant disabilities (supported employment is discussed in greater detail later in this chapter).

In addition to employment, recreation/leisure skills and opportunities are addressed in the ITP. Skills in this area encompass activities in which students can become involved within their own home (hobbies, cards, reading, model building, and so forth) as well as in the community either on their own or with assistance (e.g., community recreation department classes, YMCA, health club, social organizations, church groups). Because some of these experiences may involve activities that occur outside of the program time, the core team will need to address ways to support continued inclusion in these activities with creative staff assignments.

Independent living skills promote increased participation in the individual's family home with the goal of facilitating skills that will enable the student to move into supported or independent living as an adult. These activities range from basic cooking, cleaning, and laundry to budgeting, safety, and monitoring one's own health.

Transportation and mobility issues continue to be one of the greatest challenges for adults with disabilities. Support persons are constantly trying to be creative in terms of meeting transportation needs. Public transportation is expected to improve through the mandates of the Americans with Disabilities Act; however, such improvements appear slow in coming and will not solve many of the existing needs. Carpool membership (where, for example, the student contributes by paying for gas or by occasionally bringing donuts); relying on friends, family, and co-workers; walking; bicycling; or three-wheeling are all options that have been utilized in the past to deal with this major area of need.

Community access skills are also incorporated into transition services. Teaching students to use shopping areas, restaurants, public service agencies, medical offices, recreation areas, and so forth are all means of ensuring an active adult lifestyle. The instruction in transition services must focus not only on selection of activities in a variety of community environments but also on how, why, and when to use them. The intent is to facilitate the student's use of these environments independently or with the natural supports that are available to all community members.

Finally, transition services address needs in the areas of self-advocacy, social/sexual development and relationships, and further education. These areas are addressed later in this chapter.

Individual Schedules

Perhaps the most difficult aspect of implementing a transition program is arranging individual schedules to ensure that each student receives instruction that reflects the comprehensive curriculum. Because transition services are most often implemented for school-age students, programming will likely be limited to a typical period of a 6-hour school day. Within that period of time, or across different days of the week, students must be assured opportunities to gain skills and have access to the IEP/ITP-specified activities and environments.

Specific scheduling needs are accommodated by careful examination of staff ratios, transportation availability, natural supports in each environment, the needs of the student, and the exact location of other students needing similar support. Schedules will vary from student to student based on the amount of time they need to spend receiving support and instruction in any particular area. In addition, student schedules will change over time as an individual needs less support in certain areas and more in others. For example, as a student becomes more skilled and secure at a range of recreational activities, he or she will likely increase the amount of time spent in employment. In this case, the student's recreation needs have become less critical than employment needs during the program day. As students near the end of their transition program years, it is hoped that they will be building endurance in their employment setting by increasing the number of hours worked per day, while other areas of their life are addressed through natural supports outside of school time. In some situations, a student may be working full time but have no activities outside of work. This student's support will be focused on nonvocational areas. An extended day of paid support, if necessary, might be accomplished with the assistance of school or other agency staff, parents, or employers. Ideally, many of the activities will be continued through natural supports, such as co-workers, teammates, classmates, friends, and so forth.

Quality Indicators for Effective Transition Services

In order to determine the effectiveness of the program, in general, there are several factors to consider. If the program goal is to develop an individual's lifestyle, activities performed outside of programmed time must be considered (i.e., time not scheduled by school/agency personnel). It is no longer sufficient to consider only the activities of a person within school/work hours. To assess a student's total lifestyle, it is essential to receive information from the student and his or her parents or primary caregiver. Figure 2 is an example of an inventory of a student's use of time outside of service provider hours. Such information can be gathered several times annually to determine progress, changes, and continuing needs of the student.

In addition to specific student outcomes, the quality of transition services can be evaluated by determining the comprehensiveness of the services provided. A quality indicator checklist is a quick method of determining whether or not basic program components are in place and appropriate techniques are being utilized. Table 1 provides examples of quality indicator components.

Once a program has been reviewed for each of these components, continued evaluation is necessary. This can be accomplished by asking for feedback from parents, community members (employers), outside agencies (rehabilitation, state funding agency, and so forth), and students regarding their experiences with and reaction to the services. Each of these constituency groups is essentially a customer of the transition services and will be able to provide valuable information. In this manner, new relationships and partnerships may be established to provide further opportunities for current and future students.

ISSUES OF ADULTHOOD

This section of the chapter deals with issues relevant to adults at all stages, whether they are receiving transition services or support from adult services providers. Educators should have an understanding of the possibilities and limitations of services offered in their community. By knowing the individual students and what is possible in the adult services world, educators can advocate with students and families for assuring appropriate services and options. Without an awareness of community offerings, many young adults might move into adult services in restrictive environments or with limited activities.

Agency issues, family issues, and individual issues all have a number of topics to be addressed. Each of these topics could easily be entire books themselves, and the reader is advised to pursue further information on the specific topics of interest or need.

Individualized Transition Plan

I. Student Information

Name	Address	School
Social Security Number		Date of birth
Guardianship Name		Address
Persons in attendance		

II. Performance profile

Area	Strengths	Needs	Interests
Academic			
Domestic			
Home and community management			
Vocational			
Recreation/ leisure			
Communication			
Other functional skills			

Figure 2. Example of a parent (or primary caregiver) inventory used to account for time spent outside of program hours.

Area	Projected needs	Goal/activity recommendations	Service provider	Projected timeline	Date action taken	Outcome
Academic						
Domestic						
Home and community management						
Vocational						
Communication						
Other functional skills						
Transportation						
Employment						
Community living options						
Financial, insurance, medical						
Other						

(continued)

375

Figure 2. *(continued)*

We the undersigned have participated in the development of _____'s Individualized Transition Plan and agree to carry out the recommendations specified within.

Family / guardian representatives:

Student:

_____
Parent / Date

_____
Student / Date

Careprovider representatives:

_____
Title / Date

_____
Title / Date

School representatives:

_____
Title / Date

_____
Title / Date

_____
Title / Date

_____
Title / Date

_____
Title / Date

_____
Title / Date

Adult service providers/funding agencies:

_____
Title / Date

_____
Title / Date

_____
Title / Date

_____
Title / Date

_____
Title / Date

Community support representatives:

_____
Employer / Date

_____
Recreation / leisure / Date

_____
Other / Date

Table 1. Quality indicators for transition services

- ITP features include
  Student involvement
  Parent involvement
  Funding agency involvement
  Adult services provider involvement (supported living and employment)
  Goals targeted to future environments
  Delineated responsibilities and timelines
- Student's schedules incorporate all life skills areas.
- Frequent and ongoing interaction occurs daily with peers without disabilities.
- Initial assessment includes
  Person-centered planning
  Student interests
  Parent/guardian inventory
  Ecological inventories in all life skills areas
  Student repertoire inventories
  (see Chapter 4 for more specific assessment information)
- Objectives and instruction are based on data collected regularly and systematically.
- Individual instructional strategies are utilized.
- Least intrusive instructional strategies are implemented.
- Positive behavior support plans are in place if necessary.
- Decisions are based upon data that are regularly collected and reviewed.
- Each student has a method of communication.
- Administrative policies are in place, for example:
  Emergency procedures
  Work experience regulations and staffing requirements
  Funding support
- Interagency agreements have been completed and are implemented.
- Regular meetings are scheduled and attended by the core team.
- Paid and volunteer staff have received adequate training for assigned tasks.
- Sites and services are available to and utilized by persons of appropriate chronological ages without disabilities.

Agency Issues

Adult services, like education services, should include support across a range of domains. This section highlights supported employment, living arrangements, and staff considerations. However, agencies will need to consider providing support as necessary in recreation and leisure activities and in developing and maintaining relationships.

Supported Employment Employment is often a requisite status of acceptance of adults in contemporary societies. If individuals are excluded from participation in the work of a society and from completion of contributory tasks, they cannot be free from economic dependence on family or governmental subsistence. Consequently, if individuals with severe disabilities are unskilled and inexperienced in meaningful work, they cannot escape their readily sanctioned, segregated existence. Work that is carefully chosen and creatively structured to match an individual is essential to personal growth and will result in fewer institutional needs and dependencies.

Adults with significant disabilities have historically been provided with a variety of "day program" options. However, those options were generally available in restrictive, sheltered, or segregated settings (Falvey, Bishop, & Terry Gage, 1992). These settings (adult development centers, work activity centers, and sheltered workshops) were developed as a continuum of sheltered training services that individuals would "flow through" before moving into competitive employment (Bellamy, Rhodes, Bourbeau, & Mank, 1986). The continuum usually began at age 21, after services from public schools were discontinued. In the continuum, according to Bellamy (1983), the average length of stay per individual is 37 years for developmental centers, 10 years for work activity centers, and 9 years for sheltered workshops. Therefore, if a person started in the adult development center and matriculated through the continuum, he or she would be 77 years old before being eligible for paid employment in a typical community setting accessed by employees without disabilities. In other words, the continuum prohibits thousands of individuals from inclusive employment opportunities.

In 1985, the Office of Special Education and Rehabilitative Services issued a supported employment initiative indicating that supported employment should be the primary service option for adults with mental retardation. The problems inherent in the continuum of adult services and the continued high rate of unemployment or underemployment for persons with disabilities led to the implementation of a supported employment service delivery option. Conceptually, supported employment avoids the trappings of continuums and prerequisite skills. Supported employment services allow individuals, regardless of the severity of their disability, to be supported in obtaining and maintaining paid employment in the community.

Supported employment is an outcomes-oriented service delivery model. Supported employment focuses on the following outcomes in its definition (Federal Register, 1984):

Involves paid, meaningful work (i.e., work that others would be paid to do)
Features work performed in integrated settings (i.e., settings that approximate natural proportions of employees with and without disabilities)
Includes a place-and-train approach (i.e., elimination of ineffective prevocational training services)
Is appropriate for individuals who need ongoing support, not in a time-limited manner (i.e., a zero-reject service)

Employment needs are common to people regardless of whether or not they have a disability (Powell et al., 1991). These needs include a career, paid employment, opportunities for career advancement, benefits, security, training opportunities, fair bosses, friendly co-workers, safe working conditions, and a reasonable commute. For people with disabilities the following needs can be added: competent supporters, advocates, on-the-job support services, and work-related support services (e.g., assistance with other aspects of their lives that may indirectly affect their employment situation) (Powell et al., 1991). Given a clear understanding of these needs, employment service providers can move forward in their attempts to provide quality supported employment opportunities.

Belief that supported employment is a viable option is the first step toward delivery of successful services. Service providers must place a strong value on inclusion and meaningful work, or the logistical challenges of involving people with the most severe disabilities will be perceived as insurmountable barriers. Without the philosophical value base, most efforts will be rendered futile. If service providers value the concept, however, accepting and creatively working through the logistical challenges becomes the motivation, excitement, and reward.

Supported employment may be offered through a number of models, depending on a person's needs. Individual placement, that is, placing and supporting a single individual with significant disabilities in a particular employment site, allows the greatest individualization, inclusion, and independence (Bishop, 1991). Small-group placements (3–4 people with disabilities) and mobile crews are viable options that allow more on-the-job supervision but may inhibit maximal interaction opportunities with peers without disabilities. Furthermore, individuals placed in a group setting may be restricted in their productivity because of the need to save enough work for other group members (Bishop, 1991). Affirmative industry is an option that may prove successful in rural areas or in areas of high unemployment. This model introduces to a community a needed business that happens to employ a small number of people with disabilities and a greater number of people without disabilities. The business is developed and maintained by an agency or organization funded to provide services to adults with disabilities. The community benefits from the new business and from increased employment opportunities for all.

Regardless of the type of supported employment model implemented, several key components are needed. Each component is a necessary mechanism for providing supported employment services. It is important to note, however, that the components do not occur in a linear sequence and frequently overlap in implementation. A description of each component follows.

Marketing and Job Development Promoting supported employment in the community and developing jobs with specific employers require a shift in perspective on the part of service providers. As opposed to a more typical human services style, staff need to assume businesslike approaches in their efforts to institute supported employment. This marketing of the model requires creating, promoting, funding, and distributing services that accommodate the needs of the employment community as well as the needs of the consumers who have disabilities.

While marketing introduces and promotes the concept, job development is the process of actually securing specific jobs that can be matched with individuals seeking employment. Most development techniques are those commonly associated with acquiring jobs, such as making telephone calls, following newspaper ads, using personal connections, attending service club meetings, utilizing employment placement services, and canvassing door to door. Supported employment job development differs from job development in regular placement agencies in the concept of *job carving*. Typically, job developers seek positions that are being advertised or have existing standard job descriptions. For persons with severe disabilities, job development sometimes requires studying existing jobs and businesses and then creating (or developing) jobs that are not currently in existence or that are not currently an intact position. This notion of job carving is the "process of breaking jobs down into their key components and reassigning those pieces in more efficient or understandable ways" (Griffin & Sherron, 1992, p. 198). This is not to say that unnecessary or artificial jobs are created. By actually studying the business, a good job developer may see more efficient and effective ways to distribute responsibilities among personnel.

Job Match   The process of pairing an individual with a specific job is called *job match*. Creating a successful job match involves careful individual assessment and analysis of job-site requirements. The information gathered for the job match focuses not on task-specific skills but on job-related factors that can truly influence job success. The reason for not focusing on task-specific behaviors is two-fold. First, the fields of special education and rehabilitation have developed sophisticated instructional and training strategies that enable individuals with significant disabilities to complete complex tasks (Snell, 1993; Wolery, Ault, & Doyle, 1992). Second, research by Gaston (1988) and Greenspan and Schoultz (1981) has demonstrated that individuals with severe disabilities lose their jobs not because of poor task performance but more often because of factors related to social skills such as interactions with co-workers and customers or responding to directions from supervisors. Therefore, job match considers personality, setting preferences, and other psychosocial issues.

Job Retention Support   Training for the new employee at the job site can be achieved by either using a job retention specialist (provided by the transition/adult services agency) or relying on natural supports (i.e., an existing employee in the workplace) (Nisbet & Hagner, 1988). In addition to providing intensive instruction on specific job tasks, the job retention specialist may also need to provide support in work-related functions such as clocking in and out, leaving and returning from breaks on time, and, perhaps most important, facilitating relationships with co-workers.

Technology   In addition to, or in place of, assistance from personnel, individuals with disabilities can receive support through the use of assistive technology. Assistive technology allows some individuals to participate more fully in a greater range of tasks, have more control over their own lives, and interact more effectively with others. Assistive technology can range from off-the-shelf, simple devices such as head pointers and computer equipment to highly individualized devices developed to help an individual with a particular task. Plans for using assistive technology include assessing and identifying appropriate equipment, financing the equipment, and teaching use and maintenance of the equipment.

Follow-Up Support   Once an individual has been employed successfully, support personnel must examine the opportunities for career advancement or at least a change in tasks or settings. As with any employee, individuals with disabilities will tire and become bored if not challenged to learn new tasks and to grow professionally and personally. Additional areas of follow-up support may include changes in transportation, inclusion in activities outside of work with co-workers, and support with money management and Supplemental Security Income (SSI) reporting. Once an individual is employed, he or she can be supported to further enhance other aspects of life as well.

Supported employment options for people with disabilities have increased dramatically over the last few years. Positive outcomes for individual employees, employers, co-workers, and families have resulted in an increase in opportunities for meaningful paid employment. Wehman, Kregel, and Revell (1991) surveyed 50 states and found that approximately 20% of all day program service providers intended to convert resources into integrated employment opportunities or at least to offer these opportunities as one component of their services. In addition, the survey determined an increase from 300 to more than 2,600 services that were providing community employment opportunities with support for people with disabilities.

Living Arrangements   Historically, persons with significant disabilities have had a limited set of living options: continue to live with their families into adulthood, or move to congregate living facilities, ranging from 6-person group homes to long-term core facilities of 100-plus residents, convalescent homes, and institutions. Persons with severe disabilities have not had the options available that same-age community members have enjoyed. While family members without disabilities moved into their own homes and established themselves in the community, the family member with a severe disability stayed at home or was "placed" in a segregated facility. Persons with severe disabilities have lived in places governed by rules made by others and regulations designed to protect their interests, but which make an unnatural living environment. Another option, "independent living," provided instruction in skills needed to live in the community. This option was traditionally available only to those that were deemed to have the potential to live independently and focused largely on skills that were considered prerequisites to moving out. The *supported living* model developed in order to normalize the process of establishing a home for everyone, regardless of their current or potential levels of independence.

O'Brien and O'Brien (1991) define supported living as providing people with disabilities with the individualized help they need to live successfully in the living arrangement (place and people) of their choice. The assistance offered by supported living agencies is based on what each individual needs and wants. Targeted areas of support encompass objectives that the individual, friends, family, and agency staff believe will contribute to the individual's quality of life. These may include meeting neighbors, learning to take public transportation, finding a house or apartment, managing an attendant, going to school, or any number of other activities, large or small, that contribute to one's quality of life. Supported living agencies share several commonalities in the way that they deliver services and the population they serve.

Supported living agencies provide services to anyone with the desire to live in his or her own home. They do not discriminate based on the intensity of support needed or a person's perceived readiness skills. A second essential feature of supported living is that the support services are driven by the person who receives the supports. The agency takes direction from the person regarding who will work for him or her, where the individual will live and what form the support takes, and what services are delivered. The supported living agency and the individual continue throughout the relationship to give each other feedback and to work toward goals defined by the individual (O'Brien & O'Brien, 1991).

This collaboration yields a number of different options for the delivery of support. Supported living agencies should always attempt to cultivate natural supports to the greatest extent possible. As in other areas of a person's life, the support that someone receives from people who are not paid has an enhanced normalized quality. The collaboration should weave together a fabric of natural supports, generic community services, and hired support persons to provide all necessary services. The individual plays a key role in all decisions regarding who will be part of his or her support services, including the hiring and firing of employees directly involved with the person through interview and evaluation opportunities. Support persons may be neighbors, roommates, community members, co-workers, and/or live-in or visiting attendants who assist the individual throughout the day.

Staff Considerations   Issues in supporting people with disabilities change across ages. Respect and dignity, critical components of any staff–individual relationship, become important in a different way when the individual is an adult. Empowering individuals to make informed choices while at the same time teaching and supporting them to make responsible choices requires a delicate balance.

The foundation for any staff training is an organization that clearly defines the philosophy, goals, and services that embrace the values of respect and dignity for every person and the right to make choices and decisions about one's life regardless of the severity of the disability. The organization's culture and management of staff must also reflect the same philosophy and values; that is, respect is provided to every staff member, and every staff member feels empowered by the organization. Management interaction style, methods of delegation, directions provided by supervisors, staff inclusion in problem solving, and decision making are all ways that demonstrate that the goal of respecting all community members within an organization can be accomplished.

Some suggestions follow for support staff who work with transition or adult-age individuals. These suggestions are organized into three categories: working with students/adults, working with other community members, and working with other staff members.

Working with students/adults:

- Focus on the individual's positive qualities rather than on limitations.
- View those who are being served as equal adults, as opposed to "kids" in need of our compassion.
- Perceive the staff role as that of service provider or advocate, as opposed to care provider or trainer.
- Individualize services rather than trying to fit people into structured services.
- Involve the student or adult in the decision-making process (e.g., ask what he or she wants and needs; provide choices and respect the individual's choices; allow "no" to be an option).
- Talk with individuals, not about them.
- Assist individuals to demonstrate their competencies in the community.
- Listen more than you talk.
- Assist or facilitate rather than do.
- Facilitate interdependence within the community rather than dependence on a program or service provider.
- Respect people's confidentiality.

Staff working with other community members:

- Communicate about the program by describing the services provided, not the limitations of the people served.
- Redirect attitudes of sympathy or pity into respect for achievement and greater opportunity.
- Maintain natural proportions so that community members perceive each person as an individual rather than members of a labeled group.
- Avoid the use of labels.
- Model the highest level of respect for the persons being served by participating in positive interactions, age-appropriate activities, and dignified communication styles.
- Reduce the visible distinctions between the roles of staff and the persons receiving support.

Staff working with each other:

- Support each other without commiserating negatively about the persons receiving support.
- Respect and reinforce each staff member for abilities, hard work, and contributions.

- Assist each other in developing skills that empower others to become self-advocates.
- Work cooperatively, and provide constructive input and feedback to each other so that all staff can reflect a common philosophy.
- Communicate effectively without betraying confidentiality.

If staff members can value these considerations and incorporate them into their daily existence, people with disabilities can be assured of interactions and support that enhance their dignity. In addition, staff members who treat others with such respect are more likely to gain respect for themselves and to experience greater personal job satisfaction.

Family Issues

Leaving the educational system involves changes that affect families as well as individuals with disabilities (Thorin & Irvin, 1992). The following section highlights some of these changes for families in terms of relationships and bureaucracies.

Changing Relationships   As an adolescent makes the transition into adulthood, parental involvement should evolve into parental support. Typical adolescents demand passage into adulthood that brings with it subtle as well as overt changes in the relationship with their parents. These changes are important for adolescents and young adults with severe disabilities as well. Parents and service providers need to encourage this passage into adulthood by taking on rules that are supportive rather than directive and authoritative. This may mean that the decisions and preferences of the young adult are considered primarily, with parental preferences being considered secondarily. Parental roles and responsibilities change relative to the age of the child, the family's cultural, ethical, and moral values and needs, and the relationships of other family members.

As their child with disabilities grows into adulthood, parents may face other issues, especially the right to grow up, full citizenship, and relationships with and implications for siblings (Turnbull & Turnbull, 1990). The right to grow up challenges parents to "let go," to empower their sons or daughters to have greater control over their own lives and further independence in making choices. Full citizenship requires continued advocacy on the part of parents to ensure not only equal opportunities but equal results in terms of their child's meaningful employment opportunities, housing choices, full community participation, and meaningful or intimate relationships.

Sibling relationships are to be considered as well. Powell and Gallagher (1993) summarize the concerns of brothers and sisters of adults with disabilities as acceptance from their own family, genetics, long-term care or continuing involvement with the sibling with disabilities, and supporting that sibling in leading and enjoying a high quality of life. Educators and service providers should be aware of these needs and be prepared to help families deal with them.

An additional important concern for parents as they age is one of determining legal guardianship or conservatorship. When individuals reach the age of 18, they become a legal adult with the responsibilities of being accountable for their own actions in areas such as finances, medical decisions, and contractual arrangements. Each individual is his or her own legal guardian regardless of the level of ability, unless a family member or appropriate advocate completes court proceedings to have that right taken away from the individual and awarded to a designee. This is a very difficult decision, as it essentially means taking away a basic right that is highly valued in our society.

Some individuals may have disabilities that truly prevent them from making such complex decisions on their own behalf. There are many other individuals, however, for whom the decision is not so clearly defined. Choosing to allow the young adult to remain "unconserved" (i.e., a fully responsible adult) is a way to reinforce the acknowledgment of adulthood and to empower the individual to fulfill that role. However, worries over who will be available to support and guide the decisions that the individuals might make after the parents are deceased causes some families to begin the court proceedings if for no other reason than to prevent any potential "ward of the state" circumstances. Parents, young adults with disabilities, and other support members should work together carefully in determining what actions are most beneficial for the individual.

Changing Bureaucracies   In addition to relationships changing between parents and their young adult children, parent and family life is affected by changes in bureaucratic systems. By the time a child is in a secondary school program, the parents are "old hands" at the educational system and all of its jargon, rules, regulations, and paperwork. School schedules remain consistent, transportation is secure, and teachers who hold valid credentials make up the daily routine of children with or without disabilities. But as adulthood nears, parents of children with and without disabilities realize that life will never be quite so consistent and secure.

For parents of children with disabilities, the realization of change may come abruptly when their son or daughter no longer receives school-age services. This is yet another reason why transition planning is so critical during the last few years of school eligibility. By involving parents as part of the core team, they have an opportunity to begin to learn the rules, regulations, and jargon of a whole new bureaucracy. Issues such as "How involved should I be?" and "How involved can I be?" resurface when attempting to develop relationships with a whole new group of professionals and services (Moore, 1993).

For those individuals and families encouraging full community participation for their sons or daughters, issues of permanence can cause considerable parental anxiety (Moore, 1993). One look at segregated institutions or sheltered workshops indicates that they were built and founded with the notion of permanence in mind. Supported employment, supported living, and real-life adulthood are based on changing as the individual changes; supports needed will change from year to year as options and skills increase.

Individual Issues

Regardless of agency and family issues, adult services delivery needs to focus on the needs and wishes of the adult with disabilities. Enhancing the quality of life for each adult should be the goal of service delivery. To assure that this occurs, the Futures Plan or MAPs or circle of friends process is essential. As discussed in Chapters 4 and 10, this process identifies the goals, dreams, and fears of the individual. In addition, the process identifies how and when each of the items will be addressed.

Areas of adulthood for individuals with disabilities that are often overlooked by agencies and families are self-advocacy and relationships. These topics are briefly addressed in the follow section.

Self-Advocacy   Self-advocacy provides a means for individuals and groups to speak for themselves and educate one another about the rights and responsibilities of full citizenship (Gould, 1985). Supporting self-advocacy for people with disabilities may mean identifying self-advocacy skills as specific goals in an individualized program and/or participating in a self-advocacy group.

Speaking for oneself as a person with a disability means participating in planning the meetings that affect issues related to one's life; being an active, respected decision maker and problem solver; expressing wants and needs; and sharing dreams and fears with people who are directly or indirectly involved in the life of the individual. Educating and being educated by other people with and without disabilities about the rights and responsibilities of citizenship in a community help to keep individuals updated on current legislature, barriers in the local community, and recent successes of individuals or groups promoting disability rights.

In addition, self-advocacy enhances one's contribution to the community. Members of self-advocacy groups not only provide support to one another by relating experiences of similar frustrations but also encourage collaborative efforts to effect greater change at local, state, and national levels.

Allen (1988) has outlined the following characteristic skills in self-advocacy:

1. *Control over the timing of events*—for example, determining when to go to bed, when to eat a meal, or when to change jobs.
2. *Making personal choices*—for example, choosing what to wear, what music to listen to, with whom to live.
3. *Opportunity to evaluate services and programs*—for example, participating in program reviews and accreditation processes, completing regular evaluations of staff members, selecting the service providers from whom to receive support.

4. *Choosing environments and methods of training*—for example, deciding whether to use personnel supports or assistive devices, choosing what stores to shop in, choosing the neighborhood in which to live.
5. *Involvement in the hiring of staff*—for example, interviewing and hiring personal attendants, paid roommates or neighbors, or supported employment job coaches.
6. *Attendance in all planning meetings*—for example, circle of friends, MAPs or PATH meetings, individual program planning meetings (IEP or ITP meetings).
7. *Opportunity for self-charting and self-monitoring*—for example, using a picture-coded daily planner, monitoring nutritional and dietary needs, planning and scheduling medical appointments.
8. *Receipt of assertiveness and self-advocacy training*—for example, attending People First meetings, asking that service providers help to facilitate the development of a local self-advocacy group, participating in community classes on assertiveness skills.

Relationships   Adulthood is a time when people rely on a variety of mutual relationships to support and enhance their lives. Relationships range from paid support to casual friendships, best friends, intimate lovers, or spouses. Despite the fears and worries of family members and agency workers, adults with disabilities have the same needs for and rights to intimate relationships that adults without disabilities experience. The role of those "other parties" is to once again determine how to best support and facilitate opportunities for developing and maintaining relationships at all levels.

The development of specific curriculum materials addressing the skills necessary for friendships and sexual relationships (Los Angeles County Office of Education, 1987; Valenti-Hein & Mueser, 1992) has provided easier access for skill development for adults with disabilities (see Chapter 10). The challenge, however, seems not to lie in the skill development as much as in the opportunity for relationships to be developed and sexuality to be expressed. Many adult services agencies include social/sexual skills "training" as part of their services, but the support necessary for an individual to participate in an intimate relationship is frequently lacking.

Given the increased opportunity for adults with significant disabilities to live in housing arrangements of their own choosing, their greater participation in the meetings that plan their own future, and increased self-advocacy skills, the need for supporting intimate relationships grows greater. As adults with severe disabilities are working toward achieving equal status in the community, they have the right for equal status in relationship opportunities as well. Adults with severe disabilities are involved in intimate relationships with support, are choosing to become married, and are choosing to be supported as parents. These choices are rights and should become integral components of the supports offered by service providers and families.

The following case study provides an example of one man's story as he works to develop a lifestyle for himself.

CASE STUDY: CESAR

Cesar has seen many changes in the way that education and other services are offered to persons with disabilities. Cesar's disability labels include cerebral palsy and mental retardation. When he attended elementary school, he went to a special education segregated campus. As educators learned the value of integration, he moved to a regular campus where he participated during lunch, recess, art and other non-academic classes with students without disabilities. His base for instruction continued to be the special education classroom. For one or more periods per day, he had community-based instruction. During his high school years, Cesar had his first experience of inclusion in the regular high school. Although he still received behavioral support and instruction from the special education teacher, he attended classes with everyone else. At age 18 he transferred from high school to a transition program, where he stated that he wanted to get a job and consider going to the local junior college, where his friends from school were going.

Throughout Cesar's life, the education system influenced the expectations that Cesar's family had for him. They once thought that Cesar would always have a life quite different from that of his brothers and sisters. As the years went on, his parents began to hope for the same things for Cesar that they desired for their other children, including that he would be able to live in his own home. These hopes and fears were discussed when his inclusion facilitator developed a "circle of friends" team for Cesar (see Chapter 4 for circle details).

Cesar's friends and family especially supported Cesar's desire to have his own apartment. As Cesar passed through his young adult years, ages 18–22, his friends began to move out of their family's homes. Several moved to go to college, while others began to save money to move out. This seemed the next logical step for Cesar.

Cesar's parents admitted to having many fears and hesitations about Cesar's next step, but that it was very exciting as well. They now say that having regular circle of friends meetings helped them through that time. They felt assured that Cesar would have people looking out for his well-being and helping him to advocate for himself. In addition, they noticed that after Cesar started to attend his self-advocacy group he became more expressive about his desires. At first it seemed to be a little disturbing to see Cesar "acting up." He had never refused to eat his mother's tofu chili before! Again, it was the circle that pointed out that Cesar's advocacy efforts were positive, if occasionally inconvenient. After he began to assert himself more, Cesar's parents felt their relationship with him begin to change, as had theirs with his brothers and sisters. Cesar's parents continued to be active in his life, but they began to empower him to make his own decisions.

They maintained the role of valued advisors, but let Cesar make his own decisions. They describe that process as difficult but rewarding. At times, he made sound decisions and at other times he made decisions that were not so good, but everyone learned from his mistakes.

Cesar recounts that he has always wanted to live in his own apartment like his brother Hector, who went away to college. He had heard others say in the past that he would not qualify for an "independent living program" because he needed a great deal of assistance on a long-term basis. He also knew that his use of a wheelchair excluded him from some programs, while his sudden outbursts ruled him out for others. During one of his transition planning meetings, Cesar's case manager discussed the possibility of a supported living program that provides services regardless of the type or level of disability.

Supported living appealed to Cesar because of the notion of building supports around his needs. The agency and the person receiving supports work in a partnership to design the services that the person needs and desires. His financial needs were supported through several state and federal funding sources, as well as his supported employment income. Cesar liked the idea of hiring the support persons who would be working with him. They even said that they would assist him to find a place with a pool, that allowed dogs, and was within walking distance of the mall. Cesar interviewed and hired a live-in attendant as well as a part-time relief attendant. Cesar went through a few relief attendants before finding the right one. More than once he needed the supported living agency to fill in when one of his relief attendants did not show up or when he was between attendants. His live-in attendant, Rod, has always been great; they quickly established a positive rapport as roommates.

The supported living agency also assisted Cesar to apply for Housing for Urban Development (HUD) rental assistance. Although the waiting list can be 1–2 years, it will be worth the wait. When Cesar gets his HUD certificate, he will have to pay much less rent, and his attendant's half of the rent will be free because of Cesar's needs. The supported living agency utilized the services of the local Center for Independent Living to look over the request and to help monitor the process.

Objectives that Cesar identified with the supported living agency include meeting new people by joining organizations, budgeting, making milk shakes, supervising his attendant, having a dinner party for friends, cooking with the use of a switch, and getting an environmental control unit. Cesar enjoys his home. He has met many of the neighbors when he and Rod take the dog for a walk or when they sit on the porch in the evenings. By being visible in the neighborhood, he and Rod are included in many of the parties and other functions available, such as the Neighborhood Watch program.

Cesar spends some of his time with the Sierra Club getting involved with environmental concerns and going on the accessible hikes. Through his activism with the Sierra Club, Cesar met a person who eventually became his employer.

Impressed with Cesar's commitment and dependability, Rebekah approached him and offered him a job at her music store. There, he had the help of a job developer who collaborated with the floor manager to establish the details about Cesar's job. His work includes unpacking shipments, brining them to the floor, labeling merchandise, and helping customers with questions.

Cesar receives services from a supported employment agency to assist him at his job, as well as in several areas of his life, and to fully include him in his community. He has developed goals and objectives with the support of his circle of friends. His goals entail enrolling and participating in preferred classes, maintaining preferred employment, and attending self-advocacy meetings.

Cesar receives assistance at his job to develop technological adaptations to increase his productivity when labeling merchandise. He also receives support to self-monitor periodic behavior disruptions. Cesar is now working only 20 hours a week and has requested assistance to locate additional employment opportunities.

Cesar attends classes at the local community college. When he and his family talked about his love of music and singing at a circle meeting, Veronica (a support staff member from his supported employment agency) suggested that he join the community college choir. Veronica was already a member of the choir, so she invited Cesar to join her and helped him get enrolled.

As a part of his support services, Veronica works to support Cesar at the college. They assist him with necessary adaptations in his voice and choir classes, by practicing his music prior to each class, and by helping him to meet and develop relationships with other choir members and college students. Veronica balances her different roles while at the college. She is also a member of the classes and works hard to not be viewed as Cesar's "special helper." She assists Cesar to make the connections necessary to be successful instead of being the sole provider for the assistance he needs. Her own connections and friendships at the college have naturally benefited Cesar as well. Other students enjoy spending time with him and they seem to share similar interests beyond his love for music. Cesar goes to parties and concerts with classmates and often has lunch on campus with one or two of the other students from his class.

Cesar is eligible to receive support from the college's Office for Students with Disabilities. The staff in the office assist him to register for his classes, to complete class assignments, and to coordinate tutor services. Cesar recently invited Nadine, one of the office staff, to attend his next circle of friends meeting.

By attending college, Cesar's opportunities and interests continued to expand. Pablo, a classmate from the voice class, invited Cesar to attend a meeting on campus for Latino students. After attending a few meetings, Cesar decided that he wanted to learn more about Latin American history and issues and registered for a Latin American history class. A friend who eats lunch occasionally with Cesar invited him to join the college's entertainment club. Every Tuesday evening the club meets to plan events such as attending television game shows, concerts, and fund-raising activities. Once a month, the club enjoys an evening at a concert or other special event together. Cesar receives assistance from his support services providers to set up transportation that is accessible for his wheelchair. Often the transportation company is late or does not show up. Cesar dreams of owning a van with a wheelchair lift so that he can have more reliable transportation.

Cesar discusses his dreams and challenges with other members of his self-advocacy group. He attends his meeting every other week with other individuals with disabilities. The group members discuss issues affecting their lives, affirm each other's feelings and rights, and work to become better informed in local government and community issues. Although issues of employment, transportation, and intimate relationships still present challenges for Cesar, he is able to participate more fully in the community than he or his family ever thought possible.

SUMMARY

As students with significant disabilities age out of the education system, a number of changes occur that affect individuals and families alike. Transition services are provided to students in their teenage and early adulthood years in order to ensure that the skills and supports necessary for adult life in the community are being addressed. As inclusion into the schools is a major focus of educational supports, inclusion into the community is a major focus of adult services providers.

Besides transition services, this chapter has addressed issues of adulthood in terms of agency support, family roles, and individual needs. The agencies providing services are supporting adults with severe disabilities to participate in all of the decisions affecting their lives, including employment issues and living arrangements. Families are asked to be supporters in the decisions that are being made, to encourage greater community involvement, and to foster relationships outside of the family. Individuals are becoming greater self-advocates and seeking quality lifestyles that include paid employment in the community, roommates and housing of their choice, and relationships that may include marriage and parenthood.

REFERENCES

Albin, J.M. (1992). *Quality improvement in employment and other humans services: Managing for quality through change.* Baltimore: Paul H. Brookes Publishing Co.

Allen, W.T. (1988). *The right to be heard: Ways to increase consumer participation in the service system: A guide for case managers.* Sacramento, CA: Association of Regional Center Agencies.

American Association on Mental Retardation. (1992). Americans thing people with disabilities are good for the economy. *News & Notes, 5*(1), 1–8.

Americans with Disabilities Act of 1990 (ADA), PL 101-336. (July 26, 1990). Title 42, U.S.C. 12101 et seq: *U.S. Statutes at Large, 104,* 327–378.

Bates, P. (1989). *Illinois transition planning program and program guide.* Carbondale: Illinois Transition Project, Southern Illinois University.

Bellamy, G.T. (1983). *Competitive employment training.* Paper presented at a conference by the California chapter of The Association for Persons with Severe Handicaps, San Diego.

Bellamy, G.T., Rhodes, L., Bourbeau, P., & Mank, D. (1986). Mental retardation services in sheltered workshops and day activity programs: Consumer benefits and policy alternatives. In F.R. Rusch (Ed.), *Competitive employment issues and strategies* (pp. 257–271). Baltimore: Paul H. Brookes Publishing Co.

Bishop, K.D. (1991). *The integration and employment status of adults with disabilities in supported employment.* Unpublished doctoral dissertation, University of California, Los Angeles/California State University, Los Angeles.

Brown, L., Rogan, P., Shiraga, B., Albright, K., Kessler, K., Bryson, F., Van Deventer, P., & Loomis, R. (1986). A vocational follow-up evaluation of the 1984–86 Madison Metropolitan School District graduates with severe intellectual disabilities. *Monograph of The Association for Persons with Severe Handicaps, 2,* 2. Seattle, WA.

Carl D. Perkins Vocational and Applied Technology Act of 1990, PL 101-392. (1990). Title 20, U.S.C. 230/note: *U.S. Statutes at Large,* 753–843.

Education for All Handicapped Children Act of 1975, PL 99-142. (August 23, 1977). Title 20, U.S.C. 1400 et seq: *U.S. Statutes at Large, 89,* 773–796.

Falvey, M., Bishop, K., & Terry Gage, S. (1992). Mental retardation. In M. Brodwin, F. Tellez, & S. Brodwin (Eds.), *Medical, psychosocial and vocational aspects of disability* (pp. 165–178). Athens, GA: Elliott & Fitzpatrick.

Federal Register. (1984, September 25). Developmental Disabilities Act of 1984. Report 98–1047, Section 102(11)(F).

Gaston, D. (1988). *What are the reasons for job termination of people with mental retardation who are severely handicapped?* Unpublished master's thesis, California State University, Los Angeles.

Gould, M. (1985). Self-advocacy for youth in transition from school to work and adult life. In M. Gould & G.T. Bellamy (Eds.), *Transition from school to work and adult life* (pp. 78–89). Eugene: University of Oregon Specialized Training Program.

Greenspan, S., & Shoultz, B. (1981). Why mentally retarded adults lose their jobs: Social competence as a factor in work adjustment. *Applied Research in Mental Retardation, 2,* 23–28.

Griffin, C., & Sherron, P. (1992). Finding jobs for young people with disabilities. In P. Wehman, *Life beyond the classroom: Transition strategies for young people with disabilities* (pp. 189–208). Baltimore: Paul H. Brookes Publishing Co.

Individuals with Disabilities Education Act of 1990 (IDEA), PL 101-476. (October 30, 1990). Title 20, U.S.C. 1400 et seq: *U.S. Statutes at Large, 104,* 1103–1151.

Kerachsky, S., & Thornton, C. (1987). Findings from the STETS traditional employment demonstration. *Exceptional Children, 53*(6), 515–521.

Los Angeles County Office of Education (L.A.C.O.E.). (1987). *Family life curriculum.* Downey, CA: Author.

Moore, C. (1993). Letting go, moving on: A parent's thoughts. In J. Racino, P. Walker, S. O'Connor, & S.J. Taylor (Eds.), *Housing, support, and community: Choices and strategies for adults with disabilities* (pp. 189–204). Baltimore: Paul H. Brookes Publishing Co.

Nisbet, J., & Hagner, D. (1988). Natural supports in the workplace: A reexamination of supported employment. *Journal of The Association for Persons with Severe Handicaps, 4,* 260–267.

O'Brien, J., & O'Brien, C. (1991). *Perspectives on community building*. Lithonia, GA: Responsive Systems Associates.

Peraino, J.M. (1992). Post-21 follow-up studies: How do special education graduates fare? In P. Wehman, *Life beyond the classroom: Transition strategies for young people with disabilities* (pp. 21–70). Baltimore: Paul H. Brookes Publishing Co.

Powell, T., & Gallagher, P.A. (1993). *Brothers and sisters: A special part of exceptional families*. Baltimore: Paul H. Brookes Publishing Co.

Powell, T., Pancsofar, E., Steere, D., Butterworth, J., Itzkowitz, J., & Rainforth, B. (1991). *Supported employment: Providing integrated opportunities for persons with disabilities*. White Plains, NY: Longman.

Rehabilitation Act Amendments of 1986, PL 99-506. Title 29, U.S.C. 701 et seq: *U.S. Statutes at Large, 100*, 1807–1846.

Rehabilitation Act Amendments of 1992, PL 102-569. (October 29, 1992). Title 29, U.S.C. 701 et seq: *U.S. Statutes at Large, 100*, 4344–4488.

Snell, M.A. (1993). *Instruction of students with severe disabilities* (4th ed.). New York: Macmillan.

Thorin, E.J., & Irvin, L.K. (1992). Family stress associated with transition to adulthood of young people with significant disabilities. *Journal of The Association for Persons with Severe Handicaps, 17*(1), 31–39.

Turnbull, A.P., & Turnbull, H.R. (1990). *Families, professionals, and exceptionality: A special partnership*. Columbus, OH: Charles E. Merrill.

Valenti-Hein, D., & Mueser, K.T. (1992). *The dating skills program*. Worthington, OH: IDS.

Van Deventer, P., Yelinek, N., Brown, L., Schroeder, J., Loomis, R., & Gruenwald, L. (1981). A follow-up examination of severely handicapped graduates of the Madison Metropolitan School District from 1971–1978. In L. Brown, D. Baumgart, I. Pumpian, J. Nisbet, & A. Schroeder (Eds.), *Educational programs for severely handicapped students* (Vol. XI, pp. 1–177). Madison, WI: Madison Metropolitan School District.

Wehman, P. (1992). *Life beyond the classroom: Transition strategies for young people with disabilities*. Baltimore: Paul H. Brookes Publishing.

Wehman, P., Kregel, J., & Barcus, M. (1985). From school to work: A vocational transition model for handicapped students. *Exceptional Children, 52*(1), 25–37.

Wehman, P., Kregel, J., Barcus, M., & Schalock, R.L. (1986). Vocational transition for students with developmental disabilities. In W.E. Kiernan & J.A. Stark (Eds.), *Pathways to employment for adults with developmental disabilities* (pp. 113–127). Baltimore: Paul H. Brookes Publishing Co.

Wehman, P., Kregel, J., & Revell, G. (1991). *National analysis of supported employment implementation: FY 1986–1990*. Richmond: Virginia Commonwealth University, Rehabilitation Research and Training Center.

Will, M. (1983, November). *Programming for the transition of youth with disabilities: Bridges from school to working life*. Paper presented at the national conference of The Association for Persons with Severe Handicaps, San Francisco.

Wolery, M., Ault, M.J., & Doyle, P.M. (1992). *Teaching students with moderate to significant disabilities: Use of response prompting strategies*. White Plains, NY: Longman Publishing.

CREATING HETEROGENEOUS SCHOOLS

A Systems Change Perspective

RICHARD A. VILLA, JACQUELINE S. THOUSAND, AND RICHARD L. ROSENBERG

The earlier chapters in this volume have focused on strategies and characteristics of various elements of inclusive educational practices. The most effective schools and school systems are those that have engaged in intentional restructuring to move from a dual, segregated, categorical, and generally splintered system of special and general education services to one that is unified and inclusive, considering the whole person and system in the design and delivery of services. This chapter focuses on effective strategies that schools and individuals can use when implementing this change.

Although the views about changing school systems are as diverse as they are many, these views converge in their emphasis on promoting and valuing diversity and heterogeneity among children and adults. Along with promoting and valuing diversity as an underlying assumption or goal of school change, this chapter examines a model for facilitating school change that expands upon previous models of change.

A VALUES-BASED INVENTIVE MODEL OF SCHOOL CHANGE

Since 1950, divergent approaches to creating improvements in organizations have been articulated, tested, and refined. Schools are cultures existing within sociopolitical and economic contexts, so guidelines that can be individually applied to each system are more useful than a rigid universal formula for change (Deal & Peterson, 1990). Systems change efforts are driven by spoken and unspoken values (Sergiovanni, 1990). This chapter offers a change process most useful for restructuring schools for inclusive education for all students and represented as four phases: visionizing, introducing, expanding, and selectively maintaining the change and change processes (Villa & Thousand, 1992). Each of these phases is discussed below. The strategies described in each phase are meant to be not prescriptive, but dynamic and catalytic for achieving fundamental change in schooling practices.

Phase One: Visionizing

Visionizing is a term used by Sidney Parnes (1988) to describe creative problem-solving and solution-finding processes for encouraging innovative excellence in any field. The term was selected to identify the first step in school change because it represents the desired outcome of this initial state—a shared vision of preferred conditions for the future. It also was selected because it is an action verb. As an action verb, it suggests the active struggling for a dream or vision for the future. Such visions must be conceptualized, shared, and publicly owned by a school community.

Within the context of school change, visionizing is an act of creating and communicating a compelling vision of a desired future state. Visionizing involves clarifying and defining the current situation and securing commitment to a future (Bennis & Nanus, 1985). The concept of visionizing is commonplace in today's leadership for school reform, although it was rarely discussed prior to the works of Peters and Waterman (1982) and Blumberg and Greenfield (1980). Change initiatives are guided by a vision of preferred futures, and although organizations are often governed by belief and faith, rationality and outcome also influence their structures.

Visionizing involves people building a new shared core covenant (Sergiovanni, 1990). A covenant is

> a binding and solemn agreement by principals, teachers, parents, and students to honor certain values, goals, and beliefs; to make certain commitments to each other; and to do or keep from doing specific things. It is the compact that provides the school with a sense of direction, on the one hand, and an opportunity to find meaning in school life, on the other. (Sergiovanni, 1990, p. 20)

Given a covenant, school personnel can motivate themselves to reshape their behavior and the norms that governed past behavior. In general, unexamined past visions or cultures tend to be glorified and romanticized. By leading people to examine and alter history, individuals leading schools can help people discover that schools that have not changed or evolved may no longer be effective. This is the first step of the change process.

Two types of "vision" drive change within schools: organizational excellence and universal vision. *Organizational excellence* concerns the creation of the best, most effective school or school district possible. *Universal vision* extends the concerns beyond a local context to the promotion of fairness and equity everywhere. Although the equity concern may have a specific focus (e.g., students with disabilities, students of diverse cultural background), it is the emphasis upon the more universal moral dimension that characterizes the universal "visionizer." Schools successful in restructuring for inclusion of all students have often been led into change by those who hold both organizational and universal visions.

Leaders in a change movement must initially promote a school climate that fosters feelings of safety and unity rather than mistrust or competition among "leaders" and "followers." They also need to create opportunities for school personnel to demonstrate mastery and commitment to the school in ways that appeal to and satisfy the needs of all those affected by the changes. Furthermore, they need to inspire a willingness to risk changing through appeals to the intrinsic human need for importance and significance in one's work.

Time, resources, and energy must be devoted to those people who actively embrace the desired future. Leaders both within and outside of the school or school system should describe the vision in an ethical, theoretical, practical, legal, and research-based way to assist others in adopting the vision. This information can be communicated through in-service training events, visits to schools that have adopted similar visions and successfully transformed themselves, and similar instructive activities.

Communication of a vision is accomplished through two functions: 1) marketing, that is, making people who are not doing the conceptualizing aware of the change; and 2) development, that is, soliciting input and feedback from peripheral people who will need to support the change (Schlechty, 1990). A visionizer needs to employ marketing and development tactics that are most likely to expand the number of people who believe in the vision. The educational visionizer's role, therefore, is to conduct marketing and development efforts outside of the school—getting "good press" with a wide audience, including the local community, other school districts, professional associations, and the public at large. An effective marketing tactic is to engage representatives of each of a school's "stakeholder" groups (e.g., parents, students, teachers, guidance counselors, instructional assistants, administrators, specialized support personnel) in a process of articulating the vision in the form of a school mission or vision statement (Deal & Peterson, 1990). Another tactic is to capitalize upon incidents of resistance and conflict as forums for explaining the vision or to structure opportunities for people to air their differing views during faculty meetings, in-service training sessions, or other professional events (Villa & Thousand, 1990).

Each school or district needs to categorize its beliefs according to its own needs. Diversity, empowerment, recognition and rewards, decision making, belonging, caring, integrity, and excellence are some of the categorical headings for vision statements used by many schools and school districts (Patterson, Purkey, & Parker, 1986). This is an example of a vision statement:

> Every student can learn, and every student will learn if presented with the right opportunity to do so. It is the purpose of school to invent learning opportunities for each student each day. . . . Continuous improvement, persistent innovation, and a

commitment to continuing growth should be expected of all people and all programs supported by school district resources and school district resources should be committed to ensure that these expectations can be met. (Schlechty, 1990, pp. 131–132)

In their vision statements, successfully restructured schools typically include concepts that promote inclusive thinking and heterogeneous practices, including those articulated by Villa and Thousand (1990):

1. All children can learn.
2. All children have the right to be educated with their peers in age-appropriate heterogeneous classrooms within their local schools.
3. It is the responsibility of the school system to meet the diverse educational and psychological needs of all students. (p. 202)

Phase Two: Introducing

The second phase of a school change effort involves introducing the change. The desired outcomes of this phase are to unfreeze (Lewin, 1951) current practices and to help people understand that systemwide change will occur. This change can be facilitated, in part, by recruiting and supporting early experimenters to create successful examples of the desired future state that people within or outside of the organization can study and imitate. The more active various individuals and groups have been in creating the vision discussed in Phase One, the less elaborate Phase Two will need to be.

It is at this point that efforts to construct a new culture begin (Deal, 1987). In order to create new rituals, practices, symbols, heroes, and heroines, it is particularly important to introduce new language and labels, language that is not associated with the "old way," but language that is educative (Schlechty, 1990). If, for example, the desired change is for all children to be part of the general education process regardless of ability, it is more educative to refer to this change as *inclusion* than as *mainstreaming* since mainstreaming has represented part-time placement of students in general education or dumping students with disabilities in general education classrooms without the necessary supports to be successful.

Initiating change requires change agents who can create cognitive dissonance, discomfort, chaos, and even a sense of urgency or rage among school personnel and the community (Schlechty, 1990). This may be done by loudly and publicly pointing out each time an old solution (e.g., adding on a new isolated professional for each new category of children with disabilities introduced into the school) no longer works to achieve the desired vision, that is, inclusive and heterogeneous learning opportunities for all children (Skrtic, 1991). It may be done by fact finding, sharing those facts with key people, and possibly stirring up community pressure (e.g., sharing the local, state, or national student outcome data that indicate a disproportionate number of ethnic minority students, especially African and Latino students, are placed in special education).

Change agents may stir up the community by creating forums for parents, students, state department of education representatives, and university and business personnel to discuss their dissatisfaction with educational inequities (e.g., tracking, segregated programs for categories of students, racial, ethnic, and economic discrimination) or the declining performance of high school graduates. It is also important to highlight the prospects of success for teachers and students that the desired future will bring. One of the most effective ways to motivate school personnel to engage in a major change (e.g., welcoming students with severe disabilities to their local "home" school general education classrooms) is to alert them to the inevitability of the change by having the leadership set a not-so-distant date by which the change will be put in motion (e.g., telling the staff that these students will transition to home schools in September of the following school year) and thereby creating the time to get ready.

Change led by outrage requires initial leaders to express strong feelings about achieving the system's mission, to focus attention and energy on the foremost priorities, and to communicate that people in the system are free to take actions as long as they are moral, ethical, and consistent with the articulated visions. Leadership by outrage and passion works to initiate change because, as others observe and feel their leaders' outrage, their own potential for outrage is kindled within themselves.

The initiation of a planning process is a powerful method for getting change under way. It signals that things will no longer be the same; it gets people to really believe that change will occur. Whatever planning approach a school district adopts, it is important for action to follow quickly. Action plans for change may take many forms and may employ various decision-making procedures. Strategic planning (Cook, 1990; Kaufman, 1991) is one systematic approach for moving people from a vision to action. Guiding principles of strategic planning are

- Pay attention to and gather as much relevant information about the world outside of the school as possible because information about external economic, social, and cultural trends is critical.
- Spend time carefully examining the current internal strengths and weaknesses of the school organization because the school organization already has its resources for, as well as detractors from, successful education.
- Use participatory decision-making processes whenever possible, and be sure all relevant stakeholder groups are represented and communicated with on a regular basis, because people are the core of change.
- Regularly schedule meetings to review progress, make necessary modifications of the plan, and assign new teams to develop action plans for additional needed strategies, because change is a dynamic process. The driving and restraining forces will change over time, and the outcomes of actions for change are unpredictable.

- Periodically examine and review the vision to help everyone stay on track. Use the media (e.g., television, newspapers) to influence the community because the vision or mission may get lost or muddied over time or as new people enter the school system or community.
- Develop a detailed and measurable action plan that includes implementation timeliness and identifies the person(s) responsible for each action included in the action plan.

There is little argument that people benefit from having examples to observe and imitate and to convince them that new practices can work. A beginning step can be to solicit school personnel who have demonstrated an interest in taking a chance on change to develop an "experimental" demonstration project. Human (e.g., administrative) and material support and training must be provided to these personnel as they initiate the change, for there is much to lose if the experiment fails and much to be gained if it succeeds. Once the demonstrator has been observed as successful, the stage is set for Phase Three, Expanding, during which schoolwide or districtwide implementation begins through the recruitment, training, and support of additional experimental groups.

If an innovation has already been repeatedly demonstrated, it may be possible to take an "all at once" approach to organizationwide implementation. This is likely to be successful if individuals are at a technical and emotional state of readiness to adopt an innovation of the magnitude being proposed and if the organization has accomplished its visionizing and other initiating tasks (e.g., spread the vision, prompted the initiation of cultural change, fostered a climate of trust, secured needed supplies). The fewer of these conditions that are met, the more sensible it is to break the change effort into steps.

Starting small and adopting a stepwise implementation strategy requires greater endurance on the part of everyone involved, as it stretches the time between the initiation and the selective maintenance of an innovative practice. A stepwise strategy also requires critical examination of the proposed interim steps and outcomes to determine their potential for interfering with full implementation of the innovation. For example, school personnel intending to create heterogeneous learning environments for students with disabilities occasionally make the following mistake. Instead of initiating the desired outcome, that is, placing students in age-appropriate classes with needed supports, a short-term special class "homeroom" is created for students from more segregated classes and schools. Unfortunately, once this class is in place, educators and others often view it as educationally appropriate. Why else would everyone advocate or settle for it? Subsequent resistance to the next steps (e.g., phasing out and eventually eliminating the segregated class) then obstructs rather than facilitates the achievement of the desired end results (e.g., equitable heterogeneous schooling opportunities for all children, regardless of their differing abilities).

In summary, what is most important during the initiating phase of any change is that people notice that change is under way. These introductory steps should be salient enough for the change to be taken seriously but not so massive that anxiety is created.

Phase Three: Expanding

The objectives of the expanding phase of the change process are twofold: 1) to expand the number of people engaged in behaviors that represent the desired future and 2) to transform the culture so that others share a moral commitment to the new way, or covenant. To attain these objectives, leadership must communicate an expectation that everyone will receive needed training and coaching. Coaching is a form of teaching others about innovations by giving them constant feedback about their progress in adopting and implementing the innovation. Leadership must empower and reward individuals for engaging in desired practices. Evaluation questions of importance to the various stakeholder groups must be constructed and answered.

No matter how exciting an innovation or appealing the materials, activities, or expected outcomes associated with it, educators need training to understand clearly how to use the innovation. Such training needs to include ongoing modeling, guided practice, and feedback (Hord, Rutherford, Huling-Austin, & Hall, 1987). Furthermore, for any innovation to become the new culture, people must come to understand that the innovation is significant to their personal and professional growth (Sarason, 1971). Within the context of school reform, this places training at the heart of strategies for both changing the culture of a school and increasing the number of people who can perform the desired new behaviors and perform them correctly.

Leaders of change must oversee the formulation and ratification of a comprehensive in-service training agenda designed to increase knowledge about best practices and develop positive attitudes (Hord et al., 1987). Although initially training may be organized and delivered to the innovators and early adopters in the school, eventually everyone involved (e.g., teachers; administrators; instructional assistants; educational, secretarial, and related services staff; students; parents) needs to receive a common core of instruction. No one involved with the change should be exempt from participation in such training events if large-scale and long-lasting change is the aim. In addition, ongoing coaching must follow the training activities to ensure that personnel, parents, and students gain the necessary awareness, knowledge, comfort level, and skills to implement the changes.

In the initial stages, people are more concerned about how a change will affect them on a personal level (during later stages, they will focus on promoting the effectiveness of the innovation). The implicit recognition that each individual matters is essential. What quells fears and motivates movement in the direction of the Phase One vision will be unique from person to person, but the type of attention provided each participant can be tailored accordingly to match personal needs and responses.

Central to recruiting new believers and performers at the expanding phase is the employment of empowerment strategies. Such strategies include locating opportunities for people to share their skills with others; inviting people to become members of decision-making teams; encouraging others, including students, to fine-tune innovations and to invent ways of not just "doing it right" but "doing it even better"; and encouraging and helping people to act on their concerns, rather than simply to expend their time and energy worrying about their concerns.

Incentives and rewards in recruiting participants to change are essential; however, overreliance on extrinsic rewards (e.g., money, honors) to encourage participation and performance can interfere with change. When extrinsic rewards are used, it is critical to distribute them so they are shared because public recognition of one individual over others fosters competition and destroys rather than promotes the desired unity in cultural change. Alternatives to these rewards are those that are more intrinsic, such as pride in one's professional growth and the accompanying recognition by respected colleagues, students, or parents; recognition of one's own increased effectiveness as indicated by improved student performance or teacher–student interactions; and feelings of personal satisfaction and mastery.

Rewards should be given for any behavior consistent with the vision and its underlying values as well as any behavior that represents or promotes real progress (e.g., a better place for students and teachers). Suppose, for example, a school community's vision is to create heterogeneous learning and working conditions for children and adults. Collaboration among members of the school community is an ethic and practice consistent with and conducive to such a heterogeneous schooling vision and, thus, one worthy of rewarding (Thousand & Villa, 1990). To make the use of collaborative processes more intrinsically rewarding for school personnel, leadership could provide ongoing training to promote skill development, bring together people from within and outside of the system to discuss collaboration issues and strategies, structure time for teams to meet collaboratively, and create opportunities for collaborators to serve as technical assistants and trainers of others (Hord et al., 1987).

Phase Four: Maintaining

Maintenance of change is not ensured until steps have been taken to make certain that innovations do not fade away and practices revert to where they were before. The final phase of a change effort involves weaving new practices into the day-to-day operational patterns of a school so that they continue to be routinely employed by the majority, widely accepted as legitimate, and supported by regular allocations of time and money. This final phase is based upon three assumptions: 1) maintenance does not just happen; 2) use and mastery of new practices are not enough to ensure their maintenance; and 3) planning for maintenance needs to begin early, that is, during the initiating phase (Eiseman, Fleming, & Roody, 1990).

Schools should regard this last phase as an ongoing effort to seek and adopt even better solutions that emerge as educators use, modify, and improve upon original visions and accompanying innovations (Crandall, Eiseman, & Louis, 1986). Educators should be supported at this point to be reflective practitioners who make decisions and modify educational practices based upon stated goals and observed student outcomes (e.g., if students don't learn the way we teach, we teach the way students learn). In addition, educators should be given the time and resources to actively study the teaching and learning process and seek continued renewal and stimulation by entertaining further change activities. The final phase of the change process is involved less in "casting change in stone" than in maintaining change processes so that innovations can continue to be modified and new innovations are welcomed.

Changes and practices that should be maintained are those for which the school community shares a common vision, the change is appropriate for achieving that vision, and evidence of positive outcomes has occurred. Some factors that facilitate successful maintenance of the change process and the specific innovations were identified by Eiseman et al. (1990) in a study of 12 innovative schools in 10 American states. Ten key facilitators emerged (highlighted in italics):

> High administrative commitment tends to lead to both *administrative pressure* on users to implement the innovation, along with *administrative support*, which often show up in the form of *assistance* to users. Both the pressure and the assistance tend to lead to increased *user effort*. Researchers repeatedly found that the harder people worked at an innovation, the more *committed* they grew; that commitment was also fueled by increasing technical *mastery* of the innovation.
>
> Commitment and mastery both lead toward increasing *stabilization of use*; the innovation has "settled down" in the system. That stabilization is also aided if administrators decide to *mandate the innovation*, which also naturally increases the *percentage of use* to something approaching 100 percent of eligible users. . . . Where administrators were committed, they also took direct action to bring about *organizational change* . . . by altering the structure and approach of inservice training, writing the innovation's requirements into job descriptions, making new budget lines, appointing permanent coordinators for the innovation, and making sure that needed materials and equipment would continue to be available in succeeding years. (Eiseman et al., 1990, p. 3.3)

There are also several ways to accelerate change to achieve progress. First, a significant financial investment should be made in an ongoing aggressive training agenda that addresses values and incorporates modeling and coaching of innovative practices. Second, new personnel should be hired based upon their commitment to the desired vision. Third, those who remain resistant throughout the change process could be encouraged to explore alternatives such as early retirement or employment elsewhere. Fourth, in order to spread dissatisfaction with the status quo, the leaders should affiliate and build coalitions with advocacy groups and capitalize upon other outside pressures for change. The negative consequences of current ineffective practices should be publicized, because in order to consider alternatives, one must first be dissatisfied with the present state or at least some elements of the present state. Finally, there must be frequent opportunities for visionizers and early adopters to share their vision and skills with reluctant or new members of the school community.

A description of a school district that restructured, from a segregated to an inclusive school district, using the inventive model for change is provided below.

SYSTEMS CHANGE: AN EXAMPLE OF HOW IT CAN HAPPEN

Phase One: Visionizing

District 54 is the largest elementary school district in Illinois, with 5 middle and 23 elementary schools. In 1990, the administration of the District 54 Special Services Division identified that very few options were available for children labeled severely and profoundly disabled. The service delivery options available at that time were segregated classrooms in either segregated or "regular" buildings, with none being within students' neighborhood schools.

The administration of District 54 decided to form a 36-member committee, which they called the Leadership Team for Special Services System Change (LT/SSSC). The team met on a monthly basis for the first year. Committee membership—designed to give representation as much as possible to all stakeholders across the spectrum of perspectives on inclusion—included parents of children both with and without disabilities, teaching and support staff from various schools throughout the school district (including teachers' union representation), administrators, and community members. The LT/SSSC was charged with identifying service delivery options for all students with disabilities. The monthly meetings included guest speakers as well as members who shared their impressions from visits to sites where inclusive education was already being implemented. At the end of the school year, the committee presented their findings to each other, as well as highlights of the year's observation, and discussed specific plans for inclusion,within District 54. With a consultant from an outside agency, a long-range plan was initiated. The process was to divide into three teams to create vision/mission statements. The "nominal group process technique" for group decision making (Scholtes, 1993) was then employed to blend the subsequent three statements into one statement for District 54. Next, LT/SSSC members created a "futures plan" for District 54, which involved identifying their dreams for District 54, determining where the district wanted to be in one year, articulating what was necessary to build strength to reach those dreams, identifying who needed to be enrolled, and creating measurable outcomes to ensure that inclusion was being effectively implemented in the district. The committee prepared a report for the school board that included the recommended vision statement and a proposed course of action with regard to providing inclusive educational options within District 54. The following vision/mission statement created by the LT/SSSC was adopted by the school board in April of 1993:

> School District 54 will value diversity and foster belonging by understanding and accepting all students. A process will be developed to provide a wider array of educational options, support, and resources for each school community to address the individual needs of its students.

Phase Two: Introducing

The introducing phase of inclusive education was initiated by having local, state, and national speakers make presentations to the LT/SSSC. Personnel from many of the individual school sites as well as staff with specific roles (e.g., psychologists, communication specialists, resource specialists, social workers) had access to the various speakers. Staff development activities proved to be a key to sharing the vision/mission of District 54, providing school personnel with the supports they requested.

In the introducing process, some staff expressed concerns that inclusive education would mean "dumping" students into already overcrowded classes or reverting back to 1960s-like "mainstreaming" when needed supports were not provided. Some of the staff and even some committee members were also concerned that schools would be "pushed" into inclusion prior to the necessary preparation of staff. As part of one activity the team implemented to address the above concerns, the LT/SSSC created the term *supported education* to refer to inclusive education in a way that emphasized the provision of supports to students, families, and staff whenever and wherever needed.

Parents who desired supported education for their children were provided with this option. Supported education was clarified as a child-centered approach in which the needs of each child are considered and met through special education supports and services. Figure 1 represents the district's organizational strategy to ensure that the necessary quality supports would be provided to all students in their home schools.

With strong commitment to quality supports between the LT/SSSC and local school staff, the dedication to supported education spread across the district. Additional teams, known as school site teams (SSTs), were developed, including general and special education teachers and other representatives (e.g., communication specialists, resource teachers, psychologists, social workers, counselors, instructional assistants) from particular schools. The SSTs provided additional training and support to building personnel to facilitate the availability of necessary resources, adaptations, and curricula for students returning to their home schools. One additional team, the Supported Education District-Wide Team, made up of special services administrators, supported education facilitators, behavior specialists, and low-incidence specialist/consultants, was established to

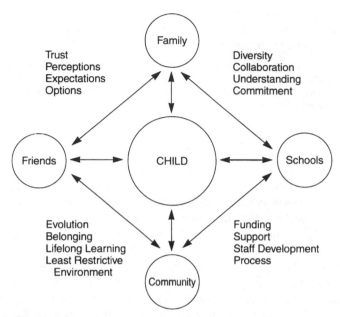

Figure 1.   Child-centered approach for supported education developed by District 54.

articulate and monitor what was occurring in schools at the present time and determine what additional support(s) and staff development activities were necessary for the future.

In the first year, four families asked that their children be returned to their home schools and be fully included. Following staff recommendations, two additional families agreed to have their children returned to their home school with needed supports. School site teams were provided with training on circles of friends, support, future planning process (see Chapters 4 and 10 for details on these strategies), and collaborative team building (see Chapter 3 for strategies). Transition and support plans were developed for home schools, and staff of home schools received training in team building, conflict resolution, and curriculum adaptations and modifications.

The Assistant Superintendent and Director of Special Services held regular meetings with SSTs, the teams of educators to whom they provided training in each building. An asset to the change process was the strong involvement of the students' parents at all levels and steps of the transition team and team building process. This minimized misinformation as well as reduced the anxiety brought about with change. The LT/SSSC was kept informed of the supported education efforts throughout the year by the Assistant Superintendent and the Director of Special Services. Additionally, the LT/SSSC's work was presented annually to the school board. The positive results at this stage grew from open communication from the field, parents, administrators, and outside consultants.

Phase Three: Expanding

Parents and the SSTs identified eight more students to receive supported education services in the second year of implementation of the project. In addition, those in buildings that had not yet received the "year one" training requested this training, and support staff were identified to assist in providing supported education services. A number of parents continued to request at IEP meetings that their children receive supported education at their home schools.

As a consequence of its efforts, the district was awarded a grant through the Illinois State Board of Education to study and expand inclusive services throughout the entire district. This enabled the district to expand, as well as link with a statewide network (i.e., Project Choices) for inclusive education. The grant also provided a means to offer financial support to building sites to initiate, implement, or expand inclusive education possibilities via staff development resources and release time.

Through parental choice, each year additional students with disabilities receive supported education opportunities. The change process was carefully planned and orchestrated by the district administration, principals, and school site teams. Ongoing in-service training and collaborative team building planning meetings were some of the major efforts to expand the change process within the district. Principals throughout the district became very supportive of the process.

This district's supported education model is not meant to be a recipe for other districts. But, team building has been a key to success. Although there have been problems and challenges along the way, teams at both school and district levels worked together to address issues as they occurred and to successfully generate practical solutions.

Phase Four: Selectively Maintaining

Supported education has become a standard rather than an exception within District 54. At the end of the year and long before the next school year begins, the school site teams determine the supported education needs for the next year. Future planning and IEP planning processes have proved to be critical to the success of the district. Articulating supports for the identified students for upcoming years and providing summer training events to assure the support is present for the next grade and/or the receiving school is critical.

Each summer there have been intensive workshops and planning sessions offered (volunteer as well as paid) for staff to become better prepared in collaboration, teaming, conflict resolution, curriculum adaptations, and other related topics. These trainings have been held within the school district. Some staff have also been supported to participate in national trainings in other states in order to be aware of additional quality inclusive educational options.

Each year more students are provided supported education. With the students' progress in school has come the need to change the service delivery model at the high school level. Staff have begun to initiate the change process with the high school district where the students will go after completing middle school in elementary District 54. Undoubtedly the high school district will need to go through the same phases of systems change, beginning with visionizing similar to that of District 54. The successful experiences of District 54 in moving through the change process can be shared, and the high school district can benefit from District 54's documentation of the process and articulation of outcomes.

In 1994, District 54 made a dramatic move that clearly signaled its commitment to its inclusive education mission. Until that time, District 54 participated in a Cooperative Special Education Services region. In Illinois and in other states, special education services are provided on a regional and/or cooperative services basis, where districts pool their resources and have another organization provide the supports. Generally, this has resulted in segregated services outside of students' neighborhoods and even sometimes outside of home school districts. This was the case with the cooperative serving District 54. Because of this, the District 54 School Board of Education unanimously voted to withdraw from participation in the Cooperative Special Education Services region. The decision to withdraw from the cooperative was a powerful indicator of the district's commitment to provide students quality educational opportunities and whatever supports are needed for successful education in their home schools. This withdrawal bolstered the energy and commitment of district personnel, the building teams, the parents, and the students to create supported education options in District 54.

District 54 continues to work toward full implementation of its vision/ mission statement. As a school district in the process of systems change, it has had to learn that each phase of the change process is essential.

CHARACTERISTICS OF AND STRATEGIES FOR CHANGE AGENTS

Within any successful change process, there will always be at least one person, if not more, who functions in the role of change agent. Change agents, whether from within or outside of the school or school system, assume leadership responsibilities for facilitating the change process. Change agents identify whom to involve and at what point to involve them. As a general rule, planning should involve the largest number and variety of people inside and outside of the school as possible. This means inviting parents, business people, former graduates, retired community members, and consumers (i.e., the students themselves) to join the planning team. Planning teams comprise those stakeholders who form a group (formally or informally) to systematically plan and monitor the change process. Strategies for planning have been articulated in Chapter 3.

Deciding whom to court and engage in various phases of a change process is a critical leadership skill. To overlook principals in the visionizing phase, for example, may result in problems of ownership for change at the initiating and subsequent phases. However, to involve some people at the earliest stages may be counterproductive. For instance, some members of the school community may be greatly invested in maintaining the old culture and familiar educational practices. To involve them too early could thwart the creative processes critical to the visionizing and initiating phases of change. A delicate balance needs to be achieved between recruiting early and limiting creative visionizing.

Often students are overlooked as stakeholders and partners in school change processes. These stakeholders have the most to lose or gain with the changes and, therefore, must be part of the change process. In addition, students can pose as much resistance to change as reluctant adults. Recruiting and facilitating their involvement in this process is essential for success. Change agents need to consider carefully how best to introduce prospective changes to students, how to enroll them in planning and implementation activities, and how to solicit their evaluation of the impact of change on their school life. If change objectives are to be personally or socially relevant to students, they must be enrolled in the process of setting and evaluating the objectives. Including students as partners in school change efforts acknowledges that students are among a school's richest and most refreshing sources of innovative ideas.

Change agents face a "time dilemma" because of two opposing realities. On the one hand, schools reform is long overdue. Furthermore, today's world changes so rapidly that quick responses to the often unpredictable new needs of students and schools are necessary. In sum, there is little time to delay the change process and the changes that are needed. On the other hand, change is a process that requires patience. Change is a process rather than an occurrence or an event, and it occurs over time. The failure of some past educational reform efforts may perhaps be explained by change agents' lack of understanding of these two contrastive forces or their lack of patience or tenacity to persevere.

Change agents are more likely to be successful in their efforts if they adopt several essential perspectives. These strategies are described below.

Focus on Individuals

Change is primarily about individuals (e.g., teachers, principals, students, parents) and their beliefs and actions rather than about programs, materials, terminology, or equipment. Change is highly personal; it affects people. It will be viewed differently by each participant and will require individualized personal and professional growth. Change requires its facilitators to focus on the individuals affected by the changes because what matters most in school improvement programs are the people themselves (Clark, Lotto, & Astuto, 1984). The change process must concentrate on the students and their needs.

Because each member of the school community is unique, no two people can be expected to react in the same way to change. Some will more willingly and rapidly engage in new practices than others. Supports to individuals experiencing change, therefore, must be highly personalized, and each person's progress must be individually assessed. By attending to an individual's personal and practical concerns (e.g., How will this affect my classroom practices? How much of my time will it require?), resistance to change efforts may be reduced.

Typically, among the most important supports for individuals will be the opportunity for and the experience of professional growth in knowledge, skills, and beliefs that are positively associated with the desired future state. Ongoing training, modeling, coaching, and feedback are essential for moving people along in a change process.

Be "Up Front" and Teach Others How to Actualize a Vision

Change can only occur if everyone in the organization is made aware of the fact that change will be taking place; that changes in roles, rules, and responsibilities will result; and that positive personal and other outcomes can be expected (Sarason, 1990). Change is facilitated when change agents have both the disposition and the skills to honestly and clearly articulate to members of the school community the goals, timelines, and procedures each person needs to employ and promote the changes (Senge, 1990). An effective change agent is a direct, upfront communicator who knows how to articulate desired future states.

Expect the Unknown and "Go with the Flow"

Facilitators of school change must have an implicit sense that a school is an organism in which the components (i.e., the work of the educators) may be "tightly coupled" (interdependent) or "loosely coupled" (independent) (Skrtic, 1991, p. 163). In more "tightly coupled" organizations, adjusting even a small part will immediately affect other parts, and the outcomes of the adjustments will always be somewhat unpredictable. Therefore, change agents must be comfortable with the unknown and the unexpected, be flexible, and "go with the flow." Ideas about how long change will take, the steps to be taken along the way, and the exact nature of the final outcomes will inevitably be adjusted and readjusted throughout a change process.

Know Your Assumptions about Change

Central to any healthy organization is self-examination of unconscious assumptions or mental models about how the world, the organization, and change operates (Senge, 1990). Facilitators of change, then, need to be disposed to regular self-examination of their mental models. Some assumptions about change more likely to foster than impede progress include the following (Fullan, 1991; Senge, 1990):

Assume that no amount of knowledge will ever clarify what action is the "correct" one to take.
Assume that changing the culture, not implementing specific innovations, is the real agenda.

Assume that your ideal of what change should be is not necessarily the one that should or will be implemented.

Assume that for any innovation to result in lasting change, individuals in the system must work out their own meaning of the innovation.

Assume that people need pressure to change and opportunities to react, form, and express their own positions, interact with others who are changing, and receive technical assistance.

Assume that conflict is inevitable and fundamental to change.

Assume that lasting change takes years (Fullan, 1991), if not decades (Senge, 1990).

Assume that not all people will change; nevertheless, increasing the number of people who do change is the goal.

Assume that lack of implementation is not necessarily a rejection of the change or its underlying values; other factors (e.g., inadequate supports, need for more training, personal crises, insufficient time elapsed) may be the cause.

Assume that any plan you formulate must be based on the above assumptions.

Take Risks and Act Courageously

Much about the nature and process of change remains to be discovered. Thus, people interested in school reform are faced with acting without knowing what exactly the process or the outcomes will be. In other words, they are faced with taking risks that are as likely to lead to failures as they are to successes. Yet, the biggest risk to the educational system and to children is not taking one. Before taking on a leadership role, people interested in initiating school reform must acknowledge the courage they will need to challenge people's long-held assumptions, to collaborate, to negotiate compromises, to specify needed practices and strategies, and to attempt the unknown (Sizer, 1991).

EVALUATION

Evaluation needs to be regular and ongoing throughout all phases of any change process. Its purposes are many and diverse. Clearly, one purpose is to determine whether change is occurring and whether that change represents progress. Another is to determine future actions needed to deal with the challenges as they occur, as well as the successes. Specifically, at the expanding phase, a key role of evaluation is to facilitate a change in the culture by signaling to everyone what is and what will continue to be valued, respected, expanded, and expected in the future. Evaluation then serves marketing and development functions at the expanding phase, guiding additional people to the organization's vision and emerging culture.

For evaluation to be optimally effective, it is important for everyone, students included, to be evaluators. Furthermore, evaluation questions should be those the stakeholders involved with and affected by the change may consider important. For example, educators, parents, students, school administrators, related services personnel (e.g., speech-language therapists, vision specialists), or community members may be interested in evaluating long-range student outcomes (e.g., graduates' employment or continued education; postsecondary civic contributions; reduction in the gap between educational achievements of graduates of differing racial, ethnic, and economic backgrounds). In addition, they may have an interest in determining the impact of the change effort: Does the implementation and modification of innovations continue to yield positive outcomes? Do circumstances still require the practices? Do the changes represent genuine progress, creating a better state of affairs for children and adults?

The leadership in school reform efforts may wish to devote considerable effort to measuring more effective and process-oriented variables: How worried or concerned do staff seem to be at various points during the change process? How comfortable are the participants with using key innovations and processes (e.g., creativity, collaborative teaming processes)? To what degree do staff perceive the change effective? Examining all of these personal issues can be useful to further progress.

Any evaluation agenda must be flexible and open. Sometimes outcomes are quite unexpected. For example, in the early 1980s, when Vermont schools began restructuring to include students with severe disabilities, several positive unexpected outcomes emerged (Thousand et al., 1986). After 2 years of returning to general education classrooms in their local home schools, several students who had been segregated in special programs made so much academic and social progress that they were no longer eligible for special education services. Others experienced unexpected health improvements and corresponding improvements in school attendance. In order to determine and, over time, update what becomes important to evaluate, everyone needs to remain attentive to the unexpected. The leadership in the reform efforts should recruit qualitative researchers who are able to observe and extract the meaning of what people in schools are doing and saying on a day-to-day basis, rather than base evaluation exclusively on quantitative data (e.g., standardized test scores or a list of the curriculum objectives achieved) that focus on counting incremental steps in isolation from the holistic, complex, interactive, human teaching–learning process.

CONCLUSIONS

It is easy to become overwhelmed by the monumental and complex nature of inventing or reinventing schools that are both caring and effective. Nevertheless, Senge (1990) instructs, time and choice come to us all:

> Choice is different from desire. Try an experiment. Say, "I want." Now, say, "I choose." What is the difference? For most people, "I want" is passive; "choose" is

active. For most, wanting is a state of deficiency—we want what we do not have. Choosing is a state of sufficiency—electing to have what we truly want. For most of us, as we look back over our life, we can see that certain choices we made played a pivotal role in how our life developed. So, too will the choices we make in the future. (p. 360)

Effective school organizations can be built, and they are built by individuals who choose to be stewards of a larger vision. We can be hesitant. Or we can be courageous and choose to engage what we do know about change processes to create a brighter educational future for all children.

REFERENCES

Bennis, W., & Nanus, B. (1985). *Leaders: The strategies for taking charge*. New York: Harper & Row.

Blumberg, A., & Greenfield, W. (1980). *The effective principal: Perspectives on leadership* (2nd ed.). Boston: Allyn & Bacon.

Clark, D.L., Lotto, L.S., & Astuto, T.A. (1984). Effective schools and school improvement: a comparative analysis of two lines of injury. *Educational Administration Quarterly, 20*(3), 41–68.

Cook, B. (1990). *Bill Cook's strategic planning in American schools*. Rosslyn, VA: American Association of School Administrators.

Crandall, D., Eiseman, J., & Louis, K. (1986). Strategic planning issues that bear on the success of school improvement efforts. *Educational Administration Quarterly, 22*(3), 21–53.

Deal, T. (1987). The culture of schools. In L. Shieve & M. Schoenheit (Eds.), *Leadership: Examining the elusive* (pp. 3–15). Alexandria, VA: Association for Supervision and Curriculum Development.

Deal, T., & Peterson, K. (1990). *The principal's role in shaping school culture*. Washington, DC: U.S. Government Printing Office.

Eiseman, J., Fleming, D., & Roody, D. (1990). *The school improvement leader: Four perspectives on change in schools*. Andover, MA: The Regional Lab.

Fullan, M. (1991). *The new meaning of educational change*. New York: Teachers College Press.

Hord, S., Rutherford, W., Huling-Austin, L., & Hall, G.. (1987). *Taking charge of change*. Alexandria, VA: Association for Supervision and Curriculum Development.

Kaufman, R. (1991). *Strategic planning plus: an organizational guide*. Glenview, IL: Scott, Foresman.

Lewin, K. (1951). *Field theory in social science*. New York: Harper & Row.

Parnes, S.J. (1988). *Visionizing: State-of-the-art processes for encouraging innovative excellence*. East Aurora, NY: D.O.K.

Patterson, J., Purkey, S., & Parker, J. (1986). *Productive schools systems for a nonrational world*. Alexandria, VA: Association for Supervision and Curriculum Development.

Peters, T., & Waterman, R. (1982). *In search of excellence: Lessons from America's best run companies*. New York: Harper & Row.

Sarason, S. (1971). *The culture of the school and the problem of change*. Boston: Allyn & Bacon.

Sarason, S. (1990). *The predictable failure of school reform: Can we change course before it's too late?* San Francisco: Jossey-Bass.

Schlechty, P. (1990). *Schools for the 21st century: Leadership imperatives for educational reform*. San Francisco: Jossey-Bass.

Scholtes, P.R. (1993). *The team handbook: how to use teams to improve quality*. Madison, WI: Joiner Associates, Inc.

Senge, P. (1990). *The fifth discipline: The art and practice of the learning organization*. New York: Doubleday/Currency.

Sergiovanni, T. (1990). *Value-added leadership: How to get extraordinary performance in schools*. New York: Harcourt Brace Jovanovich.

Sizer, T. (1991). No pain, no gain. *Educational Leadership, 48*(8), 32–34.

Skrtic, T. (1991). *Behind special education: A critical analysis of professional culture and school organization*. Denver: Love.

Thousand, J., Fox, T., Reid, R., Godek, J., Williams, W., & Fox, W. (1986). *The homecoming model: educating students who present intensive educational challenges within regular education environments* (Monograph No. 7-1). Burlington: University of Vermont.

Thousand, J., & Villa, R. (1990). Sharing expertise and responsibilities through teaching teams. In W. Stainback & S. Stainback (Eds.), *Support networks for inclusive schooling: Integrated interdependent education* (pp. 151–166). Baltimore: Paul H. Brookes Publishing Co.

Villa, R., & Thousand, J. (1990). Administrative supports to promote inclusive schooling. In W. Stainback & S. Stainback (Eds.), *Support networks for inclusive schooling: Integrated interdependent education* (pp. 201–218). Baltimore: Paul II. Brookes Publishing Co.

Villa, R., & Thousand, J. (1992). Restructuring public school systems: Strategies for organizational change and progress. In R. Villa, J. Thousand, W. Stainback, & S. Stainback (Eds.), *Restructuring for caring and effective education: An administrative guide to creating heterogeneous schools* (pp. 109–137). Baltimore: Paul H. Brookes Publishing Co.

Villa, R., Udis, J., & Thousand, J. (1994). Rethinking responses to and for children experiencing behavioral and emotional challenges: A constellation of resources, supports, and services. In Thousand, J., Villa, R., & Nevin, A. (Eds.). *Creativity and collaborative learning: A practical guide to empowering students and teachers* (pp. 369–390). Baltimore: Paul H. Brookes Publishing Co.

INDEX

Page numbers in italics denote figures; those followed by "t" denote tables.

415